ADVANCE PRAISE FOR *HEA[*

Anyone who works with troubled children and their families should not miss this book. *Healing the Fractured Child* weaves together comprehensive theory and neurobiology that substantiate practical treatment guidelines for children and their families. The complexity of symptoms, diagnoses, assessment, and use of medication and a variety of innovative treatment approaches for stabilization, trauma processing, and integration are explored and come to life through the clear, practical, and touching clinical illustrations peppered throughout the book. Fran Waters has drawn on her vast clinical experience and thorough knowledge of current perspectives on dissociation and child therapy to write an integrative, readable, and immensely useful masterpiece, a gift to the field of child psychology and psychotherapy and to the many therapists, children, and parents who will benefit from her wisdom.
—Pat Ogden, PhD, Founder, Sensorimotor Psychotherapy Institute

Healing the Fractured Child provides an invaluable source of information for all professionals and nonprofessionals interested in childhood dissociation. Based on her many years of experience in this field, Waters takes us from an explanation of dissociation and related theories to the behaviors that may be noticed by a parent, teacher, or doctor, through the assessment quagmire and the challenges of parenting, to the important work of emotional regulation and the identification of self-states, bringing in consideration of where medication can or cannot assist and describing the hard work of trauma processing, to integration, possible relapse, and back again to even stronger internal integration. The intricately described clinical examples provide a plethora of ideas for working with these children and offer readers the encouragement and hope so important for working with children who experienced trauma.
—Sandra Wieland, PhD, RPsych, Editor of *Dissociation in Traumatized Children and Adolescents, Second Edition: Theory and Clinical Interventions*

Healing the Fractured Child is a skillfully written, comprehensive, and remarkable volume. It is well grounded in theory and full of rich, practical applications and detailed case examples. Waters's outstanding work will expand clinicians' capacity to understand and assess dissociation as well as to effectively accompany children in their healing journeys. It is an essential resource for therapists of all orientations working with trauma and dissociation.
—Ana M. Gómez, MC, LPC, Author of *EMDR Therapy and Adjunct Approaches With Children: Complex Trauma, Attachment, and Dissociation*

This book is a compilation of years' worth of clinical work with traumatized, dissociatively fractured children, and the author's sensitivity and accumulated wisdom are on every page. With her integrative model, Fran Waters makes the behaviors of these traumatized children—which are seemingly incomprehensible and often misdiagnosed—understandable and even logical. Therapists, parents, and others who are in a position to interact with the dissociative child can benefit from this book with its down-to-earth and practical explanations and intervention strategies. It belongs in the library of all who treat these children and those who treat adult survivors of childhood abuse. Brava!
—Christine A. Courtois, PhD, ABPP,
Licensed Psychologist, Independent Practice, Washington, DC

Frances S. Waters, DCSW, LMSW, LMFT, a clinical social worker and a licensed marriage and family therapist in private practice in Marquette, Michigan, is an internationally recognized educator, trainer, consultant, and clinician in the areas of childhood trauma, abuse, and dissociation.

She was the past president of the International Society for the Study of Trauma and Dissociation (ISSTD), and she is currently the faculty director of the Child and Adolescent Psychotherapy Training Institute and the cochair of the ISSTD's Child and Adolescent Committee. She has authored numerous articles and chapters and serves on the editorial board of the *Journal of Child and Adolescent Trauma,* as well as on the advisory board of the Leadership Council on Child Abuse and Interpersonal Violence.

Fran Waters is an executive producer and a participant of several training videos on childhood trauma, abuse, and dissociation targeted toward mental health professionals, caretakers, teachers, child protective services workers, forensic evaluators, and prosecutors. She received the 2008 Media Award from the American Professional Society on Abuse of Children for her production of "Trauma and Dissociation in Children," which was geared toward forensic evaluators and prosecutors. She is the recipient of ISSTD's Presidential Award and is a fellow of the ISSTD.

HEALING THE FRACTURED CHILD

DIAGNOSIS AND TREATMENT OF
YOUTH WITH DISSOCIATION

Frances S. Waters, DCSW, LMSW, LMFT

SPRINGER PUBLISHING COMPANY
NEW YORK

Springer Publishing Company, LLC
11 West 42nd Street
New York, NY 10036
www.springerpub.com

Acquisitions Editor: Sheri W. Sussman
Composition: Westchester Publishing Services

ISBN: 978-0-8261-9963-8
e-book ISBN: 978-0-8261-9964-5

16 17 18 19 20 / 5 4 3 2 1

The author and the publisher of this Work have made every effort to use sources believed to be reliable to provide information that is accurate and compatible with the standards generally accepted at the time of publication. The author and publisher shall not be liable for any special, consequential, or exemplary damages resulting, in whole or in part, from the readers' use of, or reliance on, the information contained in this book. The publisher has no responsibility for the persistence or accuracy of URLs for external or third-party Internet websites referred to in this publication and does not guarantee that any content on such websites is, or will remain, accurate or appropriate.

Library of Congress Cataloging-in-Publication Data
Names: Waters, Frances S., author.
Title: Healing the fractured child : diagnosis and treatment of youth with dissociation / Frances S. Waters.
Description: New York, NY : Springer Publishing Company, LLC, [2016] | Includes bibliographical references and index.
Identifiers: LCCN 2015040802| ISBN 9780826199638 (hard copy : alk. paper) | ISBN 9780826199645 (ebook)
Subjects: | MESH: Dissociative Disorders. | Adolescent. | Child. | Stress Disorders, Traumatic.
Classification: LCC RJ506.D55 | NLM WM 173.6 | DDC 618.92/8523—dc23 LC record available at http://lccn.loc.gov/2015040802

Special discounts on bulk quantities of our books are available to corporations, professional associations, pharmaceutical companies, health care organizations, and other qualifying groups. If you are interested in a custom book, including chapters from more than one of our titles, we can provide that service as well.

For details, please contact:
Special Sales Department, Springer Publishing Company, LLC
11 West 42nd Street, 15th Floor, New York, NY 10036-8002
Phone: 877-687-7476 or 212-431-4370; Fax: 212-941-7842
E-mail: sales@springerpub.com

Printed in the United States of America by McNaughton & Gunn.

This book is dedicated to all the children and families who trusted me to work with them and to share their stories. I have learned from them and been inspired by their strength.

CONTENTS

Contributors

Diane Raven, BS, MA, Consultant and Former Clinical Therapist/Director of Art Therapy, Youth Residential Services, Great Lakes Recovery Centers, Behavioral Health Services, Negaunee, Michigan

Adrian J. Stierum, MD, Child and Adolescent Psychiatrist, Orthopsychiatric Center, De Fjord, Lucertis, Rotterdam, The Netherlands

Foreword

In 1996, in an endorsement of the book *The Dissociative Child,* Joseph Noshpitz, one of the forefathers of present-day child psychiatry, wrote, "These authors have lit a candle in a dark cave" (solicited endorsement; Noshpitz, personal communication, 1996). Now with Frances S. Waters's book *Healing the Fractured Child: Diagnosis and Treatment of Youth With Dissociation,* the lights in the cave may have finally been turned on. This book is a significant step forward in the developing field of dissociative disorders, adding a comprehensive treatment compendium to the five existing books on the topic: Shirar (1996), Silberg (1998), Putnam (1997), Wieland (2015b), and Silberg (2013). Waters's contribution may very well move this marginalized field of dissociation in children into the mainstream of the field of child clinical psychopathology.

Waters desensitizes the reader to the oddness or bizarre quality of dissociated selves in children by reference to classic child developmental literature. It turns out that Bowlby (1980) clearly described children with dissociative reactions in his work, and these are the observable phenomena in the astute clinician's office in 2016 as well.

Frances Waters allows us insight into her remarkable career by illustrating interventions with children whom many child practitioners would have given up on. Frances Waters's treatment of the most aggressive, regressed, and impaired children uses the Star Theoretical Model (STM) to inform her work. She focuses on the theoretical contributions of Satir (1965), Bowlby (1980), and Erikson (1963), highlighted by recent neurobiological research and the growing field of dissociation studies.

Waters's scholarly summary of the differential diagnosis issues between dissociative disorders in children and attention deficit hyperactivity disorder, pediatric bipolar disorder, psychotic disorders, obsessive-compulsive disorders, eating disorders, and reactive attachment disorder is the most comprehensive in the literature to date, and illustrates that a trauma-informed perspective can radically alter our conventional approaches to a variety of childhood conditions.

It is moving to read Frances Waters's detailed descriptions of trauma processing with dialogues between Waters and clients' different self-states, which show the young people's incredible insight, self-knowledge, and sensitivity. One is in awe of these young people who, despite their suffering, feel the motivation to heal and thrive under Waters's sensitive therapeutic guidance. Reading these case histories makes it clear that the power and resiliency within children are powerful forces and that clinical skill in tapping into the well of resourcefulness in young people can yield amazing clinical rewards. Waters illustrates how to tap into that well of resiliency and healing through creative engagement with the child and teen ego states, which hold memories of trauma, but also may hold powerful protective resources and insight.

As Sobol and Schneider (1998, p. 192) stated, "An image developed and changed through art-making may alter or amend internal imagery." Frances Waters, along with Diane Raven, presents a detailed map of how to use art interventions to encourage self-awareness and ultimate integration for traumatized and dissociative teens (Chapter 11). Art therapists and child therapists who have abundant art materials in their offices can use or adapt many of these techniques in their own offices. The combination of a variety of media in the same projects—masks and paintings, rocks and clay—helps the clients portray their own discontinuity of self and gives a concrete language for expressing internal fragmentation. It is clear how powerful these strategies can be, and I intend to incorporate some of them immediately in my own practice, as I expect many practitioners reading this book will do after becoming familiar with this clear description of art interventions.

For therapists who work with eye movement desensitization and reprocessing (EMDR), Waters provides a detailed methodology for the incorporation of sensitivity to dissociation within the EMDR model (Chapter 12). This will definitely be a useful addition to the literature in bridging these two clinical methodologies. Similarly, psychiatrists asked to augment treatment through medication will appreciate the in-depth discussion of psychiatric medications coauthored by Adrian J. Stierum (Chapter 9).

One of the most powerful points illustrated in Waters's book is that one ignores the traumatic roots of childhood behavioral disorders at great peril. The urgency and importance of this lesson are illustrated in a recent clinical experience from my own practice. My client, 8-year-old Robert, was evaluated at a well-known treatment center in my city, and that clinical evaluation was to be used with mine as part of the court's determination of his treatment needs and the suitability of his placement with his maternal grandparents after his parents' tragic death in a car accident. Robert displayed intermittent aggressive behavior that seemed unpredictable: He would attack his maternal grandparents, shouting "Watch out!" These aggressive episodes alternated with regressed behavior in which he spoke like a baby, curled in a ball and weeping. His paternal grandparents argued that this out-of-control behavior indicated that the home of the maternal grandparents was inappropriate to his needs. The report from the well-known treatment facility in my area emphasized that the maternal grandparents clearly needed parenting training in which they would be taught to reinforce his positive behavior and ignore his angry behavior. The obvious grief reaction of the child and the importance of the words "Watch out!" (which were the last words he heard his parents say before the crash) were ignored. The treatment philosophy of this center was to treat the observable behavior no matter what the child was experiencing internally.

In contrast, my report emphasized a trauma-focused approach, wherein Robert could safely play out his traumatic memories with support, encouragement, and validation. I argued his behavior did not reflect on the suitability of his placement. My approach, like that of Frances Waters, encouraged attention to his changing states and recognition that his aggressive state was a fear-based, state-dependent reaction that evoked its own set of state-dependent memories of the accident. To simply ignore these episodes would be a way to invalidate the central defining experience of Robert's young and tragic life. The judge, unsure whom to believe, ordered the child to stay where he was and engage in both forms of treatment, but the maternal grandparents soon came to realize that the behavior modification approach was accomplishing little and often antagonized Robert when he most needed support and validation.

Yet, how many other times is a behavioral approach like this one ordered for children like Robert who have suffered tragedies of family members' death; sexual, physical, or emotional abuse; witnessing community and domestic violence; or sudden separation from loved ones? How many clinicians who deal with children are taught to rely exclusively on simplistic treatment ideologies that are actually causing children more harm by ignoring the traumatic roots of their behavioral presentations? I wish I could answer that the trauma-informed movement in public mental health has saturated the delivery of mental health care to children, but we are not there yet.

Yet, paradoxically, when the posttraumatic nature of the symptom presentation becomes evident, there is often reluctance among treatment facilities or providers to accept the client. An article in the *New York Daily News* on November 19, 2015, reported on a 12-year-old girl with dissociative identity disorder diagnosed by three psychiatrists, who was refused entrance to 16 treatment facilities (Salinger, 2015). She languishes in a juvenile detention center in Indiana, while all the child and adolescent mental health services in the surrounding area feel ill equipped to handle her case.

However, the expertise to handle children and adolescents with dissociative disorder exists, and it is time for this previously marginalized field of expertise to reach the mainstream of psychiatric services. Based on consultation calls that I receive from treatment centers around the world, there is awareness that these dissociative clients require a specialized approach, that the expertise to handle them is rare, and that there is a growing need for centers that treat psychiatrically impaired teens to gain expertise in treating dissociative disorders in youth. Recent calls to me seeking consultation about this specialized treatment have come from Israel, Turkey, Hong Kong, the United Kingdom, Canada, and multiple states within the United States. When I explain some of the foundational concepts of treating dissociative disorders in these consultations, it is as if a lightbulb turns on. Practitioners recognize that the process of radical self-acceptance and the integration and processing of experienced pain and trauma, emphasized by practitioners who treat dissociation, are intuitive and logical. Growth-enhancing approaches such as those described by Waters in this book promote respect for the individual's adaptive capacities without blaming, categorizing, and labeling and are powerful psychotherapeutic interventions. In a recent consultation, when I suggested that the therapist praise a traumatized teen for his ability to fight back, rather than just set limits on the teen's aggressive behavior, the therapist smiled with delight and recognition. "Arthur will love that!" he recognized immediately, and laughed with relief that he could say out loud what he intuitively understood: This severely traumatized boy needed affirmation that moving out of helplessness into mastery was essential for self-preservation, and although his aggression was misdirected initially, the impulse to care for himself was a necessary survival tool that this young teen could acknowledge in himself with gratitude, while still working on learning to curb its intensity.

The world around us seems to be getting more violent all the time. The Internet provides a ready medium for those who wish to harm children to document and disseminate evidence of their crimes. Increasingly, the level of trauma our children experience boggles the imagination. Frances Waters models courage in the face of the most seemingly intractable symptoms and gives hope that even these children, exposed to the most horrific abuse or events, have the potential to heal with sensitive awareness of how they have coped with trauma. Waters's book is essential reading for all clinicians who treat children. Let us all hope for a time when one of the primary pathways that children demonstrate in reaction to trauma—dissociation with its associated fragmentation and identity confusion—is recognized widely, and the emotional pain of the youngest members of our population is treated with the sensitivity and care shown by Frances Waters.

Joyanna Silberg, PhD
Senior Consultant, Childhood Trauma
Sheppard Pratt Health System
Baltimore, Maryland

REFERENCES

Bowlby, J. (1980). *Attachment and loss, Vol. 3: Loss: Sadness and depression*. New York, NY: Basic Books.

Erikson, E. H. (1963). *Childhood and society* (2nd ed.). New York, NY: W. W. Norton.

Putnam, F. W. (1997). *Dissociation in children and adolescents*. New York, NY: Guilford Press.

Salinger, T. (2015, November 19). Indiana girl, 12, killed stepmother because creepy clown character 'Laughing Jack' told her to do it. *New York Daily News*. Retrieved from http://www.nydailynews.com/news/crime/indiana-girl-12-killed-stepmom-laughing-jack-article-1.2440821

Satir, V. (1965). The family as a treatment unit. *Confinia Psychiatrica, 8*, 37–42.

Shirar, L. (1996). *Dissociative children: Bridging the inner and outer worlds*. New York, NY: W. W. Norton.

Silberg, J. (Ed.). (1998). *The dissociative child: Diagnosis, treatment, and management* (2nd ed.). Lutherville, MD: Sidran Press.

Silberg, J. (2013). *The child survivor: Healing developmental trauma and dissociation*. New York, NY: Routledge.

Sobol, B., & Schneider, K. (1998). Art as an adjunctive therapy in the treatment of children who dissociate. In J. L. Silberg (Ed.), *The dissociative child: Diagnosis, treatment, and management* (2nd ed., pp. 219–230). Lutherville, MD: Sidran Press.

Wieland, S. (Ed.). (2015b). *Dissociation in traumatized children and adolescents: Theory and clinical interventions* (2nd ed.). New York, NY: Routledge.

PREFACE

Healing the Fractured Child: Diagnosis and Treatment of Youth With Dissociation is a comprehensive book on child and adolescent dissociation that provides the reader with a window into the fractured minds of traumatized children and adolescents and offers an effective pathway toward healing. This book delves into the inner workings of vulnerable children's use of dissociation—an adaptive defense when fighting or fleeing is simply not an option. An in-depth discussion of the Star Theoretical Model (STM), an inclusive theoretical model that examines five intersecting theories—attachment, neurobiology, developmental theory, family systems, and dissociation—provides a solid foundation for understanding how and why children dissociate and also a road map to guide traumatized children toward successful recovery. The attachment theory is given special attention in the STM, signifying the critical relationship between children and their healthy caregivers, as a strong attachment provides the anchor for children to dissolve dissociative defenses and for them to begin to process traumatic experiences.

Because dissociation can result in a confusing array of symptoms, these children are frequently misdiagnosed, resulting in years of failed treatment episodes, multiple placements, and despondent children and caregivers. Several chapters cover a thorough analysis of traumatized children's convoluted behaviors by examining overlapping symptoms and differential diagnoses, dissociative warning signs, and a thorough assessment process for accurate diagnosis, all of which are dynamically illustrated with actual cases.

Throughout the book, rich clinical vignettes, telling drawings, and meaningful dialogue between therapist and child highlight the intricate therapeutic process from assessment to final integration. Innovative, varied, and specialized therapeutic techniques that are designed for each child's unique inner world are described; these techniques engage all parts of the child in healing and integration. Clinical examples of dissociative children from varied backgrounds and ages and with a high rate of comorbidity, such as destructive behaviors and substance abuse, are provided with specific interventions. Because infant trauma is often overlooked as the origin of children's memory and behavioral and emotional disturbances, special attention is given to illustrating innovative, evidence-supported techniques to access hidden infant states that often encapsulate the child's most disturbing and retractable symptoms.

The journey of four children's healing—Rudy, Lisa, Cathy, and Briana—is followed throughout the book. Other clinical vignettes are described as well, illustrating techniques that are often simple, yet powerful, to perform and easily adapt to other dissociative children. Special emphasis is given to stabilization techniques that are tailored to the child's interests; the use of these techniques is reinforced throughout the trauma processing stage for mastery of traumatic experiences and facilitates integration. Although adjunctive therapy with medication cannot cure dissociation in clients, special attention is devoted to carefully examining the judicious and safe use of medication for stabilization of highly dysregulated, dissociative children. A psychodynamic approach that is specially designed to treat traumatized children with dissociation and that combines other treatment modalities, particularly eye movement desensitization and reprocessing (EMDR) and art therapy, is given particular attention, with numerous case illustrations that demonstrate its success.

This invaluable resource provides mental health clinicians and other health care professionals with a wealth of knowledge and tools to effectively treat this troubled client population.

Acknowledgments

I am most grateful to my family for having supported me throughout this process. My husband, Bill, gave me his university library card so that I could have access to all of the materials needed to write this book, picked up materials for me at the library, and tolerated the time it took for me to complete this book. My son, Anthony, spent hours reviewing the chapter on differential diagnosis while using his doctoral degree in psychology to question, correct, or clarify what I wanted to say. I humorously told him it was "payback" time. My other son, Vincent, was always interested in my progress and firmly supported me throughout this process.

I am very thankful for Stephanie Dallam's scholarly editing skills, commitment, and lots of hard work to make this book much better. Her efforts were invaluable. I thank my two contributing authors, Diane Raven and Adrian J. Stierum, for their contributions to this book. Diane shared her innovative art interventions, which will be a major contribution to the field in helping youth reveal their inner life and safely express through art what would have otherwise been difficult to do. Adrian's thorough review of medications with dissociative children and case studies is an invaluable contribution to the field that has not been written about in almost 20 years! I am grateful to Robbie Adler-Tapia for her contributions to my chapter on EMDR (Chapter 12). She generously supplied cases and materials to keep me better informed about EMDR therapy. She also encouraged and guided me through the publication process.

I am deeply indebted to my colleagues and friends who are involved in child/adolescent treatment. Joy Silberg, Madge Bray, and I met in 1990 and have been kindred spirits, forging ahead in sharing knowledge and developing the field. Joy has been an invaluable and esteemed collaborator, as we have shared trainings and writings for the past 25 years! Her consultations and encouragement to write this book are immeasurable. I am better for what I do because of her innovations and contributions to the field. Madge Bray's creativity always amazes me. I am most thankful for her gift to me of her specially designed "dissociative doll" with little parts. It has become a prototype for all other similar dolls and has been an invaluable tool in my practice.

I had the honor to meet Renee Potgieter-Marks in the late 1990s; I have valued her creativity and insight, and I treasure our ongoing trainings and fun times together afterward! I am richer for her contributions and collaborations. I am also indebted to wonderful colleagues and cochairs of ISSTD's Child Adolescent Committee, Sandra Wieland and Na'ama Yehuda. Their persistence and dedication helped to get committee tasks done, as well as ensured their participation as copresenters with me. Also, their writings have advanced the field. Other members of the Child Adolescent Committee, Sandra Baita, Brad Stolbach, Bengt Soderstrom, and Els Grimminck, have enriched my growth by fertilizing ideas, collaborating, and sharing in trainings. I appreciate other members of the committee, Robert Slater, Robert Muller, and Frances Dougherty, for their devotion to serve and participate in committee work.

I learned so much in my early days from esteemed colleagues. In the 1980s, Mary K. Peterson, infant mental health specialist, collaborated with me about infants and attachment, introducing me to the significance on their development of infants' primary relationships to their parents; this has tremendously influenced my work and writings. Phyllis Stien, psychiatric nurse and dear friend who specialized in early childhood, family therapy, and neurobiology, patiently taught me about the neurobiology of trauma, brain structures, and their functions, which provided me the foundation to better understand the intricacies of the brain and to write about this topic. We also had lots of fun presenting together. I am grateful for the support of other local colleagues, Hannah Steintz and Kelly Laasko.

I particularly am most grateful to the late Roger McKinley and late Ann Bailey, who were my mentors. When I was faced with my first case of childhood dissociative identity disorder (DID) in the mid-1980s, I was fortunate to connect with them, who unselfishly gave endless hours of their time to collaborate with me and to participate as cotherapists with initial cases of dissociative children I treated. They taught me about dissociation, and we became a team in those early days. Also, I learned so much from Rick Kluft in those early days, and I continue to do so from his trainings and writings. His deep understanding of the fractured mind and how to engage the client with various techniques are what I have adapted to children. Frank Putnam's writings, theories, and trainings have added to my understanding and are the basis of my work with children. The dedicated work and writings of Christine Courtois have added depth to my understanding of trauma and dissociation. Ralf and Irina Votz, Pat Ogden, Janine Fisher, Bessel van der Kolk, Peter Levine, and Robert Scaer have enhanced my understanding of how the body holds the trauma and is the portal toward recovery. I have adapted their techniques to children and hundreds of children have benefited. Kathy Steele, Ellert Nijenhuis, and Onna van der Hart's theory on structural dissociation and research have added to my deep understanding of how the mind can divide to survive. Steve Frankel, Phil Kinsler, Phil Kaplan, and Bob Geffner have enriched my understanding of forensic evaluations that I have applied to my assessments of dissociative children. I am particularly indebted to Steve Frankel for his time in collaborating and guiding me on many cases of traumatized, dissociative children. Bob Geffner's endless drive, energy, and devotion to educate clinicians about trauma and dissociation always amaze me. Kevin Connor's spirit and drive in the early days and currently to move the field forward in education and training have been an inspiration to me over the past 30 years and provided me with opportunities to conduct trainings.

I am also grateful to ISSTD's leadership—past presidents and board members—who have guided me in this field throughout the years.

Regarding technical support, I appreciate Northern Michigan University's research librarian, Mike Strahan, for giving me many hours to learn a reference program for my book, and to obtain numerous articles and books. I am also most appreciative of Michael Weinhold's ongoing support and advice in technology, and assistance in preparing all of the figures for this book.

My dear friends, Rosanne Cook, Ann Russ, and Diana Magnuson, have been great supporters of me during this process, listening to my excitement, frustrations, and challenges. They kept me going.

Although my life's work has been influenced by many more—too numerous to mention—I appreciate all that they have done to contribute to my growth!

Introduction

In the early 1980s, I developed a successful treatment protocol for sexually abused children, and then I ran into a roadblock in treating a child. In 1986, after 1½ years of working with severely traumatized 8-year-old Eliza (name has been changed to protect her identity), she simply was not making progress. I was dumbfounded. Fortuitously, the psychiatrist, Dr. Lu Kuhnhoff, at the local mental health center where I worked at the time had attended one of the early international conferences sponsored by the International Society for the Study of Multiple Personality and Dissociation, now called the International Society for the Study of Trauma and Dissociation (ISSTD). On her return to the clinic, Dr. Kuhnhoff provided a 2-hour in-service on indicators and symptoms of dissociation. I attended it, along with a small group of clinicians. I was intrigued by this strange phenomenon and thought that perhaps I would see one in my lifetime. Little did I know what would transpire with my caseload and where I would be almost 30 years later!

Back to Eliza. . . . One day, Eliza walked into my office as if it were her first time. She looked at my bookshelf and toys, inquiring what they were. This was not the Eliza I had known. And it was thus truly her first time in my office! I then began to ask whether she heard voices, and she responded that she did. I took a deep breath and wondered where to go from there. I then inquired about her name, and she told me that her name was Samantha. I was a bit stunned and was not sure how to proceed, but since she liked to draw, I asked her to draw a picture of her voice and tell me about it.

I began to recognize that Eliza's dissociation was not a rare condition among other traumatized children whom I treated. I developed a treatment protocol for treating dissociative children and adolescents that not only included their traumatic experiences but also included "all parts of them." I pursued ongoing consultation and education by attending yearly the ISSTD's international conference and have not missed a conference since 1988.

Since those early days until the present, I have found it disheartening to see severely traumatized children and adolescents suffer with years of unsuccessful treatment, multiple diagnoses, and failed placements. When they finally come my way, many are well into their adulthood. Although I have written in the field and trained internationally, I decided it was time (a bit overdue) to write a comprehensive book on assessing and treating dissociative children. My hope is that this book will encourage clinicians (and researchers) to examine dissociation as a central feature in a long list of comorbid symptoms that children with complex trauma demonstrate.

Throughout this book, I emphasize that all treatment interventions should be geared toward unity of the fractured child. I stress the importance of developing internal awareness, cooperation, and participation across all parts of the self (referred to primarily as self-states in my book and also referred to as ego states, alters, parts, or introjects) in resolving traumatic experiences. I emphasize the importance of attachment and the family in the healing of the child's fractured mind. Rich clinical examples are described throughout the book with some cases, such as Rudy, Lisa, Cathy, and Briana, being followed in each phase of treatment. These case examples and many more in the book provide a window into the internal world of dissociative children and a pathway toward healing.

In Chapter 1, I focus on the Star Theoretical Model (STM), a comprehensive model of five theories—attachment, neurobiology, developmental theory, family systems, and dissociation—that in combination explain the development and treatment of dissociation in children and adolescents. At the top of the star shape is attachment, which is given paramount importance, as the attachment style of the child to parents/caregivers can either contribute to the child's reliance on dissociation or provide the foundation to help the child release dissociative defenses. I draw heavily on Bowlby (1980), the father of attachment theory, and his description of children who display dissociative symptoms when separated from their mothers. I describe a comparison between Bowlby's psychosocial stages of loss and mourning (1960) and children who also endure other traumatic experiences, and how these children react similarly by further segmenting off these painful affects, thoughts, and behaviors into self-states.

In the STM, I also draw wisdom from other prominent researchers (e.g., Schore, 2009) who examine the connection between frightening and abusive parents and the development of dissociation in youth. Discussion on the dynamics of attachment relationships between the child and maltreating caregiver, and the science of mirror neurons between a child and significant others, can shed light on the development of a child's self-states that mirror abusers, nonabusers, and so forth.

In the STM, the neurobiology of trauma is a central theory to understanding dissociation. I discuss Porges's (2011) triune autonomic stress response system, which explains the most primitive, automatic defense system—freeze, immobilization, dissociation—when a child is exposed to trauma and cannot utilize other defenses of fight or flight. The impact of trauma on the child's developing brain and the impairment of critical memory systems that shed light on memory disturbances are reviewed, including groundbreaking research on how traumatic memories are stored differently, thus making them inaccessible (Jovasevic et al., 2015).

Numerous theories on dissociation and development of discrete states and how they overlap with attachment (e.g., Putnam, 1997) are highlighted and influence my work. Erikson's (1963) psychosocial stages of development are the basis of my developmental theory. I expand Erikson's model by incorporating into my developmental model the theories of dissociation and how trauma impacts a child's developmental stage, particularly at the time of the trauma, resulting in self-states that are stuck at that developmental stage. Finally, Satir's (1965) theory of family systems is the basis of my approach to families. Her principles and strategies are timeless and recognize that the identified client, the child, is often reacting to a dysfunctional family. She stresses the importance of examining the interactional patterns in the family that contribute to the child's symptoms, regardless of whether they are dissociative.

Chapter 2 covers a comprehensive list of warning signs related to dissociative symptoms and behaviors, and contributing circumstances that can cause or influence the use of dissociation. These warning signs describe specific behaviors that include core dissociative symptoms of amnesia, hallucinations, memory disturbances, and presence of self-states, as well as co-occurring symptoms and behaviors that often mask dissociative presentations. The warning signs are illustrated by numerous clinical examples from my caseload. This chapter provides a broad framework that can inform clinicians to consider these signs and circumstances when evaluating traumatized children for early detection of and treatment for dissociation.

Chapter 3 continues to draw on Chapter 2 by specifically examining overlapping symptoms of dissociation with more commonly known diagnoses, and how this often leads to misdiagnosis of dissociation in children. A discussion occurs about how children with complex trauma can have multiple domains of impairment, leading clinicians to base their diagnoses on the most florid symptoms, for example, inattention (attention deficit hyperactivity disorder [ADHD]), volatile mood swings (bipolar disorder), attachment disturbances (reactive attachment disorder [RAD]), hallucinations (psychosis), and many others, instead of seeing the compilation of symptoms and their relationship to a dissociative disorder. Research studies are critically examined to help the clinician discern the difference between overlapping symptoms found in other diagnoses and how they may actually be indicative of a dissociative disorder. It is stressed that recognizing these differences can lead to early detection of dissociation and a more promising recovery.

Chapter 4 provides a detailed description of areas of assessment; the use of valid, normative assessment tools; and careful, thorough questioning of the child and parents. This chapter introduces Rudy and Lisa, and it continues the discussion on Briana and Cathy. Many other cases are also described to provide examples of the diverse presentations that children can exhibit with dissociative behaviors. This chapter also provides guidance on how to question children about their dissociative behaviors.

Chapter 5 lays the groundwork for assessing and treating children with dissociation. It provides overarching principles of how to successfully work with traumatized children. A brief introduction into the phase-oriented treatment, beginning with stabilization and ending with integration, is provided. Special emphasis on developing metacognitive skills to help children reach integration is given.

Chapter 6 begins the description of the treatment process of dissociative children by focusing initially on the family and next on resolving attachment disturbances. I discuss the importance of building a secure attachment with parents or caretakers as an anchor for traumatized children to be able to release their dissociative defenses and face the horrors of their past traumatic life. Parenting strategies, formulated on brain-based parenting (e.g., Hughes & Bylin, 2012) and Satir's (1983) approach to family systems, and strategies to manage dissociative symptoms are discussed. This framework provides the clinician with an integrative approach in managing the complexity of family work that will enhance treatment of the dissociative child. Challenges in working with families are discussed, and specialized techniques to engage the parents are offered. The chapter concludes with a description of a perplexing case of a "detached teenager" and the successful outcome.

Chapter 7 begins with the provocative case of Rudy ascribing his attempt to strangle his sister to his "invisible team." This example sets the stage for a discussion on how dissociative self-states can drive a child to behave in dangerous, erratic ways. I begin with defining classifications of "lion self-states," perpetrating parts of a child that can wreak havoc on the child and his or her family's life. Questions designed to assess such states are presented. My dialogue with Rudy is detailed to illustrate his internal world where cognitive errors formed from his early traumatic life in an East European orphanage. This chapter, Phase 1 of treatment, provides detailed strategies for stabilization that enhance internal awareness, cooperation, and communication, and offers empowerment techniques that lay the foundation for later trauma processing.

Chapter 8 builds on Chapter 7 by offering more detailed strategies for stabilization that specifically focus on calming the child's overactive stress response system and managing triggers. Numerous exercises, such as containment, safe place/safe state, connecting with the body, building self-reflection (e.g., EARTH), and expanding the window of tolerance, are described. These techniques help equip the child with resources to be emotionally present and to be able to manage strong affect, particularly during trauma processing. Eight overlapping tasks are outlined to help the child manage triggers. Numerous case examples, including Cathy's and Briana's, are elucidated with the use of these strategies, including dialogues between the child and the therapist.

Chapter 9, which is coauthored with Adrian J. Stierum, is the first chapter since 1997 (Nemzer, 1998) that has been written on the use of medication in dissociative youth. Although medication will not cure dissociation in children, it is considered an adjunctive, time-limited therapy to help the child function until the trauma can be processed. This chapter follows the *Clinical Manual of Child and Adolescent Psychopharmacology*, second edition, edited by McVoy and Findling (2013), the official American Psychiatric Association (APA) guidelines, when discussing the use of medication. Numerous case studies illustrate specific symptoms and behaviors in which certain types of medication are useful. Cautionary guidelines for use, including side effects and health risks to the child's developing brain, are also discussed with the emphasis on increasing treatment sessions and stabilization techniques prior to administering medication.

Chapter 10 begins with a quote, "When I think of the bad stuff, I don't feel bad anymore." This chapter, Phase 2 of treatment, describes nine guidelines of areas that are used to assess readiness for trauma processing, such as a child's current level of comorbidity and use of stabilization techniques, evaluating meaning of implicit memories, and past unresolved attachment. The remainder of the chapter involves detailed descriptions of four stories of children's trauma processing using interventions tailored to their needs.

Chapter 11, coauthored with Diane Raven, is a description of a successful collaborative treatment effort between Raven, former art director at Great Lakes Recovery Center for Adolescents (a substance abuse residential program), and myself in providing intensive treatment for traumatized youth with comorbid substance abuse. Raven's innovative, inspiring art therapy interventions are illustrated with step-by-step instructions and case examples. These interventions are designed to help traumatized adolescents describe their internal life and begin to face their traumatic past. The issues that arose in art therapy were then addressed in intensive psychotherapy provided by me. The case of Emily demonstrates how art therapy combined with individual and family therapy can hasten recovery. Reproductions of Emily's art that depict each stage in her therapeutic process through integration are included.

Chapter 12 focuses specifically on the use of eye movement desensitization and reprocessing (EMDR) therapy with traumatized, dissociative youth throughout the treatment process. This chapter describes a comparison between adaptive information processing (AIP) theory and EMDR phases with dissociative theory and three-phase treatment of dissociative children. Details of each phase of treatment using EMDR therapy with emphasis on stabilization are provided. Numerous case studies illustrate the process with special emphasis on resolving early trauma with EMDR therapy.

Chapter 13, the final chapter, dealing with Phase 3 of treatment, focuses on integration techniques. This chapter opens with an eloquent description of what integration was like for a 10-year-old girl. Specific techniques to promote integration, including the use of metaphors (such as the child's favorite dessert or sport), are detailed with case descriptions. Numerous detailed examples of the process of how children became integrated are provided. The book ends with guidelines for assessing integration, postintegration relapse, and, finally, an inspiring poem authored by an integrated child.

The aim of this book is to provide a solid basis for assessing and treating children with dissociation by providing rich clinical cases and specialized interventions that lead to trauma resolution and, finally, integration of the fractured child.

PART I

THEORY

THE STAR THEORETICAL MODEL
AN INTEGRATIVE MODEL FOR ASSESSING AND TREATING CHILDHOOD DISSOCIATION

> *Children love and want to be loved and they very much prefer*
> *the joy of accomplishment to the triumph of hateful failure.*
> *Do not mistake a child for his symptom.*
>
> —Erik Erikson

THIS QUOTE BY ERIKSON RESONATES with the message I hope to convey in this book. Children are children and we must not define them by their symptoms. We need to look deep within them to see what they are truly communicating via their behavior and symptoms. Consider the symptoms of the following children:

At ten years old, Geraldine was found wondering in a dazed state with severe amnesia. She did not know who she was or where she was. She had a severe headache and realized that her mother was not with her (her mother had died 2 years earlier), and that she was on the wrong bus. (Bowlby, 1980, p. 338)

When Laura returned home, she banged on the door calling "Mummy, *Mummy!*" When her mother opened the door, Laura looked at her blankly and said, "But I want <u>my</u> mummy." For the next two days Laura seemed not to recognize her mother and, although not unfriendly, was completely detached. (Bowlby, 1980, p. 409)

During Kate's second week of placement in foster care, she expressed fear of getting lost, was clingy, cried more easily and at times seemed preoccupied and dreamy. On one such occasion, she murmured, "What is Kate looking for?," a remark that seemed to indicate that she was temporarily losing track of the identity of the person for whom she was yearning and searching. (Bowlby, 1980, pp. 395–396)

Remarkably, these brief case descriptions are not from research on dissociation, but rather from a study by John Bowlby, the father of attachment theory, on the impact of maternal losses on children. Bowlby (1980) noted that after being separated from their mothers, many children demonstrated profound detachment from their mothers who, in turn, complained that their children treated them as strangers. Bowlby described these children as having blank looks on their faces, confusion about their identity (e.g., Kate referring to herself in the third person), and apparent amnesia for their mothers after periods of separation. The symptoms he described are currently recognized as dissociative responses resulting from pronounced relational losses at an early age.

In the mid-1990s, I had been treating dissociative children for a decade and recognized that a comprehensive theoretical model was needed to understand the complexity and nuances of the multiple influences that impact traumatized children's reliance on dissociation. One theory seemed insufficient to explain dissociative symptoms in traumatized children, but a combination of theories from different fields provided a comprehensive framework for accurate assessment and successful treatment. I therefore developed the Quadri-Theoretical Model (Waters, 1996), which interlinked four prominent theories—attachment, child development, family systems, and dissociation. This model has recently been revised to include neurobiology as the fifth theory and is now called the Star Theoretical Model (STM; Figure 1.1).

The model describes pathways that either lead to or influence the use of dissociation in children and adolescents, and it guides the assessment and treatment of children with dissociation. The star shape represents the children who are exposed to trauma. This is not to say that all traumatized children utilize dissociation or develop a dissociative disorder. Rather, the STM was developed to describe pathways in those situations in which children do develop dissociation. The attachment theory was intentionally placed at the top of the star to signify the paramount role that parent–child attachment plays in contributing to a child's reliance on dissociative coping mechanisms when traumatized. The strength of the parent–child attachment bond also influences the child's ability to heal.

It is important to note that although each of the five theoretical models describes significant dynamics pertaining to development of dissociation

**Star Theoretical Model for assessing and treating childhood
dissociation based on five theories**

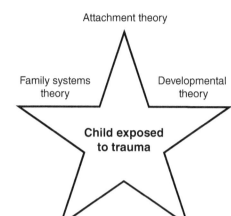

Figure 1.1 *Star Theoretical Model for assessment and treatment
of childhood dissociation.*

in children, it is the *integration* of the five theories that formulates my diagnostic and therapeutic approach. Prior to explaining my model, I describe
dissociation and examine the etiology of dissociation from different theoretical perspectives.

DEFINITION OF *DISSOCIATION*

Currently, the fifth edition of the *Diagnostic and Statistical Manual of Mental
Disorders (DSM-5)* defines *dissociation* as a disturbance in the ongoing
continuity in the normal integration of consciousness, memory, identity,
emotional, perception, body representation, motor control, and behavior
(American Psychiatric Association [APA], 2013, p. 291). Dissociation occurs
on a continuum ranging from nonpathological or normal dissociation to
pathological dissociation. Examples of normal dissociation are absorption,
such as when reading a thrilling book or playing video games, daydreaming about something pleasant, or "highway hypnosis," such as losing track
of time when driving on a long stretch of highway.

The distinguishing characteristic between nonpathological and
pathological dissociation is that pathological dissociation comprises some

degree of a "structural division" within the self, causing disturbances in consciousness, memory, perception, and/or identity. For example, someone may think about a traumatic event, yet feel detached or numb (depersonalization), or may view the event with some distortion (derealization), such as a tunnel vision. In its most severe form, dissociation may manifest as segregated self-states with separate states of consciousness or awareness. Self-states (also called parts, ego states, or alters) are segmented states of consciousness within the child that may present as different beings that can either take executive control of the child's body or influence the child from within. These states are instinctively created to carry unwanted, disturbing traumatic-associated material (e.g., affect, behavior/function, sensations, and/or memories) so the child can survive intolerable circumstances. Self-states can perform necessary functions for the child when the child is unable to cope; the child may view himself or herself as having a different age, gender, and viewpoint from those of the presenting child–client. These states can present in therapy as distinct changes in affect, speech patterns, demeanor, and body language, and each state may respond differently to the therapist (see International Society for the Study of Trauma and Dissociation [ISSTD] FAQ[1]). For a list of some Internet sites on child trauma and dissociation, refer to Appendix A.

Relationship Between Trauma and Dissociation

There are abundant research and clinical cases describing the traumatic impact of sexual abuse (e.g., Hulette, Fisher, Kim, Ganger, & Landsverk, 2008; Kisiel & Lyons, 2001; Kisiel, McClelland, & Torgersen, 2013; Macfie, Cicchetti, & Toth, 2001), physical abuse (e.g., Chu & Dill, 1990; Chu, Frey, Ganzel, & Matthews, 1999), emotional abuse (e.g., Teicher, Samson, Polcari, & McGreenery, 2006), emotional neglect (e.g., Milot et al., 2013), and natural disasters (e.g., Vásquez et al., 2012) on the development of childhood dissociation. In many of these studies, children experience more than one type of trauma.

Kisiel and Lyons (2001) studied 114 youth (10–18 years of age) who were wards of the Illinois Department of Children and Family Services and resided in residential treatment centers. Their results suggested a unique relationship between sexual abuse and dissociation. They concluded that dissociation may be the critical mediator of psychiatric symptoms and risk-taking behavior among sexually abused children. Another study found a significant correlation between sexual abuse, physical abuse and neglect, and higher levels of dissociation in foster children in San Diego (Hulette et al., 2008). Cloitre et al. (2009) researched the cumulative effects of traumatic exposure in clinical samples of 582 women and 152 children and found a direct relationship between the number of traumatic experiences and complex symptoms, including dissociation and overall self-regulatory disturbance.

The relationship between trauma and dissociation has been demonstrated cross-culturally in many different countries, including England (Farrington, Waller, Smerden, & Faupel, 2001), Turkey (Zoroglu, Sar, Tuzun, Tutkun, & Savas, 2002), the Netherlands (Muris, Merckelbach, & Peeters, 2003), Sweden (Nilsson & Svedin, 2006), and Finland (Tolmunen et al., 2007). Sar, Onder, Killicaslan, Zoroglu, and Alyanak (2014) studied the prevalence of dissociation in a psychiatric outpatient sample in Turkey and found that of the 73 adolescents examined, 45.2% had a dissociative disorder, 16.4% had dissociative identity disorder (DID), and 28.8% had dissociative disorder not otherwise specified (DDNOS[2]). A large Japanese study surveyed 1,993 schoolchildren between 11 and 18 years of age and found that 15% of children had evidence of pathological dissociation (Yoshizumi, Hamada, Kaida, Gotow, & Murase, 2010).

Infant Trauma and Dissociation

A particularly pernicious form of trauma is infant trauma. Infants can be negatively impacted by a number of experiences, such as birth trauma; painful medical procedures; early deprivation; physical, sexual, and emotional abuse; and disruption in attachment. Traditional definitions of *trauma* may fail to recognize that infants' symptoms relate to traumatic experiences. This may be due to the myth that infants and toddlers are either "resilient" or unaffected by traumatic events. In reality, the younger the children are when they experience trauma, the more likely they are to suffer enduring and pervasive problems (Perry, 2006). Although infants' pain has been either discounted or unrecognized as causing disturbance, Gaensbauer (2002) noted that newborns manifest all of the cardinal physiologic stress responses to pain. Fraiberg (1982) succinctly states that it is not possible to say that infants do not experience trauma and are "too young to feel or remember" (p. 612).

Just because infants do not have the ability to verbalize their experiences, their sensory connections are functioning even before birth.

Infants are able to hear their mother's voice and are influenced by their mother's emotional state. In addition, the implicit memory system is always operating—calculating and tabulating sensory experiences. Infants do register emotional and physical pain. Although these memories may not be conscious, they are held in the implicit memory system and often manifest somatically and behaviorally. Bowlby (1980) and Fraiberg (1982) observed infants who experienced maternal separation and deprivation, and found that they demonstrated freezing behaviors, trance states, and memory problems, resulting in total disorganization. The most potentially terrifying experiences for a young child occur in the context of their primary attachment figure, usually a parent who is abusive or neglectful (Alexander, 2013), on whom the child is totally dependent. The child has no ability to escape the trauma, except by dissociating, an automatic, primitive response, as described in the Polyvagal Theory section by Porges (2011). Further research described a disorganized attachment style in infants that is characterized by dissociative behavior resulting from exposure to frightening parents and/or frightened parents (Main & Hesse, 1990; Ogawa, Sroufe, Weinfield, Carlson, & Egeland, 1997). However, today, many clinicians fail to recognize these as dissociative behaviors related to traumatic experiences and instead ascribe them to other diagnoses.

In summary, these studies point to the need to take a comprehensive trauma history and assess all children, including infants, for dissociation whenever they come to the attention of mental health professionals.

Conceptual Models of Dissociation

Since the early 19th century, a number of models have emerged that conceptualize the formation and treatment of dissociation. All these models are based on the premise that pathological dissociation derives from traumatic experiences. I incorporate many of these models into my conceptualization of dissociation as well.

Janet's Concept of Dissociation

Although there are other early contributors to our understanding of dissociation (i.e., Ferenczi, 1933/1949; Freud, 1893/2001), Janet's concepts have greatly influenced our current understanding of dissociation (see, e.g., van der Hart, Nijenhuis, & Steele, 2006; van der Kolk, van der Hart, & Marmar,

1996). Janet (1907) used the term *hysteria* to refer to an individual's retraction of his or her field of consciousness, with segregated internal systems, each with their own sense of self. Janet recognized the role of traumatic experiences in an individual's constitutional vulnerability and integrative failure (van der Hart & Dorahy, 2009). Janet also recognized the intrusiveness of traumatic memories, which may be automatically replayed when activated, along with the fact that, at times, the individual may be unable to recall the traumatic memories (van der Hart & Dorahy, 2009). To treat hysteria, Janet developed the phase-oriented treatment model, which has been carried over into contemporary practice guidelines (ISSTD, 2011).

Putnam's Defense Model and Discrete Behavioral States

Putnam (1997) defined *dissociation* as a complex psychophysiological process that alters the accessibility of memory and knowledge, along with the integration of behavior and a sense of self. Putnam (1997, pp. 67–75) views dissociation as a defense mechanism with three major tasks: (a) the automatization of behavior in the face of psychologically overwhelming circumstances; (b) compartmentalization of painful affects and memories; and (c) estrangement from self in the face of potential annihilation. The mind becomes overwhelmed with fear, and the child functions on an automatic pilot—going through the experience without conscious thought or feeling. The child is not fully aware of what she is really experiencing and may become numb or depersonalized ("It's not me"). The child can compartmentalize either parts or all of the experience across affect, behavior, sensation, and memory, because facing it would overload the child's coping abilities. Holding the trauma in one's conscious memory would present a dangerous dilemma, particularly if a child depends on the abuser for care. It is safer for the child to not know or not to feel. Although separating from the trauma is adaptive, this separation of the self impairs the process of developing internal self-awareness and mindfulness.

Putnam's (1997) Discrete Behavioral States Model views self-states as discrete states of consciousness, each with ". . . a specific and unique configuration of a set of psychological, physiological, and behavioral variables" (p. 152). The term *discrete behavioral states* originates from the study of infant behavioral states (Wolff, 1987) as infants transition from one activity to another (e.g., sleeping to waking; distressed to neutral). How the child responds to these behavioral states is dependent on his mother's ability to read his cues and appropriately respond to his needs. For example, if the mother responds to her infant in a calm, predictable, nurturing manner, then templates are created for the baby to have a smooth transition from one behavioral state to another. Smooth transitions help the infant to modulate affect between behavioral states. However, if the mother is unpredictable, confusing, frightening, or abusive, then the child will develop fear-based alterations of behavioral state pathways, leading to discrete behavioral states of dysregulated affect and behavior separated in consciousness or knowledge of other states.

Putnam defines *pathological dissociation* as ". . . a category of trauma-induced discrete behavioral states that are widely separated in multidimensional state space from normal states of consciousness" (p. 173). Treatment interventions include working with the child's discrete states of consciousness, facilitating modulation between them, developing integrative functions across self-states, and resolving traumatic memories.

Structural Dissociation

Van der Hart et al. (2006) developed the theory of Structural Dissociation, which builds on the early works of Jackson (1931/1932) and Janet (1907). Their theory recognizes that trauma-related dissociation involves the personality having at least two self-organizing systems of psychobiological states. Each self-organizing system has its own sense of self that lacks integrative functioning between the other systems. Structural dissociation of the personality is composed of actions systems that are goal directed, adaptive, and defensive. These action systems are divided into the "apparently normal" personality (ANP) and the "emotional" personality (EP). The ANP is involved in managing daily life, such as working and attending school. The ANP is associated with avoidance of the traumatic memories, and if they have some knowledge of them, they experience detachment, as if it did not happen to them. The EP contains the traumatic memories, and associated traumatic affect, thoughts, behaviors, and sensations. The EP remains fixated at the time of the trauma and is dedicated to the survival from "predatory" threat. It often becomes stuck in the sensory experience of the traumatic memory and is unaware of the passage of time. With severe, chronic trauma, each ANP and EP can further divide into many ANPs and EPs that take on additional actions for the self.

The Structural Dissociation Model has mainly been used with adults but has also been found to be useful in understanding dissociative children (see Stolbach, 2005; Wieland, 2015a). It provides a framework for conceptualizing different self-states in children, which are viewed as action systems that are formed to help the child survive. Treatment involves evaluating each action system and then breaking down amnestic barriers between systems as the trauma is processed and resolved so that integration can occur.

Ego State Theory

Watkins and Watkins's (1997) ego state theory conceptualizes ego states along a continuum from normal to pathological. They define an *ego state* as "... a body of behaviors and experiences bound together by some common principle and separated from other such entities by boundaries which are more or less permeable" (Watkins & Watkins, 1988, p. 69). The ego state theory recognizes a range of boundaries between ego states varying from normal to pathological, such as impermeable barriers resulting in amnesia between the ego states. When clients have impermeable boundaries, they are considered to have an ego state disorder. Impermeable boundaries between ego states usually occur as a survival response when children are confronted with overwhelming trauma. These pathological ego states can have a sense of separateness, assume executive position, be highly motivated to protect their existence, and be in conflict with other ego states or the primary person. Ego states can contain affect (e.g., sad, mad, scared) or behavioral roles (playful, student, abuser). They can also identify with someone important to the child (e.g., nonabuser or abuser, aunt, hero figure). Treatment involves individual therapy to reduce the rigidity of the boundaries between states, lessening conflicts between ego states, and promoting mutual understanding through interstate communications (Watkins, 1993).

Affect Avoidance Theory

Affect avoidance theory (Silberg, 2013) relies on developmental literature, including Putnam's Discrete Behavioral States Model, attachment theory, affect theory, and interpersonal neurobiology, to explain how and why traumatized children develop dissociative coping strategies. The affect avoidance theory views dissociation as an adaptive response to trauma. Silberg noted that if the child experiences terror or distress in connection with the caregiver, the affects aroused are often intense. Over time, the affect itself becomes so painful that avoidance programs take over, triggering automatic defensive behaviors that may have been learned at a time and place when it was adaptive to engage in these behaviors. The mind becomes organized around shifting identities or self-states that segment the intense affect off from awareness. Silberg (2013) defines *dissociation* as follows: "The automatic activation of patterns of action, thought, perception, identity, or relating (or 'affect scripts'), which are overlearned and serve as conditioned avoidance responses to affect arousal associated with traumatic cues" (p. 22).

According to Silberg (2013), it is the reactivation and repetition of this pattern that develops rigidity within traumatized children, causing memory problems, fluctuating behaviors, shifts of consciousness, shifting identities, and somatic disturbances. The rigidity and impermeability of these affect scripts, stimulated by multiple triggers in the environment, make them highly resistant to intervention. These patterns of responding may become organized as shifting identities or self-states.

From this perspective, the treatment of dissociative states requires an interpersonal process that changes the restrictive ways in which the mind has come to organize itself. It requires the presence of an attuned therapist and an engaged family. Treatment emphasizes avoiding trauma-based cues and attending to select information from the environment that facilitates increasing self-determination and freedom from automatic responses learned in the traumatic past.

Betrayal Trauma

Betrayal trauma theory (Freyd, 1996) builds on the attachment theory to explain why dissociative amnesia can be an adaptive survival mechanism. The theory posits that betrayal by a trusted caregiver is the core factor in determining the use of dissociative defenses and developing memory deficits for childhood trauma. Freyd proposes that humans are sensitive to betrayal, and when one is betrayed, the normal reaction is to feel pain and avoid further contact with the betrayer. However, when attachment processes are involved, such a response may not be in the victim's survival interests. If abused children processed betrayal by an essential caregiver in the normal way, they would be motivated to stop interacting with the betrayer. However, if a child was to withdraw from a caregiver on whom he or she is dependent, the child's life would be placed in even greater danger. As Freyd points out, "A child who distrusts his or her parents risks alienating the parents further, and thus becomes subject to more abuse and less love and care" (p. 10). In these circumstances, Freyd (1996) suggests that the need to survive may prevail over the need to avoid betrayal. Consequently, victims of intimate betrayals learn to cope with inescapable conflict through internal disconnection (i.e., dissociation), rather than through external avoidance. Thus, the betrayal trauma theory posits that violence perpetrated by someone on whom the victim is dependent will be associated with memory disruption, dissociation, and other cognitive dysfunctions in order to help the victim maintain the necessary, albeit abusive, attachment (see Freyd, 1996).

Summary

All of these models recognize the need to break down amnestic barriers between parts of the self, be they ego states, self-states, or action states, and each of these models has informed my work. The betrayal trauma theory plays a significant role in the STM (described next), particularly under attachment, when I compare Bowlby's (1960) five stages of psychological responses to grief and mourning with similar stages that dissociative children experience from interpersonal violence. Let us examine the model I developed to assess and treat childhood dissociation.

THE STAR THEORETICAL MODEL FOR ASSESSING AND TREATING CHILDHOOD DISSOCIATION

The STM integrates five prominent theories—attachment, neurobiology, developmental theory, family systems, and dissociation—to describe pathways that lead to or influence the use of dissociation in children and adolescents. It complements the prior theories of dissociation outlined earlier; however, my theory relies more heavily on the interlinking between attachment, child development, neurobiology, and family system theories.

Dissociation: A Creative Escape Hatch

Houdini, an escape artist and stunt performer, was a master at devising illusions that made animals and people disappear (Gibbons, 2014). Our logical sense said that they could not really disappear—that he must be using a trapdoor of some kind. Houdini became popular, because his tricks defied all reason and left audiences in awe as the trapdoor was so well concealed.

In many respects, dissociation is a secret trapdoor that allows a child who cannot physically escape from a terrifying experience to mentally exit the situation. However, dissociation is not a trick. It is an instinctive, biological survival mechanism (Porges, 2011) involving immobilization and freezing that is activated when the threat is so great, and the fear is so overwhelming, that the child feels death is imminent (Putnam, 1997). The child escapes the only way that affords him or her the ability to be able to go on with life. The child separates from the experience so that "it didn't occur," "it didn't happen to me," or if it did, "it didn't bother me." It is an automatic escape hatch that can be activated so the child does not have to know when knowing is too unbearable. The child may at times know bits and pieces of the trauma; at other times, the child may not even know that it occurred! Although dissociation is adaptive at the time of the trauma, later, it can interfere with the child's effectiveness in navigating the world.

An example of how dissociation can manifest in a child can be found in the case of Kaitlyn,[3] a 5-year-old girl abused by her stepbrother, Charlie. Kaitlyn eloquently described dissociation when referring to an internalized abusive self-state she called "Charlie." Kaitlyn chose a puppet of an alien to represent the Charlie voice inside of her head. She put her small hand in the puppet and exclaimed, "It's all Charlie's fault!" I motioned with a hermit crab puppet asking, "What do you mean it is all Charlie's fault?" She pounded the alien puppet's head with her free hand and said, "That mean Charlie makes me do bad things." I asked her what kind of bad things he made her do. Kaitlyn looked a bit perplexed and answered, "I can't remember." I responded, "You know he makes you do bad things, but you can't remember?" She nodded her head in agreement and added, "But I know one thing, he gets louder, louder and louder, and then he shoves out!" as she raised her head upward. I reflected her words, "He makes you do bad things and he shoves out. What happens next?" She looked at me, pondering a moment and then said, "He gets louder and louder and then my mind walks away and he's in my mind!" I responded, "He gets louder and louder and then your mind walks away and he is in your mind. What happens then?" She shrugged her shoulders, again looking perplexed, and answered, "I don't know."

Kaitlyn innocently and yet poignantly disclosed what dissociation is like. She related how Charlie hijacks her mind as he "gets louder and louder" and she then did not know what happened next. It was confusing and frightening for Kaitlyn to be plagued by a threatening, persistent voice telling her to do bad things, for which she has no control and no memory once "he shoves out."

The mechanism by which traumatized children are able to develop different self-states appears to be a creative way to escape from unmitigated terror, helplessness, confusion, and emotional and physical pain. It certainly surpasses any of Houdini's tricks. At the same time, the existence of self-states with different genders, ages, and roles can seem unimaginable and hard to comprehend. Putnam (1997) stated, "Alter personalities are real. They do exist, not as separate individuals but as *discrete dissociative states of consciousness*. When considered from this perspective, they are not nearly so amazing to behold or so difficult to accept" (p. 90, italics added). Putnam then quoted Coons (1984), who stated, "Only when taken together can all of the personality states be considered a whole personality" (p. 90).

Let's examine next the neurobiology of trauma.

Neurobiology: Impact on Memory and Fragmentation

Although we can listen carefully to what traumatized children tell us about memory disturbances, observe them, and make conjectures about what is happening inside them, new neurological discoveries provide some scientific answers. There are many neurobiological systems operating within each of us to ensure our survival and development. Understanding these systems can provide some insight as to memory disturbances and the development of dissociation and self-states.

Numerous researchers have recognized the impact of chronic traumatic stress on memory and brain structures (e.g., hippocampus, amygdala, prefrontal cortex, corpus callosum) (Bremner, 2005; DeBellis et al., 1999; Frewen & Lanius, 2006; Nijenhuis & den Boer, 2009; Reinders et al., 2003; Vermetten, Schmahl, Lindner, Loewenstein, & Bremner, 2006). Stress can lead to the deactivation of certain critical structures in the brain that encode and consolidate memories into the conscious memory system, accounting for memory problems and dissociative responses (Bremner, 2005; Perry, 2001; Vermetten et al., 2006).

A recent study has confirmed a neurological pathway for inaccessible traumatic memories (Jovasevic et al., 2015). Memories are usually stored in distributed brain networks and can be readily accessed to consciously remember an event. A process known as state-dependent learning is believed to contribute to the formation of memories that are inaccessible to the normal consciousness. This process has received empirical support from Jovasevic et al.'s study.

To better understand the mechanisms underlying state-dependent fear, the researchers used a mouse model of contextual fear conditioning. Glutamate is the primary chemical that helps store memories across distributed brain networks. Glutamate and gamma-aminobutyric acid (GABA) work in tandem to control levels of excitation and inhibition in the brain, and, under normal conditions, remain balanced. Hyperarousal, which occurs when we are terrified, causes glutamate to surge. GABA, on the other hand, is calming and balances glutamate receptors in the presence of stress. However, extra-synaptic GABA receptors also exist. Based on prior research, Jovasevic et al. hypothesized that the ability to remember stressful experiences might be mediated by extra-synaptic GABA receptors in the brain.

To test this, Jovasevic et al. gave mice a chemical, gaboxadol, with extra-synaptic GABA receptors that induce a state similar to mild inebriation. The mice were then placed in a box and given a brief, mild shock. The next day, the mice were placed in the same box without the chemical administered beforehand. The mice moved about freely, unafraid, indicating they did not recall the shock. Later, the mice were given the chemical and again placed in the box. This time when they entered the box, they froze in fear anticipating another shock. Thus, when the mice were returned to the same brain state they were in when they received the shock, they remembered it.

The study demonstrated that when the extra-synaptic GABA receptors were activated with the drug, they changed the way the stressful event was encoded. Extra-synaptic $GABA_A$ receptors promoted subcortical, but impaired cortical, activation during memory encoding of the fearful event. Thus, the brain rerouted the memory using completely different molecular pathways and neuronal circuits to store the memory. The researchers said their findings imply that in response to trauma, some people will not activate the glutamate system but instead activate the extra-synaptic GABA system (Scutti, 2015).

According to one of the researchers, Jelena Radulovic, "The brain functions in different states, much like a radio operates at AM and FM frequency bands" (*ScienceDaily*, 2015). She noted that it is as if the brain is normally tuned to FM stations to access memories, but needs to be tuned to AM stations to access traumatic memories. The memory of the traumatic event cannot be accessed unless the same neural pathways are activated once again, essentially tuning the brain back into the AM stations. This research provides insight about how self-states can coexist with different memories and emotions.

Furthermore, studies have demonstrated neurobiological differences in self-states of DID patients. Reinders, Willemsen, Vos, Den Boer, and Nijenhuis (2012) looked at self-states with brain imaging. They found striking neurobiological differences in authentic self-states in DID patients compared with a control group of healthy high and low fantasy-prone adults simulating self-states in role-play. In reviewing brain imaging studies, Frewen and Lanius (2006) found that dissociation involves a disconnection in the neural pathways usually linking self-awareness with somatosensory awareness, which could lead to the development of dissociative identities in traumatized children.

Polyvagal Theory

The autonomic nervous system (ANS) also plays a role in dissociation. This system works automatically without a person's conscious effort. Stephen Porges, originator of the polyvagal theory, has extensively studied the ANS, a neuroendocrine–immune structure that enables survival. The ANS innervates the internal organs (e.g., the heart and digestive system) and regulates their functions. It was previously believed that the ANS had two main divisions: sympathetic and parasympathetic. For the most part, the sympathetic nervous system stimulates body processes (e.g., increases the heart rate) and the parasympathetic inhibits body processes (e.g., slows the heart rate). However, Porges (2011) discovered a third branch of the ANS, which he calls the social engagement nervous system, that promotes connections to others through responding to interpersonal cues.

According to Porges (2011), these three branches of the ANS produce phylogenically ordered responses that are instinctual and unconscious. The most primitive branch of the ANS is the parasympathetic nervous system. It is associated with primal survival strategies of primitive vertebrates, reptiles, and amphibians and remains functional in humans. It encompasses the unmyelinated portion of the vagus nerve that regulates the digestive and reproductive systems, and it creates a metabolic baseline of operation to manage nutrients getting to the cells. When activated by fear, it initiates a shutdown response involving immobilization, feigning death, and/or dissociation. Above in the evolutionary chain is the sympathetic system that enables mobility for finding food and defending against threats. It is responsible for fight or flight behaviors. The most advanced branch of the ANS is the social engagement system. It is mediated by the myelinated portion of the vagus nerve and fosters social communication and maternal bonding via facial expressions, vocalization, and listening.

Porges quotes Jackson's theory of dissolution (1958), which explains diseases of the nervous system: "The higher nervous system arrangements inhibit (or control) the lower, and thus, when the higher are suddenly rendered functionless, the lower rise in activity" (Jackson as cited in Porges, 2011, p. 162). For example, when an individual is under threat and cannot be rescued, the most recent section of the ANS from an evolutionary standpoint, the social engagement system, shuts down. The sympathetic nervous system is then automatically activated. It increases the heart rate and pumps blood to the muscles, preparing the individual to either fight or flee. If it is not feasible for the individual to defend himself or herself, then the sympathetic nervous system shuts down and the most primitive portion of the ANS, the parasympathetic nervous system, is activated and initiates a freeze response. As a last resort for survival, it causes a general shutdown of the body, leading to immobilization, feigning death, and/or dissociation.

This hierarchical functioning of the nervous system explains survival strategies often observed in abused children. For example, when a child is abused by a caretaker, the social engagement response is violated and cannot function. The child is unable to seek support. Further, when the vulnerable child is unable to defend himself or herself by fighting or fleeing, the child will revert automatically and instinctively to the most primitive response: immobilization and dissociation.

Use-Dependent Development of the Brain

A theoretical work by Bruce Perry, a psychiatrist who has done extensive research on traumatized children, provides a conceptual framework for understanding how childhood trauma can result in long-term changes in the functioning of children's nervous systems. Perry's model explains how over time transitory states can become enduring traits. According to Perry,

Pollard, Blakely, Baker, and Vigilante (1995), repetitive neural activation caused by repeated exposure to threatening stimuli causes sensitization of the nervous system. The more a neural network is activated, the more there will be use-dependent internalization of new information needed for survival. Perry et al. explained, "The more frequently a certain pattern of neural activation occurs, the more indelible the internal representation" (p. 275).

This use-dependent activation can be viewed as a template through which future input is filtered. Use-dependent internalization of a state of anger or fear, for example, may explain how children can have certain self-states that they identify as "the fearful one," or "the angry one." Perhaps this may also explain self-states that identify with the perpetrator or with hero characters, as children may internalize representations of these figures when they are abused. Over time, these internal representations are reinforced and become self-states that are activated whenever trauma-related cues are present. Due to sensitization, stress-induced activation of these internal representations can be elicited by decreasingly intense stimuli, resulting in the child developing hyperarousal or dissociative reactions in response to minor stresses (Perry et al., 1995).

Mirror Neurons

An understanding of why traumatized children may mimic or take on certain characteristics of others, including the mirroring found in self-states, can be explained by the discovery of mirror neurons in the brain (Gallese, Fadiga, Fogassi, & Rizzolatti, 1996; Rizzolatti, Fadiga, Gallese, & Fogassi, 1996). While studying macaque monkeys, researchers found that when one monkey was grasping for food and another monkey was observing it with the intention to grab food, the identical neurons fired in both monkeys. Iacoboni (2009) noted that core circuitry in mirroring is the superior temporal cortex, inferior parietal lobule, and inferior frontal cortex.

This landmark discovery has increased our understanding of human interactions, including facial imitation, perception, and action (Casile, Caggiano, & Ferrari, 2011). Iacoboni (2009) found evidence to suggest that there are mirror neurons that code facial actions. This innate ability to imitate others may help us better understand the people around us. According to Iacoboni, mirror neurons "provide a prereflective, automatic mechanism of mirroring what is going on in the brain of other people that seems compatible with our ability to understand others effortlessly and with our tendency to imitate others automatically . . ." (p. 658). Children who are dependent on others for survival, particularly their parents, often seek to mimic them. Iacoboni hypothesized that children may be prewired to imitate their parents in order to gain their favor.

Mirror neurons and children's desire to imitate and please caregivers who may also be abusive have implications for dissociation. When parents vacillate from being nice to being abusive, the child who is prewired to mirror is in a double bind. The child may deal with this bind by developing self-states that mimic the different presentations of their parents to manage contradictory working models of attachment (see Blizard, 2003). The presence of a prewired system to mirror others may also explain why traumatized children internalize self-states that mimic cartoon heroes they watch repeatedly on television or pet animals from whom they receive comfort. I have had a number of children who had self-states that were hero figures or pet animals. Animal self-states were often internal representations of a beloved pet that was either killed by the child's abuser or that had comforted the child when abused.

Attachment Theory

> . . . [M]other-love in infancy and childhood is as important for
> mental health as are vitamins and proteins for physical health.
> —John Bowlby (1953, p. 182)

The attachment portion of my model is primarily derived from the works of Bowlby, along with the findings of other researchers who have built on his work (e.g., Main & Hesse, 1990). Attachment is described as an emotional bond to another person. Bowlby (1982b) indicated that attachment is an enduring psychological connectedness between human beings. He defined *attachment behavior* as an instinctual drive of the infant to connect to the parent for survival. It is any behavior that the person engages in from time to time to obtain or maintain a desired proximity, particularly during times when security and closeness are needed to cope with challenges (Bowlby, 1982a). Attachment and attachment behavior are dynamics operating within the life span of the individual. Knowing that the attachment figure is available and responsive provides security for the individual. The lack of a lasting attachment or attachment bond can have a profound impact on the child's personality development, causing the child to be disturbed.

A secure attachment is formed through a repetitive interplay between mother and child in which the mother is in attunement with her child and the child's needs are met with consistent nurturing responses. Bowlby (1980) believed that the formation of a secure attachment with the mother in a child's early years provides the child with the capacity and confidence for managing stress and developing intimacy with others. Thus, the mother lays the foundation for the child's ability to form other relationships. The mother also becomes the regulatory mechanism for the child's own expressions and thus helps the child manage transitions.

Recent contributions from neuroscience support Bowlby's assertions that attachment is instinctive behavior with a biological function, that emotional processes lie at the foundation of a model of instinctive behavior, and that a biological control system in the brain regulates affectively driven instinctive behavior (Schore, 2000). Schore stated,

> . . . attachment experiences, face-to-face transactions of affect synchrony between caregiver and infant, directly influence the imprinting, the circuit wiring of the orbital prefrontal cortex, a corticolimbic area that is known to begin a major maturational change at 10 to 12 months and to complete a critical period of growth from the middle to the end of the second year. This time-frame is identical to Bowlby's maturation of an attachment control system that is open to influence from the developmental environment. (p. 30)

Schore (2000) noted that the circuit wiring of the orbital frontal system rapidly evaluates environmental stimuli and monitors the internal state with the purpose of managing environmental disturbance. According to Schore, "Attachment theory is essentially a regulatory theory, and attachment can be defined as the interactive regulation of biological synchronicity between organisms" (p. 23). It is through this interplay (whether positive or aversive) that the child develops internal working models of representation of the self and an attachment figure (Bowlby, 1973).

Ainsworth, Blehar, Waters, and Wall (1978) originally identified three attachment classifications—secure, avoidant, and ambivalent. However, Main and Solomon (1986) recognized a new attachment classification, disorganized attachment, that has significance to this discussion. Main and Solomon found that toddlers reacted in a disorganized manner toward their mothers who were frightened or exhibited frightening behavior (e.g., abusive, neglectful, contradictory, or intrusive) toward them. Infant disorganized attachment behaviors bear close resemblance to clinical phenomena that are usually regarded as indicative of dissociation (Hesse & Main, 2000). The children would extend their arms to their mothers while also turning their heads away in the middle of approaching their parents. They would suddenly become immobile and unresponsive with a blank look on their faces and then collapse. Children with disorganized attachment show contradiction in movement patterns, as if they are pursuing two incompatible goals simultaneously (Liotti, 2004, p. 5). Main and Hesse (1990) argued that parents who act as figures of both fear and reassurance to a child contribute to a disorganized attachment style. These children are unable to develop an organized style of attachment, as their maltreating parents confront them with an inescapable paradox: The parents are potentially the only source of comfort for their children, while simultaneously frightening their children through their abusive behavior.

Disorganized attachment behaviors are considered indicators of trauma-induced stress and anxiety. Studies conducted by Carlson, Cicchetti, Barnett, and Braunwald (1989), as well as by Lyons-Ruth (1996) found that almost 80% of infants in maltreatment samples show evidence of a disorganized attachment style. Numerous clinicians and researchers have recognized the significance of attachment disorders to the development of dissociation (Barach, 1991), particularly disorganized attachment (Liotti, 1999, 2004, 2006, 2009; Lyons-Ruth, 2003; Lyons-Ruth, Dutra, Schuder, & Bianchi, 2006; Lyons-Ruth & Spielman, 2004; Main & Hesse, 1990; Ogawa et al., 1997; Schore, 2000, 2009; Siegel, 1999). Blizard (2003) noted that disorganized attachment forms the basis for individuals who were abused by their parents and developed alternating, self-states with incompatible, idealizing/devaluing, or victim/persecutor models of attachment.

An example of how dissociation can affect attachment relationships can be found in the case of Becky. This case also shows how a self-state can become a container for negative affect associated with abuse and threaten the child's attachment to her nonabusive caregivers. Becky, a pleasant and cooperative child, had a secure attachment to her parents until she entered kindergarten. After starting school, her demeanor dramatically shifted and she would display fits of anger, refuse to wear her favorite clothes, and act detached from her parents. After Becky disclosed that her male school bus driver had been sexually abusing her after all the other children had been let off the bus, she was brought to me for therapy.

When I asked Becky about the dramatic changes in her behavior, she reported hearing an angry, harassing, male voice that frightened her. At the same time that she heard the voice, inside her mind she would see a face with "mean, red eyes." The voice told Becky she was stupid. Becky said that he would take control over her. This angry part had completely different clothing preferences than Becky. He was responsible for her negative thinking and uncontrollable rages. In addition, he was not attached to her parents, which profoundly impacted Becky's relationship with them. It appeared that the state held Becky's rage regarding her abuse. Becky drew a picture of herself with wide, vacant eyes and a large red mouth opened wide, depicting her terror both over the abuse and over the angry part inside her. She wrote, "I am really scared" (Figure 1.2).

Becky's dissociative escape strategy was to completely segment herself off from the repetitive, terrifying experience. In doing so, she developed a part that only knew rage and eventually turned it on her. Becky's parents had noticed a dramatic change in their daughter but were completely baffled as to what was going on until she finally disclosed what had been transpiring daily on her school bus. Once she disclosed the

Figure 1.2 *Becky's drawing of how scared she was. (Used with permission.)*

existence of a self-state that would completely take control over her mood and behavior, her parents were finally able to understand their daughter's complete personality transformation and be supportive of her.

Bowlby's Research on Children Separated From Their Mothers

Bowlby, who believed in cross-fertilization between research and therapy, made systematic observations of children separated from their mothers with the help of his assistant, James Robertson, a trained observer. Robertson filmed young children in residential nurseries or hospitals to track their responses regarding separation from their mothers during their stay. The results were groundbreaking and relevant to contemporary science on trauma and dissociation. Bowlby (1980) noted that after separation from their mothers for extended periods, many children demonstrated profound detachment from their mothers, who, in turn, complained that their children treated them as strangers. Bowlby described these children as having blank looks on their faces with apparent amnesia for their mothers after periods of separation (see the case descriptions that follow). Bowlby (1961) ascribed their responses to a "splitting of the ego" in which one part recognized that the mother was lost and another part did not recognize that the mother was lost (p. 486). He used the term *detachment* to explain this phenomenon. The contemporary term is *dissociative splitting*.

In the third volume of his book *Attachment and Loss*, Bowlby (1980) presented three cases involving children who were separated from their parents in the second year of life. These children demonstrated signs of dissociation that are relevant to the comparison model I describe later in this chapter. The following are brief synopses of each of these cases.

Laura
Laura, who was the subject of Robertson's 1952 film, *A Two-Year-Old Goes to the Hospital*, was almost 2½ when she was admitted to the hospital for 8 days to correct an umbilical hernia. She had been given specific instructions from her mother not to cry, which was reinforced by the nurses who redirected Laura's attention away from missing her mother (Bowlby, 1980). Most of the time, Laura was described as alone in her bed, looking sad, clutching her teddy bear, but not crying. However, her true feelings came out when she talked of an urgent wish to see a steamroller that was interspersed with "I want to see my Mummy!" While Laura's mother visited her every other day, on the third and fourth visits, Laura looked blank

and made no attempt to interact with her mother until her mother was there for a while. Bowlby noted that each day Laura was experiencing increased helplessness and hopelessness with the lengthening separation from her mother.

Laura experienced another traumatic period of loss and separation 4 months later. She was sent to stay with her grandmother for 4 weeks while her mother had a new baby. Laura had no contact with either parent during this period. When Laura returned home, she banged on the door calling "Mummy, Mummy!" When her mother opened the door, Laura looked at her blankly and said, *"But I want my Mummy."* For the next two days Laura seemed not to recognize her mother and, although not unfriendly, was completely detached (Bowlby, 1980, p. 409).

Kate

Kate, a 2½-year-old girl, was fostered by a couple for 27 days (Bowlby, 1980). Prior to placement, Kate's parenting was described as rigid with a father who disciplined in quiet but threatening tones, and a mother who was softer but had high expectations of her daughter. Kate's parents insisted that she be a good girl and not cry when placed in a foster home. Bowlby also surmised that her parents might have threatened not to love her if she did not listen. No details regarding what initiated her placement were provided, but generally children are placed in foster homes due to maltreatment. During Kate's second week of placement, she expressed fear of getting lost, was clingy, and cried more easily. Bowlby noted that she ". . . at times seemed preoccupied and dreamy. On one such occasion, she murmured, 'What is Kate looking for?' a remark that seemed to indicate that she was temporarily losing track of her identity of the person for whom she was yearning and searching" (p. 395).

Bowlby surmised that Kate, who was inhibited from expression, feared that she might get lost and that her parents might not want her back if she was naughty—creating extreme fear in a 2½-year-old. I agree with Bowlby's impression that she feared that she might get lost, but it also seems apparent to me that she felt lost from herself! Dreamy behavior and referring to the self in the third person can be indicators of fragmentation and dissociation. Kate's referral to herself in the third person may have been due to a self-state that was unaware of Kate's longing for her mother along with her feelings of loss and grief. Because Kate was highly inhibited from expressing her distraught feelings for fear of retaliation, she had no recourse but to segment them off. She may have already been vulnerable to dissociation due to being raised by parents who took a harsh and punitive approach toward parenting. If she also suffered other forms of maltreatment, this would have made her even more vulnerable to dissociation.

Owen

Bowlby (1980) and his colleagues (Heinicke & Westheimer, 1965) studied Owen, who had just turned 2 when he was placed in a residential nursery after his mother was hospitalized. His mother came from an unstable home and had an unhappy childhood. She grew up feeling inadequate and insecure. Owen's mother reported that he cried incessantly as a baby, at one point described him as a "little menace," and threatened to pack up the children and send them to an institution. Owen spent almost 12 weeks in the residential nursery while his mother recuperated from surgery. Although his mother returned from the hospital after 5 weeks, she never visited him. Owen's father, on the other hand, visited him regularly.

When Owen was first placed in residential care, he cried a lot (Bowlby, 1980). During the second week of his placement, Owen cried less and appeared emotionally detached. He would not say a single word to his father when he visited him. After his father left, Owen sobbed quietly for a few moments and then sat staring. In the succeeding weeks, Owen's dissociative responses worsened to the point that he seemed to not recognize his father when he visited. Regarding his attachment to his mother, there was evidence that Owen was thinking of her. According to Bowlby, at times, he would quietly utter "Mummy" and call for her when he thought he heard her voice down the corridor.

Finally, Owen's father took him home. Bowlby (1980) reported, "When his mother greeted him with 'Hello, Owen' he again appeared not to hear; instead he remained silent and expressionless on his father's knee . . ." When his elder sister came bursting into the room to greet him, he turned away from her. She remarked, "It's not Owen's face. It is a different face." Over several months, Owen was able to slowly reconnect to his mother and ask for comfort but was extremely obstinate and many battles ensued.

Traumatic Grief in Children

Bowlby favorably quoted Engle (1961), who stated, "Loss of a loved person is as traumatic psychologically as being severely wounded or burned is physiologically" (as cited by Bowlby, 1980, p. 42). Bowlby found this quote applicable to the young children he studied who experienced sudden separation from their parents. An example of the debilitating impact of maternal separation on infants can be found in a grim and profoundly disturbing black and white silent film from the early 1950s called *Psychogenic Disease in Infancy* (Spitz, 1952). After 3 months of maternal separation, infants were shown displaying developmental regression and somatic rigidity. After 5 months, infants were lethargic, immobile, and arrested in weight and growth, with vacuous faces and bizarre finger movements. They were unable to sit, stand, walk, or talk. One infant continuously rocked on his back, which reminded me of Rudy (described later in this book) who was in an orphanage from birth until he was adopted at 18 months of age. At age 6, Rudy still compulsively rocked on his elbows and knees.

This separation or loss of a parent can lead to traumatic grief, which Bowlby termed *pathological mourning*. According to Bowlby (1961),

The main characteristics of pathological mourning is nothing less than an inability to express overtly these urges to recover and scold the lost object, with all the yearning for and anger with the deserting object that they entail. Instead of its overt expression, which though stormy and fruitless leads on to a healthy outcome, the urges to recover and reproach with all their ambivalence of feeling have become *split off* and repressed. Thenceforward, *they have continued as active systems within the personality* but, unable to find overt and direct expression, have come to influence feeling and behavior in strange and distorted ways; hence many forms of character disturbance and neurotic illness. (p. 485, italics added)

Bowlby (1961, p. 485) recognized that traumatic grief can become segregated within the personality and then influence the child's behavior and feelings in "strange and distorted ways." Robertson and Bowlby (1952) noted that during a prolonged separation, attachment behavior toward the mother can suddenly vanish, with the child treating his mother as if she were a stranger, and then the attachment behavior can suddenly reappear with the child clinging to his mother with fear and anger that he may lose her again. They termed the absence of attachment behavior as *detachment*. According to Bowlby (1982a), detached children did not seek comfort when hurt. Bowlby explained,

[T]he signals that would ordinarily activate attachment behavior are
failing to do so. This suggests that, in some way and for some reason, these signals are failing to reach the behavioral system responsible for attachment behavior, that they are being blocked off and the
behavioral system itself thereby immobilizes . . . the whole range of
feeling and desire that normally accompanies it can thus be rendered
incapable of being aroused. (p. 673)

Bowlby (1982a) contended that this detached behavior is derived
from unconscious mental processes that selectively shut off specific information without the person being aware that it is happening. There is
blocking off of the signals both internally and externally that would allow
the child to love and be loved. Bowlby called this phenomenon "defensive exclusion" (p. 674).

In my view, this signal failure may be due to amnestic barriers or
impermeable boundaries between different self-states that prevent the
activation of the attachment behavior. Bowlby's description is reminiscent
of a toddler who formed a dissociated state that was not "born" from his
mother and was not developed within the context of any attachment figure. The state was developed to help the child survive by not wanting his
mother, because if he did then he would experience further loss and grief.
Because these systems were created in the absence of any nurturing figure, the self-state did not know to seek comfort when hurt.

Bowlby's Case Study of Geraldine: Undiagnosed DID
Although Bowlby (1980) focused most of his research on loss and mourning in preschoolers, he also analyzed loss and mourning in an older child,
Geraldine, and found evidence of clear dissociative states. Although
Bowlby did not have the advantage of current nosology of dissociation,
he uses the term *deactivation* and the concept of "segregated systems"
when describing two separate personalities in Geraldine, whose mother
died of cancer when she was almost 8 years old (pp. 338–349).

Aside from losing her mother, Geraldine came from a chaotic home.
Her mother was described as an extremely bright, difficult, demanding,
domineering, and stubborn woman with a volatile and periodically uncontrollable temper. Geraldine's father was an alcoholic, and there were often
violent fights between her parents, resulting in several separations. At

one point, after Geraldine's father was hospitalized with pneumonia, her mother packed their belongings and left without telling him.

Two years after her mother's death, 10-year-old Geraldine was found wandering in a dazed state with severe amnesia. She did not know who she was or where she was. She had a severe headache and realized that her mother was not with her, and that she was on the wrong bus. She asked a stranger to take her to the hospital and her neurological exam was normal. However, Geraldine had no recall of her mother's terminal illness and subsequent death, or of her other wandering episodes. After her amnesia, she lost all of her math ability. A year later, at almost 11 years old, Geraldine entered therapy. She presented in therapy with a calm, self-assured demeanor with a vocabulary beyond her years, but offered little about herself. She factually stated that she knew her mother was dead but could not remember her mother's death and had no associated affect.

Geraldine's demeanor would change dramatically during her therapist's absences or during anniversaries of her mother's death. When her therapist was away, Geraldine verbally attacked her father, blaming him for his neglect, something that she had never voiced earlier. Her father remarked that her behavior was so much like her mother's that he thought his wife had returned from the grave. At other times, Geraldine was depressed, cried often, engaged in serious fights with peers, and blamed her therapist for leaving her. The anniversaries of her mother's death seemed to open the door to Geraldine's memory for what her life was like with her mother. She began to talk about her mother's unavailability and neglect and described herself as lonely and having to care for herself when her mother was alive.

Later in therapy, Geraldine recovered her memory of the last days of her mother's life and her mother's funeral. Geraldine expressed intense grief. With the support of her therapist, Geraldine was slowly able to erode the amnestic barriers and began to allow herself to experience the previously disassociated feelings. Geraldine eloquently described what she called three phases of her life and recovery:

At first, I blotted out all feelings—things happened that were more than I could endure—I had to keep going. If I had really let things hit me, I wouldn't be here. I'd be dead or in a mental hospital. I let myself feel nothing and my thoughts were all involved with fantasies, fairy tales, and science fiction. Then in the second phase, my feelings took over and ruled me. I did things that were way out. And the third phase, now, is that my feelings are here. I feel them and I have control over them. One of my big assets is that I can experience things with genuine feelings. At times it hurts but the advantages, the happiness, far outweigh the pain. (Bowlby, 1980, p. 342)

Geraldine's statement is very similar to statements that I have heard repeatedly from traumatized, dissociative children during their recovery.

Analysis of Geraldine's Case
Bowlby (1980) recognized that Geraldine had developed two segregated systems of consciousness (self-states) after her mother's death with separate memories, affect, and behaviors. The personality that developed after her mother's death knew her mother was dead, but did not remember it and had no affect over her loss. This was a part that was created after Geraldine was at the breaking point with overwhelming grief. The other self-state, the grieving child who recalled her mother's dying and death, was hidden and unconscious, but surfaced when she was triggered by her therapist's vacations and on the anniversaries of her mother's death. The intense grief and mourning that this part felt was too unbearable for her to manage at the moment of her mother's death, thus necessitating the creation of the part of her that had no memory or attachment grief.

Geraldine's exposure to interpersonal violence within the home prior to her mother's death laid the foundation for using dissociative mechanisms, especially when witnessing her mother's volatile temper and violent fights with her father and sister. Geraldine's attachment with her mother would meet the criteria of disorganized attachment. Her mother was frightening in her unpredictable moods and behaviors. Geraldine survived by becoming nondemanding and unexpressive. She feared abandonment by her mother, who had previously taken the children and left her father without warning. Geraldine told her therapist, "How could I ever be mad at Momma—she was really the only security I had. You really have to side with the parent who looks after you" (Bowlby, 1980, p. 342). Even though the security was tenuous at best, it was all that she had.

As Geraldine was connecting with her grief, she remarked to her therapist, "With Mamma, I was scared to death to step out of line. I saw with my own eyes how she attacked, in words, and actions, my Dad and sister and after all, I was just a little kid—very powerless" (Bowlby, 1980, p. 342). Geraldine had an intense fear of stepping out of line with her mother.

However, as with any child in such an environment, Geraldine was in a perpetual dilemma. She feared her mother even though her mother was her only security. These are the very conditions that can cause a child to dissociate. Geraldine had no choice at such an early age but to segment off her feelings for risk of losing the fragile bond she had with her mother.

These cases highlight how parental separation, loss, and maltreatment can cause children to split off from expressing their feelings in order to survive. This is especially true in children who have an ambivalent or disorganized attachment with their parents prior to the separation. Although this fragmentation helps the child cope, it comes at a great expense to his or her psychological and physical well-being.

Bowlby's Internal Working Models and Development of Dissociated Self-States

Bowlby (1973) defined what he called *segregated states* as "states of the mind" (p. 203). According to Bowlby (1982b), the child develops internal working models from caretakers and significant others. These models begin to develop within the first few years of life and become incorporated into the child's identity. The development of these working models is an unconscious process based on children's expectations about how the physical world operates, how their mother and other significant people may be expected to behave, and how all of them interact with each other. Children then make plans on how to respond to their parents (including attachment behavior) based on perceptions of how accessible, responsible, and acceptable they are to them (Bowlby, 1973).

Children can develop different and incompatible internal working models based on fear-provoking situations with parents who are frightening, neglectful, or abusive. Children abused by caregivers can develop two incompatible working models of the abuser: one who is the loving parent and the other who is the abuser. They can also develop incompatible models of their self—one as the victim and the other as the apparently normal child who attends to daily functions (van der Hart et al., 2006). These incompatible models may result in the development of distorted and biased perceptions in future relationships.

Psychological Responses to Grief and Mourning

Robertson and Bowlby (1952) originally recognized three phases that children experienced when separated from their mothers: (a) protest (related to separation anxiety), (b) despair (related to grief and mourning), and (c) denial or detachment (related to segregated systems). Later, Bowlby (1960) studied the stages of grief and mourning that older adults experienced over the loss of their spouse or another loved one and noted a similarity with children's responses to maternal loss and lengthy separation. Based on this new research, Bowlby (1960) revised his model into five stages of psychological responses to grief and mourning. These stages are: (1) thoughts and behaviors still directed toward the lost object; (2) hostility directed toward others; (3) appeals for help; (4) despair, withdrawal, regression, and disorganization; and (5) reorganization of behavior directed toward a new object. Bowlby recognized that the child's intense and unresolved grief over the loss of a parent is the underlying dynamic in these stages.

Star Theoretical Model Compared to Five Stages of Psychological Responses to Trauma in Dissociative Children

I have found patterns similar to Bowlby's (1960) five stages of psychological responses to grief and mourning in dissociative children who have also experienced interpersonal trauma such as physical, sexual, or emotional abuse, and witnessed domestic violence. Because they provide a useful framework, I have incorporated these psychological stages into the STM. My model also incorporates Bowlby's concepts regarding attachment, internal working models, and segregated states. Bowlby recognized that segregated states could occur in response to various situations in which the child's bond with the parent is disrupted, including rejection, maternal depression, the arrival of a new baby, separation from a parent, or other similar situations. I include maltreatment on this list in my model.

Loss and grief is inherent in all traumatic experiences, particularly in interpersonal trauma perpetrated by a caregiver or someone a child trusts. When a child is abused by a parent, in many ways the child has lost that parent, as the child can no longer trust the parent to keep him or her safe. Protesting does not bring the attachment figure back. The child is left with feeling fearful, helpless, depressed, and desperate. The child reverts to the most primitive, survival response—engaging the parasympathetic ANS (Porges, 2011) and dissociates. The child thus seeks to escape the trauma by splitting off the experience and associated emotions from conscious awareness into segregated systems. This is an unconscious, instinctive survival mechanism that protects the child from unbearable loss and grief associated with the trauma.

In my comparison model, traumatic events can be dissociated across the domains of affect, cognition, behaviors, sensations, and relationships and, in severe cases, leads to the development of self-states. Self-states can range from fragments of the self with limited roles, behaviors, and affect, to more developed states that take executive control over the child's body.

Not all maltreated children experience each of the five stages of psychological responses of grief and mourning, or experience them sequentially, or display segmented discrete states. Rather, the STM recognizes these as psychological responses to be considered when evaluating children who have been exposed to trauma. Furthermore, this comparison model can be a guide during assessment and treatment to alert the clinician to the child's reactions to traumatic loss and mourning, and, consequently, the development of dissociative states to be coped with. I describe each of the stages to aid the clinician in understanding the underlying dynamics associated with the child's self-states.

Stage 1: Thought and Behavior Still Directed Toward the Lost Object
In Bowlby's (1960) stage 1, the child protests loudly in the hopes of being reunited with the parent. All thoughts and behavior are directed toward reunification with the parent. In my comparison model, when abused, the child experiences grief over the loss of the desired, idealized perception of the parent. The child blames himself or herself and feels unworthy of love, which can lead to feelings of depression. (A similar dynamic can occur even if the abuser is not a primary caretaker.) These unbearable feelings and contradictory perceptions of still desiring the love of the caregiver while fearing him or her are too difficult for the child to manage. In order to maintain the child's attachment to the parent, the child has to segment off the abusive experience along with the feelings of abandonment, betrayal, rejection, and loss of safety. The child compensates by developing self-states representing the abuser and/or the unbearable affect associated with the abuse. By segmenting this information from the child's awareness, the child is able to maintain attachment to the abusive parent and avoids the unbearable pain of parental abuse.

Stage 2: Hostility Directed Toward Others
In stage 2, Bowlby (1960) described children in residential care exhibiting hostility toward anyone who tried to nurture them. They would vacillate

between rejecting care and clinging to the nurses. This contradictory behavior is frequently found in dissociative children who can display loyalty to an abusive parent, while also being angry with them. The child faces a dilemma. He feels hostile toward his parent for abandoning him psychologically and/or physically and for being maltreated. However, he fears further rejection and retribution if he shows hostility. At the same time, he desperately wants to be loved and comforted. He thus has to dissociate his feelings of fear, anger, and hostility to protect himself from further rejection or harm. This hostility can become segmented into a self-state that exhibits aggression, anger, distrust, and suspicion of others. The hostile state hates feeling afraid because that feeling makes the child feel vulnerable. The fear then becomes segmented into a fearful state that feels impotent, dependent, and wanting to please others to avoid rejection and harm. The fearful state seeks out comfort and is loyal to the perpetrating parent for fear of rejection, whereas the hostile state despises the fearful state for its weakness. Consequently, when the different states are activated, the child can vacillate between closeness, hostility, and aggression.

These responses can become generalized toward all caregivers, including foster and adoptive parents who try to nurture the child. As a result, the child's presentation can be very confusing. One moment the child may be showing intense fear toward his caregiver, and then suddenly the child may shift to seeking out comfort. When comfort is provided, the child may feel threatened and switch to the hostile self-state—hitting, kicking, and swearing at the caregiver. If it is too threatening for the child to express his hostility outwardly, he will turn it inwardly with self-harming behaviors such as head banging, cutting, burning, purging, or substance abuse.

The hostile self-state can appear whenever the child is unconsciously reminded of the grief caused by the traumatic relationship. This places further strain on a nonabusive caregiver who tries to comfort the child, as attempts to nurture the child may trigger extreme distrust in a hostile self-state. If these extreme shifts between desiring closeness and meeting it with hostility persist into adulthood, the individual may be diagnosed with having borderline personality disorder.

Stage 3: Appeals for Help
In Bowlby's (1960) stage 3, the child's appeals for help are unmet and the child becomes resigned to the fact that the absent parent is unavailable. When this reality sets in, the child feels much despair. He feels immobilized

with fear and distrust and is thus unable to reach outwardly for help, as this seems too dangerous and unpredictable. However, his overwhelming need for nurturing and comfort propels him to seek "internal" ways to satisfy this need. In my model, the child develops an internalized self-state—that is, a helper, an idealized parent, a comforter, or a hero figure—to rescue him. Reliance on an internal helper enables the child to feel safer, particularly when outside help has not been consistently available. I have frequently found helper states in children who resided in orphanages during their infancy and toddlerhood. Because they had no consistent caretaker, they sought refuge from within and created internal comforters/rescuers when they were hungry, cold, or lonely.

Stage 4: Despair, Withdrawal, Regression, and Disorganization
In stage 4, Bowlby (1960) found that toddlers who were separated from their mothers exhibited despair, withdrawal, regression, and disorganization. Bowlby stated, ". . . there is no experience to which a young child can be subjected more prone to elicit intense and violent hatred for the mother figure than that of separation" (p. 24). Bowlby noted research conducted by Heinicke (1956), who studied children between 16 and 26 months who were placed for short periods in a residential nursery with a limited number of nurses caring for them. Heinicke observed the children seeking their mothers throughout their stay with the majority of children exhibiting crying for their lost mothers, autoerotic activity, and intense aggression. In his research, Bowlby observed children vacillating between withdrawal, apathy, regression, mourning, and aggression.

In my comparison model, the chaotic, disorganized responses often found in traumatized children can be attributed to rapidly switching self-states that may contain different affects (e.g., depression, hostility, fear, anger), varied behaviors (e.g., detachment, aggression, seeking support), and erratic skill performance in areas such as schoolwork, sports, and self-care. The self-states may also present at different levels of maturity and express different preferences regarding food, clothing, and so forth. These children are often highly sensitized to subtle traumatic cues. Thus, these state changes can occur without warning, making these children appear highly dysregulated and disorganized.

The underlying feelings that the child is trying to cope with are unmanageable despair, shame, and grief over being betrayed and the concomitant loss of safety, trust, and care. There is often a younger self-state that displays regressive behavior that appears to be the original self or a self-state that was created at the time of the trauma. I recall a 10-year-old girl who had been severely abused from infancy until she was age 8. She had a complex configuration of self-states that would rapidly switch in response to minor stresses. One moment she would be curled up in a fetal position sucking her thumb and in the next moment she would be standing up and shouting profanities at her adoptive mother. These mercurial self-states can wreak havoc on the child's ability to form attachments. The disorganized child's self-states are based on a conflicting need for closeness and fear of closeness.

Furthermore, because these self-states can be formed for particular survival tasks (e.g., such as going to school, comforting the child, defending against any perceived threat), they were *not created within a contextual relationship* with others. Therefore, these self-states did not develop an internal working model of what it means to relate to another person. They are purely operating in a survival task-oriented mode and thus often exhibit detachment or inconsideration toward caregivers. Because of these behaviors, the children often appear to have reactive attachment disorder (RAD), marked by inhibited, emotionally withdrawn behavior toward adult caregivers with limited positive affect, along with irritability, sadness, or fearfulness. Because of fluctuating states of affect and contradictory attachment behavior, these children can make contradictory statements in short succession, such as "My mom is always mean to me. . . . She is nice to me."

Stage 5: Reorganization of Behavior Directed Toward a New Object
In the last stage, Bowlby (1960) indicated that reorganization takes place partly in connection with the image of the lost object and partly in connection with a new object or objects. This is the final phase of mourning in which the lost object returns or a new object—another person—is found to which the child can attach. Bowlby indicated that if the child can attach to one adult, the mourning ceases; however, if the child is exposed to numerous adults (via placements or numerous caretakers), the child can become self-centered and will have shallow relationships over his or her lifetime.

Stage 5 corresponds to the later phases of treatment in my model (trauma processing and integration) as described in Chapters 10 and 12. This stage involves grieving the traumatic losses and pain across all parts of the child.

Based on my clinical experience with children and adults, I have learned that self-states are initially formed to protect the original self (the very young child) who experienced the early trauma. This young part of the child may be hidden. For recovery to occur, this hidden self (as well as other states) must be uncovered, helped to process the trauma, and allowed to grieve their losses. This usually occurs in the latter stage of treatment after considerable reframing of defensive self-states into collaborators and engaging their participation in processing the traumatic events. The key for recovery is to access self-states that have served to protect the child and working with these self-states to let go of their defenses so that grief work can occur. (A case that exemplifies this process is that of Martha described in Chapter 6.)

In a supporting, loving environment, the self-states who serve to protect the hidden, hurt young child—the original self—from the raw pain of traumatic losses will be able to let down their defenses and support the young child and other self-states to experience and master their pain and losses. Once the pain of the traumatic experiences and loss of attachment figures are processed, then trust in self and others can be established. This will open the door for the child to develop the capacity to form enduring attachments as an integrated individual. This process is described throughout this book.

Unless this last phase is completed, self-states can continue to disrupt the child's ability to form meaningful relationship with parents, even when the child has a loving caregiver. Defensive self-states may attempt to sabotage the attachment process with current caregivers as well as with others. As a result, the child will continue to display vacillating and chaotic reactions toward caregivers and peers, and will have significant difficulty in managing relationships as an adult.

Developmental Theory

Erik Erikson is the father of developmental and ego psychology. I rely on Erikson's developmental framework as the basis of my developmental theory, particularly because his main focus is the development of ego identity—the "conscious sense of self" that is developed through social interactions (Erikson, 1968). According to Erikson, ego identity is constantly changing due to interactions between the body (genetics), mind (psychological), and cultural influences. A person's identity is shaped by human experiences and interpersonal interactions, in which new experiences are continually being assimilated, resulting in solidifying, modifying, or disrupting earlier patterns of beliefs, affect, and behavior. Erikson's theory provides a basis for understanding how identity formation is disrupted by trauma.

Erikson's (1963) eight stages of psychosocial development encompass the life span of the individual. New experiences and information are obtained from daily interactions with others and impact the ability to be competent in each stage of psychosocial development. These stages parallel biological maturation and cognitive development. They are mastered within the context of significant relationships and therefore overlap with attachment and family theories.

Erikson's psychosocial eight stages are: (1) basic trust versus basic mistrust in infancy, (2) autonomy versus shame and doubt in toddlerhood, (3) initiative versus guilt in early childhood, (4) industry versus inferiority in preadolescence and late childhood, (5) identity versus role confusion for the adolescent period, (6) intimacy and solidarity versus isolation in young adulthood, (7) generativity versus self-absorption in adulthood, and (8) integrity versus despair in old age. These stages are particularly helpful in understanding the enormous challenges that traumatized children face, as trauma disrupts the child's development—particularly when it is incurred at the hands of a caregiver. Erikson's framework is complementary to Bowlby's attachment theory and together they form the essence of my approach to treating dissociative children.

Erikson (1963) outlined an order and timing for these psychosocial stages with the parents playing a major role in the child's early stages of development. Each stage builds on the preceding stage and paves the way for accomplishing subsequent stages. An individual achieves a stage of development after dealing with a biological crisis. In order to move through each stage, the individual experiences tension and conflicts within the "relational context" that effect resolution and competency. Ideally, the crisis should be resolved in order for development in the next stage to proceed. By mastering each stage, a person develops ego strength. However, failure to master a stage can result in less ability to manage the next stage, thereby leading to an unhealthy personality and a diminished sense of self. According to Erikson, if a crisis at an earlier stage is not fully mastered, it will likely resurface later in life.

Table 1.1 shows the significant relationships that play a role in the individual's success in mastering each stage along with favorable and unfavorable outcomes. Because early and chronic childhood trauma often thwarts the achievement of many of these stages, it is important to examine

Table 1.1 *Erikson's Eight Stages of Development*

Stage (Age in Years)	Psychosocial Dialectic	Primary Activity	Significant Relationships	Favorable Outcome	Unfavorable Outcome
0–1	Trust vs. mistrust	Consistent, stable care from parents	Main caregivers	Trust and optimism	Suspicion, withdrawal, and fear of future events
2–3	Autonomy vs. shame and doubt	Consistent, stable care from parents	Main caregivers	Sense of autonomy and self-esteem	Feelings of shame and self-doubt
4–5	Initiative vs. guilt	Environmental exploration	Family, social institutions	Self-direction and purpose	A sense of guilt, anxiety, and inhibition
6 to puberty	Industry vs. inferiority	Knowledge acquisition	Family, neighbors, peers, and school	Sense of competence and achievement	A sense of inferiority and inadequacy at doing things
Adolescence	Identity vs. role confusion	Coherent vocation and personality	Peers, group affiliations	Integrated self-image	Confusion over who and what one really is
Early adulthood	Intimacy vs. isolation	Deep and lasting relationships	Friends, lovers, partners, and family	Ability to experience love and commitment	Inability to form affectionate relationships; self-absorption, isolation
Middle adulthood	Generativity vs. stagnation	Productive and creative engagement in society	Offspring, family	Concern for family, society, and future generations	Concern only for self— one's own well-being and prosperity
Late adulthood	Ego integrity vs. despair	Life review and evaluation	Humankind and extended family	Sense of satisfaction; acceptance of death	Dissatisfaction with life; fear over death

Adapted from Erikson (1963).

the timing of children's trauma and to explore how the trauma influenced their ability to master the stage they were in when the trauma occurred and how the trauma affected their subsequent development.

Similarities Between Erikson's and Bowlby's Models

Erikson's developmental model is complementary to Bowlby's model of attachment. Bowlby emphasized the first few years of life as having a profound impact on the identity formation of the child, whereas Bowlby (1980, 1982b) agreed with Erikson that the development of identity is a lifelong process that is primarily influenced by relationships. Pittman, Keiley, Kerpelman, and Vaughn (2011) provide an extensive comparison between Bowlby's and Erikson's models. In their seminal article, they noted that the importance of a secure attachment is recognized in Erikson's psychosocial stages. Although attachment research has focused mainly on infancy and early childhood, and developmental theories have tended to emphasize identity issues in adolescence and young adulthood, both theories recognize that early relationships are extremely influential in an individual's life. Healthy attachments provide individuals with the ability to successfully accomplish each phase and prepare them for managing the next phase.

Comparing Erikson's Model With the Star Theoretical Model

Both Erikson's theory and the STM are primarily concerned with the construction of identity and the relational influences impacting that process; however, the STM also emphasizes the impact that traumatic experiences can have in disrupting the child's ability to develop a cohesive identity. The STM thus focuses more closely on how the fragmentation of identity can impair a child's capacity to master developmental conflicts. The developmental portion of the STM holds that when a child is traumatized, the child can develop internal states with specific characteristics across multiple domains: behavioral, affective, relational, cognitive, spiritual/beliefs, and neurobiological (Figure 1.3).

The STM contends that each self-state can have divergent thoughts, feelings, relational capacity, and beliefs, along with neurobiological differences that can impair the child's ability to effectively achieve developmental stages. To add complexity, certain self-states can be at different

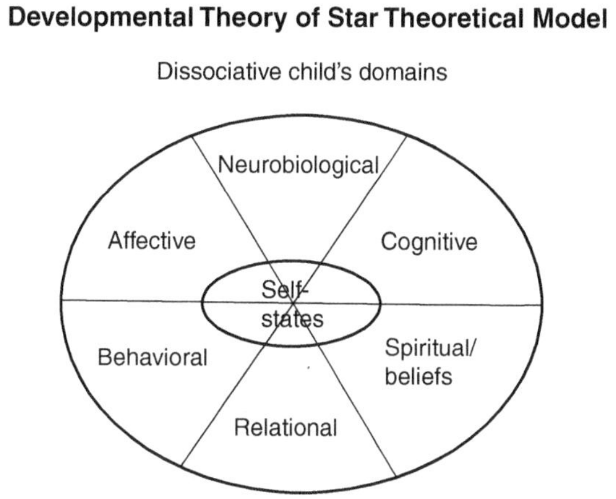

Developmental Theory of Star Theoretical Model

Dissociative child's domains

Figure 1.3 *Developmental model of the dissociative child across domains.*

levels of development, further thwarting the child's ability to form a cohesive identity. Therefore, when evaluating a traumatized child, in addition to recognizing the child's current age-appropriate psychosocial stage, *it is important to know the child's psychosocial stage when the self-state was developed because that self-state can be stuck at that stage.* This self-state can then interfere with the child's ability to deal with current developmental crises. For example, a 12-year-old with early and chronic trauma can have a self-state stuck at the developmental level of a 3-year-old, if this is when the trauma first occurred. The presence of this self-state will then impair the child from performing at his or her appropriate age level. My model holds that for successful treatment, the 3-year-old self-state will need to be included in the treatment process so that the child will be able to process the traumatic event that caused the self-state's creation and therefore master subsequent developmental stages. Then, the self-state can integrate within the child, forming a cohesive identity.

Family Systems Theory

> *Feelings of worth can flourish only in an atmosphere where individual differences are appreciated, mistakes are tolerated, communication is open, and rules are flexible—the kind of atmosphere that is found in a nurturing family.*
>
> —Virginia Satir (n.d.)

Satir's profound words are what we all strive for in our personal and professional lives. We recognize that children's feelings of self-worth are primary to their health, and that we, in both big and small ways, must communicate this message to them. I had the honor to learn about Satir in my undergraduate work and, to this day, I find her model to be solid and timeless. I, therefore, largely base the family systems portion of the STM on her theories and approaches.

It has long been established that family interactions play a significant role in the pathology of children, who are often the identified patients (Satir, 1983). Satir's model of family therapy fits well with Bowlby's and Erikson's models, as each recognizes that children should not be defined by their symptoms. Satir viewed the identified client as carrying the distortions, pain, discomfort, and obstruction of growth that are found within the family system. Thus, Satir (1983) contended that the family needs to be treated as a unit when a child presents as the problematic client.

Satir postulated that a symptom is a report about the person wearing it, about the family, and about the rules in the family system. Accordingly, to understand the child's symptoms, all family members at certain times need to participate in family therapy sessions, as a symptom in any family member is a sign of a dysfunctional family system. The therapist's task is to understand the family rules that govern each person's behavior. This requires a safe environment for exploring family rules, along with family members' fears, and limiting behaviors.

Satir (1965) contended that each family member is unavoidably committed to the system of the family by the nature of the family member's origin and dependency. Satir understood that the openness, flexibility, clarity, and appropriateness of the family's rules will determine whether developmental and life cycle changes that children and parents face will be managed in a healthy manner. In an open family system, rules promote change openly, directly, appropriately, and clearly. Conversely, in a closed family system, distortions, denial, and maintaining the status quo are prominent. When confronted with change, a closed system will maintain past, ineffective ways of interaction, thus inhibiting effective management of the demands of relationship and life cycle changes. The resultant pathology is often exhibited in the identified patient, who is often a child. I have found that due to their innocence, young children are more likely to reveal the family's dysfunctions and secrets than older family members. Once these are revealed, change can occur.

When working with families, we need to recognize that we are working with three generations: the parents' history, the current family, and the future family that the children will create when they become adults. It can be very valuable to look at the chronology of the family (comparable to a psychosocial history of individuals) and create a genogram with notations on intergenerational histories of trauma, mental illness, substance abuse, legal problems, and so forth. It is also important to explore with each parent what patterns they bring into the current family structure so that we can help the parents become conscious of repetitive patterns that may hinder growth. With adoptive children, we often have to surmise the rules they learned from their biological (and possibly foster) families. Children often reveal the rules they have learned via their communication patterns and behaviors. Having an open discussion with children about what they have learned can help promote healthier communication patterns.

Communication encompasses verbal as well as nonverbal behavior. The therapeutic aim is to close the gap between inference and observation and to document the relationship between patterns of communication and symptomatic behavior. The therapist's role is to help family members clearly communicate their needs, wishes, and expectations while being on the lookout for contradictory messages.

Satir (1983, pp. 124–125) outlined three therapeutic beliefs about human nature: (a) every individual is geared to survival, growth, and obtaining closeness with others, no matter how distorted these may look; (b) what society calls sick, crazy, stupid, or bad behavior is really the person's signal of distress and call for help; and (c) human beings are limited only by the extent of their knowledge, their ways of understanding themselves, and their ability to relate with others. Satir adhered to a growth model that is based on the notion that people change through interactions with other people and through an exploration of their inner life by exploring their own thoughts, intentions, and perceptions of others. The therapist's role is to be the leader of the process but not the leader of people. Satir also recognized the importance of therapists exploring their own inner life, while exploring the life of the family. Satir's guiding principles provide a foundation for our work with traumatized children and their families.

SUMMARY

The Star Theoretical Model (STM), comprising five theories—attachment, neurobiology, child development, family systems, and dissociative—is an integrative, comprehensive model that critically analyzes each of these theories and their corresponding relationships to understand the formation of dissociation and to conceptualize pathways toward treating the fractured child. This model can assist in formulating an accurate diagnosis and effective treatment course for children and adolescents with dissociation as demonstrated throughout this book. The underlying premise is that dissociation is an automatic, unconscious defense mechanism (based particularly on the neurobiology of trauma) that helps the child to survive unmitigated fear, helplessness, despair, shame, and grief over immense relational betrayal and other forms of trauma in which the child fears annihilation. The child's mind segments off horrifying experiences in order to survive. Attachment theory is intentionally placed at the top of the star figure of STM to emphasize the paramount importance of being astute to the deleterious impact of traumatic experiences on the child's ability to attach with caregivers and others and also to recognize that healing takes place in a safe, secure environment of compassionate and committed caregivers. Throughout this book, specialized techniques aimed at repairing attachment disturbances, stabilizing the dissociative child, processing traumatic experiences, and finally integrating the child's mind are described with numerous rich clinical cases. In particular, the reader will learn about the progression of therapy in four cases—Rudy, Briana, Cathy, and Lisa—as their dissociative barriers are removed. The ultimate goal is for the dissociative youth to resolve past traumatic experiences and to become an integrated, cohesive individual who has the capacity to develop healthy attachments and to become a fulfilled and productive member of society.

NOTES

1. Available at www.isst-d.org/?contentID=76
2. Earlier research and clinical cases used *DMS-IV* (DDNOS) but with the current *DSM-5*, most of these cases would likely meet the criteria for OSDD.
3. All the names of the children in this book have been changed to protect the children's identities. In addition, any identifying details have been altered.

PART II

ASSESSMENT

2

WHAT'S GOING ON WITH THIS CHILD?
RECOGNIZING WARNING SIGNS
OF DISSOCIATION IN TRAUMATIZED
CHILDREN AND ADOLESCENTS

FROM THE FIRST SESSION, 5-YEAR-OLD Tony would bounce into my office carrying his constant companion, his teddy bear. As he ran around, he would grab the trucks and cars, bang them together, and throw them around the floor. Suddenly, he would stop, stare off into space for about 5 seconds, and then resume this frenetic movement. This sudden stillness repeated itself several times during his play. Then one day, he came into my office and sat quietly on my couch, looking around in a reserved manner as if my office was foreign to him. He furtively glanced around and shyly asked whether he could play with the toys. It was clear that this Tony was not the same rambunctious child I had encountered earlier.

An adolescent babysitter sexually abused Tony when he was 3 years old. He never really achieved successful potty training and had frequent soiling accidents at school and at home. He was unaware of them until they were brought to his attention. His teacher noted his erratic behavior and academic performance. At times, he simply could not sit still and was hyperactive—fidgety, falling off his chair, and talking out of turn. At other times, he seemed frozen, in his own world, and unresponsive. He was a bright boy and at times, he was able to perform well in learning words and numbers, but then the next day, he would sit with a blank look on his face unable to recall what to do. He was diagnosed with attention deficit hyperactivity disorder (ADHD) and was on a stimulant; however, the medication did not seem to make much difference. Tony's parents were concerned that his problems were related to his early trauma and brought him to see me. Tony is typical of the many dissociative children who I have treated who exhibit fluctuations in mood, behavior, performance, and memory along with disconnection from their bodily functions.

I have compiled 16 warning signs that are suggestive of dissociation in children and adolescents (Waters, 1991). Some of these warning signs pertain to conditions that can cause dissociation and to corresponding symptoms and behaviors that mask dissociative symptoms, whereas other signs pertain to core dissociative symptoms, such as memory and identity disturbance, auditory hallucinations, depersonalization, and derealization. Some are adapted from a dissociative predictor list compiled by Kluft (1985), whereas others are adapted from a list of symptoms and behaviors seen in childhood dissociation compiled by Peterson (1990). Indicators of self-states are included in several of the warning signs as they relate to specific symptoms. Core symptoms of dissociation carry significant weight toward diagnosing dissociation, whereas a compilation of all of the warning signs provide clinicians with information to thoroughly consider dissociation in children. As with any diagnostic criteria, some may be present, whereas others may not be.

As with other assessments, care should be taken to sensitively explore disturbing signs that a child exhibits not only with children but also with caretakers, family members, teachers, and relevant professionals. Recognizing the meaning of these warning signs is a beginning step toward determining the presence of dissociation in children.

WARNING SIGNS SUGGESTIVE OF DISSOCIATION IN CHILDREN

1. History of Childhood Trauma

A history of childhood trauma is commonly found in dissociative disorders; this history may include sexual, physical, or emotional abuse, abandonment, neglect, witnessing interpersonal violence, painful medical conditions and interventions, natural disasters, and/or exposure to war. When children experience trauma, it overwhelms their limited coping abilities and they may rely on dissociation as a way to escape overwhelming fear and helplessness. There are significant variables that influence a child's degree and reliance on dissociation. These include factors such as age (the younger the child, the more vulnerable he or she is to relying on dissociation); the child's physical and mental limitations; the severity and chronicity of the trauma; dependency on the perpetrator for survival and nurturing; the overall environmental climate/support; and whether the child dissociated at the time of the trauma (i.e., peritraumatic dissociation). Carefully exploring how a child coped at the time of the trauma provides a gateway to examine continual reliance on dissociative defenses.

For example, some questions to consider when evaluating Tony are as follows: Did he mentally remove himself from the sexual abuse by focusing on his teddy bear—his constant companion? Did he block out the sensory experience of the sexual abuse so as to not feel the pain? Is it possible that Tony is triggered when he feels sensations related to the need to use the bathroom? Could he be incontinent due to depersonalization in order to avoid a traumatic reminder of his abuse? If Tony dissociated at the time of the trauma, it makes it much more likely that he will continue to rely on dissociation as a coping mechanism. Peritraumatic dissociation is a significant precursor for the development of trauma-related disorders (Birmes et al., 2003; van der Hart, van Ochten, van Son, Steele, & Lensvelt-Mulders, 2008; Vásquez et al., 2012).

Pediatric medical trauma has been less well recognized as a factor in causing dissociation with limited studies (Diseth, 2006; Stolbach, 2005). Others and I (Yehuda, Stolbach, & Waters, 2008) have treated many medically traumatized children as a result of birth traumas, debilitating and life-threatening illnesses, and painful medical procedures. These children respond similarly to children who have been abused and can demonstrate significant disturbance in affect, behavior, consciousness, and memory. Ricky, a 4-year-old I treated, is one such example. He had a traumatic birth and then a botched circumcision without anesthesia that took months to heal. At age 2, Ricky had penile reconstructive surgery for cosmetic reasons. He was a highly dysregulated, frail child who experienced severe constipation. A specially designed sensorimotor play therapy helped Ricky heal from the traumatic experiences he had experienced early in life (Chapter 13).

2. Level of Parental/Caregiver Support Available and Mechanisms Used to Survive

When questioning children and families about traumatic events, it is important to ascertain whether a supportive person was present to comfort or rescue the child at the time of the trauma, as a comforting presence can assuage the use of dissociation. Unfortunately, caregiver support is often lacking in child abuse—particularly sexual abuse, which is usually done in secrecy. If no support was available to the child during the traumatic event, it is important to sensitively inquire about what the child did to manage such a frightening experience. You may learn that the child blanked out, saw herself watching from the ceiling, was numb and did not feel what was happening to her body, or developed a helper part to comfort her. In some cases, the child may be unable to recall the specific details of the trauma. Assessing how the child coped, including using any internal resources, when there was a lack of caregiver support will provide important diagnostic guidance for further questioning.

3. Glazed Look in Eyes or Blanking Out

As with Tony, dissociative children often experience brief episodes of stillness or glazed eyes that last for seconds (or longer), whereas a moment earlier the child was animated or engaged. Noticing these episodes and questioning the child about his or her awareness of what transpired just before the child blanked out aid in the assessment. Sometimes, traumatized children display pseudoseizures in which they fall to the floor, exhibiting jerky movements, and lapse into unconsciousness for seconds or longer. Silberg (2013) has described such episodes as "dissociative shutdown" (pp. 128–147).

I worked with a sexually abused 9-year-old boy, Ryan, who had pseudoseizures (Waters, 2015). He had recurring severe "spells" of awakening in the middle of the night for several hours, during which he would shiver, throw up, experience diarrhea, and have an intense headache. The next day, Ryan would wake up feeling fine with no memory of these episodes. Although a seizure disorder was considered and ruled out, a self-state "Crabby Ryan" appeared, who reported experiencing these strange spells. Crabby Ryan held the somatic reaction to the anal rape that Ryan had experienced when he was 3. It does behoove the clinician to rule out a seizure disorder as part of the differential diagnosis of dissociation, but from my clinical experience of working with traumatized children their EEGs are usually found to be within a normal range.

Often, children will relate that they were unaware that they were blanking out or say, "Hey, I do that all of the time. I don't know why I do that." This may suggest more severe dissociation such as a presence of a self-state. See Chapter 4 for information on how to further assess memory disturbances.

4. Eyes Roll Back or Flutter

Unusual eye movements, such as eye rolls or flutters, may be an indicator of internal communication or awareness of a self-state's presence. For example, during abnormal eye movements, some children have reported to me that they hear internal voices calling their names or telling them they are stupid. There may be a more severe shift that accompanies the eye movements in which a self-state takes executive control over the child with associated changes in affect, memory, and behavior. As with "blanking out," it is important to ascertain what occurred right before and after the eye roll or flutter.

With some amusement, I recall Sally, a mischievous 8-year-old DID girl with a history of severe and chronic trauma. Sally was a "pro" at rapidly switching between self-states—particularly when she misbehaved. When these switches occurred, Sally's eyes would roll back until only the whites of her eyes were visible. At these times, Sally happily went inside and out came Tom to take the rap. Tom was understandably quite angry with Sally. Little did she realize that the eye roll was giving away her "trick." Using some humor with her about her manipulation, I pointed out that Tom was not happy with her and she really could not escape from Tom, who was a part of herself. She would have to deal with Tom regarding her shenanigans, as he was not happy to take the consequences for her actions. I further indicated that if she thought she was getting away with her misbehavior by disappearing inward, she was not. She was still responsible, because "all" of her would be in time-out. After our talk, her switching and "fleeing the scene" subsided as did her eye rolls.

5. Reports Auditory Hallucinations When Asked (Usually Will Not Self-Report)

I briefly mentioned that the eye roll or flutter is often associated with hearing voices. These warning signs are interrelated and often occur simultaneously with dissociative children. It is important to note that auditory and visual hallucinations associated with dissociation are often misconstrued as a form of psychosis. Although there are some similarities in symptomotology, a detailed description of the differences that exist between schizophrenia and dissociation is provided in Chapter 3 on differential diagnosis.

Hearing internal voices is a strong marker of dissociation in children with complex trauma (Sar, Onder, Killicaslan, Zoroglu, & Alyanak, 2014; Silberg, 2013; Wieland, 2011). These voices can represent self-states that communicate internally to the child and can be harassing. For example, a child may report, "There is an angry voice that tells me to do bad things. I try not to listen to it but I can't stop it!"

If a child reports hearing a voice talking to him or her, it is important to assess what degree of influence this voice has on the child's behavior, thoughts, and emotions. If the child reports that the part completely takes over—"The angry part takes over and I go away. I don't know what happens then"—the child may fit the criteria for DID. Further questioning, observation, history gathering, and administering a dissociative checklist will assist in understanding the meaning of voices and degree of dissociation occurring. Chapter 4 on assessment provides further guidance on interviewing children for dissociation.

6. Reports Internal Visual Hallucinations

The child may report internal visual hallucinations, such as faces, floating objects, clay figures, scary heads, a devil, an angel, and so forth. Internal visual hallucinations may coincide with the report of auditory hallucinations, both of which can be strong indicators of the presence of self-states (Silberg, 2013; Wieland, 2011). Younger children are more likely to reveal seeing frightening visions of scary figures, images, or shadows (such as floating heads, faces or eyes, or a devil), contrary to teenagers who are often hesitant to report hallucinations for fear of being viewed as "crazy." Asking questions about visual hallucinations in a sensitive and empathetic manner can provide a safe atmosphere for teenagers to disclose such experiences.

When I explored these kinds of experiences with dissociative adolescents, several reported that they had seen these visions when younger and thought they were imaginary playmates (see also Silberg, 2013). As we explored these hallucinations, the adolescents realized that these "imaginary friends" were actually self-states that formed at the time of the traumatic event and continued to play a significant role in managing their trauma.

Children and adolescents have described vivid images of what they see and often are willing to draw them. Such drawings can provide clues regarding a self-state's strength, affect, role, and level of development. Children, particularly younger children, often report seeing only heads; or if they see a body, it can be quite distorted in shape. Some children draw figures resembling hero figures or scary monsters with sharp teeth. Some pictures may be of a sexualized self-state that was developed to cope with sexual abuse. Figure 2.1 provides one such example. This picture was drawn by an 8-year-old girl with DID, Tara, who was prostituted by her mother during her preschool years. She fills up the entire page with this sexualized image of her face with large eyes without pupils, depicting a haunting, vacant look. Written above her large scarlet lips (that also look like splayed legs) is the word "love," suggesting that sex is love. In this picture, she not only depicts her sexualized self-state but also portrays the profound impact of her sexual abuse.

Figure 2.1 *Eight-year-old girl's picture of a sexualized self-state. (Used with permission.)*

Some children have depicted self-states by drawing themselves with multiple arms, legs, and heads, as Silberg (1996, p. 92) noted in her Dissociative Features Profile evaluation as an indicator of dissociation. If children only draw heads, I wonder whether their self-states are not as elaborate or well developed, or perhaps the child had depersonalized from her body as a result of trauma, which is a warning sign described later in this chapter in the section on depersonalization.

7. Memory Problems/Amnesia

Memory problems and amnesia are key indicators of dissociation in traumatized individuals (Bremner, 2005; Chu, Frey, Ganzel, & Matthews, 1999; Coons, 1996; Goldsmith, Cheit, & Wood, 2009). Some factors that deter the child's ability to recall traumatic events are the severity and chronicity of the trauma, the child's age at the time of trauma, the child's relationship to the perpetrator, and the development of self-states that contain the traumatic memory.

Memory problems can range from not remembering the trauma to also not remembering nontraumatic events and behaviors. For example, children may not remember what they said to someone or what others said to them, angry outbursts, or misbehavior. They may also not remember doing their homework and not recognize a completed assignment. In some cases, children may forget much of their past, including holidays, birthdays, vacations, schools attended, former teachers, and childhood friends.

Dissociative children can also have fluctuations in their memory in that they may recall activities at one time and not at others. Some may have only sketchy memories of past and present events or may only experience sensory aspects of an event, such as a bodily sensation (e.g., choking), without a contextual framework, to comprehend the meaning of the sensation.

If the traumatic experience is contained in a self-state, each self-state may contain a distinct level of consciousness and a separate memory system, inhibiting shared knowledge of the past and present. For example, if a self-state contains an aspect of a traumatic memory, this knowledge may only be accessible when that particular state is activated. If the memory is triggered by some current event, this event can activate the emergence of the self-state that contains the relevant memory. This is similar to the state-dependent learning theory in which it is easier to remember information when the physiological and mental state that the person was in when they learned the information is duplicated (Eich, 1980; Jovasevic et al., 2015). Consequently, the influence or appearance and disappearance of self-states can account for traumatized children having sporadic memories for past and current events.

Jimmy, a 12-year-old boy who was severely traumatized starting in infancy, provides an example of amnesia due to the presence of a self-state. Jimmy was previously diagnosed with ADHD and conduct disorder. He was referred to me for his intermittently explosive temper. During the evaluative process, Jimmy's father confessed to shaking and screaming at Jimmy since infancy and inflicting more severe beatings as Jimmy got older. Jimmy also witnessed extreme domestic violence and would try to intervene, resulting in further beatings. The abuse continued until the father was removed from the home, just prior to my assessment. I asked Jimmy to draw a picture of what his anger looked like since this was the presenting problem. Drawing can also be helpful in lowering children's anxiety about treatment. We did not have time to discuss the picture before the session concluded.

At the follow-up session 5 days later, I asked Jimmy to explain his picture. He held the picture, looked at it, and then put it down on the couch. He leaned forward with his hands clasped under his chin and said in a matter-of-fact way that he did not remember drawing this picture. I asked if he could explain this. He told me that he sometimes "blanks out" and does not remember doing things.

I asked him to tell me about those times when he "blanks out." In a prosaic manner, Jimmy said: "I got into a fight with my dad and the next thing I knew was that I was on the roof of our house. I don't remember climbing the television antenna and getting on the roof. I know about other times when I would do this to be by myself, but not that time. I just blanked out."

Therapist: "When was the first time you realized that you blanked out?"

Jimmy: "Well I remember as far back as third grade. I got stressed out because I had to draw a castle to hang up on the wall. Next thing I knew, the castle was drawn."

Therapist: "You don't remember drawing it?"

Jimmy: "No, I don't remember drawing it."

Therapist: "How do you explain this?"

Jimmy: "I don't know."

Therapist: "How do you feel about this?"

Jimmy: "Awkward."

Therapist: "Are there other times when this has happened?"

Jimmy: "Yeah, I had to clean my room and, then the next thing I knew, my room was cleaned."

Therapist: "You don't remember doing it?"

Jimmy: "No."

Therapist: "Could your sisters or parents have cleaned your room?"

Jimmy: "No, they weren't home."

Therapist: "What do you feel just before you blank out?"

Jimmy: "Stressed out and angry."

Therapist: "Do you ever feel afraid?"

Jimmy: "No, just stressed out and angry." (Fear that would have been activated by his father's violence appeared to have been completely segmented off from his awareness; thus, Jimmy only felt "stressed out and angry." The overwhelming feelings of "stressed out and angry" precipitated a shift in states—a pattern he exhibited frequently.)

I then returned to Jimmy's drawing and asked him to explain it. He picked it up off the couch and held it in his hand, studying it closely. His picture showed swirling colors of reds, yellows, greens, and blacks with a small black box in the corner. I was startled when he said in a monotone voice. "This drawing is what it is looks like just before I come to after blanking out" (Figure 2.2). He then elaborated and said, "I see myself floating on something—this cloud thing, this spinning circle with all of the swirling colors that explode. I see some darkness at the bottom. When I wake up, I leave that zone. I feel like I am still floating. My feet up to my neck go numb. I'll sit up and look around and see where I am at."

While I asked him to draw his anger, Jimmy instead had drawn his dissociative experience of coming back to present awareness after blanking out. Another part of Jimmy was present in this session, a part that had no memory of having drawn this in the previous session.

It was not until this interview with Jimmy that I realized that I was dealing with a different aspect of him. This one appeared to simply be a

Figure 2.2 *Jimmy's picture of swirling colors when he is returning to consciousness after blanking out. (Used with permission.)*

"reporter," devoid of affect. He provided extensive examples of past and current times of frequently losing time and finding out that he had done something. I realized how important it is to observe affective differences and subtle changes in mannerisms with children, as well as memory problems. Since then, I have routinely asked my clients about pictures and activities they did in our previous sessions. Many traumatized children have not recalled pictures they had drawn or even their videotaped session.

8. Refers to Self as "We" or in the Third Person or Demonstrates "Regressed Behavior"

Because young traumatized children engage in fantasy play and misuse pronouns, it is tricky to ascertain what they mean if they speak about themselves in the third person or use plural pronouns. Without careful assessment, it is difficult to determine whether what they are demonstrating is a projection of themselves or elaborated self-states. For example, a child may refer to herself as "we" when describing a traumatic event or say "Her did that," when talking about a self-state. Dissociative children may also say, "The baby is sad about daddy hurting her," and engage in vivid play about the baby's anger, while otherwise being disconnected from their feelings about their trauma. If children talk about a baby, I will ask whether the baby is a pretend baby while assuring the child that it is okay to pretend. Nondissociative children will casually agree that the baby is a pretend baby. This is contrary to dissociative preschoolers who will adamantly insist that the baby is real, and will often report that they see the baby. They may proceed to comfort the baby through their play with a baby doll, or spontaneously switch to the baby state with striking developmental differences that can be misconstrued as "regressed behavior."

When a baby state emerges, there are often remarkable differences in the child's presentation. The child may display apparent developmental delays in speech (baby talk), motor deficits (unable to walk or walks with an awkward gait), and loss of previously acquired knowledge, such as names of toys, people, and so forth. They may also have trauma-related somatic disturbances in which they may feel pain or be void of bodily sensations. The following clinical case highlights amnesia and regressed behavior that suggested that Nancy was portraying a self-state and not pretending to be a baby.

I treated Nancy, a petite 3-year-old, in the 1980s. Nancy was a very articulate, well-coordinated, and intelligent child who I had been treating for 6 months. Nancy had been sexually abused at 1½ years old by her father and later sexually revictimized by her mother's boyfriend when she was 3.

One day, Nancy came into the play therapy room and suddenly began crawling and babbling like a baby as she awkwardly picked up toys. She explored toys that she had previously played with as if she was seeing them for the first time. Then, Nancy held up her arms uttering "Potty." I picked up her tiny body to take her to the bathroom thinking this was odd and perhaps she was displaying regressed behavior, not recognizing the dissociative symptoms. When we walked by her foster mother of 6 months, I stopped to let her know that we were heading to the bathroom. Nancy became frightened when she saw her foster mother, turning her head away and wrapping her arms tightly around my neck. Her foster mother looked at her with startled confusion. Suddenly, I realized that Nancy was in a different state and this one did not know her foster mother! I reread the forensic report that I had written a couple of months earlier and noted that Nancy had "exhibited regressed behavior" when reporting her sexual abuse. I had failed to recognize that the regressed behavior represented a self-state, despite having treated several older dissociative children at that time. This case highlights how attuned an evaluator must be and not assume that a baby/toddler behavior is merely "regressed behavior." I have since learned that dissociative symptoms are common among very young, highly vulnerable children, as they have no other recourse to manage their trauma (Bowlby, 1980; Fraiberg, 1982; Putnam, 1997).

9. Imaginary Playmates Reported as Real

Imaginary playmates are pretend friends present in the healthy development of young children. They serve emotional and social needs of children by assuming many creative roles in play and exploration. They provide a vehicle for the child's projection of feelings and thoughts through creative play. Children normally outgrow imaginary playmates at around age 7 when they enter school and become more socialized. However, Taylor, Carlson, Maring, Gerow, and Charley (2004) found that one third of 7-year-olds continue to have imaginary friends and that these can persist into their teen years.

The meaning and purpose of imaginary playmates needs to be carefully explored to ascertain whether these are self-states—particularly if amnesia is associated with their presence. Imaginary playmates have been reported in dissociative children with self-states (e.g., Frost, Silberg, & McIntee, 1996; McLewin & Muller, 2006). Frost et al. (1996) and McLewin and Muller (2006) note that imaginary friends in dissociative children tend to be antagonistic, possess skills that the child does not display, take control over the child, and often persist into adolescence. Silberg's (2013, p. 252) Imaginary Friends Questionnaire can provide guidance in determining whether the reported imaginary friends may be self-states.

An evaluator must also understand young children's linguistics, because children do not have sophisticated language skills to describe their internal experiences. Children will often use familiar words or phrases, such as "imaginary friends," to denote self-states, as they have no other language to express their experiences. We must not assume that traumatized children mean that their imaginary or pretend friends are indeed such because of our own assumptions; instead, we must explore what "imaginary friends" mean to them. It is also important to be accepting of what children report, and to help them find meaning for their experiences, while the evaluation continues to discern whether there is dissociation.

Questioning older, traumatized children about past or current imaginary friends is also important, as it can provide helpful information in determining the presence of self-states. When I interviewed a number of traumatized male and female adolescents about imaginary friends, many of them described having imaginary friends during childhood only to realize that these dissociative states continued to exist. Some of these self-states remained their original, young age, whereas others aged and performed different functions as needed for survival. Clark, a 14-year-old with DID who had been verbally and sexually abused by multiple perpetrators, reported a host of imaginary friends who would put on elaborate plays throughout his childhood until the seventh grade, when he began using alcohol and drugs. The "imaginary friends" had different names and characteristics and had helped him escape from his feelings of despair and loneliness. His family confirmed witnessing him putting on these plays by himself, changing his voice and mannerisms as he portrayed the different imaginary friends. However, when we penetrated his amnesic barriers and explored his internal voices, Clark realized that his imaginary friends were actually his present-day self-states. One remained 7 years old, whereas the others had aged with him. As this example shows, it is important not to assume that traumatized children's reference to their imaginary friends is only fantasy. Instead, the clinician should explore their meaning, as imaginary friends may actually be self-states. Detecting self-states when

children are younger and providing appropriate treatment will facilitate early recovery with a more favorable prognosis for the future.

10. Sense of Depersonalization and/or Derealization

Steele, Dorahy, van der Hart, and Nijenhuis (2009), who view many forms
of depersonalization and derealization as alterations of consciousness
and memory related to ownership of self and a distortion of one's body,
described them as:

> (1) the existence of an observing and experiencing ego or part of the
> personality (Fromm, 1965); (2) detachment of consciousness from the
> self or body (i.e., feelings of strangeness or unfamiliarity with self,
> out-of-body experiences); (3) detachment from affect, i.e., numbness;
> (4) a sense of unreality such as being in a dream; and (5) perceptual
> alterations or hallucinations regarding the body. (Noyes & Kletti, 1977)

There is research that links depersonalization to a history of trauma
(e.g., Simeon, Guralnik, Schmeidler, Sirof, & Knutelska, 2001). Depersonalization is also correlated with anxiety and depression (Baker et al.,
2003), and closely linked to somatoform dissociation (Simeon, Smith,
Knutelska, & Smith, 2008).

Although depersonalization is an adaptive measure, it can present numerous problems for depersonalized children. They frequently
describe feeling disconnected from or lacking conscious awareness of
parts of their bodies. These children may act as if their head is cut off from
the rest of their bodies—a separation from their somatic self. This is often
a protective defense strategy to ward off traumatic reminders related to
assaults to the body. Consequently, they may not have control over their
bodily functions (i.e., bladder and bowels), or not feel pain when they are
self-injured or accidently injure themselves. Young children who have been
physically assaulted often appear to have some neurological deficits, as
they frequently bump into, stumble, and trip on objects or even over their
own feet. They divorce themselves from their physical self, and, consequently, do not know where their bodies end and the world begins! Their
depersonalization leaves them prone to injuries.

I vividly recall Briana, a bright 17-year-old girl diagnosed with DID
who had severe depersonalization. Briana was sexually and physically

abused by multiple perpetrators between the ages of 7 and 16. She also witnessed domestic violence between her parents beginning at an early age. Briana was numb to her body and her feelings. She desperately wanted to feel connected to herself but also wanted to avoid feeling her pain. She vacillated from one maladaptive, compulsive behavior to another, including cutting, bingeing, and purging, excessive exercise, and drug and alcohol abuse. Briana was particularly distressed that she could not feel sadness after the Columbine shootings, a tragic event that left the entire United States in mourning.[1] She complained, "Fran, everyone is crying about the shootings. I don't feel anything. I wish I could feel!" Briana, like other similar children, was faced with a conundrum: To feel is to feel real. But to feel real is to feel pain. (Briana's recovery process is highlighted throughout this book.)

Traumatized children may also show evidence of derealization—a sense of unreality or unfamiliarity with one's environment; a distortion of the perception of time or of one's surroundings, as if seeing events with tunnel vision, from a distance, or as blurry and distorted. Time can seem to be frozen during these moments.

Both depersonalization and derealization can involve alterations of consciousness and memory. Jessica, a college student who was diagnosed with other specified dissociative disorder (OSDD; previously dissociative disorder not otherwise specified [DDNOS]),[2] eloquently summarized her experience of depersonalization and derealization. She reported one of the many traumatic incidents of emotional abuse by her father when she was a teenager. Her father was in her face for hours haranguing her. She said, "I told him I had to get up for school in the morning, but he wouldn't let me go." She reported having tunnel vision—only seeing his mouth moving. She internally heard a crying child, while a helper part answered her father's demands, which she, herself, could not hear. Jessica told me, "I couldn't hear him but a part of me could and knew how to answer him. I don't know how I did that. I was always afraid of my dad."

When evaluating children, querying them about any numbness or distorted perception of the environment will provide a window into how they coped with traumatic experiences and will aid in designing a treatment protocol to help them reconnect with their senses. Children cannot effectively master personal or environmental challenges without the awareness of their physical self and their surroundings.

11. Extreme Mood Switches, Which May Be Unprovoked or Minimally Provoked

Extreme switches in mood are a common symptom in dissociative children that can lead to a misdiagnosis of bipolar disorder. Traumatized children with OSDD (replaces DDNOS) may have self-states that contain specific feelings, such as anger, sadness, shame, happiness, and/or hurt. When something triggers a strong emotion, the dissociative child often switches to a self-state that holds that emotion. This can cause the child to rapidly fluctuate from one extreme mood to another depending on what self-state has been triggered. The presenting child may not have conscious awareness of these shifts or when they emerge. If the child does know about that self-state, he is unable to have any control over that part. If the child does maintain executive control of his body, he may realize that he is suddenly raging, but may not be conscious of the influence of the self-state, and, consequently, be unable to understand or control his affect and behavior.

Making matters even more complicated, rapid shifts in affect can appear for seconds, minutes, or days, and then suddenly disappear without clearly defined triggers. For example, a self-state who carries rage for past beatings and verbal abuse can be reminded of a traumatic memory when an adoptive parent, teacher, or peer says or does something that can seem innocuous (a perceived critical tone or an unexpected touch), resulting in the child exhibiting an exaggerated reaction. If the child is then reprimanded, another state may suddenly appear that is sad or depressed and is unaware of what transpired; or, if aware, feels helpless and depressed over lack of control and being reprimanded.

Such shifts in mood may also be accompanied by amnesia and seriously impair the child's relationship with others. Often, those around the dissociative child are perplexed, critical, rejecting, or frightened by the child's sudden, apparently unprovoked emotional outburst and are uncertain about to how to respond to the child. It can be very difficult for those observing the child to detect that the child's mood changes are related to self-states, because self-states can be close in age and sound similar to the child's core personality. Contrary to DID adults who have more florid presentations of self-states, children's self-states are characteristically less developed. The shifts are thus less dramatic in presentation, and, therefore, it is easy to ascribe their mood shifts to being oppositional, moody, or just having a bad day.

To assess for self-states that may be related to shifts in mood, evaluators need to ask children whether they have "little or no control over" mood shifts, and if they "don't know why" the sudden and extreme mood shifts occur. The influence of self-states contributing to dramatic affective shifts needs to be uncovered in order for the child to gain mastery over his or her emotional life. Guidance on differentiating between a dissociative disorder and a bipolar disorder is provided in Chapter 3.

12. Extreme Behavioral Changes in Voice, Face, Handwriting, Food, or Dress

Similar to the previous warning signs on mood shifts, extreme behavior changes may also be associated with a self-state's presence. When a self-state either internally influences the child or takes executive control over the child, there can be sudden, behavioral shifts that can be slight or dramatic, lasting for only seconds or for days. Dissociative children can have extreme behavioral changes in almost every aspect of their life, including: developmental and skill level depending on the "age" of the self-state (e.g., handwriting, academics, language, extracurricular activities), relationships with others (e.g., caretakers, peers, relatives, teachers), and preferences in food, clothing, toys, and activities.

Ryan, the previously mentioned boy who was anally raped at age 3, provides an example of a child with dramatic shifts in skill level and food preferences (Waters, 2015). At age 9, Ryan was an enthusiastic and accomplished hockey player. During a weekend hockey tournament, unknown to his parents, Ryan's self-state "Crabby Ryan" appeared and was resistant to putting on his hockey gear. Ryan played badly during the game and fell down throughout the tournament. Afterward, he ordered pizza with pineapple and ham, contrary to Ryan's normal preference for a pepperoni and cheese pizza. His parents noted it was odd that Ryan was having such a difficult weekend. They learned in the follow-up family session that Ryan did not recall that weekend at all; however, "Crabby Ryan" appeared in the session and was able to tell us all about that weekend.

Another example of shifting preferences can be found in Kaitlyn, the 5-year-old girl with DID (described in Chapter 1). Every morning, Kaitlyn changed her clothing dozens of times when preparing for school until she finally collapsed sobbing. She experienced a total meltdown that lasted for approximately 45 minutes over an internal conflict between her and her male self-state, Charlie, who wanted to wear pants instead of a dress to school.

13. Disavowed Witnessed Behavior; Accused of Lying and Sincerely Denies It

When conducting an individual interview with a traumatized child, it is important to ask whether he has been accused of doing something that others say they saw him do, but for which he has no memory. Exploring the circumstances surrounding these times and what triggered them can provide relevant information pertaining to a pattern of memory disturbance and presence of a self-state that is responsible for the misbehavior.

As described earlier, children with self-states can rapidly shift from one state to another. Self-states can have separate memory systems with amnestic barriers between them. Therefore, if one state with a different memory system emerges and engages in, for example, a destructive behavior and then quickly leaves, the emergent personality will not know what just transpired. If an adult witnesses the destructive behavior and the child adamantly disavows the behavior, the child is often accused of lying and manipulating to avoid consequences. The dissociative child often becomes outraged or extremely distraught for being unfairly accused, and persistently denies the behavior even *after* receiving the consequences, which usually do not provide any gain. It is easy for a frustrated parent to assume that the child is lying; however, when assessing traumatized children, memory disturbances need to be considered rather than simply assuming that the child is being deceptive. Furthermore, a thorough evaluation that assesses for whether children experience other instances of amnesia and other dissociative indicators can assist in untangling the issue of lying versus dissociation.

Ryan, the 9-year-old hockey player mentioned earlier, provides an example of disavowed witnessed behavior (Waters, 2015). The school principal witnessed Ryan hitting a girl while standing in line. The principal confronted Ryan, who adamantly denied hitting her, and then collapsed to the ground sobbing. The principal called me, stating, "Ryan really doesn't know that he did it." At the time, I had thought that Ryan only suffered from depersonalization that accounted for his encopresis. On further exploration of the event at school, Ryan revealed that he had a part of him that he called "Friendly Ryan," who was his protector. This part thought that the girl had knocked into him on purpose and viewed her as a threat. In my practice, I have treated many children who were unaware that a protective/aggressive state took control, attacked another student, and then "quickly left the scene."

14. Complaints of a Severe Headache Before a Change in Behavior

I have treated a number of children who have complained of severe headaches when they experienced intense and unmanageable feelings, internal conflicts between self-states, or when a self-state was trying to take control. If the child complains of headaches, it is important to inquire about what is occurring internally when the headaches occur.

Martha, an 8-year-old child, had incapacitating headaches. Martha was a failure-to-thrive toddler with an extensive history of physical, emotional, and sexual abuse by numerous people from infancy until she reached age 3. She would get debilitating headaches when a sexualized self-state would attempt to take control of her body and engage in sexualized play with other children. This had been an ongoing problem for Martha and the activation of this self-state caused her much anxiety and conflict, requiring that she lie down, completely immobilized. She would then fall asleep to avoid having the sexualized state take control. (Martha's case is described throughout the book.) Evaluating for sudden headaches and their underlying dynamics may point to overwhelming and frightening internal conflicts that account for such somatic complaints.

15. Inadequate Progress Despite the Child Being in a Safe, Nurturing Environment

Traumatized children who are in a safe environment and are in psychotherapy but not making consistent, adequate progress should be evaluated for dissociation. Unless dissociative defenses are uncovered and treated, these children will usually continue to have persistent symptoms and be unable to learn from past experiences, regardless of therapeutic interventions and appropriate consequences for their behavior. Unfortunately, many patients, including children who I have treated, have suffered years of wasted lives and incurred enormous health care costs due to missed diagnosis of a dissociative disorder and improper treatment (Brand, Loewenstein, & Spiegel, 2014).

16. Prior Diagnoses and Treatment Failures

Multiple prior diagnoses and previous treatment failures overlap with the earlier indicator of inadequate progress in treatment, but deserve special emphasis. Dissociative children can have numerous symptoms that appear, disappear, and reappear, and new symptoms can emerge at any time. Often, the most pronounced, intractable symptom takes center stage and becomes the focus of treatment. The shifting of mood and behavior can relate to the presence or influence of self-states that contain those symptoms. How much disruption they cause often determines the diagnosis. Thus, shifting self-states can account for children with multiple diagnoses ranging from ADHD and conduct disorder to bipolar disorder or schizophrenia over their treatment course. Extensive discussion on overlapping symptoms and the frequent misdiagnosis of children with dissociative disorders will be described in Chapter 3.

In summary, these warning signs cover the conditions that can cause dissociation, as well as core dissociative symptoms and co-occurring symptoms and behaviors that often mask dissociative presentations. Familiarity with these warning signs will enhance proper evaluation for dissociation so that children can receive appropriate treatment and care. Otherwise, these children will often experience repeated treatment failures and feel like failures. They will experience helplessness, worthlessness, and shame for their lack of progress. Over time, their parents will become frustrated, burned out, and unable to cope with their children's behavior, resulting in their removal. Consequently these children will often experience a cycle of multiple placements.

NOTES

1. On April 20, 1999, two senior high school students, Dylan Klebold and Eric Harris, entered their school in Littleton, Colorado, with an arsenal of weapons and killed 12 students, one teacher, and themselves.
2. Waters's clinical cases with DDNOS have been updated to OSDD per *DSM-5.*

3

DECIPHERING WHAT IS DISSOCIATION
DIFFERENTIAL DIAGNOSES

A MOTHER CAME TO MY office highly distraught and frightened by her 6-year-old daughter, Kyra. She described Kyra as suddenly shifting from being a calm child to getting the most hateful look in her eyes:

> She threatened to kill me! She talks to herself in a strange voice. She doesn't act like herself. She acts schizophrenic! She does sexual things to her younger brother and to our dog but denies them even when I catch her! I brought her to other counselors, but she didn't get better. She was put on lots of medications, but nothing helped her. She was diagnosed with oppositional behavior disorder and bipolar disorder.

The mother reported that Kyra was sexually abused by a relative beginning in infancy until 2½ years of age when Kyra disclosed vaginal and oral penetration. The mother said that Kyra's previous therapists neither explored the sexual abuse with Kyra nor assessed for dissociative symptoms.

Individuals exposed to trauma over a range of time spans and developmental periods suffer from a myriad of psychological problems that are not included in the traditional diagnosis of posttraumatic stress disorder (PTSD) (Courtois, 2004). Significantly, Stien and Kendall's (2004) model on complex trauma cited alterations in consciousness, memory, and identity to move the field forward in recognizing dissociation. Then, the National Child Traumatic Stress Network (NCTSN) compiled a white paper on complex trauma in children (Cook et al., 2005). Cook et al. categorized seven domains of impairment in children exposed to chronic trauma: attachment, biology, affect regulation, dissociation, behavioral control, cognition, and self-concept. Within each of these domains there can be a plethora of debilitating symptoms and diagnoses, including depression, anxiety, conduct disorder, bipolar disorder (BP), substance abuse, revictimization, and self-destructive and risk-taking behaviors, . . . ad infinitum!

Moreover, these problems are usually categorized as comorbid conditions rather than being recognized as essential elements of complicated post-traumatic adaptations (Courtois, 2004).

A child with complex trauma, including a dissociative disorder, drew a self-portrait depicting her pain and confusion. She was crying and saying, "Help Me." On her shirt, she wrote, "I don't feel like myself" (Figure 3.1). This is a common reaction with other traumatized, dissociative children.

Research on children with dissociation points to high comorbidity (e.g., Kisiel, Stolbach, & Silberg, 2013; Putnam, Hornstein, & Peterson, 1996) and overlapping symptoms (e.g., Sar, Oztürk, & Kundakci, 2002). Dissociative children often meet at least one or another of the diagnostic criteria (Sar, Onder, Killicaslan, Zoroglu, & Alyanak, 2014). Hornstein and Putnam (1992) examined 64 youth and found that the average number of psychiatric diagnoses a child received prior to a dissociative disorder diagnosis was 2.7. Diagnosis of a dissociative disorder in children and adolescents is often ignored, as clinicians are not well acquainted with what dissociative behaviors look like. Also, more commonly recognized symptoms can overlap or mask dissociation, making it more challenging to decipher

Figure 3.1 *Self-portrait of a child with complex trauma. (Used with permission.)*

dissociative symptoms. Furthermore, clinicians must rely on traumatized children's limited ability to put their experiences into words. Yehuda (2005) pointed out that dissociative children can have speech and language deficits along with fluctuations in consciousness and memory that compromise their capacity to disclose their dissociation.

Moreover, unless the clinician specifically asks about dissociative symptoms, children rarely volunteer to share this information. Reports from frustrated and exhausted caregivers, who may misunderstand or misinterpret their observations about their children's behavior, can mislead the evaluator. Therefore, for an accurate diagnosis of confounding symptoms, the therapist must be informed about complex trauma and dissociation. They must carefully explore what the underlying meaning is of mercurial and contradictory symptoms seen in dissociative children that can appear with such force and suddenly recede in a flash! It requires a paradigm shift from looking at the symptoms as an illustration of what defines children to instead examining what the symptoms suggest is going on *within* them. Because these children can fit numerous diagnoses, *the focus must not be on a segment of the behavior, but rather on what the sum of the behavior means.*

Chapter 2 examined the warning signs, such as hallucinations, extreme mood switches, and memory problems, that can suggest the presence of dissociation. In this chapter, I examine overlapping symptoms and comorbidity of dissociative disorders with PTSD, attention deficit hyperactivity disorder (ADHD), BP, psychosis or schizophrenia, obsessive-compulsive disorder (OCD), eating disorders, substance use disorders, and reactive attachment disorder (RAD) to help the clinician discern unique differences for accurate diagnosis.

DISORDERS THAT HAVE SYMPTOMS THAT OVERLAP WITH DISSOCIATION

Posttraumatic Stress Disorder

According to the National Survey of Children's Health (NSCH, 2011/ 2012),[1] almost half the children in the United States, close to 35 million, have experienced at least one or more types of childhood adversity that are likely to affect their physical and mental health as adults (Stevens,

2013). Other studies (Saunders, 2003; Turner, Finkelhor, & Ormrod, 2010) indicated that in the United States, one fifth of youth have been exposed to at least one type of victimization, and many are exposed to several types involving multiple perpetrators (Grasso, Greene, & Ford, 2013). Victimization encompasses sexual, physical, and emotional abuse, neglect, witnessing domestic violence, some form of disruption of attachment, or impairment of caregivers due to illness, drugs, and incarceration. As stated earlier, children often present with complex symptoms that PTSD or other singular diagnoses do not adequately address (D'Andrea, Ford, Stolbach, Spinazzola, & van der Kolk, 2012). Unfortunately, from my clinical experience, many children who have suffered multiple traumatic events were not even diagnosed with PTSD, but were instead given a diagnosis that was reflective of their most disruptive symptom, such as conduct disorder, oppositional diagnosis, BP, or ADHD.

The *Diagnostic and Statistical Manual of Mental Disorders*, fifth edition (*DSM-5*; American Psychiatric Association [APA], 2013) has expanded the PTSD diagnosis to include children aged 6 years and younger with symptoms of dissociative reactions (e.g., flashbacks in which there may be a complete loss of awareness of surroundings), depersonalization, and derealization. Hopefully, these changes will improve recognition of the relationship between PTSD and dissociative symptoms. If children with PTSD show dissociative symptoms, it is critical to assess for other symptoms such as identity alterations and memory impairment that may warrant the diagnosis of a dissociative disorder.

Attention Deficit Hyperactivity Disorder

When children experience repetitive trauma, they often have deficits in attention and concentration, resulting in a diagnosis of ADHD (Barletto Becker & McCloskey, 2002; Ford & Connor, 2009). Children with complex trauma frequently function in a state of hypervigilance, preoccupied with the fear of being harmed. This preoccupation draws their attention away from learning and assimilating new experiences and can impair their ability to concentrate on schoolwork. Instead, they attend more to tone of voice, body posture, and facial expressions (Perry, Pollard, Blakely, Baker, & Vigilante, 1995). Furthermore, when children are chronically exposed to threatening environments, they become sensitized to trauma-related sensory cues and are easily triggered by minor traumatic reminders. When triggered, they can become hyperaroused or dissociated, which can lead to abnormal organization of neural systems that interfere in attention and memory (Perry et al., 1995).

The literature to date indicates that there appears to be a relationship between ADHD and trauma in children. There have been many other studies linking child abuse with ADHD symptoms (e.g., Briscoe-Smith & Hinshaw, 2006; Ford, Ellis, Davis, & Fleischer, 2007; McLeer, Deblinger, Henry, & Orvaschel, 1992; Merry & Andrews, 1994). Merry and Andrews found an unexpectedly high rate of ADHD, double that found in the community population, in children 12 months after disclosure of sexual abuse. In another study, ADHD was the most frequent diagnosis found in sexually abused children. Forty-six percent of a sample of sexually abused children met ADHD criteria, and 23% of the sexually abused children met ADHD and PTSD criteria (McLeer et al., 1992). Ford and Connor (2009) distinguished between PTSD and ADHD while noting that despite an overlap in symptoms, they each have independent phenomenologic, diagnostic, etiologic, and neurobiologic characteristics. Because of the large overlap in symptoms, it is recommended that children diagnosed with ADHD be routinely assessed for a trauma history (Ford & Conner, 2009; Harrison & Wilson, 2005).

It does not appear that ADHD predisposes children to trauma. A 4-year prospective study determined that boys identified as ADHD were not at higher risk for a traumatic experience than the comparison group of children without ADHD (Wozniak et al., 1999). Endo, Sugiyama, and Someya (2006) studied the presence of ADHD both before and after child abuse, as well as the relationship between ADHD symptoms and the presence of a dissociative disorder. Their study demonstrated that a majority of child abuse victims (67%) met ADHD criteria for inattention after their abuse, whereas only 27% met these criteria before experiencing abuse. These findings suggest that the ADHD symptoms were in response to the trauma.

A number of studies have examined the correlation between inattention and dissociation in abused children (e.g., Cromer, Stevens, & Deprince, 2006; Endo et al., 2006; Kaplow, Hall, Karestan, Dodge, & Amaya-Jackson, 2008; Malinosky-Rummel & Hoier, 1991). Endo et al. found that child abuse victims who were diagnosed with a dissociative disorder met ADHD criteria for inattention more frequently than nondissociative victims of child abuse. A dissociative disorder was the most frequent diagnosis (59%), ADHD was diagnosed in 18% of abused subjects, and 71% of children diagnosed with ADHD had a comorbid dissociative disorder. Malinosky-Rummel and Hoier noted an overlap between traumatized children who scored in the significant range on dissociative checklists and on specific items in the Child Behavior Checklist (CBCL; Achenbach, 1992), a tool commonly used to measure ADHD. These symptoms included inattention, feeling in a fog, staring, and daydreaming. The question of whether these ADHD symptoms are the result of alterations of consciousness, identity, and perception remains to be explored.

Kaplow et al. (2008) tested a prospective model of attention problems in sexually abused children. They found two paths that predicted attention problems in abused children: being sexually abused by someone in the family and/or dissociation measured immediately after disclosure. Cromer et al. (2006) examined executive attention and dissociation in foster children and found that there were common deficits in tasks that required response inhibition in high dissociation and ADHD samples; however, dissociative children were better able to perform complex tasks that require planning than children diagnosed with ADHD. Their findings point to the possibility that dissociation and ADHD may be differentiated by performance into tasks primarily requiring planning, strategy, or multiple rule sets as dissociation is not associated with pervasive impairment in cognitive performance.

In summary, ADHD and dissociative disorders appear to be distinct but frequently comorbid disorders. Most of the overlap appears to be in the area of inattention. Given the overlapping symptoms between ADHD and dissociation, all children diagnosed with ADHD should routinely be assessed for a trauma history. If there is a significant trauma history, rather than assuming the child has ADHD, clinicians should explore whether the attention problems are associated with PTSD and dissociative symptoms, such as alterations of consciousness.

Bipolar Disorder

One of the most debilitating symptoms of complex trauma in children is dysregulation of the affective system. Traumatized children often operate in a fear mode and are highly sensitive to minor triggers, emitting a cascade of chemicals, some of which can cause hyperarousal (i.e., flight or fight responses) and others that cause dissociative symptoms such as freeze and immobilization responses (Perry et al., 1995). Lanius et al. (2003) found that reduced activity in the anterior cingulated cortex and thalamus found in patients with PTSD may underlie emotional dysregulation. In a review, Frewin and Lanius (2006) found reduced activity in the anterior cingulate cortex as well as in the medial frontal cortex in patients with PTSD. These brain structures are involved in several key emotional processing functions and may impact the ability to modulate automatic affective responses to cues, which remind survivors of their traumatic experiences.

An overactive amygdala, a part of the brain associated with fear conditioning, may play a role as well (Bremner, 2002; Rauch et al., 1996). Vermetten, Schmahl, Lindner, Loewenstein, and Bremner (2006) noted that patients with PTSD have a smaller hippocampus, which plays a role in learning and memory and damping stress reactivity. All of these structures influence self-regulation, and their impairment may cause traumatized children to experience extreme mood fluctuations.

The presence of dissociative self-states that contain different affects could be seen as further complicating the traumatized child's regulatory system. When a self-state becomes activated, the child can exhibit sudden and extreme mood fluctuations that are often out of the child's control and sometimes even out of the child's awareness. For all of these reasons, it is not uncommon for traumatized children to be misdiagnosed with a BP.

Although there is a spectrum of BP in the *DSM-5*, generally BP is instability of mood characterized by mania or hypomania and major depressive episodes, or cyclical periods of mania or hypomania and depression usually lasting weeks or months. Under a differential diagnosis section for BP, the *DSM-5* recognizes anxiety disorders, PTSD and schizophrenia spectrum and other related psychotic disorders, ADHD, and substance use disorders to be ruled out, but dissociative disorder is not one of the specifiers as a possible cause of mood irregularity.

In the previous decade, there was a dramatic change toward more permissive, less rigorously applied standards in diagnosing children with BP. The rate of diagnosis of pediatric BP has increased 40 fold in the past 10 years (National Institute of Mental Health [NIMH], 2007). This has resulted in considerable controversy surrounding this diagnosis. Moreover, upward of 90% of children diagnosed with BP are treated with medication for which there has been little testing for effectiveness or safety in children (Olfson, 2007).

A seminal article by Parry and Levin (2011) critically examined multidimensional factors that influence the overdiagnosis and misdiagnosis of pediatric BP. Contributory factors included popular books, the media, and the pharmaceutical industry, along with the failure to examine the impact of developmental trauma and attachment factors on affect regulation. Some popular books on pediatric BP have derived their data by surveying parents who visit online bipolar websites (e.g., Lederman & Fink, 2003) or surveying parents who visit online websites and examining corresponding pediatric reports (Papolos & Papolos, 2000). Although trauma and dissociation were not examined in these studies, Lederman and Fink's online survey revealed that 14% of the children were adopted, which may suggest that these children could have experienced early trauma that would impact affect regulation. Lombardo's (2006) book on BP mentions overlapping symptoms with dissociation but indicates that dissociation is uncommon. Conversely, I suspect that dissociation is more likely unrecognized and undiagnosed in children.

Birmaher et al. (2006) studied BP in 263 children older than 2 years of age and found that youth with BP demonstrated high lifetime rates of psychosis with poor prognoses, indicating the need for intensive and prompt treatment when psychosis is present. Regrettably, a traumatic history and discernment between psychotic and dissociative symptoms were not mentioned and did not appear to be evaluated in their study; this may account for the children's poor prognosis, as treatment is very different for BP, psychosis, and dissociation. Birmaher et al. (2009) studied 413 youths diagnosed with bipolar spectrum disorders. The children suffered episodic illness with subsyndromal and intermittently syndromal episodes of depression, mixed symptoms, and rapid mood changes. However, again, the researchers did not evaluate whether mood fluctuations could be related to trauma and dissociation.

Failure to take trauma histories (and screen traumatized children for dissociation) is of particular concern, as a number of studies have found a link between a history of trauma and adult BP (e.g., Blader & Carlson, 2006; Hyun, Friedman, & Dunner, 2000; Levy, 2007). Since many of the traumatic events began in childhood, it is possible that the origin of the adults' affective dysregulation was trauma based.

Oedegaard et al. (2008) administered the Dissociative Experiences Scale (DES) to patients diagnosed with BP-II or a major depressive disorder (MDD). Patients diagnosed with BP-II scored higher on the DES than those diagnosed with MDD. In addition, there was a subgroup in both the BP-II and MDD groups who had cyclothymia and higher levels of dissociative symptoms. Oedegaard et al. concluded that more serious dissociative disorders may be on a continuum with bipolarity. Researchers acknowledged that they did not obtain a trauma history from their participants but recognized traumatic events associated with dissociative symptoms. I cannot help but wonder whether the significant scores on the DES may signify a dissociative disorder that was misconstrued as BP-II given the overlapping symptom of mood cycling.

D'Andrea et al. (2012) discussed distinctions between BP and dissociation. They stated:

> The affect dysregulation associated with even rapid-cycling bipolar disorder occurs on a much slower time course than the lability and moment-to-moment state shifts expected in traumatized children. Similar to depression, the psychotic symptoms associated with bipolar disorder are mood-congruent and not characterized by the fragmentation, depersonalization, and derealization associated with dissociative states. Whereas manic states are characterized by grandiosity, the symptoms associated with maltreatment are characterized by a sense of the self as damaged or defective. (p. 194)

Medication is the main treatment used to regulate mood swings in BP; however, if the mood swings are a result of rapid switches between self-states, medication will not eliminate or cure self-states. Specialized treatment for dissociation that addresses self-states is the recommended standard of care (see guidelines for treatment of children and adults with dissociation at www.isst-d.org). Pavuluri et al. (2006) examined the response to lithium treatment in youth diagnosed with BP who had a history of sexual and physical abuse. They found a lack of response to the medication. Perhaps this was due to the mood swings resulting from unprocessed trauma and dissociative mechanisms, rather than being due to biologically based BP.

Harris (2005) warned that it is not enough to assume that children's mood cycling is a biological condition that warrants a diagnosis of a pediatric BP and treatment with medications. She advised that clinicians must build skills in understanding family systems and individual psychodynamics so that the complexity of each case is carefully explored. As an example, she reports on the case of an 11-year-old boy diagnosed with BP. He had intense mood swings that were characterized by severe aggression. After a careful history was gathered, it was found that he had been recently returned to his biological parents after living with his grandparents in the Dominican Republic, where he incurred severe beatings for

2 years. Harris found that the boy was dissociating due to subtle triggers related to teasing by his peers and limit setting by his teacher. He reported that during these episodes "I just see red. . . . I don't really know where I am or what I'm doing. . . . I don't really feel in my body."

This case exemplifies the dozens of cases that I have seen in children who experienced significant traumas that were unexplored or dismissed as irrelevant, and who exhibited intense mood swings that were dissociative in origin but misdiagnosed as a BP (Waters, Laddis, Soderstrom, & Yehuda, 2007). If a history of trauma and dissociation remains undetected, then the underlying causes for mood and behavioral dysregulation will not be addressed with an appropriate treatment modality. Although psychotropic medication can support psychotherapeutic treatment, it does not resolve interpersonal trauma suffered by a child.

D'Andrea et al. (2012) advocated for a developmentally appropriate trauma diagnosis while stating:

> [V]ictimized children with diagnoses of conduct disorder, bipolar disorder and ADHD do not respond to disorder-specific treatments as well as other children with those diagnoses and do respond to trauma-focused interventions addressing the core disturbances of affect dysregulation, attention and consciousness, interpersonal skills and attributions and schemas . . . (p. 194)

In summary, there is a strong need for more research and education among clinicians on the overlapping symptoms of mood dysregulation, traumatic experiences, and dissociation. Research and clinical assessments that methodically utilize valid and normative childhood trauma and dissociative measures (Chapter 4), and that explore detrimental family dynamics would greatly benefit the field and the families we serve by helping clinicians accurately distinguish between pediatric BP and dissociative disorders. The misdiagnosis of dissociative children with BP will be discussed in several cases studies in the upcoming chapters.

Hallucinations

Many clinicians are not familiar with dissociative hallucinations in which traumatized children report hearing voices or seeing images. As a result, these hallucinations are often attributed to schizophrenia, a biological condition with a usual onset in late teens or early 20s for which environmental issues play a minor role, without considering a possible traumatic origin and the potential for a dissociative disorder (Foote & Park, 2008). Because the treatment trajectories of psychotic and dissociative hallucinations are vastly different, it is critical that the clinician is able to differentiate between the two.

Moskowitz (2011) and Ross et al. (1990) offered a valuable historical perspective on two opposing paradigms when diagnosing clients with hallucinations. The dominant view is that hallucinations are exclusively biologically based symptoms of psychosis. This view has greatly influenced the *DSM* and overshadowed the pioneering work of Bleuler (1911/1950, cited in Ross & Keyes, 2004), who described schizophrenia as a "split mind disorder." Bleuler's description of schizophrenia is consistent with our current understanding of dissociation:

> If the disease is marked, the personality loses its unity; at different times different psychic complexes seem to represent the personality . . . one set of complexes dominates the personality for a time, while other groups of ideas or drives are "split off" and seem either partly or completely impotent. (as cited in Moskowitz, 2011, p. 349)

As more research has been done on trauma and dissociative disorders, there has been increasing recognition that auditory and visual hallucinations can result from dissociation. This recognition has greatly contributed to accurately diagnosing dissociative patients with psychotic-like symptoms (Ross et al., 1990).

Read, van Os, Morrison, and Ross (2005) performed a comprehensive review of the literature from 1872 through 2004 and found a considerable overlap between diagnostic constructs of PTSD, schizophrenia, and dissociative disorders—particularly with regard to hallucinations. Overlapping symptoms in dissociation and schizophrenia include positive or Schneiderian first-rank symptoms such as "made" or unwilled actions, thoughts, and feelings; thought withdrawal; thought insertion; thought broadcasting; and hallucinations (Laddis & Dell, 2012; Ross et al., 1990). Numerous studies and clinical vignettes have described these types of symptoms in dissociative children and adolescents with DDNOS and DID and found them to be associated with the presence of self-states (e.g., Coons, 1996; Hornstein & Putnam, 1992; Putnam, 1997; Sar et al., 2002; Sar, Akyüz, Oztürk, & Alioğlu, 2013; Silberg, 1998, 2013; Wieland, 2011).

Sar and Oztürk (2009) noted a distinctive feature in the presentations of dissociative clients who have psychotic symptoms. These clients usually have insight into their illness and their reality testing is intact except during a dissociative episode. Sar and Oztürk (2009) stated:

> The dissociative patient's reported claim of containing another person's existence, or of having more than one personality, cannot be considered a delusion. Such claims do not originate from a primary thought disorder, but rather from experience itself—the actual experience of the other as "not me" (Sullivan, 1953). In contrast, the delusions of a schizophrenic patient are thought to be the result of a primary disturbance of thought content. (pp. 536–537)

There are also a number of studies that have found a link between childhood trauma and schizophrenia. Spence et al. (2011) found a significant rate of childhood trauma in patients diagnosed with schizophrenia, but they did not rule out a dissociative disorder in their sample. A longitudinal twin study in the United Kingdom (Arseneault et al., 2011) found that psychotic symptoms at age 12 were associated with cumulative childhood trauma; however, again the authors did not explore dissociation as a possible etiology for the children's auditory and visual hallucinations. Schäfer et al. (2006) found that dissociative symptoms in patients with schizophrenia spectrum disorders are related to childhood trauma.

Studies with adults have demonstrated a robust relationship between dissociation and schizophrenia. Ross and Keyes (2008) examined the overlapping symptoms of schizophrenia and dissociation in adults. They concluded that among individuals who have a long-standing diagnosis of schizophrenia, there is a substantial subgroup with pathological dissociation and elevated rates of childhood trauma. Vogel et al. (2009) examined dissociation in adults diagnosed with schizophrenia and found that childhood traumatic incidents were frequent and physical neglect was associated with high levels of dissociation, whereas abuse was not. This result was surprising in that abuse is so frequently associated with dissociation. This study underscores our need to explore the serious impact of physical neglect on children and its link to dissociation. Varese, Barkus, and Bentall (2012) studied 45 adults with schizophrenia spectrum disorders and compared them with healthy controls with no history of hallucinations. Hallucinating patients reported both significantly higher dissociative tendencies and childhood sexual abuse. Dissociation positively mediated the effect of childhood trauma on hallucination proneness.

These results point to the need for similar research in traumatized children. It also underscores the likelihood that some adults who have been diagnosed with schizophrenia actually have a dissociative disorder. This is an important point, as dissociation requires very different treatment than schizophrenia. In addition, unlike schizophrenia, dissociation is curable with appropriate treatment.

Alao, Tyrrell, Yolles, and Armenta (2000) presented a case study that is pertinent to our discussion on the differential diagnosis of schizophrenia and dissociation. During her 30s, Anna was hospitalized due to auditory hallucinations, delusions, and thought disorganization. She was described as paranoid for stockpiling knives in her house. During the hospitalization, she disclosed childhood and adult sexual abuse, and she demonstrated amnesia along with florid, angry dissociative states with different names and characteristics.

The description of Anna is similar to that of many dissociative children with self-states. These children often appear to exhibit delusions, thought disorders, and aberrant behavior. These disorganized thoughts and delusions may be due to the confusion caused by rapidly switching self-states that do not have continuity of knowledge of people and the environment. Dissociative children can confabulate scenarios filled with bizarre thoughts and act on thoughts that are not based on reality, but rather are derived from their traumatic histories and based on survival. When working with these children, it is important to explore a self-state's underlying motivations to see whether they make sense from a survival perspective, as often they are still living in the terror of their past. Joey, a 7-year-old boy whom I treated, was similar to Anna in that he also stockpiled knives.

Joey was severely traumatized from infancy until he was placed with caring adoptive parents at age 6. Joey's adoptive father was a hunter and a gun collector. One night, while the family was asleep, Joey quietly got out of bed. He climbed up on a table in his dad's study and retrieved ammunition stored high on a shelf. Joey found the key to the gun cabinet and loaded the correct gun with the ammunition. He then cocked the gun and placed it under his adoptive father's desk. Sometime later, as his father was sitting at his desk he dropped some paper. He leaned over and found the loaded gun. He was horrified. When questioned, Joey admitted to putting the gun under the desk. His adoptive father checked Joey's room and found that he had stashed sharp knives from the kitchen in the bottom of his toy chest and under his mattress. Joey said that the voices inside him told him to do these things. Fortunately, they only told him to load and cock the gun and not to use it! The voices came from self-states who did not know they were safe and felt the need to protect themselves. They thought that they were still living in the horrors of their former home in which they had been abused by multiple perpetrators, including their biological parents.

Dissociative children often describe auditory hallucinations as occurring internally and perceive various voices with different attributes (e.g., an angel versus a devil). On exploration, it is often found that these voices are introjects or internal representations of significant others in the child's life, for example, abusers or protectors. Internal voices can also represent segmented affective states (e.g., angry or sad parts) pertaining to the trauma. Negative voices can argue, harass, or berate the child endlessly, causing significant distraction, fear, and distress. Although voices in those diagnosed with schizophrenia are also often described as hostile (Honig et al., 1998; Putnam, 1989), it is important not to assume a hostile voice is due to psychosis. It is critical to explore the etiology of hallucinatory voices with traumatized children to determine the impact that the trauma has on the genesis of the voices, and whether the voice represents a dissociative state.

Similar to auditory hallucinations, visual hallucinations in dissociative children are usually related to self-states. In my office, children have described and drawn these self-states as floating figures, faces, and shadows that they see internally. Some children have even drawn another person coming out of their head. Children often describe their self-states as having different genders, ages, roles, and affects related to their traumatic experiences. Figure 3.2 is a picture drawn by Mathew, a 10-year-old boy with OSDD, of a menacing self-state emerging from his head. This state contained rage over his early neglect and the domestic violence he witnessed between his parents. Mathew had also found his father's body after he had hung himself.

The amount of detail in children's drawings of their self-states may provide clues to how well developed or fragmented they are. Children who draw more developed images appear to have self-states with more distinct identities and roles; consequently, these self-states may exert more influence over the child's mood, behavior, and memory. This is not to suggest that this is true in all cases. One should note that although Mathew drew his self-state with only a head, his self-state had a powerful influence over Mathew's destructive and aggressive behaviors.

Figure 3.2 *Mathew's self-state emerging from his head. (Used with permission.)*

I have also treated traumatized children who initially reported visual and auditory hallucinations coming from outside of themselves. However, on further exploration, they recognized that their hallucinations were coming from within and originated from self-states. I suspect that they externally projected their internal visual and auditory hallucinations as a result of rapid fluctuation from hyperarousal to dissociation, impairing their cognitive ability to recognize that their hallucinations came from within. Read et al. (2005) reviewed the literature on hallucinations that are trauma based and in which there is confusion between inner and outer experiences. They hypothesized that this confusion may be due to faulty source monitoring in which there is a misattribution of an internal event to an external source.

As a final note, although I have treated dissociative children who had been misdiagnosed as schizophrenic, I have not encountered a dissociative child as actually having comorbid schizophrenia. Of course, it is possible for a child to have both conditions. Van Eyes (personal communication, March 19, 2012) reported the case of a girl with DID who also had a psychotic voice that sounded similar to a loud siren that hurt her ears. When medication was given for the siren voice, the psychotic symptom resolved and she was then capable of working on her dissociative states.

In summary, when a child presents with hallucinations, it is important to determine whether these are psychotic symptoms or indicate the presence of dissociative self-states. It is crucial for dissociative children's recovery that diagnosticians become familiar with trauma-related hallucinations so that these symptoms are not misdiagnosed as psychosis and ineffectively treated as a consequence. For a more comprehensive analysis of the differential diagnosis of hallucinations, I encourage the reader to read the section on dissociation and psychosis in Dell and O'Neil's (2009) book *Dissociation and the Dissociative Disorders: DSM-V and Beyond* (pp. 519–568).

Obsessive-Compulsive Disorder

Obsessive disorder is defined as recurring, persistent thoughts, urges, or images that are intrusive and unwanted. Repetitive behaviors or mental acts that an individual is driven to do in response to obsessions or to conform to rigid rules is a compulsive disorder (American Psychiatric Association, 2013).

Historically, OCD has been viewed as an isolated diagnostic entity, void of the contextual relationship to traumatic memories and dissociation, and treated with medication and/or cognitive behavioral therapy. This had begun to shift in the past two decades with an increased focus on trauma-related disorders.

There is a growing body of research examining the relationship between trauma and dissociation with OCD (e.g., Belli, Ural, Vardar, Yesilyurt, & Oncu, 2012; Lochner et al., 2004; Pica, Beere, & Maurer, 1997; Watson, Wu, & Cutshall, 2004). Lochner et al. studied the link between childhood trauma and dissociative experiences in patients who had OCD and trichotillomania. They found that dissociative symptomatology may be present in a substantial proportion of patients diagnosed with these disorders. Belli et al. examined psychiatric outpatients with a diagnosis of OCD and found that 14% of them had depersonalization disorder, amnesia disorder, or DID. They concluded that dissociative symptoms among patients with OCD should alert clinicians for the presence of a dissociative disorder. Pica et al. reviewed the psychological literature and found that dissociative and obsessive-compulsive individuals have similar difficulties in attending to new facts, responding to changes in the environment, and assimilating peripheral information into preexisting schemas about the self and the world. They theorized that both dissociative disorder and OCD may be linked to rigidity in the organization and integration of cognitive/perceptual experience.

I studied eight dissociative children with severe trauma who also met the criteria for OCD (Waters, 1999). Table 3.1 includes the names, ages, types of trauma, and dissociative diagnosis, along with the types of compulsions or obsessions these children experienced. All of these children suffered two or more types of chronic trauma during their preschool years. All of the children except one had more than one compulsion or obsession with an average of three compulsions per child. Half of the children identified self-states who were responsible for the compulsions and obsessions. One of the subjects, Briana, had experienced four types of trauma and had five different compulsions as noted in Table 3.1. Her assessment and treatment are discussed throughout this book.

I developed my own theory to help explain the high rates of OCD in children who have experienced complex trauma (Waters & Stien, 2000). I believe that OCD is a means to cope with unbearable trauma-related dissociated affect (e.g., fear, shame, guilt, helplessness), self-deprecating thoughts, offensive behaviors, and disturbing sensations. The OCD symptoms may be encapsulated in one or more self-states. The obsessions and compulsions are an attempt to release aspects of the trauma and to gain mastery over them. However, the attempt fails, causing a more negative affect, especially shame, which, in turn, increases the obsessions and compulsions. This cycle cannot be interrupted until the dissociated material and any associated self-states have been uncovered and the trauma has been processed and resolved. Until then, the child does not have control over the various states and is involved in a futile battle to gain control over them.

Compulsions and obsessions can serve a variety of purposes, including: (a) self-soothing (e.g., rocking, riding a bike in circles for hours, rubbing silky material); (b) cleansing to erase the sexual abuse feelings of being dirty (e.g., handwashing or bathing repetitively during the day); (c) distraction from unwanted affects, thoughts, or memories (e.g., engaging in repetitive behaviors such as counting); (d) substitution as in replacing one compulsion for a less undesirable one (e.g., finger tapping and counting to avoid the compulsion to look at male and female genitalia [Waters, 2000]); (e) managing feelings of vulnerability (e.g., by checking locks or

Table 3.1 *Children With Dissociative Disorders and OCD Following Traumatic Experiences*

Subject[a]	Age	Trauma	Dissociative Diagnosis	OCD Symptoms
Tammy	9	CSA, PA, EA, N	DID	Trichotillomania (pulling out of eyebrows/eyelashes)
Monica	9	CSA, PA, EA, N	OSDD	Finger tapping, counting, sexual obsessions
Kristine	7	CSA, PA, EA, WV	OSDD	Picking hands, picking wrists
Briana	17	CSA, PA, EA, WV	DID	Sexual obsessions, bulimia, compulsive exercise, substance addictions, compulsive cleaning
Lynn	19	CSA, EA, WV	DID	Compulsive cleaning, compulsive exercise, obsession with food (anorexia), praying for hours, rubbing silky fabrics
Heather	9	CSA, PA, EA, N	DID	Picking excrement, nose, and ears
Betty	5	CSA, WV	OSDD	Trichotillomania (pulling out eyebrows/eyelashes)
Ava	14	CSA, PA, EA, WV	OSDD	Cracking knuckles, tying shoelaces, sucking on something

[a]All names are pseudonyms.

CSA, child sexual abuse; DID, dissociative identity disorder; EA, emotional abuse; N, neglect; OCD, obsessive-compulsive disorder; OSDD, other specified dissociative disorder; PA, physical abuse; WV, witnessing violence.

Adapted from Waters (1999).

compulsively exercising 8 hours a day to feel strong); and (f) reenacting the trauma to gain a sense of mastery or control (e.g., sexual compulsivity or promiscuity, excessive masturbation).

Traditional cognitive behavioral therapy and pharmacological interventions alone have been found to be ineffective when treating OCD in patients with childhood trauma and dissociative disorders (McNevin & Rivera, 2001). Although traditional therapies have value for many who suffer with OCD, they do not tend to be effective for traumatized, dissociative children. These children do not get relief until the underlying dissociative processes and the purpose that the obsessive-compulsive behaviors serve are uncovered. When specific obsessive-compulsive symptoms are targeted with psychodynamic interventions that uncover the traumatic origin of those symptoms (including the presence of any self-states), then meaningful and enduring change can occur. The focus in these cases is on resolving trauma-related affects, behaviors, and sensations along with integrating any identity alterations that contribute to the OCD.

Eating Disorders

The connection between eating disorders and dissociation is well recognized in the literature (e.g., Farber, 2008; Lightstone, 2004; McShane & Zirkel, 2008). Somatic symptoms of dissociation can be found in binge eating (Fuller-Tyszkiewicz & Mussaph, 2008) as the result of a disruption of body-based awareness and bodily functions.

Demitrack, Putnam, Brewerton, Brandt, and Gold (1990) found evidence to suggest that neurochemical changes in dopaminergic, serotonergic, and opioid systems may be associated with the clinical expression of dissociation in patients with eating disorders during the acute phase of their illness. Lightstone (2004) examined the relationship between compulsive eating patterns and dissociative symptoms and found that bingeing and purging resulted in increased negative affects and feelings of low self-worth, which, in turn, furthered the use of dissociative mechanisms in a cycle of shame, compulsive eating, and dissociation.

Dissociative mechanisms, particularly depersonalization and the existence of a dissociative state driving the eating disorder, can have debilitating and even lethal results. For example, if the dissociative component of an eating disorder such as anorexia remains unrecognized, treatment failure can occur, resulting in the starvation of the child. In these cases, the youth does not have a unified sense of consciousness, identity, integrated thoughts, feelings, bodily responses, and actions that accurately reflect the repercussions of their eating disorder. A self-state often assumes direct control over the body either by bingeing or by internally controlling food intake. The youth is often unaware of the self-state's presence and its powerful influence over their relationship with food. I have learned to not make assumptions regarding the unconscious processes that may underlie the motivations of a self-state–driven eating disorder, as often the self-state is formed for only one purpose and, consequently, does not have an accurate understanding of the consequences of the behavior. I worked with a 17-year-old female with anorexia who had a self-state that controlled her eating disorder and her memory! See Chapter 13 for a detailed description of Sarah's treatment. This part took away her memory so she could not continue her perfectionistic, hard-driving behavior because her 7-year-old self-state wanted to play (Waters, 2005) and was also trying to remain small.

Farber (2008) reported on the presence of an abusive self-state in a boy whose eating disorder stemmed from a continued attachment to his abusive parent. The boy attempted to maintain an attachment with the "still loved," but abusive and neglectful parent by developing an internal introject of his parent, who inflicted pain on him, through bingeing and purging. The powerful, instinctual drive to be attached can overrule any concern about the damage that one is inflicting on the body.

On the other hand, children may develop eating disorders to protect themselves from their abusers. I treated a sexually abused, dissociative teenager who would vacillate between starvation and bingeing as a form of self-protection from her father's sexual advances. Her behavior stemmed from alternating beliefs that if she were small and asexual looking, he would leave her alone; and if she were large and unattractive, he would leave her alone. Neither worked.

Although traumatized children engage in these desperate self-protective measures, they ultimately fail, resulting in increased helplessness and shame that can reinforce the cycle of self-harming with food. A careful exploration of the role of traumatic experiences in the etiology of eating disorders—including impaired attachments, dissociation (especially depersonalization and contributory self-states), somatic distortions, and cognitive distortions—is crucial for successful intervention.

Substance Abuse

It has been long recognized that victims of severe trauma often resort to substance abuse to manage traumatic memories, negative affects, and associated behavior. Adolescents with significant trauma histories are particularly vulnerable to abusing substances given developmental stress-ors, such as a need for independence from their parents, peer pressure to engage in illegal drugs, and poor affect regulation. I have provided consultation and specialized outpatient treatment with severely addicted adolescents with a history of various forms of trauma and dissociation. It is horrifying what adolescents will put into their bodies to escape from their memories and numb their emotions. The sad dilemma is that although it feels safe to numb oneself with substances, it also causes ado-lescents much distress, as drugs and alcohol cause a disconnection from both themselves and others—the very connection they really want and strive for, but are too terrified to experience.

A review by Giaconia, Reinherz, Paradis, and Stashwick (2003) found that clinical and community studies consistently demonstrate that 50% to 75% of adolescents with substance use disorders have also experienced serious traumas, and that between 11% and 47% have PTSD. Giaconia et al. (2000) studied teenagers with substance use disorders–PTSD comor-bidity and found that they had significantly poorer health and more somatic complaints, anxiety, and withdrawn behavior than those with substance use disorders alone. Grossman (1997) studied 207 adolescents in a juvenile detention facility or a psychiatric hospital and found a high correlation between severity of childhood sexual, physical, and emotional abuse with dissociative symptoms with an increased use of mood-altering substances and risk for developing an addictive lifestyle.

I have treated a number of adolescents who had a substance-abusing self-state who engaged in reckless, impulsive behaviors that were beyond the adolescent's initial awareness or control. One case that comes to mind is that of Daren, a 15-year-old diagnosed with DID who severely abused both drugs and alcohol. Daren was amnestic to stealing a car, driving inebriated, along with being dragged out of the car and handcuffed by police, and incarcerated. The next day, he found himself sitting in a chair at a locked delinquency facility wondering how he got there. As we explored the internal voices that he reported had been present for years, he learned that one of the voices that he had heard was the substance abuser. This self-state had the complete memory of driving while inebriated and being apprehended by the police.

It is challenging to determine whether a substance-abusing adoles-cent's amnestic episodes are solely related to the effects of the substances or whether dissociative blackouts may be occurring. For this reason, it is important to administer dissociative checklists and explore the client's

early trauma history, along with episodes of amnesia and other dissociative symptoms, prior to the onset of the substance abuse or during
recovery. These assessments are well suited to substance abuse residential treatment programs, as these provide opportunities for ongoing
observations of the adolescent for the presence of dissociative symptomatology while the youth is maintaining sobriety.

The need for better assessments of adolescents in substance abuse
treatment programs is highlighted by a study conducted by Diane Raven
and Megan LaDuke at Great Lakes Recovery Center (GLRC), a residential
adolescent substance abuse center in Michigan (Raven, LaDuke, & Waters,
2014).[2] Many of the severely disturbed adolescents had significant childhood trauma that was either unrecognized or untreated prior to placement.
They entered treatment with multiple psychiatric diagnoses that included
BP, ADHD, conduct disorder, oppositional defiant disorder, OCD, MDD,
PTSD, emerging cluster B personality disorder, seizure disorders, somatoform disorders, mood disorders, and sleep disorders. Ironically, it was
rare for an adolescent to have been diagnosed with DID or OSDD (one
in 10 during the years of Raven's tenure) when, in fact, trauma-induced
symptomatology was common in this population.

To properly assess, evaluate, and provide appropriate treatment for
these substance-abusing adolescents, Raven et al. (2014) sought to determine the role of trauma in the youth's problems. The Trauma Symptom
Checklist for Children (TSCC) was administered to a sample of 145 adolescents between the ages of 12 and 17. However, seven assessments were
discovered to have invalid scores, leaving 138 valid participant assessments to be evaluated. All adolescents in this sample had also previously
experienced traumatic events. After administering the TSCC, responses
were converted into T scores and analyzed for clinical significance and
symptomology in each of the 10 clinical scales. The clinical scales included:
Anxiety (ANX), Depression (DEP), Anger (ANG), Post-Traumatic Stress
(PTS), Dissociation (DIS), Dissociation-Overt (DIS-O), Dissociation-Fantasy
(DIS-F), Sexual Concerns (SC), Sexual Preoccupation (SC-P), and Sexual
Distress (SC-D).

The focus in examining the results of this study was the DIS scale
and subscales. Within the DIS scale, there are two subscales: DIS-F and
DIS-O. The DIS scale is a measure indicating the degree of mild to moderate dissociative symptomatology that a child reports experiencing,
including endorsements of symptoms such as emotional numbing and
derealization (Briere, 1996). However, children with elevated scores in

DIS-F present differently from those with elevated scores in DIS and DIS-O, with symptoms related to high degrees of daydreaming, fantasy, and pretending to be someone else (Briere, 1996). DIS-O also includes a sense of detachment with reduced emotional response and affect (Briere, 1996).

The results of the TSCC indicated the highest overall levels of clinical significance, particularly in the categories of DIS and DIS-O where clinical significance is defined as T scores at or above 65 (Figure 3.3). Overall, 30.43% of participating adolescents were clinically significant in either DIS or dissociation subscales DIS-O and DIS-F (DIS, 23.91%; DIS-O, 26.08%; DIS-F, 13.78%) where many also scored in more than one DIS scale. Results for all DIS scales also demonstrated subclinical significance, T scores 60–65, with 27.53% of all participants showing subclinical significance, but significant symptomology, in at least one of the DIS scales. Data demonstrated subclinical scores, with 13.76% in DIS, 13.76% in DIS-O, and

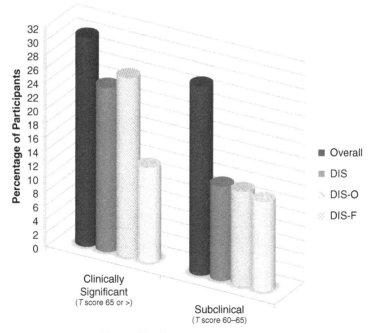

Figure 3.3 *Trauma Symptom Checklist for Children (TSCC) rating of dissociation in adolescents being treated for substance abuse.*

13.04% in DIS-F. In addition, the percentage of symptomology in both males and females was highest in the clinical scales of PTS, DIS, and DIS-O (Figure 3.4).

Clinical significance was further assessed to compare male and female presentations. Male participants indicated the highest levels of clinical significance in DIS-O, whereas female participants were most clinically significant in reports of DIS. Other significant clinical scales for female participants were DIS-O and ANG. Male participants also showed prominent clinical significance in DEP and DIS. Levels of symptomology out of all TSCC categories were highest in PTS. Considering the significance of scores being highest in PTS and the DIS scales, further inquiry was completed to assess for the percentage of adolescents who indicated symptomology in PTS with clinical significance in the DIS and ANX scales. Results demonstrated that approximately 17.4% of participating

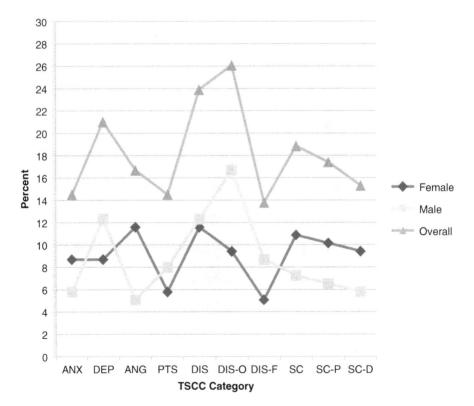

Figure 3.4 *Trauma Symptom Checklist for Children (TSCC): Clinical significance in males versus females.*

adolescents who indicated symptomology in PTS were also clinically significant in the dissociation categories and ANX. Differences between the clinical significance of PTS scores and ANX scores were marginal, though the percentage of adolescents who demonstrated clinical significance in ANX was higher than those who exhibited clinical significance in PTS. In light of the aforementioned results and with consideration of PTSD also being an anxiety disorder, it would be prudent to further analyze what these emergent findings may suggest and how they may or may not be associated with dissociation and trauma. (Treatment with this population using art therapy is described in Chapter 11.)

Overall, research has shown that substance abuse is correlated with significant trauma histories and high levels of dissociation with significant comorbidity of impulse control, suicidality, depression, and anxiety. In previous decades, the conventional wisdom was that mental health issues should be treated prior and independent of substance abuse issues (Souza & Spates, 2008). Surprisingly, some substance abuse treatment providers stubbornly hold onto this notion despite research showing that integrated treatment for comorbid disorders leads to more positive outcomes than treating the disorders serially (Bukstein & Horner, 2010; Libby & Riggs, 2008). Studies show that when the primary diagnosis is effectively treated (e.g., PTSD), co-occurring symptoms such as substance abuse will also show improvement (Coffey, Schumacher, Brimo, & Brady, 2005; Gershuny, Baer, Jenike, Minichiello, & Wilhelm, 2002; O'Donnell, Creamer, & Pattison, 2004).

Reactive Attachment Disorder

Many traumatized children, particularly those in foster and adoptive placements, are diagnosed with RAD because of attachment impairments resulting from early neglect and abuse. The *DSM-5* (APA, 2013) has placed RAD in the trauma and stressor-related disorders and separated it into two distinct disorders: RAD and disinhibited social engagement disorder (DSED). RAD more closely represents internalizing disorders with depressive symptoms marked by inhibited and emotionally withdrawn behavior toward adult caregivers with limited positive affect, irritability, sadness, and/or fearfulness. In contrast, DSED more closely resembles ADHD, as children readily approach and interact with unfamiliar adults and display a willingness to go off with them with minimal or no hesitation.

Little research has been done on the relationship between RAD and dissociation. For several decades, the literature has recognized the prevalence of dissociative symptoms in disorganized attachment; however, only in the previous decade, research was done on examining RAD in traumatized children (Hornor, 2008; Shi, 2014; Stinehart, Scott, & Barfield, 2012; Zeanah et al., 2004). Unfortunately, this research did not examine the prevalence of dissociative symptoms in these children, making it difficult to determine its relevance to attachment impairment.

A search of the literature revealed two case studies that discuss dissociation and RAD (Hardy, 2007; Hinshaw-Fuselier, Boris, & Zeanah, 1999). Hardy described the case of John, an 8-year-old boy who had an early history of physical, sexual, and emotional abuse and neglect, multiple failed therapeutic placements, and exhibited extremely aggressive and disruptive behaviors. Drawing on Schore's (1994, 2002) work on the neurobiology of attachment, Hardy recognized that John's mother did not provide adequate regulation of his internal affective states, resulting in an internal collapse and dissociation. John had an inconsistent sense of self along with an inability to perceive and understand the emotional states of others.

Hinshaw-Fuselier et al. (1999) described 18-month-old fraternal twins, Bobby and Claire, whose dissociative symptoms were meticulously tracked. The twins were observed to have increased episodes of staring. Their trance-like episodes and freeze responses occurred multiple times a day, lasting from seconds to 2 to 3 minutes at a time. These dissociative symptoms escalated during a 2-year span with multiple different placements and exposure to additional trauma. The authors noted that minor frustrations could cause a dissociative episode, particularly with Claire. The authors noted that initially the twins met criteria for RAD but over time, the diagnostic picture became less clear with multiple placements and inconsistent attachment behaviors. These case studies highlight how important it is to explore whether dissociative symptoms may underlie a child's erratic attachment behaviors, particularly when a diagnosis for RAD does not fully represent what is occurring.

Given the overlap between attachment problems and dissociative symptoms in children with histories of maltreatment (e.g., Liotti, 2006; Lyons-Ruth, 2003), I question whether RAD should be included as a subtype of a dissociative disorder or whether there should be a dissociative subtype of RAD. I have seen dissociative children vacillate rapidly between close attachment, complete detachment, avoidance, resistance, and hostility to a parent within a single day! These children can also hug a stranger who comes in their sight 1 minute and in the next moment react by curling into a fetal position. The main difference that I have found between dissociative children and children with RAD is that dissociative children exhibit more fluctuations in attachment style and contradictory attachment behaviors and affect with their parents due to shifting self-states, memory impairment, and perceptional distortions. For example, a dissociative child can have a close bond with the parents, but a self-state that is unfamiliar with the parents or that is still stuck in a trauma-based defense may appear briefly. This self-state may respond to the parents by either avoiding or attacking them—behavior for which the rest of the child is amnestic. Another state can be very outgoing, impulsive, and overly friendly to strangers without any awareness of the possibility of risk.

One such case is that of Dexter, a 4-year-old with DID who had a history of early, chronic physical and emotional neglect. Dexter had been previously diagnosed with RAD after multiple failed placements (including a previous adoptive placement), due to destructive and impaired attachment behaviors. As Dexter snuggled in his current adoptive mother's arms and engaged in eye gazing with her, she smiled and said, "He's not reactive attachment."

After one of his amnestic, destructive episodes, I saw Dexter in a family therapy session with both of his adoptive parents present. I asked Dexter whether he could check inside of his mind to see whether he could learn about what caused the destructive behavior. Dexter began to tell us about his self-states. His adoptive mom recognized Dexter's three distinct self-states and their different attachment styles with her and her husband. Dexter was able to attach to her, whereas his three self-states were not able to do so. Their behavior varied from avoidance to hostility. Dexter would rapidly shift from one state to another, displaying significant fluctuations in attitude, behavior, and memory. One female self-state had assumed a maternal role and comforted Dexter when he had been neglected. She was threatened by and hostile to Dexter's parents. The other two self-states carried rage, aggression, and memories of the neglect as well as witnessing considerable domestic violence. Although both of these self-states carried Dexter's rage, they also identified with Dexter's abusive biological father and were particularly resistant to attaching to Dexter's adoptive father. (Chapter 12 on EMDR describes how Dexter's self-states were able to resolve their traumatic attachment to the biological parents and develop an attachment to the adoptive parents.)

Because of the link between dissociation and disorganized attachment, it is critical to carefully explore any dissociative mechanisms operating, including the presence of self-states, when examining children with severe attachment impairments and vacillating attachment styles. I believe that many foster and adoptive placements have failed because of unrecognized and untreated dissociation that can greatly interfere in children's ability to form meaningful relationships with their caregivers.

Chapter 4 will provide guidance on interviewing the traumatized child, including specific questions to ask the child that will help determine whether dissociation may be responsible for the child's symptoms.

NOTES

1. Available at www.childhealthdata.org/learn/NSCH
2. The researchers would like to acknowledge their appreciation to GLRC for their permission to conduct research with their clients.

Uncovering the Child's Fractured Self
Assessing for Dissociation

"I hear these voices. I can't make them go away. They scare me and tell me to do bad things. Then I can't remember what happens next."
— 9-year-old boy with dissociation

HEARING VOICES IS A FREQUENT disclosure that children with dissociation have made to me. They feel out of control of their voices. It is a confusing, frightening, and helpless experience that often plagues these children daily or multiple times a day. This chapter explores ways to help children reveal their inner world, make meaning of their disturbing symptoms, and elicit significant information from caregivers and others for accurate assessment.

THERAPEUTIC APPROACH

In addition to developing a knowledge base regarding complex trauma and childhood dissociation, it is important to approach traumatized children in an inquisitive, open, collaborative, and empathic manner. Traumatized children are particularly sensitive to adult responses and are understandably wary of being judged or rejected. However, if you assume a nonjudgmental, open posture without any assumptions, and the children sense that you are genuinely interested in them, their fears and dissociative defenses will decrease. Moreover, they are more likely to reveal what internal and external dynamics are impacting them.

Another critical element in facilitating a child's openness is the *therapist's attunement with the child,* by which questions are paced based on the child's reactions. Becoming attuned to the child's subtle shifts in affect, behavior, and somatic movements—such as pauses in the child's responses, eye flutters, and slight shifts in body posture—will provide clues to the child's internal state of tension, confusion, and conflict, as well as a gateway into the child's inner life. Becoming attuned helps you to develop "synchronicity" with the child by adjusting your questions and comments to reflect what you are noticing in the child. Sensitively exploring subtle shifts and empathizing with the child can facilitate the child's willingness to explore underlying motivations or causes of shifts in affect and behavior, and memory problems associated with trance states.

Over the years, this approach has led to children disclosing extensive dissociative symptoms in initial sessions and experiencing immediate relief after finally feeling understood. They smile. Their bodies relax. They make eye contact with me. The clinician's synchronicity with the child promotes the therapeutic alliance and positive transference that will be carried forward even during the struggles that inevitably occur in the treatment process. If the therapist can maintain this synchronicity while assessing and treating dissociation, the treatment success will be enhanced as long as the child is in a supportive, safe environment.

Furthermore, this therapeutic approach provides powerful modeling for parents, who are often frustrated and depleted. They frequently believe that their children are capable of controlling their behavior and are intentionally misbehaving and avoiding responsibility for their actions. It is a difficult therapeutic balance to empathize with both caregivers and their children during family interviews while also attending to the frustrations and confusion of both over the children's disruptive behaviors. Providing psychoeducation about trauma and dissociation—particularly normalizing dissociation as an adaptive mechanism for survival from aversive experiences—can encourage caregivers to collaborate with therapists and become "therapeutic partners" (Waters, 1998a).

AREAS OF ASSESSMENT

Assessing a child for dissociation is a complex process of gathering data from the child and others who have interacted with the child. This includes conducting a series of interviews with the child, caregivers, relatives, and significant others, such as teachers, former mental health and health care professionals, and receiving relevant reports after obtaining the necessary releases from parents. Assessment also involves administering checklists to parents and children, as these can be invaluable tools for confirming dissociative symptoms.

To assess traumatized children, I use the Star Theoretical Model that covers areas of attachment, family relations, child development, neurobiology, and dissociation, as described in Chapter 1. The following areas are examined in an assessment:

1. Quality of the child's attachments with his or her parents and their responses to their child
2. Complete child developmental history, including any form of trauma from prebirth to present and its impact on the child's development and relationships
3. The child's medical history, including any intrusive or painful interventions, illnesses, brain injuries, or neurological problems
4. The child's academic history and peer relationships
5. The child's previous treatment and diagnoses
6. Any legal or Child Protective Services involvement
7. Family relationships and communication patterns, including any interpersonal violence between family members
8. Family and environmental influences that increase or decrease risk for trauma and the use of dissociative defenses, including forms of discipline and stressors related to the extended family, such as financial, medical, or legal problems
9. Parental history and relationships with family of origin, including any early attachment disruptions and history of trauma

The clinician should not assume, however, that asking about trauma or dissociative symptoms will automatically result in disclosure. Some children with histories of trauma are either unwilling or unable to indulge in disclosure early in the process. Disclosure may only occur as the child comes to know and trust the therapist (Courtois, 2004). In other instances, the presenting child may not be aware of the trauma, as the memory may be held in a different self-state. In addition, if the trauma happened within the family, the child may have been instructed not to talk about it by a family member or may avoid bringing it up to protect the family secret. These types of family dynamics can promote dissociation.

The parent history is an important and often neglected area of assessment. Understanding the parent's personal history can help avoid future problems and can identify parents who would benefit from a referral for their own therapy. It is also critical to assess the caregivers' commitment and attachment to the child, and their ability to understand, support, and persevere in managing the challenges of caring for their traumatized child.

I also explore the warning signs of dissociation discussed in Chapter 2 with the child, caretakers, school personnel, and other relevant individuals. Within these warning signs are five classifications of dissociative symptoms that Silberg (2013, p. 36) lists for the diagnostician to consider: (a) perplexing shifts in consciousness, (b) vivid hallucinatory experiences, (c) marked fluctuations in knowledge, moods, or patterns of behavior and relating, (d) perplexing memory lapses for one's own behavior or recently experienced events, and (e) abnormal somatic experiences. For example, it is important to inquire about any episodes of any trance behaviors, persistent denial of disruptive or explosive behavior even after being disciplined, and memory problems beyond ordinary forgetfulness of significant and/or daily events (e.g., birthdays, school activities, not recognizing their homework, or being unable to recall how to do homework that was performed well earlier). Inquiries about any extreme fluctuations in mood, behavior, and likes and dislikes, particularly when accompanied by amnesia, are also important signs of dissociation. Obtaining the details of these episodes will help link these types of fluctuations and their origin.

Although it is common to perceive the child's denial of problematic behaviors as avoiding responsibility, which may be the case, it is also important to know that disrupted memory is a strong feature of dissociation, particularly when there is a presence of a self-state. We have to be open to all possibilities to better differentiate what is occurring with the child.

Any signs of identity confusion in traumatized children also should be explored, such as signs of auditory hallucinations, children referring to themselves in the third person or by another name, talking to themselves, and exhibiting changes in voice, mannerisms, and imaginary playmates. It is also important to inquire about somatic disturbances, such as periods of unexplained pain in extremities, or an inability to walk, see, or hear that has no organic cause. Although I ask these questions initially, I will repeat them to children and their caregivers during the process of therapy, particularly when dissociative symptoms are observed or suspected.

Dissociative symptoms may not be initially apparent for a number of reasons. Dissociative defenses may remain hidden until something triggers such behavior. Subtle signs may not be detected nor clearly understood by the child or the therapist. It may take children time to become conscious of their behaviors. In addition, they may not have the ability to reflect on or report their internal experiences due to their dissociation and language impairments (Yehuda, 2005, 2015). It can be helpful to assume the role of a detective and enlist the child as an "assistant" to ascertain what is impacting the child's symptoms—including any trauma, dissociation, and any environmental and familial influences that may promote dissociative behaviors. Astute observation over a period, coupled with an understanding of what dissociation looks like, is required to effectively detect dissociative signs.

Adolescents may be reluctant to report hallucinatory and amnestic episodes for fear of being viewed as "crazy." Reassuring them that these experiences have also been described by other youth with similar traumatic histories, and are treatable, can help allay these fears. Normalizing their experiences helps relieve the worry that they are being judged. It also gives them permission to expound on their inner world. These children are desperate to be understood and to make meaning out of their confusing and scary experiences. When they feel safe from recrimination, it is like opening the floodgates and they will divulge extensive information that they had never previously given to anyone.

THE INTERVIEWING PROCESS

Because of the complex symptoms associated with extensive trauma histories, I may ask the parents or caregivers to initially come in alone so I can gather the child's history and more quickly understand what underlying dynamics may be influencing the child's symptoms. In addition, this spares children from listening to their parents describe in detail their problematic behaviors to me. I also want to assess the caregivers' commitment and attachment to the child, and their ability to understand and tolerate their child's disruptive behaviors while maintaining a safe and supportive environment. This also gives me the opportunity to assess the parents' capacity to become therapeutic partners with me (Waters, 1998a), and how involved they can be in the sessions (with their child's agreement).

I will then interview the child and parents together to assess their relationship, their quality of attachment, and review their concerns along with other challenges that they face that need special attention. Beginning these sessions in a neutral manner by first asking the child about his or her interests, hobbies, favorite games and television programs, any hero characters, or people they admire helps build rapport (Adler-Tapia & Settle, 2008). This information can later be used in empowerment and stabilization techniques, described in Chapters 7 and 8. I provide reassurance that recovery is possible with time, patience, and investment. I stress to parents that their child's symptoms are a cry for help and as a team we will explore the underlying meaning of the symptoms and develop a plan for effective intervention. I will also interview the child alone, as some topics may be difficult for the child to express in front of the parent. If a young child is uncomfortable in separating from her parent, then I will see the child along with her parent until the child is comfortable being seen alone. My aim is to provide a welcoming and reassuring environment to help children express what is disturbing them.

Questions to Ask Parents About Dissociative Symptoms[1]

The following is a list of questions to ask parents that will assist in identifying dissociative symptoms in children. They are also available in Appendix C. Depending on parental responses, some questions may not be necessary. This is a guide for the clinician to use with discretion. Although the questions apply to both boys and girls, for simplicity, male gender is used.

- Does your child have extreme switches in mood and behavior? If so, describe these and what you notice about his behavior and affect. Does he seem different during these episodes; if so, in what ways?
- Does your child deny his aggressive or disruptive behavior even when you have witnessed it? How does he respond to you at these times? Does he continue to deny his behavior even after he is disciplined? Does he deny other behaviors or situations that are not problematic (e.g., conversations or family/social/school activities)?
- Does your child have memory problems for events that he should recall, such as holidays and birthdays, past or present?
- Does your child adamantly deny that you told him to do his homework or chores when you are facing him, engaging with him in

conversation, and he is not occupied with any other activity, such as electronic games?

- Does your child look and behave differently at times that are not attributable to physical illness? Describe these times in detail.
- Does your child prefer a favorite food, activity, clothing, and so forth, but at other times hate it? Please describe in detail.
- Do you see your child staring, unresponsive, and as though he is in his own world (not including when playing video games or watching television)? How often and for how long does this happen? Afterward, can he explain where his mind was?
- Do you notice any changes in the child's eyes (e.g., blinking, fluttering, eye rolling) and/or notice changes in voice and/or mannerisms during these times? Please describe. Are there other changes associated with these mannerisms (e.g., memory, mood, or behavior disturbances)?
- Has your child ever told you that he hears voices or sees things or people that are not heard or seen by others? Please describe. Do you notice other changes during these times (e.g., memory, mood, or behavior disturbances)?
- Have you heard your child talk to himself? Does he sound as though he is using a different voice? Does he seem younger or older, or act very differently? Does he have memory problems during these episodes?
- Does (or did) your child have imaginary playmates? When were you aware of them? Describe what you have noticed. Does your child have memory problems and/or act differently during this time?
- Does your child have somatic complaints that do not have a medical cause? Please describe. Do you notice other changes during these times (e.g., memory, mood, or behavior disturbances)?

Interviewing the Child

Traumatized youth generally have a lot of anxiety when meeting a therapist, particularly if they had experienced previous unsuccessful treatment. I provide many activities for children to engage in while I am assessing them. Squishy toys are helpful sensory toys that can release some anxiety. Drawing; playing with clay, a dollhouse, and a sand tray are therapeutic forms of expression that they can engage in as we get acquainted. If children do report internal voices, at some point during the evaluation I will show them a specially designed androgynous, "dissociative doll" that has an opening in its head for little dolls with different feelings that can be inserted and closed with a tie string. The doll also has a pocket in its heart for a doll to be inserted that represents the child's particular feeling at that moment (Figure 4.1).

This doll is especially useful for helping children to begin to express the different voices and feelings they experience. I begin to educate them

Figure 4.1 *"Dissociative doll" with little dolls depicting varied feelings.*

that all of the voices and feelings, even the ones that seem scary, are a part of them that helped them survive in some way, even though it may not seem that way currently. I explain that, as we work together, we can figure out what purpose the voices serve so that all parts can learn to get along with each other. Although a child who has a harassing voice may be dubious about this, it does bring some relief to know that there is help and a solution.

In their children's book on dissociation, *All the Colors of Me*, Gomez and Paulsen (in press) use a rainbow analogy to represent the shiny child who is born and then develops different feelings and thoughts represented in various colors of the rainbow. When bad things happen, these colors become mixed-up emotions that separate from the other rainbow colors, and one color may not notice what the other color did to deal with those mixed-up feelings. They further explain that when the mixed-up colors are no longer present, all the colors can connect with the "bright shiny me" and work together to enjoy their own rainbow. This story can give hope to the child and let the child know that our major goal of therapy is to strive toward harmony and unity—an important goal that I want to immediately emphasize in the evaluation phase.

Observing for Dissociative Shifts

Dissociative children can display subtle shifts in consciousness when switching from one state to another. If a self-state's age is close to that of the biological age of the child, detection of such shifts can be challenging. You may notice a change in voice inflection or the presence of unusual mannerisms, such as facial twitching, eye rolling, or changes in body posture. In the case of Ryan, when an angry state emerged in a family session, Ryan straightened his posture and licked his lips (Waters, 2015). Memory lapses are more easily detected, as Ryan's angry state knew about the hockey weekend for which Ryan had no memory.

The following are the signs that may accompany state shifts:

- Staring or a glazed look in the eyes
- Rapid blinking, fluttering, or eye rolling
- Other facial changes such as biting one's lip or a stern look
- Vocal changes in tenor, inflections, or language use (e.g., baby talk)
- Changes in body posture, such as changing from a relaxed posture to a stiff one, or from coordinated to clumsy

- Contradictory statements in short succession (e.g., "I don't get along at all with my mom. We get along alright," or "I hate soccer. I like playing it.")
- Dramatic changes in activity preferences (e.g., enjoys drawing in the office, then later claims to hate it)
- Shifts in awareness of what was just said by either the child or the therapist
- Confusion, significant discrepancy, or denial of an earlier report of traumatic and nontraumatic events

Questioning Children About Dissociation

It is important to be aware that assessment questions can be triggering to traumatized children. These questions may cause children to spontaneously blank out or experience shifts in self-states, particularly when they pertain to traumatic reminders (i.e., mentioning the name of the perpetrator, events, or symptoms related to the traumatic event). Shifts in affect and thought processes can be due to internal confusion or conflict that may relate to a self-state of which the child may or may not be consciously aware. Self-states can have varied preferences for food, dress, activities, and relationship disparities with parents, siblings, friends, teachers, and so forth. They can have divergent skill levels in academic and social performances depending on their age, how they were formed, and their purpose. Some shifts may be subtle whereas others may be more extreme. Dissociative children can switch so rapidly that it is easy to overlook such shifts or attribute them to other reasons, such as the child being nervous or having a cognitive impairment. Assessment questions should be geared to exploring shifts that occur in the session as well as a general exploration of sudden changes or shifts that traumatized children experience in their daily life.

Auditory and visual hallucinations should be asked about, as in any mental status exam. If endorsed, follow-up questions about the details of the hallucinations are recommended to ascertain frequency, triggers, details of what is said and seen, as well as the impact that this has on the child. When I specifically inquire about hallucinations, I present these questions in a nonchalant manner while explaining that I have worked with many children who have described similar experiences. I explain that these experiences occur because of stress and upsetting events. Normalizing these types of experiences helps to put children at ease and to talk about their hallucinations.

The following are the suggested questions to explore dissociative symptoms with children and adolescents. Silberg (2013) provides a similar list of questions. Depending on the age and developmental level of the child, modification or reframing of the questions will need to occur. It is also important to pace the questions according to the child's ability to manage them.

Suggested Questions to Ask Youth Suspected of Being Dissociative[2]

The following are questions to explore dissociative symptoms with children and adolescents. They are also available in Appendix C.

- Have you ever had imaginary friends? Did (or do) they seem real to you? If so, in what way?
- Do you find yourself zoning out and not aware of what is happening in the here and now? If the answer is affirmative, follow up with these questions:
  - How often does this happen? What is going on just prior to zoning out? What are you feeling or thinking just before you zone out? How long do these periods last? What is the shortest and longest amount of time? Where do you go in your mind? (Child may not know.) Do other people notice this, such as parents, teachers, and if so, what do they say to you? Do you have control over it or does it just happen?
- Do you sometimes not remember drawing, playing games, doing chores, homework, problem behaviors, or other activities that others indicate you did? If the answer is affirmative, follow up with these questions:
  - How often does this occur? What seems to be occurring when the memory problems happen (e.g., are you mad, under stress, having a conflict with someone)? During these episodes, do you hear any voices or see things that are not present later?
- Do you have a hard time remembering scary or bad things that happened to you? If the answer is affirmative, ask the child to elaborate. (Be aware that you may not want to pursue too many details about trauma, as the child may be neither ready to disclose these details

nor strong enough to handle the disclosure. You may witness some dissociative shifting that is diagnostic. Notice the child's reactions and follow sound therapeutic guidelines and principles.)

- Do you ever have a hard time recognizing or remembering your parents, siblings, friends, teachers, and so forth? If the answer is affirmative, follow up with these questions:
  - When does this tend to occur (e.g., when you wake up in the morning, at bedtime, during times of stress)? Who do you have a hard time remembering or recognizing? Do you hear voices during these times? What are you feeling and thinking when this occurs? How often does this occur? Do you tell anyone about not remembering people?

- Do you have a hard time remembering something you did, such as homework? Do you get homework back and not remember doing it? Please describe those times.

- Do you ever see things or people and later realize that what you saw was not there or you are not sure whether they were there? If the answer is affirmative, follow up with these questions:
  - Please describe what you saw. When do you see them? How often do you see them? What were you doing, feeling, or thinking at the time? When you saw them (insert what was said), did you hear voices at the same time? If so, what did they say?

- Some kids who have been through similar situations have reported hearing voices either inside or outside of their minds. Have you had this happen to you? If the answer is affirmative, follow up with these questions:
  - Do the voices seem friendly, angry, sad, scared, and so forth? What do they say? How often do you hear them? What happens just before you hear them? What feelings do you have when you hear them? What thoughts do you have when you hear them? Do you talk to them?

- Do you ever see things, objects, or people and later realize that what you saw was not there or you were not sure whether they were there? If the answer is affirmative, follow up with these questions:
  - Please describe what you saw. When do you see them? How often do you see them? What were you doing, feeling, or thinking at the time? When you saw objects or people, did you hear voices at the same time? If so, what were they saying?

- When you had (insert recent behavioral problem), what was going on inside of your mind? Ask the child whether he would be willing to draw what he *experienced in his mind* at that time.

After attending one of my trainings, Amy Kordus, a domestic shelter youth counselor, asked 11-year-old Tony what was going on in his mind when he pushed his only friend against the school locker, causing the friend to suffer a possible concussion. After she got a general answer about pushing the boy, Ms. Kordus gave him a blank sheet of paper and asked him to draw what he felt happened in his mind at the time. With parental permission, Ms. Kordus was able to relate to me what Tony described. Tony reported, "It feels like my brain has a switch. When that switch is turned on, I feel like it is going a million miles an hour, like gears won't stop turning." His drawing of his brain depicted three gears in the back part of the brain with large, fast circles around the gears, showing how fast they were turning. Ms. Kordus asked him what happened to the instructions his mother gave him about "keeping your hands and feet to yourself" to help him avoid getting into trouble at school. He said that his brain moved so fast that it kept going away from the instructions his mother had given him. He then drew a split down the middle of his brain and called it the "force field," which prevented his mother's words from getting to his brain. This force field appears to represent a barrier.

Ms. Kordus added eyes to Tony's drawing and a stick figure representing the friend whom he pushed. She said, "Your eyes are here, what do you see when your brain is moving so fast?" He revealed further dissociative symptoms, saying that he did not see anything until the incident was over, because he "blanked out." Ms. Kordus followed up by asking Tony whether he had ever blanked out prior to this incident. Tony replied that he had when another student called him "a psycho," which resulted in him strangling the other student. Ms. Kordus asked Tony when he first remembered having the force field, and he said that he had it when he was 2 years old and strangled his younger sister. She asked whether he heard voices and Tony reported that he heard a voice telling him, "You are bad. You're going to hell. You were happier before you had sisters." Tony drew a tongue in the back of his head to represent the voice talking to him. The voice blamed his sisters for his unhappiness and misbehavior. He drew a camera on the outside of his brain, because he felt as though there was a camera on the outside, looking into his life, showing him what

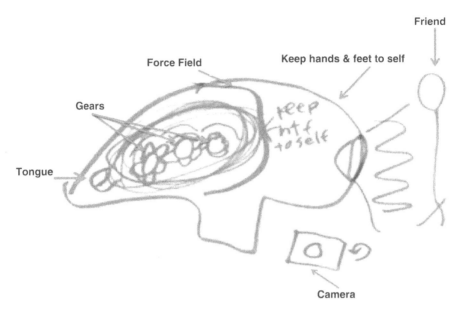

Figure 4.2 *Tony's picture of his brain. (Used with permission.)*

had transpired. He seemed to be describing some depersonalization as well, as if a part of him were looking at himself (Figure 4.2).

This is a poignant example of how a series of simple but potent questions about the internal workings of the child's mind and a drawing can illuminate dissociative defenses. As with many dissociative children, Tony suffered severe and chronic trauma and previous unsuccessful treatment, including several inpatient psychiatric admissions. He experienced a traumatic birth, resulting in a skull fracture, witnessed severe domestic abuse between his mother and her male partners, and moved over a dozen times. Could his pattern of strangling others be related to how he felt during his birth when his skull was fractured or due to witnessing strangulation when his mother's boyfriends assaulted her? Tony had been on medication since early childhood, including a mood stabilizer and stimulants for attention deficit hyperactivity disorder (ADHD). Unfortunately, Tony's prior treatment and medications did not address his trauma or the dissociative mechanisms that impaired his ability to control himself. This singular intervention provided a pathway for understanding Tony's fractured mind so that appropriate intervention could begin.

TRAUMA AND DISSOCIATIVE ASSESSMENT TOOLS

Assessment tools are invaluable in further exploring childhood dissociation. The following are useful trauma and dissociative assessment checklists for children, adolescents, and caregivers that have good validity and
reliability. When items score in the significant range, discussing the child's
answers with him or her can elicit further details.

Self-Report Checklists

Trauma Symptom Checklist for Children

The Trauma Symptom Checklist for Children (TSCC) (Briere, 1996; for
ages 8 to 16 with normative adjustments for 17-year-olds) has six clinical
scales: Anxiety, Depression, Post-Traumatic Stress, Dissociation, Anger,
and Sexual Concerns with two subscales on Dissociation-Overt (DIS-O)
and Dissociation-Fantasy (DIS-F) that can signal a need for a more thorough evaluation of dissociation by using one of the dissociative checklists described later in this chapter. It has excellent reliability (Finkelhor,
Ormrod, Turner, & Hamby, 2007).

The UCLA Posttraumatic Stress Disorder Reaction Index

The UCLA Posttraumatic Stress Disorder Reaction Index (PTSD-RI; Steinberg & Brymer, 2008; Steinberg et al., 2013) was recently updated to correlate with the *Diagnostic and Statistical Manual of Mental Disorders,* fifth
edition's (*DSM-5*; American Psychiatric Association [APA], 2013) revised
criteria for PTSD. This comprehensive index contains child–adolescent
self-report and parent-report checklists for exposure to various traumatic
events with a rating for degree of traumatic impact on the child, and a
rating for corresponding preoccupation with PTSD symptoms.

The Adolescent Dissociative Experiences Scale

The Adolescent Dissociative Experiences Scale (A-DES; Armstrong,
Putnam, Carlson, Libero, & Smith, 1997) is a commonly used checklist
to assess for dissociative symptoms. The 30-item questionnaire uses a

0 to 10 rating scale for severity of various dissociative symptoms. It is scored by summing each item's score and then dividing the total by the number of items (30). A score of 4 or above is considered to represent pathological dissociation. It has excellent reliability and validity with sexually abused children (Keck Seeley, Perosa, & Perosa, 2004), as well as with children from other cultures (Shin, Jeong, & Chung, 2009; Yoshizumi, Hamada, Kaida, Gotow, & Murase, 2010). A copy of the A-DES is provided in Appendix B.

A-DES Correlates to MMPI-A on Clinical Study of Briana
At age 13, Briana (introduced in Chapters 2 and 3) had a high level of comorbidity, including obsessive-compulsive disorder (OCD), depression, substance abuse, and an eating disorder, which was worsened by a sense of depersonalization when she starved, binged, and purged. In a collateral interview, Briana's mother, Rita, endorsed numerous dissociative symptoms she had observed in Briana, including denial of witnessed behavior, trance states, and extreme mood and behavior switches in which Briana would act similar to a little girl one moment and a raging pseudo-adult the next.

Although Briana displayed memory problems, extreme mood and behavior shifts, and numbing, it was not until she was sober at age 16 that she was administered the A-DES. She scored 6.13, well above the cutoff of 4 for dissociative pathology. Briana rated herself a 10 based on the following criteria: not recognizing herself in the mirror; going somewhere or doing something and not knowing why; people noticing that she acts differently; and her past is a puzzle with missing pieces. Items for which she rated herself a 9 pertained to being in a fog or spaced out, things around her seeming unreal, and being confused about whether or not she did something. She also rated herself well above 5 in severity for many of the other items related to memory, lost time, and depersonalization. Interestingly, she gave herself a 0 on hearing voices in her head and feeling as though there are different people inside of her. However, later in treatment, she revealed self-states (Chapter 8).

It is interesting to note the correlation between the Minnesota Multiphasic Personality Inventory–Adolescent Version (MMPI-A; Butcher et al., 1992) administered to Briana when she was 13 years old and the A-DES administered much later. On the MMPI-A, she received four diagnoses: psychoactive substance abuse; dysthymia; conduct disorder, undifferentiated type; and identity disorder. A concern over a developing eating disorder was noted. MMPI-A interpretations showed Briana demonstrating highly erratic mood and behavior swings, confusion about herself and her identity, and a lack of understanding and control over her emotions and thoughts—all of which were consistent with dissociative symptoms. Although Briana responded positively to child sexual abuse items, she did not receive a diagnosis of PTSD. The results of the MMPI-A were also consistent with those of complex trauma (Cook et al., 2005) in that Briana showed evidence of impairment in six domains (attachment, affect regulation, dissociation, behavioral control, cognition, and self-concept). Multiple diagnoses such as those seen in the case of Briana are common in children with complex trauma.

Adolescent Multidimensional Inventory of Dissociation V.6.0

Another dissociative checklist is the Adolescent Multidimensional Inventory of Dissociation V.6.0 (A-MID; Dell, 2004, 2006), a comprehensive 218-item questionnaire that rates 23 dissociative symptoms and has 27 scales organized into five clusters: (a) dissociation scales, (b) parts and alters scales, (c) validity scales, (d) characterlogical scales, and (e) functional/impairment scales.[3]

This checklist was particularly illuminating when administered to Sarah, a 17-year-old female, during an intensive 2-day evaluation. Sarah was previously diagnosed with a severe eating disorder and dissociative amnesia when she lost complete memory of her prior life. She was also unable to retain any current memory and, thus, was significantly impaired in all areas of her life. Although Sarah did not rate significantly on the A-DES, the A-MID accurately portrayed that she had a hidden, young dissociative state. More details of Sarah's treatment and integration are provided in Chapter 13.

In summary, the A-MID is a comprehensive tool that appears to be more sensitive than the A-DES in detecting atypical presentations of dissociation.

Children's Dissociative Experiences Scale and Posttraumatic Symptom Inventory

The Children's Dissociative Experiences Scale and Posttraumatic Symptom Inventory (CDES-PTSI; Stolbach, 1997) is a self-report measure designed for 7- to 12-year-olds. However, Stolbach has found it helpful with adolescents as well (personal communication, May 2006). This checklist is easy for children to fill out and valid for differentiating traumatized children from nontraumatized children. Although there are no valid norms for dissociation, I have found this to be a friendly, helpful checklist in detecting dissociative symptoms in young traumatized children. For younger children who do not read, I read the questions in a matter-of-fact way so as to not skew the results.

Children's Perceptual Alteration Scale

The Children's Perceptual Alteration Scale (CPAS; Evers-Szostak & Sanders, 1992) is a self-report measure of dissociation for children who are 8 to 12 years old. It was derived from the Perceptual Alteration Scale for adults (Sanders, 1986) and is a helpful measurement for childhood dissociation as well as for normal development and childhood psychopathology.

Structured Clinical Interview

Structural Clinical Interview for **DSM** Dissociative Disorders

The Structural Clinical Interview for *DSM* Dissociative Disorders (SCID-D; Steinberg, 1994) requires training to perform and takes about 30 to 90 minutes to administer, depending on the child's experiences. The interview can be used with adolescents who can maintain sustained attention and have an average or higher level of cognitive functioning. It assesses five dissociative symptom areas: amnesia, depersonalization, derealization, identity confusion, and identity alterations.

Caregiver Checklists

Child Dissociative Checklist

A common caregiver dissociative checklist for children up to 12 years of age is the Child Dissociative Checklist (CDC; Putnam, Helmers, & Trickett, 1993). It has also been used by teachers to rate children's behavior. Domains assessed include the following: (a) dissociative amnesia; (b) rapid shifts in demeanor; (c) access to information, knowledge, abilities, and age appropriateness of behavior; (d) spontaneous trance states; (e) hallucinations; (f) identity alterations; and (g) aggressive and sexual behaviors. A total score of 12 or higher is significant for pathological dissociation. It has excellent validity and reliability across cultures (Zoroglu, Sar, Tuzun, Tutkun, & Savas, 2002). A copy of this checklist can be found in Appendix B.

Trauma Symptom Checklist for Young Children

The Trauma Symptom Checklist for Young Children (TSCYC; Briere, 2005) is a parent checklist that has excellent reliability (Briere et al., 2001). It is geared for children between the ages of 3 and 12 with eight clinical scales: posttraumatic stress symptoms (intrusion, avoidance, and arousal), sexual concerns, dissociation, anxiety, depression, and anger/aggression. Even if dissociative items are not endorsed on the TSCYC, I will administer the Child Dissociative Checklist, particularly when the young child displays dissociative symptoms.

Child Sexual Behavior Inventory

The Child Sexual Behavior Inventory (CSBI; Friedrich, 1997) is a useful parent checklist for children who exhibit sexualized behavior. It is a valid and normative checklist for children aged 2 to 12 years. Its 38 items assess a wide range of sexual behaviors, including boundary problems, exhibitionism, gender role behavior, self-stimulation, sexual anxiety, sexual interest, sexual intrusiveness, sexual knowledge, and voyeuristic behavior.

Child Behavior Checklist

The most widely used standardized measurement for caregivers and teachers is the Child Behavior Checklist (CBCL; Achenbach, 1992). It assesses internalizing and externalizing behaviors and is often used to assess ADHD. Subscales of the CBCL have been developed to assess for dissociation (Malinosky-Rummel & Hoier, 1991; Ogawa, Sroufe, Weinfield, Carlson, & Egeland, 1997; Sim et al., 2005) and for PTSD (Althoff, Ayer, Rettew, & Hudziak, 2010; Hulette, Fisher, Kim, Ganger, & Landsverk, 2008). For example, Malinosky-Rummel and Hoier's subscales include the following items that relate to dissociative symptoms: acts too young for age; cannot concentrate; cannot pay attention for a long time; confused or seems to be in a fog; daydreams or gets lost in his or her thoughts; stares blankly; and experiences sudden changes in mood or feelings.

Many other checklists are available that assess children and adolescents who have complex trauma (see Ford, 2011). When caregivers and children endorse items on checklists that suggest dissociative symptoms, I follow up on the specific items endorsed. This will often elicit examples of dissociative experiences that can be helpful in determining whether a dissociative diagnosis is warranted. When combined with a thorough interviewing process, these checklists can also be useful in forensic evaluations of child abuse cases and delinquency.

CASE EXAMPLES

Assessment of Rudy, Age 6

Rudy's adoptive mother, Carol, called me requesting treatment for her adopted 6-year-old son, Rudy. She indicated that he had a serious history of aggression at home and in kindergarten that resulted in a school suspension for 45 days. In a quiet, halting, anxiety-filled voice, Carol told me she and her husband, Joe, adopted Rudy and his biological sister, Katrina, from Eastern Europe when they were 18 months and 3 years old, respectively. Carol sounded both desperate and tired on the phone as she began to relate Rudy's lengthy history of destruction. It was quickly apparent to me that I needed to first see Carol by herself in order to gather a thorough history on Rudy, particularly regarding any early emotional and physical deprivation prior to adoption.

Carol, a full-time homemaker and in a traditional marriage with Joe, was a pleasant, slender woman who was an excellent reporter of Rudy's history. Rudy was abandoned at birth by his birth mother and immediately placed in an orphanage along with his older sister, Katrina. When Rudy was 18 months old, both siblings were placed in Carol and Joe's home, after they had visited them in the orphanage for a month. Carol reported that the orphanage was clean and she had been told that both children were well attended to, well fed, and exhibited no problems.

However, Carol reported that the children immediately exhibited signs of developmental delay, particularly Rudy, when they were placed in their home. Rudy was not walking or uttering a word. He rocked on his elbows and knees to put himself to sleep. He bounced constantly in his car seat and continued to exhibit these behaviors. Rudy didn't walk until 20 months of age and only began to say words at age 2. However, by age 3, Rudy had progressed to communicating within a normal range. Rudy's potty training was a continual problem. He soiled himself daily both at home and at school. He had recently displayed "regressed behavior," smearing feces on a wall.

Carol tearfully reported that when Rudy first came home, he was skittish around her and did not bond. Carol reported that it took a good year before Rudy would respond to her and her husband. She sadly looked away, stating, "Rudy was in his own world." I asked her whether she could describe how he looked. She said, "He was often staring off." He did not make eye contact and refused to cuddle with her. He would go off by himself and play. He especially liked to watch toy wheels spin—a behavior he exhibited in the orphanage. Rudy ignored his sister, Katrina. He acted as though she did not exist, possibly because they were kept in separate parts of the orphanage and did not develop a relationship. It took months before either one acknowledged the other.

At times, Rudy engaged in baby talk but only around his adoptive mother. He loved soft things and acted babyish when squeezing stuffed animals. Carol told me that Rudy sometimes squeezed her arm and breast. She said that when he did this, she would patiently say, "No, Rudy." She denied seeing any sexualized behaviors in him. Although this behavior is odd in a 6-year-old, it would not be unusual in an infant. I wondered whether this behavior and the smearing of feces were related to a baby self-state that formed due to the deprivation in the orphanage or perhaps as a result of the major transition to a new culture and a new family.

Carol related that she would frequently rock Rudy but he still had a hard time making eye contact. I praised her for all of her efforts to help him bond and reassured her that even though he had not yet responded, rocking was exactly what he needed, and together we would work on ways to help him attach. Without an attachment to his parents, I worried that Rudy would not be able to develop the care and empathy that were necessary to curtail his aggressive behavior toward others.

As Carol talked, I could sense her exhaustion and desperation. She resumed telling me about Rudy's aggressive behaviors. Beginning in preschool and without any known provocation, Rudy grabbed children, pushed them aside, and cut in line. At about the same time, he began to show similar aggression toward his sister. In kindergarten, Rudy choked another child and a few weeks later, he cut a child's finger with a pair of scissors, resulting in a 45-day school suspension with a part-time tutor. At the time of my evaluation, Rudy was attending school only 3 days a week for half days.

Carol described mealtimes as being very stressful. Rudy displayed considerable aggression toward Katrina before, during, and after meals. Katrina ate faster than Rudy and would leave the table. Rudy often followed her, throwing objects at her or bumping into her. Rudy behaved better when Katrina was not at the table. I wondered whether this had to do with any hunger he might have experienced while in the orphanage.

Carol also reported Rudy's positive attributes. She described him as being intelligent and inquisitive. He enjoyed learning about the human body; he also liked to take apart gadgets with gears. However, Carol reported that, if he later could not locate the gears, "it's the end of the world."

Due to Rudy's early deprivation and lack of a consistent caretaker, it appeared that he had not mastered any of the psychosocial stages of infancy and toddlerhood described by Erikson (Chapter 1). Rudy experienced the mistrust of others, appeared to internalize shame and doubt, and exhibited poor self-control that impaired him from mastering toilet training and his ability to maintain positive relationships with family and peers. I wondered whether dissociation also contributed to Rudy's problems.

Carol had sought previous mental health services for Rudy. A psychological assessment was administered and Rudy scored in the superior range on vocabulary, which confirmed Carol's report that Rudy enjoyed learning new words. Rudy was diagnosed with reactive attachment disorder (RAD). Rudy had received therapy for his problems but his condition had not improved.

I inquired about additional signs of dissociation. Carol said that sometimes Rudy had problems doing activities that he previously performed well, such as his homework and building toys. Carol reported that for the most part, Rudy would admit when he misbehaved, but it took a lot of prodding for him to admit the scissor assault at school. She acknowledged that Rudy had a lot of extreme mood changes and described him as "Dr. Jeckle and Mr. Hyde." Rudy also had exaggerated responses when he got hurt. When he bumped himself on the table, he shouted that they should get rid of the table and buy a new house! Carol also reported erratic behavior with Rudy, who could be very affectionate with her—hugging, kissing, and snuggling—yet at other times he would threaten to shoot the family when he grows up and to cut off their arms. She reported that Rudy was angered easily and at times he would turn the anger on himself by hitting himself in the head, screaming that he wanted to die, and threatening to kill himself. At other times, he would flee outside or attempt to attack his sister. Carol was frightened by his behavior. I gave Carol the CDC and Rudy scored a 15, which is above the cutoff of 12 for pathological dissociation (Putnam et al., 1993). My initial impression was that Rudy had some characteristics of dissociation that needed further exploration.

Rudy's mother accompanied Rudy to his first session. Rudy was a pleasant, handsome, and slender 6-year-old. He was fidgety with his legs and hands, but was able to pay attention. He sat next to his mother on the couch. He reported that he had come to see me to help him "to be good and stuff like that." He sat leaning against his mom, who had her arms around him. Rudy looked at her and she smiled at him. He then hugged her, demonstrating signs of attachment. Rudy talked about how angry he got at his sister, particularly when he had to share his mom's attention. I asked Rudy whether he remembered how he felt when he was in the orphanage. He candidly and succinctly and surprisingly responded, "Yes. Hungry for food and attention." This answer helped explain his increased agitation around mealtimes and his jealousy of his sister. I suspected that his need for attention, similar to that of hundreds of children who I treated and who were emotionally deprived during early childhood, was contributing to his rivalry and aggression toward his sister.

Due to the dire situation at home, I decided to immediately try an intervention to begin to heal some of his early trauma from this period of his life. I was not sure whether there was a baby state, but I was sure by his statement and his periodic infantile behavior that Rudy was emotionally stuck at an infantile stage of development. I wanted to show empathy for him and provide him a way to begin to repair his early deprivation.

Rudy was maintaining good eye contact with me and I felt we were connecting. I said, "It must be really hard to feel those feelings when you were so young and how hard it must be to have your sister around when you are hungry for mom's attention." He nodded his head and his body seemed to relax more as he snuggled into his mom. I asked him whether he felt that he had a baby part of him inside that carried all those feelings. He nodded his head. I asked whether this baby part still felt worried and scared that he would not get his mom's attention. He said, "Yes." I said that we needed to reassure that baby part of him that he was no longer in the orphanage, was safe, and got lots of hugs, food, and attention from his mom and dad. I asked him whether he would like a baby doll that would be similar to his baby part inside. He could use that doll to help that part of him feel better. His eyes lit up and he exclaimed, "Yes!" I keep a collection of baby dolls to give to children when we are doing internal healing of early trauma and I gave one to Rudy.

Without any hesitation, Rudy held the doll in his arms, smiling, as I reinforced that the doll represented his baby part inside. I said, "Rudy, you need to help that part of you by hugging him and keeping him safe. Let him know that he is loved and cared for now, and that he is in a nice home and has plenty of food." I asked his mom whether she would like to let that part of Rudy know that she loved him too. Carol fondly looked at Rudy, who was cuddling the little doll, and said, "I love that baby part of you too and I want him to know that I will help keep that part of you safe and hug that part too." I explained that holding, rocking, hugging, and keeping the baby part safe would help this part of him to grow to be Rudy's current age and become one Rudy. There was an immediate shift in Rudy. He stopped fidgeting, and he sat still for the remainder of the session. I asked him how he felt, and he said, "Calm." I asked him where he felt calm in his body. He said, "I feel calm all over."

Using a symbolic figure, such as a doll, can help traumatized children externalize what they are experiencing internally for safe expression and resolution. This can also be useful in assessments, as Rudy's positive response to comforting the baby provided confirmation that he was still struggling with his needs that were unmet during infancy. I have used this technique successfully with other traumatized children.

Although on the surface, Rudy's diagnosis of RAD may be an appropriate diagnosis, it did not capture the complexities of Rudy's conflicting behaviors and affect toward his mother. There were times when Rudy acted very attached to his mother, whereas at others, he acted as though he could care less about her and was very threatening toward her. This type of vacillation is often found in dissociative children, particularly if the child has different self-states that are either unattached or display various degrees of attachment to their caregivers. Rudy's case continues in Chapter 6 on working with the family. More discoveries about Rudy's internal world and interventions that helped stabilize him are presented in Chapters 7 and 8.

Assessment of Cathy, Age 12

Cathy leaned forward as she sat on the end of my couch. She was a slender girl with pale skin and dark circles under her sunken brown eyes. Her frail body spoke volumes of the pain she was carrying. She spoke in a polite, quiet voice, revealing the horrors of life with her adoptive father. Cathy was born to a single mother, Jane, who was a college student at the time. When Cathy was 2 years old, Jane married Ken, who adopted Cathy. Her parents had a son, Justin. From the beginning, the marriage was turbulent and marked by Ken's irresponsibility with work and finances. Ken was emotionally abusive and controlling of his wife, restricting time with her family and friends. He was physically and emotionally abusive to Cathy. He would scream at her, throw her against the wall, and beat her, leaving handprints on her bottom. Child Protective Services became involved and when Cathy was 4, her parents divorced. Jane was awarded full custody of the children. Ken was granted supervised visits that were monitored by Cathy's mother. Ken soon moved away and visits ceased.

When Cathy was 6, the family was involved in a serious automobile accident. The children were unharmed but Jane was hospitalized and in rehabilitation for months. Cathy and Justin were sent to live with their father, who had remarried, while Jane recovered. When Jane was back on her feet, Ken refused to return the children or to even allow them to visit their mother. He moved the children farther away from their mother and monitored and restricted their phone calls with her. A lengthy legal battle ensued until Cathy's mother was finally able to regain custody of her and Justin 4 years later when child abuse by their father was finally substantiated.

Cathy reported vivid memories of sadistic abuse at the hands of her adopted father; he frequently beat and screamed at her. He also deprived her of food or gave her "rotten food" to eat. He locked her in an unventilated, smoldering storage room for hours at a time. She described one night when she could not get to sleep. Her dad made a paddle out of twigs and wrote on it "the judge." He beat her with it, and she showed me a scar still visible on her leg from the beating. Cathy told me that her father proceeded to throw her into a cold shower in her pajamas to "cover up the evidence" on her body. He then forced her to sleep in the cold, wet pajamas. When she cried, he held the paddle to her face, threatening to resume beating her if she did not stop crying and go to bed. After her father went to bed, Cathy quietly got up and changed into dry pajamas. The next morning, when her father saw that she had changed her clothes, he yelled at her and sent her to her room.

When Cathy could, she secretly called her mom, sobbing and reporting the abuse, but each time her mother reported it, it was unsubstantiated due to lack of physical evidence, as the bruising dissipated. After 4 years of chronic abuse, it was finally substantiated and Jane, who had remarried, was finally able to regain custody of Cathy, who was then 11, and Justin, who was 9. Ever since, no visits to their father have occurred. However, from toddlerhood until late childhood, Cathy's ability to master her psychosocial stages was severely impaired, resulting in feelings of doubt, shame, guilt, and inferiority.

Cathy displayed dissociative and PTSD symptoms. She frequently denied witnessed events. For example, Cathy's mother witnessed Cathy jumping on her mother's bed, breaking it, but Cathy arduously denied that this occurred. Her mother reported that she would often hear Cathy roaming around the house in the middle of the night, whereas Cathy insisted that she slept through the night. Her mother further complained that she could barely awaken Cathy in the mornings and had to help her get ready for school. Cathy frequently fell asleep in class and was unable to be awakened by her teacher. Cathy's mother would be notified and had to take Cathy home. Moreover, when Cathy did sleep, she experienced nightmares. Cathy's increasing amnesia and sleep disturbances were severely impacting her daily functioning and were being noticed by her peers. Cathy was being teased at school for her odd behaviors.

During the first three interviews, Cathy divulged both her traumatic experiences and what she was experiencing internally. She was so tired, confused, and frightened that it seemed a relief for her to disclose her trauma and its impact on her. She reported memory problems such as not recalling doing her homework but later finding it completed. Since she was 10 years old, she reported experiencing vivid auditory and visual hallucinations of her adoptive father threatening and correcting her. She related, "I hear voices coming from my mind. It's really weird. I keep hearing my dad demanding me to do things." Even though she did her schoolwork, she heard him saying at school, "Do your work, or you'll be in trouble." She reported seeing a frightening hallucination of her dad standing next to the teacher with a ruler in his hand. She got up and asked the teacher whether she could go to the bathroom, but was refused. She felt constant fear and was hypervigilant with the sense that her father was always watching her and continuing to harass her.

When I interviewed Cathy's brother, Justin, he revealed that their dad had forced him and Cathy to fight each other, including throwing objects at each other. Then, his dad shamed the loser, which was usually Cathy. Justin complied, because he feared retribution from his dad. Justin said, "The worst part was hurting my sister. I felt guilty. I should have stopped it." Justin reported that his father also forced him to hit his father, stating, "Dad made me hit him with wooden swords on his feet, legs, stomach and chest. I kept hitting him because I was afraid I would get into trouble if I didn't do what he said." Justin corroborated Cathy's memories of being beaten by their father. Justin recalled hearing his sister screaming during the beatings, and he felt guilty because he was too afraid to rescue her. Although his dad did not physically abuse him, he swore at Justin, who would hide under the bed or run outside. Justin said, "Dad taught me to be mean." Both children suffered significant trauma because of their father's sadistic and masochistic behaviors, but Cathy was the primary focus of their father's abuse.

Prior to seeing me, Cathy was seen by a child psychiatrist who diagnosed her with ADHD for poor concentration and inattention at school. She was prescribed a stimulant that did not help, because Cathy's inability to focus was due to her preoccupation with traumatic memories that had not been addressed. Cathy continued to have school problems, and the psychiatrist prescribed an antiseizure drug that was also used to treat anxiety. When Cathy reported to her former therapist that she heard voices and exhibited extreme mood switches, she was diagnosed with bipolar II and was prescribed an antipsychotic that was used for schizophrenia and bipolar disorders. The psychiatrist then discontinued the stimulant and added an antidepressant. Despite just having been rescued from an environment of substantiated, severe abuse, Cathy's symptoms were not recognized as trauma related and she was not diagnosed with PTSD. Dissociation was also not considered. Instead, a cocktail of medications was prescribed that had little efficacy and Cathy's symptoms persisted. When the family relocated, her new pediatrician recognized the importance of addressing her trauma and referred Cathy to me.

I administered a variety of trauma and dissociative checklists to Cathy. On the UCLA PTSD Index for *DSM-IV*, Adolescent Version, Cathy's PTSD score was 45, well exceeding the cutoff score of 32, indicating PTSD. I learned more about Cathy's trauma when reading her response to a question related to any other really scary, dangerous, or violent situation that happened that was not covered by earlier questions. Cathy wrote,

"My dad (adoptive) would put duct tape on me and make me stand in the bathroom for 2 to 3 hours. He would pick me up by my neck and beat me against the wall. He made a paddle and beat me with it. *I DON'T THINK A DAD SHOULD DO THAT*" (emphasis in the original). It was heartbreaking to read what she experienced. I was amazed that she could even function. She met all three criteria for PTSD with significant ratings on reexperiencing and increased arousal. She also met the criteria for peritraumatic dissociation. I had her mother fill out the Parent Version of the UCLA PTSD Index, and her ratings of Cathy's symptoms correlated with Cathy's self-report.

On the TSCC, Cathy rated in the significant range for PTSD, anxiety, and dissociation. Cathy was also administered the A-DES, and she scored 6.2, well above the score of 4.0 for pathological dissociation. She rated herself a 10, the highest rating, on eight items, including the following: I hear voices in my head that are not mine; it feels as though there are walls inside of my mind; and people tell me that I do and say things that I do not remember doing or saying. She gave herself a score of 8 out of 10 on the item: People tell me that I sometimes act so differently that I seem like a different person.

Cathy was also given the CDES-PTSI and scored a 39 on the PTSI, which suggests a moderate level of PTSD. Although there are no norms for dissociation on the checklist, she scored 49, which is high. In addition, she consistently endorsed items that are indicative of dissociation, including depersonalization, amnesia, identity confusion, and alterations in perception. For example, she endorsed items such as not recognizing herself in the mirror; often staring into space; and thinking daydreams are real.

Cathy's ratings on the various checklists suggested that she was suffering from PTSD and dissociation. I gave her the diagnosis of PTSD and OSDD (formerly DDNOS) with the need to monitor her for signs of more severe dissociation. Cathy's case continues in Chapter 7 on stabilization.

Assessment of Lisa, Age 9

When Lisa's adoptive mother, Sandra, attended a workshop I conducted on children with early trauma, she approached me afterward requesting an appointment for her 9-year-old daughter Lisa (see Waters, 2013). I could see how distressed Sandra was, and what little information she gave me about her daughter was typical of other traumatized children whom I had treated. Lisa was only attending school part time due to her frequent meltdowns at school. Lisa's family had severely limited their activities due to Lisa's frequent explosive outbursts.

Sandra was seen initially to gather a complete developmental history. She reported that Lisa was highly dysregulated. When she became upset, Lisa would run to her room inconsolable. She would throw herself on the bed sobbing, "I want to die, I want to die." Prior to collapsing in her bed, Lisa's adoptive mother would approach her, but Lisa would push her mom away screaming, "Don't touch me! I hate you!" When her mother backed off, Lisa would run after her mother screaming, "Don't leave me!" Finally, Lisa would give up and run back to her room in despair. This was a typical pattern that had persisted for Lisa's entire turbulent life when anyone came near her, even as an infant.

Sandra methodically recounted Lisa's extensive history of problems. Lisa was removed from her Asian mother at birth and placed in a foster home until she was adopted at 4-months-old by Sandra and her husband, Joe, who had two biological sons. The brief history provided to her adoptive parents was that Lisa's birth mom did not know she was pregnant until her fifth month and did not tell her parents until she was in labor. Sandra recognized problems with Lisa from the moment they received her. In transport to the United States, Lisa seemed unresponsive to her surroundings and her physical state. She seemed oblivious to being overly dressed and drenched with sweat; she slept the entire trip.

Although no significant trauma history was reported, Lisa came with a swollen gum that the pediatric dentist determined was from an unknown trauma. From the moment that Sandra attempted to feed Lisa, she was orally defensive and would fight having anything put in her mouth until she was starving. Needless to say, feeding time was extremely stressful. When anyone came close to her, especially close to her mouth, Lisa violently swung her little arms and kicked her legs furiously. She also fought against having her teeth brushed. She did not develop strong facial and mouth muscles. Her tongue protruded from her mouth, and she drooled until she was 5 years old. Lisa also demonstrated visual perceptual difficulties in that she did not recognize herself in the mirror, viewing her own reflection with a blank look. When she was 3, Sandra had to teach Lisa to recognize her own image in the mirror.

Since infancy, Lisa engaged in self-abusive behavior. She would bang her head against the crib railings, causing massive bruising; bang her face on the floor, causing nosebleeds; hit her face; and scratch her arms and legs until they bled. Sandy described one incident of self-harm that happened when Lisa was 3. Lisa suffered a self-inflected nosebleed from face banging. Lisa was bleeding profusely and choking on her blood. When her adoptive mom tried to clean the blood out of Lisa's mouth with a tissue, Lisa's hysteria escalated even more. I highly suspected that these self-inflicted incidents were a reenactment of the trauma that occurred when she was an infant. Unfortunately, her adoptive mother's attempts to help and comfort her appeared to further trigger Lisa's distress.

Sandra sought professional help for Lisa beginning when she was 18-months-old. She was placed in occupational and speech therapy to treat her poor motor development, and difficulty articulating words due to poor facial muscle development. Because of Lisa's lack of attachment, her mother contacted the adoption agency for guidance and was advised to engage in holding therapy, a controversial technique of forced, prolonged holding of a child by a parent or therapist to develop attachment. Lisa's mother held her for prolonged periods while Lisa screamed, thrashed, collapsed, and passed out. On awakening, her mom continued to hold her with the same responses. Lisa did not attach to her mom and her symptoms worsened.

A psychiatrist evaluated Lisa when she was 6. He was unsure of Lisa's diagnosis but gave her a provisional diagnosis of an anxiety disorder and oppositional defiant disorder (ODD). He prescribed an antidepressant and later added an antipsychotic, but her mother discontinued them when Lisa's symptoms did not improve. Desperate, Lisa's mother sought help from a well-known and respected child guidance center that diagnosed Lisa with a developmental disorder not otherwise specified and ODD. Lisa was noted to have behavioral, sensory, emotional, cognitive, and academic problems. Lisa's early trauma was disregarded as an origin of her disturbances. The center recommended that her parents "ignore feelings" and prescribed behavioral therapy, which proved to be ineffective.

I had Sandra complete the CDC and Lisa scored 23, well above the cutoff of 12 for pathological dissociation. Sandra described classic symptoms of dissociation in Lisa, such as significant memory problems related to everyday activities, trance behaviors, extreme mood and behavioral switches, depersonalization, and considerable fluctuations in abilities.

At 9 years of age, Lisa, who was an avid, accomplished reader, was still unable to hold silverware properly. She demonstrated depersonalization and regressed behavior while eating—she would get food all over her face, arms, and body without sensory awareness. She was highly sensitive to her hair being combed, as well as to other forms of touch, and would become very agitated. Lisa had numerous nonorganic somatic complaints, including headaches, and pain in her arms and legs. She frequently would not remember her daily and sudden outbursts that appeared unprovoked. During those times, Lisa would rage for hours, saying that she wanted to die, and was completely inconsolable. When later questioned, Lisa had no memory of her behavior and had a glazed look in her eyes. When her mother would come into Lisa's room in the mornings to awaken her, Lisa would often have a blank look on her face, as if she did not know who her mother was. Her life was a daily struggle, and her committed parents were despondent and exhausted.

Lisa's ability to master the early stages of psychosocial development appeared to be thwarted by two placement changes and the oral trauma that occurred in her foster home. The use of holding therapy with Lisa at age 3 appeared to have caused additional trauma and further dissociative reactions at a developmental time when Lisa should have been working on achieving autonomy and gaining self-esteem. Lisa demonstrated signs of PTSD and dissociation. Because her trauma happened during infancy, I also wondered whether Lisa might have a frozen infant self-state behind her significant developmental impairment.

At Lisa's first session, she came into my office cooperatively. She was a petite, slender girl with long, shiny black hair. She smiled hesitantly, looking at me with her dark almond eyes. We sat on the floor and she began to play with the dollhouse. I explained that I worked with children who had difficulties similar to hers and that I would like to get to know her and help her. I asked her permission to ask some questions to which Lisa consented. After asking some general questions about what she liked to do, I asked, "Are there times that you have trouble remembering things?" Lisa looked at me and shyly said, "It takes me awhile to remember who my mom and dad are and my brothers." I told her that I worked with other kids who had this problem and I could help her with this. Lisa breathed a sigh of relief and opened up even more. She said, "I get papers back that I don't remember doing, but they have my name on them. My dad said that I did something when I was outside but I don't remember doing it." I empathized about how confusing this must be for her and continued to reassure her that I could help her. She smiled broadly and her eyes brightened as she looked at me.

That night, I received an excited phone message from her mother. Sandra said, "When Lisa returned to the waiting room, she sat down next to me and looked at me and smiled. This was the first time that she has really *looked at me!*" I think because her mother brought her to me and Lisa felt understood by me, she felt hopeful and more positive toward her mother. I was optimistic that I was on the right track with Lisa. Lisa's case continues in Chapter 7 on stabilization.

SUMMARY

Briana, Rudy, Cathy, and Lisa experienced severe forms of trauma and/or deprivation. Utilization of dissociative checklists and careful questioning about dissociative symptoms revealed important information about how they coped with their traumatic histories. Briana's interpersonal trauma occurred throughout her lifetime, and she had the highest amount of comorbidity of the four children, including five different forms of OCD. Briana was on the brink of self-destruction and dissociation was a way for her to escape her pain.

Cathy's separation from her mother due to her injuries was itself traumatic, but her placement with her abusive adoptive father sent her over the edge. Her only escape was by dissociation. Both Lisa and Rudy, who were cross-cultural adoptees, had experienced very early trauma and neglect that was unknown to their adoptive parents. They entered their new homes demonstrating profound disturbances that impacted their overall functioning, development, and ability to attach. Previous evaluators failed to associate their behavioral problems with their traumatic experiences during infancy. As a result, both Lisa and Rudy had been misdiagnosed and received ineffective treatment. This allowed their dissociative symptoms to progress to the point that it was affecting every aspect of their life and endangering their placements. Both were only able to attend school part time, were violent, and were unable to form a secure attachment with their parents. Their parents were exhausted and time was of essence in helping them.

With Lisa and Rudy, it was extremely helpful to gather a thorough history from their mothers prior to seeing them. This allowed me to learn about their trauma history and to recognize that posttraumatic and dissociative symptoms were contributing to their dysregulation, attachment impairments, and their inability to learn from their mistakes. A few key questions with Rudy and Lisa, and an immediate intervention with Rudy, opened the door to healing their internal wounds. Lisa and Rudy immediately began to develop healthy attachments with their adoptive parents. When dissociative children are in dire need of stabilization and time is of essence, critical questions that relate to the source of the child's disturbance can begin to dismantle internal barriers and initiate the healing process.

The next section of this book covers a comprehensive treatment process with much emphasis on stabilization that provides the backdrop for trauma processing and finally integration of fractured children. Special focus chapters deal with the judicious use of medication, eye movement desensitization and reprocessing (EMDR) therapy, and art therapy. To introduce this section, the following chapter covers a mindful approach to phase-oriented treatment of children with complex trauma.

NOTES

1. Adapted from Waters (2013), reprinted with permission from Springer Publishing Company. Many of these questions correlate with the International Society for the Study of Trauma and Dissociation's frequently asked questions for parents, available at www.isst-d.org.
2. Adapted from Waters (2013), reprinted with permission from Springer Publishing Company.
3. The checklist can be obtained by contacting Dr. Paul Dell at PFDell@aol.com.

PART III

TREATMENT

Mindful Approach to Phase-Oriented Treatment

When dissociative children enter therapy, they are often frightened and confused. They are also often skeptical that they will be understood, particularly if they have experienced repeated failures in placements and treatment programs. Often, they are hurt, shamed, and blamed by people who they rely on for care. They may wonder, "Is this going to happen again?" As clinicians, we need to be clear with ourselves about where we stand, and how we view our clients. We need to be clear about our principles of treatment so that we can proceed carefully and provide a successful growth experience for this vulnerable and traumatized population. In addition, we need to be cognizant about our own biases and histories and recognize how they may interfere in treating traumatized children and their struggling families.

Joyanna Silberg and Daniel Siegel are two clinicians who add insight to this discourse. In her list of treatment principles, Silberg (2013) recommends that we portray a deep respect for the wisdom of the individual's coping techniques, their potential to heal, and that our relationship with our clients is one of validation of their experiences as well as our belief that they can grow and change. This perspective is conveyed to the children in how we approach them and enter into their world as we help them move forward.

Siegel (2010) discusses the importance of being mindful as therapists so that we are conscientious and intentional in what we do, open and creative with possibilities, and aware of the present moment without judgment. It is our *presence* with our clients that is the most important element in helping them heal. Siegel recommends that we develop an inner awareness of ourselves and monitor our own life narratives so that we can build empathy, resonance, and attunement with our clients.

By recognizing that nothing ever stays the same and changes occur moment to moment, we are able to better manage transitional moments that can happen almost as fast as the speed of light with dissociative children, who can rapidly shift from one self-state to the next. Having an inner awareness of ourselves while being sensitive to the children's struggles and fears will help us model empathy and patience for them and their caregivers. It is through Silberg's and Siegel's wisdom and contextual framework that I offer my own treatment principles.

OVERARCHING TREATMENT PRINCIPLES

Focus on Primary Trauma-Related Symptoms, Rather Than on Secondary Ones

When working with dissociative children, treatment of trauma-related and dissociative symptoms should be the priority. This tenet is derived from Putnam's (1997) book *Dissociation in Children and Adolescents*. Putnam stated:

> Affective symptoms, somatization, and certain disturbances of self (e.g., low self-esteem) commonly noted in trauma victims are . . . secondary responses to dissociation and to associated post-traumatic stress symptoms . . . Treatments directed toward secondary symptoms are only palliative until the underlying primary dissociative and trauma-related symptoms are addressed. (p. 78)

This is not to say that comorbid symptoms are not treated, but true healing occurs in treating core symptoms of trauma and dissociation. Comorbid symptoms will often resolve as the treatment progresses, as many are posttraumatic reactions. For example, in the study of dissociative children with obsessive-compulsive disorder (OCD) discussed in Chapter 3, once the trauma and dissociative symptoms were successfully treated, the OCD behaviors ceased. In some cases, such as with substance abuse, treating both the comorbid symptom and trauma/dissociation simultaneously may be necessary.

Because children have the majority of their lives ahead of them, it is paramount that their dissociative and trauma-related symptoms are the primary consideration in treatment. If secondary symptoms become the focus of treatment, those symptoms are often replaced with other secondary symptoms due to children's maladaptive expressions of untreated dissociative and trauma-related symptoms. The child will not be able to resolve the trauma and become a unified self. It is a travesty to disregard children's trauma-related and dissociative symptoms, as treatment that does so will be ineffective, leaving the child facing a life of continual disharmony and chaos.

Safety Is Paramount

Safety in homes, schools, communities, and therapeutic environments is paramount for a child to begin to remove dissociative barriers and embark on the process of healing. A safe, predictable environment helps traumatized children to relax defenses, learn from past experiences, and trust that their needs will be met. Safety will stimulate social engagement and help children grow into healthy, productive citizens.

Growth and change with traumatized children occur best when there is both physical and psychological safety. Physical safety encompasses an atmosphere void of physical violence, including witnessing any violence between family members, deprivation, and neglect. It involves an environment free of yelling, swearing, shaming, criticizing, and ostracizing. Research by Teicher, Samson, Polcari, and McGreenery (2006) found that parental verbal abuse can lead to dissociation, limbic irritability, depression, and hostility. Psychological safety is the felt sense of security that a child experiences. With a traumatized, dissociative child, this means that there is no internal threat from parts of the self and no threat from the external environment that could endanger the child's sense of safety, predictability, expectations, boundaries, and overall self-integrity. These children need an environment of patience, understanding and tolerance of divergent ideas, genuine expression of concern and care, and respect for personal space.

We give messages to children in subtle and overt ways by how we look at them, our tone of voice, the words we say, and our body language. Porges's (2011) polyvagal theory, described in Chapter 1, emphasizes that children can feel threatened based on the facial expression and intonation of one's voice. An open facial expression with warm eyes can engage interactions, whereas stern eyes with a furrowed brow can elicit defensive reactions. Our messages can convey respect or disdain to children, which, in turn, will be modeled by them.

Because parents can become easily frustrated in caring for an aggressive, dissociative child, therapeutic attention needs to include teaching parents strategies to diffuse an intense situation, how to reach out to a child's dissociative state that is driving the behavior, and how to empathize with the child while providing safe alternatives for expression of affect, without engaging in aggressive behaviors to control the child. This is a tall order for tired, frustrated parents. It means that we must show respect for caregivers' dilemmas and engage them to become active partners in learning constructive ways to manage their children. This process will be described in the next chapter on working with families.

Every Behavior Has Meaning

Although traumatized children can act impulsively and destructively, their behavior has meaning, even if on the surface it does not appear so. It is often *coded and hidden*, but the behavior is trying to tell us something about what is going on internally and what external forces are impacting the child's actions. *It is our job to help the child find the underlying meaning of the behavior and the unconscious processes that are in play.* Achieving this understanding is the first step toward true transformation. That is a tall order, but if we analyze children's behavior based on the five theories that make up the Star Theoretical Model (attachment, child development, family, neurobiology, and dissociation), we can begin to make sense of what dissociative children are trying to communicate. For example, are they reenacting unresolved attachment failures with birth parents in their adoptive home? What degree of dissociation do they have (e.g., presence of self-states)? Are they or a self-state stuck at the psychosocial developmental stage they were in at the time of the trauma? Are there family circumstances that increase the child's disruptive behavior and reliance on dissociation? What neurobiological factors are operating?

An example of family circumstances exacerbating disruptive behavior can be found in the case of Elsa, an 11-year-old girl who hit, bit, and kicked her adoptive mother when told to do something that on the surface seemed quite reasonable. The adoptive parents had just separated and Elsa's destructive and aggressive behaviors escalated during this period. I worked as a consultant with Elsa and her therapist. Elsa had been removed from her neglectful birth parents at age 2. Because biting is more typical of a toddler than an 11-year-old, I immediately wondered whether Elsa had a young self-state stuck in the unresolved trauma of her birth parents' abuse and neglect, which included starvation. Interestingly, since placement with her adoptive parents at age 2, Elsa had been chronically biting her inner mouth, causing painful sores. She was also "eating" her bedding and clothes when initially placed with her adoptive parents. Was this an unconscious reaction to trying to sustain herself when there was no food?

During my assessment, Elsa revealed a hidden 2-year-old self-state. Elsa said that the 2-year-old part would bite her inner mouth and chew clothing to "eat," because she was hungry. The 2-year-old thought she was still living with her birth parents and was unaware of the adoptive family. This self-state did not share gustatory experiences with Elsa when she ate and instead experienced only hunger. The 2-year-old was encapsulated but emerged when Elsa felt anxious. The recent family disruption had triggered the 2-year-old self-state's abandonment and loss issues. Elsa then engaged in infantile behavior over which she had no control and little awareness until she was able to connect with her toddler self-state.

Educate Children and Caregivers About Trauma and Dissociation

Throughout the treatment process, but particularly in the early phase of treatment, children, parents, and teachers need to make sense of their children's dissociative behaviors. I carefully explain dissociation and address any misperceptions or fears that they may have. I explain about the neurobiology of the animal defensive system (Porges, 2011) to help them understand that when a child cannot fight or flee, the only escape is to freeze when faced with overwhelming fear and helplessness. I explain that dissociation is a freeze response and that this is really not a choice but rather an automatic, instinctive, and biological survival response that is shared with all members of the animal kingdom. I provide an example of the "deer in the headlights" in which the deer becomes immobilized in a frozen stare just before the car hits it. Another example is the collapsed, freeze position of prey "playing possum" when attacked (Scaer, 2001), in the hope that the predator will become disinterested and leave. Humans respond in the same way when faced with terror. A release of endorphins can cause numbness and block the traumatic experience from memory. Traumatized children may go away in their mind to an imaginary safe place and/or develop internal helpers to comfort them or to hold the pain, anger, rage, fear, and memories associated with the traumatic event. Dissociation thus provides them with a creative escape hatch.

I also explain dissociation with the metaphor of a power outage in a house. When the electrical circuits become overloaded, the lights go out, leaving the house in total darkness. Similarly, when a child becomes overloaded with fear, it is as though the lights in the child's mind switch off. Certain regions of the child's brain shut down, inhibiting the child's ability to speak, think, or move. I sometimes draw a picture of the brain and provide children basic information about brain regions or show them a wooden puzzle model of the brain created by Renee Potgieter-Marks. I also have a windup toy of a brain and I wind it up while explaining, as it moves in the opposite direction of the child, that "the brain walks away" when the child becomes too frightened. I compare this to a child blanking out or going away in his mind in order to not know and not feel what is happening. I tell children that this means that at the time of the trauma, their survival instincts were so good at shutting off awareness that they may have even separated from their body and therefore were not aware of what they were feeling, seeing, tasting, hearing, or smelling. They became similar to a frozen lake. These examples help children understand their dissociative responses and why they could not protest, thus assuaging any self-blame or guilt.

I indicate that, over time, these adaptive survival instincts continued to operate even when the threat was no longer present. Because the child is now so attuned and sensitive to danger, even a slight reminder—such as an unexpected touch or a teacher's disparaging tone—can cause the child to dissociate. Dissociation can become a habit, and similar to any habit, it takes time for the brain to learn new patterns of coping. I explain that with the parents' supportive participation, my job is to help the child feel safe, work through the traumatic memories, and learn new ways to respond to stress. I reassure parents and children that with all of us patiently working together as a team, healing can happen.

With children who exhibit self-states, I emphasize to parents that although there is only one child, there are aspects of the child that know or contain certain parts of the trauma that the child could not manage by himself. These self-states have *separate states of consciousness, awareness, or knowing.* Sometimes, these self-states continue to attempt to help the child manage life stressors long after the trauma occurred. These self-states may do things that are not helpful, but this is because they do not know how to do things differently, or because they think that danger is still present. Our job is to help all parts of the child learn how to behave and express feelings and thoughts appropriately as they process the trauma. This will take a lot of patience, because these self-states have established patterns developed for survival, and they will need time to learn and practice new ways of dealing with stress. I explain that it is similar to rewiring a house so that the wiring does not become overloaded. We will need to teach children how to manage their emotions and in doing so, we will literally be rewiring their brain!

I explain that dissociation is treatable and curable and that the parents play a critical role in their child's recovery. The parents' job will be to provide a safe, nurturing environment, even during stormy times. They will need to accept all parts of the child and teach the child how to trust and love, while learning how to manage their child's dissociative behavior. I assure parents that I will provide both them and their child, including all self-states, with tools to help the child gain competency over his or her mood and behavior as the child works through the traumatic events and becomes a more unified self. I again emphasize that this requires a team effort and express how pleased I am to provide them assistance.

My experience is that parents are relieved to finally understand why previous treatments and medications did not correct their child's behavior. Parents leave with a renewed sense of hope. *Rob the Robin and the Bald Eagle* (Bray & Wheeler, 2015) and *All the Colors of Me: My First Book About Dissociation* (Gomez & Paulsen, in press) are lovely books that help children understand about dissociation. (Refer to Appendix A for more resources on trauma and dissociation for children.) If the parents themselves struggle with dissociation, these explanations can help them better understand themselves and recognize that they also need to seek help so that they can be more effective with their child.

Strive for Developmentally Appropriate Activities

Dissociative children face major challenges as they navigate school and community activities. We want to help them to engage in both structured and unstructured peer activities so they can relate to other children, form genuine friendships, and learn new social skills. The dilemma is that their dissociative behaviors can interfere in their ability to participate in these types of activities. Although we want to promote engagement in activities (which may also motivate them to stay present rather than dissociate), this may not be possible with children who have self-states that take control over the child and who do not have the necessary social or physical skills. For example, a self-state may become angry and resistant to doing certain activities, may embarrass the child, or may attack other children. In cases such as these, containment strategies will need to be put in place to decrease interference from the self-states.

I am reminded of Jenny, a petite 7-year-old girl with DID. Jenny was an accomplished figure skater who performed with grace and agility. However, at the opening night of an important performance, Jenny tripped several times and was very awkward on her skates. Her adoptive mother, who was sitting in the front row, knew immediately that it was Jenny's 3-year-old self-state that was skating. Afterward, Jenny had no memory of the event and was angry and upset on learning that her younger part had taken control. The provision of empathic understanding along with therapeutic interventions that rewarded internal cooperation resolved the problem and Jenny was able to skate without this recurring. The 3-year-old self-state was rewarded for not coming out while Jenny was skating by being given the opportunity to learn how to play a game with the family.

Engage all Aspects of the Child in the Process

All aspects of the child should be engaged throughout treatment with the goal of sharing knowledge, affect, behavior, and sensations, while working toward safe resolution of the trauma and integration. One of the major reasons that treatment fails with dissociative children is because their dissociated parts are not discovered and thus not included in the treatment process. Hidden self-states can exert much power over the child's functioning without the child's awareness and control.

I refer to the internal self-states as the "inside family." As with any family, if there is one part that is disruptive or left out, then the entire family is affected. It takes a family approach that recognizes the varied feelings and behaviors of each family member to resolve problems. So it is with children who have dissociated states. An approach that engages all parts of the child in finding out what the problem is, uncovers the role each part plays in the issue, and works with all parts of the child to coordinate a solution is more likely to result in success. If a disruptive self-state is not involved in the solution, then that state can sabotage the child's attempts to control the disruptive behavior. This was the case with Elsa whose 2-year-old self-state did not have awareness of Elsa's current life. She was still stuck in her protest and rage at her biological parents and had transferred her feelings to her adoptive mother.

The recovery process can be better facilitated when there is a seamless self-awareness across all parts of the child, and this is achieved by using a team approach that promotes emotional and behavioral control. This principle will be discussed in more depth as we cover stabilization techniques in Chapters 7 and 8.

Encourage Responsibility for all Behavior Across Self-States

Severely dissociative children have memory problems and, as previously indicated, can have a part of them take over and engage in disruptive behavior outside of their control. Although these children may appear to intentionally misbehave, we must not make such an assumption with dissociative children. We have to look beneath the surface and see what is happening internally. To motivate a child to gain control over this behavior, the child needs to be held responsible for the behavior no matter what part of the child has contributed to the misbehavior. This will hopefully motivate the child to break through amnestic barriers to learn about any internal self-states contributing to the problem behaviors. I want to stress that often this is not possible without therapeutic assistance.

Consequences are an important part of motivating children to learn about internal influences that contribute to their behavior. However, the consequences must be reasonable. For example, Martha, first introduced in Chapter 2, was an 8-year-old girl whose self-state acted out sexually with her peers. Martha experienced severe headaches whenever this sexualized state attempted to take over her behavior. The consequence was that Martha could play with her friends only under close supervision until she and the self-state worked through the trauma of her severe sexual abuse and Martha was able to gain control over the behavior. Once this occurred, Martha was able to play with other children in unsupervised settings and there were no further problems with sexually reactive behaviors.

Engage Parents and Caregivers in the Treatment Process

Parental and family influences can promote or sabotage successful treatment. Therefore, motivating parents to engage in constructive approaches with their dissociative child is essential for their child to release dissociative defenses. When parents are motivated and supportive, I invite them, especially those who have young children, to directly participate in the therapy with their child's consent. This affords parents the opportunity to witness their child's disclosure about his or her trauma and internal states, and it allows parents to be instrumental in soothing their child. The clinician is also able to model therapeutic techniques that can be modified for use at home. This does not preclude having individual sessions with the child, as some children may find it easier to disclose certain information without their parents being present. Clinical judgment and sensitivity to the child's needs is paramount. Dissociative teenagers generally do best with individual therapy, given they are striving for autonomy at their developmental stage. Family sessions can be interspersed to deal with specific problems and to work on strengthening attachment across all self-states.

Promote Attachment Between Parents and the "Whole Child"

Developing attachment between the parent and all parts of the child is one of the most important principles of treatment. Before beginning trauma processing, interventions that focus on building attachment between the child and parents help provide the anchor for the child to successfully manage traumatic disclosures and remove dissociative defenses. As children, including self-states, build attachment with their parents and feel understood, they become more capable of restraining destructive impulses. A strong, healthy, and secure attachment with parents also motivates children to reveal aspects of self and their trauma. In addition, it is through parents modeling affect regulation that traumatized children learn to modulate their own affect as they work through their trauma.

Promotion of attachment behavior between adoptive parents and children's self-states, even those who are resistant, scared, or mourning an early parental loss, is particularly challenging. Many diverse dynamics may make it difficult for dissociative children to attach to their current caregivers. Dissociative children who have been removed from their biological parents often feel rejected by them and distrust others even when in need of comfort. There also may be self-states who are not aware that they are now living with new parents who are taking good care of them and instead remain fixated in their traumatic past, such as happened in Elsa's case. Furthermore, a child may have several self-states with different attachment styles ranging from avoiding closeness to seeking closeness.

Children who were abused or abandoned by their parents may develop an internal parental substitute to provide them with comfort and guidance that is in direct conflict with their current caregivers. For example, a maternal self-state can exert significant control over the child and thwart the child from attaching to adoptive parents. Potgieter-Marks (2015) stated, "In reality, no adoptive parent can win against the internal dissociative mother figure unless this part is specifically addressed in therapy" (p. 94). Therefore, it must not be assumed that over time a child will bond with his adoptive parents. Time alone will not change or release this self-state's protective role that is in competition with the adoptive parents. Working with the maternal self-state to release such an influence can pave the way for the child to accept and attach to the child's new parents, as demonstrated with Lisa, who is discussed throughout this book.

I believe that most failures in adoptive placements with traumatized children are the result of hidden or unrecognized self-states who do not have an attachment to the parents, and who, either directly or indirectly, sabotage the attachment process. Recognizing these self-states and engaging them in strategies to promote attachment with their caregivers is critical to maintaining the child's placement. Managing attachment problems will be covered in more depth in Chapter 6 on working with the family.

Promote Metacognitive Skills

Developing metacognitive skills in dissociative children promotes consciousness and consolidation of memories that lead to integration. Metacognitive skills are based on the ability to self-reflect, think about thinking, and imagine what others may be thinking. In school-age children, *metacognition* refers to the "development of and knowledge of one's own cognitive processes and their influence on learning" (Flavell, 1979, as cited in Semerari, Carcione, Dimaggio, Nicolò, & Procacci, 2007, p. 106). Semerari et al. indicated that metacognition is a self-reflective process of identifying emotions, understanding beliefs, finding links between emotions and knowledge, and identifying the motivations behind outward behaviors. Metacognition is also termed *mentalization* (Fonagy & Target, 1996, as cited in Semerari et al., 2007), in which a child creates mental representations about himself and others. This mentalization plays a role in developing the child's identity. Siegel (1999) noted that metacognition is awareness that emotions influence thought and perception, and the recognition that one is able to contain contradictory emotions about the same person or experience. This is particularly relevant to a child who has been abused by a parent and who, consequently, may simultaneously hate and love the parent. The ability to be aware of contradictory emotions is vital for the development of emotion regulation. The ability to think reflectively is also critical to being able to put the brakes on one's own behavior.

Children are best able to develop metacognitive abilities when living in a safe environment and with nurturing and attuned parents who model affect regulation, empathy, and reflective skills. Parents can teach their children to notice their feelings, bodily sensations, and thoughts and validate them while trying to help them solve dilemmas and conflicts. Even infants and preschool children can be taught emotional literacy by parents who adopt an affective tone that matches the child's words of discomfort, sadness, happiness, and anger. They can begin to put words to what the child may be feeling and thinking and offer comfort or demonstrate effective resolution. For example, when a toddler grabs a toy from an older brother, an attuned parental response is to have the child give it back to the brother, and say, "I see you are very frustrated now. You really want to play with the toy, but your brother is playing with it now. Let's find another toy to play with and when he is done, you can play with that toy. I would be very pleased with you if you did that." Another example of an attuned parental response would be, "I see you looking at your brother's toy that he's playing with. I am wondering if a part of you would like to take that toy and another part of you knows that would not be fair to do. Is that what you are feeling and thinking?"

Helping the child recognize contradictory "feeling parts" or "thinking parts" lays the groundwork for simultaneously holding opposing thoughts and feelings. The parent can also add, "If you took that toy, how might your brother feel? What would be fair to do? Perhaps you could ask to play with it, or ask him to allow you to join him to play with it. What do you think of those options?" These types of simple, problem-solving statements can have a profound impact on the child's ability to recognize his own thoughts and wishes and to learn how to resolve dilemmas and tolerate feelings until some resolution can be achieved. This type of early parenting also provides the "fuel" for a young child's brain to effectively develop the higher parts of the brain—the "thinking parts" of the brain— that are necessary to dampen arousal and reactivity to stress. With a secure attachment, the child will mirror the parent's skills and will demonstrate more self-awareness, understanding, and empathy toward others.

The therapeutic tasks with the clinician are the same. The therapist reflects back with empathy on how difficult it is for children to have contradictory and confusing feelings and thoughts. Inclusion of parents in sessions provides the opportunity to teach these skills to the child's parents.

Early Neglect and Abuse Thwarts the Ability to Develop Reflective Skills

Putnam's (1997) Discrete Behavioral States Model, reviewed in more detail in Chapter 1, has relevance to this discussion. Putnam discusses how when parents are unpredictable, frightening, neglectful, or abusive, the capacity for an infant to develop smooth transitions and awareness across behavioral states is impaired, which directly impacts the metacognitive integration of the self. Putnam further explains:

> . . . traumatic states of consciousness are widely separated in state space from normal states of consciousness on many psychological and physiological dimensions. This distance, and the powerful and painful emotions associated with traumatic states, makes it difficult for a traumatized person to retrieve information learned in other states while he or she is in a traumatic state. In general, investigations of state-dependent learning and retrieval demonstrate that the larger the differences between two states, the greater the dissociations of memory between them (Weingartner et al., 1995). Cognitive deficits and brain damage associated with trauma may also interfere with the efficacy of metacogntive processes. (p. 172)

Children who have experienced early and chronic trauma can have multiple self-states containing bits of "reality" derived from their limited knowledge and exposure to the child's ongoing life. The child's mind becomes fractured by repetitive trauma, resulting in multiple states of consciousness or "multiple minds." The mind is similar to a shattered mirror with pieces of various sizes reflecting their traumatic roles, divergent knowledge of the past and the present, and degrees of sensory, affective, and behavioral disturbances. These self-states can remain hidden until activated and then take charge. They then can collude and compete with each other for control, resulting in chaotic and erratic thinking, behavior, and emotions. Consequently, they simply do not have the capacity to self-reflect, because they do not contain the entire picture of who they are or what the world is all about.

In addition, they are often in a chronic, defensive state of heightened reactivity to *perceived* threats of harm, which further hampers their capacity to think clearly. For example, a child may begin a sentence with one thought, get triggered midsentence, which then activates a shift to a self-state who takes control. The child shifts midstream to a new thought that is either contradictory or completely off subject. These traumatic states can intrude without the child's control or awareness and take the "driver's seat," propelling the child to engage in unpredictable or bizarre behaviors derived from a traumatic origin. Their actions appear incongruent with current reality and often make no sense to anyone who is observing them. However, this chaotic presentation does make sense if we understand that this can be a sign of fragmentation and a discontinuous stream of consciousness.

Because dissociative children can have self-states with conflicting realities, beliefs, and affects, it is extremely unlikely for them to have the capacity to understand themselves, let alone accurately read others. It is simply impossible for these children to develop metacognitive abilities until they begin to connect with their shattered parts and fit these parts together to begin to get a coherent picture of themselves and the world. If these children are to function in society, it is imperative that therapeutic interventions are designed to promote metacognitive integration across "all" states of the child. This means that we must initially help the child to calm down the stress response system across all states of the self. This will increase the child's capacity to think, connect with self-states in a collaborative way, begin to understand contradictory feelings, thoughts, and sensations, and work toward becoming unified. Although developing metacognition is a complicated process with a traumatized child, the process is similar to the earlier example of the parent who helps the child reflect on his or her different motivations and conflicts, and work toward appropriate resolution. Helping the dissociative child develop internal awareness and "whole self-reflection" can be a slow, meticulous process, but the rewards for the child who is trapped in confusion and despair are immense.

This process can only occur when the child is in a safe environment and when there is a respectful, therapeutic alliance with the child. This alliance will increase the child's willingness to trust the therapist and make it possible for the child to explore the often frightening internal contradictions—ultimately leading to better self-understanding and metacognitive abilities.

Phase Treatment Model for Dissociative Children

A phase-oriented treatment model specifically designed for dissociative children will help them develop integrative functions (Waters, 1991). Stabilization is considered the first phase of therapy; trauma processing, the middle phase; and integration, the final phase. This does not mean that these phases are always conducted in a sequential, linear fashion; rather, the model outlines a particular focus and tasks in each phase, recognizing that there will be a considerable overlap between them. These three phases are explained in subsequent chapters. However, I would like to note that although integration is considered the main goal and final stage of treatment, integrative techniques and language are used throughout the treatment process. In fact, integration begins when I first meet the child and it is in the forefront of my thinking when I communicate with the child and do any interventions. For example, when I talk to dissociative children about their self-states, I refer to the self-states as parts of them to convey that "it is still them." I emphasize a sense of unity when there is disunity within the self. Detailed information about this process is provided throughout the remainder of this book.

Because caregivers play a major role in their dissociative child's recovery, the next chapter focuses on interactional dynamics, attachment dilemmas, and intervention techniques to help build a strong relationship with their child that will encourage stabilization and prepare their child for trauma processing.

6

"I Guess They're Going to Keep Me. I Tried Everything . . ."
Building Attachment and Partnering With the Family

Martha and her adoptive mother were driving home from a day of shopping. Martha (introduced in Chapter 2 with a history of severe child abuse and neglect) suddenly began to sing a song, making it up as she went along. In her song, Martha described some of the things she did to test her adoptive parents to see whether they were going to kick her out, as her previous adoptive parents had done. Martha sang the refrain, "I guess they're going to keep me. I tried everything," over and over again. Her adoptive mother listened with amusement, thinking, "Yes, Martha, you did try everything to make us get rid of you, but we didn't give up!" I think most parents who care for children with complex trauma can relate to Martha's lyrics, because these parents are tested and tested and tested. . . .

Martha was lucky, because her adoptive parents understood how her extensive sexual, physical, and emotional abuse and severe neglect made it difficult for her to trust anyone. Martha spent the first 3 years of her life vacillating between living with her biological parents and two foster home placements until she was finally placed in an adoptive home. Unfortunately, her first adoptive parents could not handle her detachment and she was placed in her current adoptive home. Her new adoptive parents armored themselves with compassion, dedication, and willingness to learn all they could about maltreated children. Stosny (1995) noted that compassion "entails *seeing beneath* defenses and symptoms (anger, anxiety, obsessions, emotional withdrawal and manipulation), *validating the hurt* causing the symptoms and defenses, and *changing the meaning* that causes the hurt" (p. 7, italics in the original). Although Stosny indicates that these are therapeutic goals, they also apply to parents caring for traumatized children.

After several years of treatment, much work had been completed on trauma processing across Martha's self-states; however, she was still emotionally shut down with unresolved grief and mourning regarding the loss of her biological parents. Even though by all standards her birth parents could be considered "monsters," Martha had a traumatic bond with them that needed to be resolved. Whenever she began to feel some of the pain of what they had done to her, a "dissociative curtain" came down. Martha's adoptive mother, Helen, and I discussed how important it was for Martha to grieve the pain associated with this loss, as it appeared to be preventing her from forming an attachment with her new family. Martha expressed her grief in a drawing of all of her self-states shedding tears (Figure 6.1). Martha titled the drawing, "The world inside!" She also wrote "Waaa Waaa" on her drawing. Martha indicated that she would often see and hear her self-states sobbing. In her picture, Martha depicted the deep pain and depression felt throughout her self-states. At the same time, Martha was unable to face the fact that her birth parents were responsible for the horrendous trauma she had suffered. She was still shielding herself from the reality of their betrayal.

Figure 6.1 *Martha drawing of "the world inside!" (Used with permission.)*

Helen and I agreed to schedule a Saturday afternoon session to work with Martha on helping her grieve the loss of her birth parents. It was a wintery afternoon as we sat in the family therapy room in the quiet clinic. Helen sat in the rocking chair with Martha on her lap; I sat facing them. Using soft, soothing tones, her mother and I remarked on how painful it must be for Martha to have been hurt by her birth parents. Each time we broached the subject, Martha eyes glazed over and she was gone. Finally, with much encouragement and soothing, Martha's eyes welled up and the tears began to flow. She wailed from deep inside of herself, reaching the core of the infant trauma that reverberated through all of her self-states. Helen held and rocked her, while reassuring Martha that she had not done anything wrong to deserve this. In a soft, soothing voice, Helen told Martha that she was a lovely child, and expressed how sad she felt for what Martha and all of her parts had gone through.

It was the breakthrough that was needed. Martha was able to let down her dissociative shield and *all* of her was able to grieve her early betrayal by her birth parents and their loss. Martha was also able to mourn the loss of her previous adoptive parents as well. As a result of this session, Martha's depression lifted and she was finally able to begin to attach to her adoptive parents. And as her song indicated, Martha no longer needed to test her adoptive parents' love for her.

Mourning the loss of the original attachment figure is often the most difficult and critical phase of the trauma processing. Over decades of working with traumatized children, I have recognized that the relational component of trauma that is described as "betrayal trauma" by Freyd (1996) is often even more painful to resolve than the horrendous acts that the child's parents commit. This type of trauma seems to get to the core of the child's self-esteem and sense of worthiness. The child is left with the plaguing thought, "What is wrong with me? Wasn't I lovable enough?"

Traumatized children will often internalize their traumatic experiences and blame themselves. They view themselves as inadequate, deserving of the abuse, and unworthy to live. These children feel that at their very core they are deficient. It takes considerable support and courage for children to face the truth of their parents' betrayal. Grieving the loss of an idealized childhood and primary relationships is a critical step of the grief work that continues as the child moves toward integration.

In Chapter 5, I described many principles of treatment, including educating caretakers throughout the treatment process about the symptoms of trauma and dissociation. In this chapter, I discuss the interplay between the dynamics within the family and those within the dissociative child, and explain how these dynamics affect children's ability to attach to their parents across all self-states. I attempt to prepare parents for these challenges and work in partnership with them so they will have tools in place to manage their child. I also provide intervention strategies to enhance parenting skills and parent–child attachment. Some parenting resources are listed in Appendix A.

Much has been written on the impact of trauma on attachment in adults and children (e.g., Blaustein & Kinniburgh, 2010; Brisch, 1999; Hughes, 2009; Kagan, 2004; Muller, 2010; Solomon & George, 1999; Stosny, 1995; Struik, 2014), attachment difficulties and neurobiology (Hughes & Bylin, 2012; Music, 2011; Schore, 1994; Siegel, 1999), and disorganized attachment and dissociation (Silberg, 2013; Sinason, 2002; Solomon & George, 1999; Wieland, 2015b). Many writings also provide treatment strategies to build attachment with traumatized children (Blaustein & Kinniburgh, 2010; Brisch, 1999; Hughes, 2009; Hughes & Bylin, 2012; Silberg, 2013; Sinason, 2002). However, when a traumatized child has dissociative states, the complexity of attachment issues is greatly compounded. Each self-state of the child can influence the success or failure of the attachment process, as reported in many clinical cases (see, e.g., Silberg, 2013; Waters & Silberg, 1997); therefore, the attachment of each self-state must be addressed.

Because parents may bring along their own history of trauma and attachment problems, examining their histories and how family members interact with one another is also critical to the success of treatment. Satir's family systems theory model (previously discussed in Chapter 1) provides a useful construct when working with families who care for traumatized children.

SATIR'S FAMILY SYSTEMS THEORY MODEL

In the Star Theoretical Model, I draw on Satir, who held that family interactions play a significant role in the development of pathology in children. Although children often enter therapy as the identified client, Satir (1983) recognized that children should not be defined by their symptoms; rather, they should be viewed as reacting to the family environment. When children are traumatized in their family of origin, the connection between their symptoms and how their parents and other family members have treated them is obvious. However, when a child is abused by a nonfamily member, or is living in foster care or an adoptive home, clinicians may fail to recognize the influence of current family dynamics on the traumatized child's behavior and symptoms.

There are a number of reasons that family dynamics are important to assess even when the child's abuse does not involve current family members. First, traumatized children bring to their new environments previously learned communication patterns and dysfunctional family rules—such as secrecy about abuse, prohibitions against expression of feelings and opinions, and the use of violence and aggression to solve problems. Previously learned maladaptive patterns and current family values and rules must be discussed so that the child understands how to effectively manage conflicts and triggers, and how to feel safe enough to be open with current caregivers. Family modeling that conveys openness, acceptance of divergent viewpoints, and empathy can be powerful building blocks toward attachment and decrease dissociative responses. Traumatized children quickly learn the new family's values and communication patterns through nonverbal and verbal behaviors. These patterns may either help them discard previously learned barriers to intimacy or reinforce previously learned maladaptive patterns of avoidance.

A second reason that family dynamics are important to assess in placement homes is because people who foster and adopt severely traumatized children bring along with them their own family histories. These histories can contribute to their child's symptoms if the family members have not worked through their own traumatic histories and attachment disturbances.

Applying Satir's Model

Satir postulated that when a child presents as the identified client, *the family needs to be treated as a unit* with a close examination of values, communication patterns, and openness and honesty. Over the years, I have come to recognize how important this is. Parents who foster and adopt severely traumatized children come to us, desperate for help. They are usually committed and present their intentions sincerely. However, because of the severity of the child's symptoms, the placement may be in peril. Consequently, the therapist may be inclined to focus on the child's pathology in order to help restore some stability to the family. However, neglecting to gather a thorough parental history of any trauma or attachment impairments is unwise, because the child's behavior can trigger the parent's own unresolved issues, causing them to react in ways that exacerbate the child's symptoms.

To help parents stay engaged, I start by attempting to instill in them a sense of hope for their child's recovery, while recognizing how difficult the process can be. I reframe the child's disturbing symptoms as a cry for help and demonstrate a compassionate perspective for the parents to adopt. I tell parents that they are "agents of change" in their family and their participation is a critical component of the therapy. I explain that as a part of the treatment of their child, I will explore parental histories along with patterns of communication and problem solving, as this is crucial information that is necessary for effective treatment. Since mixed or hidden messages can cause or exacerbate dissociative reactions, I carefully examine parental messages, verbal and nonverbal, direct and subliminal, so that they can be clearly addressed in family sessions, as deemed appropriate. When traumatic events and family struggles are denied or hidden, children will often become secretive and manipulative to avoid recrimination or rejection. I also explain that it is not uncommon for parents to have a history that results in them being triggered by their child and emphasize the importance of exploring their own backgrounds so that I can provide them with guidance. It may be difficult to get such information from foster parents or garner their full participation, particularly in transitional placements and traditional households in which the father is viewed as the head of the household.

I describe the "domino effect," explaining how the behavior of either the child or the parent can set off a chain reaction that reverberates throughout the entire family system. I encourage all family members to be included in sessions at various times to explore what each can do differently to interrupt destructive chain reactions. If the father is reluctant to participate, I stress that only the father can explain clearly what his thoughts and feelings are, and I ask for him to attend as many sessions as are feasible.

Finally, I explain that a slower approach is, in the long run, a faster approach to problem solving. I encourage patience and a willingness to stay in the therapeutic process, while assuring the family that a collaborative effort will provide the quickest results. We are more likely to find effective solutions if we first carefully explore all the variables affecting their dissociative child.

These discussions take place in a nonjudgmental atmosphere with empathic expressions of how difficult it is for parents to manage disturbed children, and how all of us are triggered by shadows of our past that can interfere with how we want to communicate and parent our children. I have encountered hundreds of dedicated parents who put forth tremendous effort to face their own traumatic pasts and dysfunctional communication patterns so they can become healthy role models for their children and partners in their children's healing, and to ultimately form a healthier family unit. There are many such examples throughout this book.

Exploring Family Histories

To put parents at ease when taking family histories, I make reference to a cartoon that depicts a conference hall with a large sign above the entrance reading "Adult Children of Normal Parents Annual Convention," humorously abbreviated as "ACNP." There are only two people in the large auditorium. This cartoon dramatically illustrates an important point: More often than not, there is some pathos in most, if not all, families.

Parental histories should include the following: the quality of attachment to their parents, siblings, peers, and spouses; a history of domestic violence, childhood trauma, legal problems, substance abuse, and/or mental illness. A plan should be developed to help parents to be mindful of their own traumatic triggers and unresolved attachment issues as they interact with their child. An excellent tool that is used for evaluating parent's quality of attachment and interactional patterns is the Adult Attachment Interview (AAI; George, Kaplan, & Main, 1996), a structured interview that requires formalized training. Psychoeducation about the influences of the parent's past on parenting, particularly interpersonal trauma and attachment disturbances, can be very helpful. Referring parents to receive their own therapy and/or participate in parent support groups is recommended if issues are identified that warrant intervention.

Although it is easy to assume that a child's early trauma history prior to placement accounts for his or her behavioral problems, even good parents can engage in abusive or frightening behavior when faced with challenges in managing traumatized children with attachment issues and aggressive problems. Parents may trigger the child, reinforcing the child's reliance on dissociation. If parents are resistant to seeking their own therapy, I explain the increased likelihood that they will react in maladaptive ways with their child, resulting in more suffering not only for the child but also for themselves and the entire family. In addition, parents who are under considerable stress can attribute the wrong intentions to their children's behavior (Struik, 2014). Regrettably, sometimes parents will remove their child from treatment rather than tackle their own issues. Rudy's and Briana's cases highlight how well-meaning parents can contribute to their traumatized child's reliance on dissociation.

Rudy's Family History

Aside from Rudy's early maternal deprivation while in the orphanage, his adoptive mother revealed that Rudy's difficulty in attaching to her was also likely due to her early treatment of him. She tearfully confessed that when Rudy and his sister came to their home, they demanded constant attention as both of them were highly dyregulated and did not listen. Rudy did not look at her and did not have dexterity or knowledge of putting food in his mouth. He cried constantly. She reverted to her own upbringing of yelling and spanking the children. She herself had a history of physical and emotional abuse by her father and witnessed considerable domestic violence in her home. She married after becoming pregnant when she was 18 years old and divorced her abusive husband a few years later. Her son by that marriage died when he was a teenager as a result of a reckless driving accident on a four wheeler. Although she received many years of therapy since her young adulthood, she was so afraid that if she was not strict with her adoptive children, they would not learn how to behave and could die as well. Under stress, she reverted to what she experienced as a child. Her honesty about her behavior and sincerity in wanting to help Rudy were assets that helped her repair the damage she had done.

We had several family sessions that included her husband and both of their adopted children. The mother tearfully apologized to Rudy and his sister for spanking and yelling at them. We then discussed how each of them felt. Rudy and his sister expressed being afraid of their mother. Rudy particularly felt he was going to die.

To aid in the healing process, I engaged the entire family in psychodrama (Blatner, 2000). The family role-played various conflicts between the siblings, particularly at mealtime. The family also role-played conflicts between the children and their parents. After each role-play, each family member reflected on how they behaved. I then asked the family members to role-play their desired behaviors with a favorable outcome. This approach yielded positive results for the entire family in resolving conflicts and building closer attachment between the members. It also helped Rudy resolve his relational trauma. Each family member would make a closing comment after each psychodrama. After the conclusion of one of the family therapy sessions, Rudy expressed an unexpected, lovely sentiment, "Thank you, God. This was a wonderful meeting." I smiled. Rudy's parents beamed. I suggested a family hug, as I had done in previous family sessions; however, this family hug was different, as it seemed to be filled with joy.

The family therapy sessions were reparative for Rudy and helped him overcome his early losses and his adoptive mother's mishandling of him. I also provided extensive collateral therapy to Rudy's mother. She was very receptive and eager to employ new ways to manage her children. She exercised calmness and patience with them when they were obstinate. The children were more compliant over time, particularly after many family sessions in which her honesty and sincerity with them helped them understand why their mother had been harsh with them in the past. Rudy and his sister accepted their mother's apology.

Briana's Family History

As noted in Chapter 4, Briana was a severely traumatized, dissociative teenager with a high level of comorbidity. Briana and her older siblings were exposed to numerous incidents of their biological father verbally and physically abusing their mother until Briana's parents divorced when she was 6. After the divorce, Briana's father made little effort to see her and when they had visits, they usually ended in an argument. Briana felt rejected by him. Briana's mother, Rita, remarried when Briana was 11 years old. Briana's new stepfather was jealous of Rita's attention to her children, particularly to Briana, and he did not make much of an effort to relate with her. Briana and her siblings had frequent and sometimes violent altercations. Although Rita was concerned and sought treatment for her daughter, she had difficulty setting clear boundaries with Briana and in being able to communicate constructively with her.

Briana and her mother had an intense, conflictual relationship due to Briana's high level of disruptive behavior and Rita's inability to manage her daughter due to her own psychological problems. Rita was often overwhelmed, depressed, and intimidated by Briana's aggression, as it triggered her own trauma history and dissociative responses. Rita had unresolved issues from her childhood that impacted her ability to parent. She had a significant history of childhood trauma that included physical, sexual, and emotional abuse by relatives and later by her first husband. Rita also had severe attachment impairment with her mother, who had been highly critical and negligent. Rita had remarried a man who was controlling and possessive of her. She also suffered from posttraumatic stress disorder (PTSD), severe dissociation, along with depression and anxiety that adversely impacted her ability to consistently parent Briana. Rita was continually triggered by her daughter's aggressive behavior and had a child state that would emerge during conflicts. Briana resented her mother's weakness and frequently took advantage of her. In addition, Briana often felt that her mother did not love her.

Fortunately, Rita was highly motivated to receive treatment. Because of Rita's commitment to heal herself and her family, each family member was in individual therapy and periodic family therapy. Rita also participated in marital therapy with her current spouse to effectively co-parent and improve their marriage.

In the next section, I provide some important strategies that I teach parents that help to overcome severe attachment impairments between parents and their dissociative children.

Developmental Milestones and Attachment Issues

As Erikson (1968) indicated, adolescence is a time of identity versus role confusion. "Who I am and how does my past and current attachment figures influence my identity" becomes a plaguing issue. Adolescence is a critical age that adoptive parents must be prepared for so they can support their teens' search for their identity, while continuing to provide a stable environment that anchors them during their tumultuous journey. Traumatized, dissociative children are particularly prone to a heightened sense of confusion about their identity related to abusive attachment figures. Adopted children may need to revisit their past and reprocess the loss of early attachment figures. By providing emotional support and guidance to their teens, parents can help them feel empowered to resolve their past instead of relying on dissociative defenses. The following case examples demonstrate two different outcomes based on how two adoptive parents responded to their children's unresolved feelings toward their biological parents.

Jamie was a 10-year-old girl who had an "open adoption" in which contact with her birth mother could occur at the discretion of her adoptive parents. As a toddler, Jamie was exposed to domestic violence and then, her father's lethal drug overdose. Afterward, her birth mother was depressed and unable to care for Jamie and her siblings. Jamie had limited contact with her birth mother, who continued to have difficulty functioning. Jamie's adoptive mother was critical of her birth mother and seemed threatened by Jamie's attachment to her, particularly when Jamie returned from occasional visits while exhibiting some oppositional behavior.

Both Jamie's adoptive parents grew up witnessing alcoholism and domestic violence between their parents. The adoptive mother was the oldest child and had to protect and care for her younger siblings. The adoptive father was passive and went along with his wife, who made decisions for the family. The adoptive mother had unresolved attachment issues with both of her parents, and particularly unresolved abandonment issues from her own mother's failure to protect her when her dad was drunk and went into fits of rage.

Although Jamie's early trauma and dissociation were resolved, issues arose when Jamie reached adolescence—the time when her adoptive mother witnessed considerable intrafamilial violence when growing up. Jamie's adoptive mother was threatened by Jamie's desire for more autonomy and refused to allow her to see her birth mother. This set off a pattern of adolescent revolt. The adoptive mother wanted Jamie to be placed in a treatment program to "fix her," and unfortunately my services were terminated. Jamie had a close relationship with me and she rebelled even more by running away and abusing substances. It was only after Jamie's attempted suicide by a drug overdose that her adoptive mother sought her own therapy.

This case example highlights how previously cooperative parents can later be triggered when their child reaches the age that they experienced traumatic issues in their own lives. If the parent's issues are not resolved, these issues can interfere in his or her ability to effectively manage the child. Although Jamie's adoptive mother was able to be the helper and rescuer by adopting Jamie, the same role she played in her family of origin, she was unable to effectively parent Jamie when she reached adolescence as Jamie's increasing desire for autonomy threatened her own loss and abandonment issues. In retrospect, if I had taken a thorough parental attachment history with Jamie's adoptive mother, perhaps she might have been willing to seek treatment earlier and might have been empathic, rather than threatened, by Jamie's need to have contact with her birth mother.

Jamie's case stands in stark contrast with that of Miranda. At age 16, Miranda wanted to reconnect with her birth mother, Sue, who Miranda had no contact with since she was adopted at age 7. Sue had been with two men who sexually abused Miranda. The first man abused Miranda when she was 18 months old; the second man abused her at age 3. Although Miranda did not know this, Sue herself had sexually abused Miranda's younger sibling. It would have been understandable for Miranda's adoptive parents to want to shield her from any further contact with her birth mother. However, Miranda's adoptive parents had secure attachments with their own parents and with Miranda. Miranda's adoptive parents understood that Miranda needed to resolve her attachment with her birth mother. When Miranda was an adolescent and asked to see her birth mother, they facilitated a visit by traveling hundreds of miles to visit Sue. After the visit, Miranda wished to have no further contact with her birth mother, who continued to deny any responsibility for what had happened to Miranda and blamed others for her problems.

Miranda felt understood and respected by her adoptive parents and, as a result of the visit, their attachment was strengthened. Miranda was not forced to choose between her adoptive parents and her birth mother, nor did she have to act out to be heard. These two cases exemplify how, when traumatized children reach certain developmental stages such as adolescence, they may need to explore their identity and revisit past attachment figures. (Miranda's case is described in more detail in Chapter 7.)

One way of helping parents become more effective therapeutic partners with the clinicians is by helping them understand the neurobiology of trauma. This understanding can help parents manage their children in ways that promote healthy attachment and help them recover from their traumatic experiences.

BRAIN-BASED PARENTING

There is a growing understanding of how to apply neurobiology to effectively parent traumatized children (Hughes & Bylin, 2012; Porges, 2011; Siegel & Payne Bryson, 2012, 2014). Brain-based parenting encourages parents to validate their children's feelings and to utilize calming techniques to stabilize hyperaroused children and help children engage the thinking part of their brains. These techniques can encourage cooperation and attachment even with highly dissociative children.

It is important that we convey to caregivers the message that their children's behaviors, while disruptive, are developed for survival, and to communicate how desperate their children are to be understood and not judged for their memory problems and changing moods and behaviors. This perspective can help caregivers overcome their own prejudices toward their children and adopt a more empathetic view of them. When caregivers understand dissociative defenses, they can better respond to their children in a manner that decreases reliance on such defenses. For example, when parents stay calm and model empathy toward their children (such as empathizing with them about how difficult it must be to have parts of themselves with such contradictory feelings, thoughts, and wishes), children will become less defensive and are more likely to calm down. In this way, parents can become powerful co-regulators of their children's arousal and over time, the children may begin to mirror their parents' calm demeanor. This will enhance children's ability to communicate with their parents about how their internal life is impacting their behavior. Better understanding will occur between parents and their child, which, in turn, will increase the attachment between them.

A cornerstone of brain-based parenting is teaching parents how their vocal and facial expressions can affect their traumatized child.

Role of Voice and Facial Expression in Engagement, Mirroring, and Empathy

Learning to modulate vocal tones and facial expressions to communicate safety is paramount when dealing with a traumatized child. Humans instinctively rely on vocal inflections and facial expressions when communicating emotional states to one another. When assessing how a person feels about us, we are often more interested in intonation of the voice than in what is actually being said (Porges, 2014a). Traumatized children have an especially heightened awareness of subtle facial expressions, vocal inflictions, and sudden body movements that may convey life-threatening danger. For example, studies have shown that physically abused children devote more attentional resources to the processing of angry faces (Pollak, Cicchetti, Klorman, & Brumaghim, 1997; Pollak, Klorman, Thatcher, & Cicchetti, 2001), and they have greater difficulty in "disengaging" attention from angry faces (Pollak & Tolley-Schell, 2003). Abused children also over attend to auditory anger cues, and they are especially responsive to facial signals of anger from their own parent (Shackman, Shackman, & Pollak, 2007). These studies suggest that abused children develop a greater sensitivity to facial expressions and auditory cues of anger as a form of adaptation to an environment in which threat signals may predict the occurrence of abuse. Furthermore, dissociative children can have highly sensitive radars that are encompassed in vigilant, angry, and protective states. These states are usually primarily invested in survival and less so in attaching to caregivers and therapists. Thus, a raised voice or a wrinkled brow can cause maltreated children to overreact with fear or hostility in situations in which no danger is actually present.

An explanation of children's sensitivity to facial and vocal cues is provided by Porges's polyvagal theory. The vagus nerve is a cranial nerve that originates in the brain stem. Its main function is to communicate the state of the organs of the body to the central nervous system (Berthoud & Neuhuber, 2000). The vagus nerve has three branches. Porges (2011) discovered that one branch of the vagus nerve, the most recent in terms of evolution, is linked to what he terms the *social engagement system*. This portion of the mylenated vagus nerve contains sensory fibers that go directly from the heart to the upper part of the face and ear muscles. It is linked with the regulation of all of the facial muscles, including those used for listening and engaging with others. According to Porges, facial expressions are manifestations of our physiology and they communicate what is going on in our body.

A parent's vocal inflections and facial expressions (involving facial muscles above the nose) can elicit feelings of either fear or safety in the child. Porges (2014a) stated,

> The upper part of the face is the giveaway. The upper part of the face tells us, in fact, whether or not people can process the words we say. If the orbital muscle of the eye . . . is working, then the middle ear

muscles are contracting, and the person can hear human voice. When it's not working . . . they are not able to hear human voices well . . . They hear the background noise of a predator. (p. 8)

For example, if a parent exhibits an angry frown and squinty eyes along with vocal tones that are low, loud, and sharp, this can automatically activate a hard-wired fear reaction in the child. Porges's theory holds that when a child feels fear, the social engagement system related to bonding and the higher cortical centers of the child's brain are deactivated. The child is, therefore, unable to effectively learn from parent's communication. When the social engagement system is deactivated, the next most highly evolved portion of the autonomic nervous system (ANS), the sympathetic nervous system that has to do with fight or flight, is activated. If the child is unable to fight or flee, this portion of the ANS is also deactivated and the most primitive portion of the ANS, the parasympathetic nervous system, is activated. The activation of the parasympathetic nervous system causes the child to automatically and unconsciously become immobilized or to dissociate. When this happens, the child is unable to process incoming information across sensory domains. This state of immobilization creates a sense of helplessness and a desire to avoid similar situations that might provoke such feelings.

Porges (2014b) observed that traumatized individuals who speak in a flat voice, lack upper facial expressions, and avoid eye contact are operating from the parapsympathetic nervous system, in a state of physiological withdrawal, and disconnected from others. Porges (2014a) poignantly noted, "If trauma disrupts the ability to feel safe with another, then the roots associated with attachment are ruptured" (p. 15). Therefore, it is imperative for parents and therapists to understand just how sensitive children are to how we look at and talk to them.

Consequently, *one of the most important principles in working with parents is to impress on them the importance of talking with their traumatized child in "modulated tones" with "calm facial expressions" regardless of the child's affect and behavior.* This is particularly relevant to children who have experienced verbal abuse. This means that the parents will need to be calm and put aside their own needs to attend to the child (Struik, 2014). Although this is challenging for the parents, in the end, their example will serve as a mirror of affect regulation to their children and facilitate their children's ability to gain mastery over their dysregulated behavior and affect. The parent's soothing voice can bring down an escalating child and, consequently, the parent can become the co-regulator of the child's affect. The child's brain will begin to mirror the parents' brain, based on the science of mirroring discussed in Chapter 1. When the child is calm, the child's higher cortical brain functions will be reactivated, thus helping the child to think more clearly and gain control over negative affect and behavior.

I model this technique for parents when their children escalate in therapy, and then later role-play with parents how to respond to their children's disruptive behaviors. The following is an example of using vocal tones and facial expressions to help an escalating child gain control of her behavior and emotions.

I treated a 6-year-old girl, Jessica, who was physically and emotionally abused by her parents. Her mother would scream and swear at her, and at times handled her roughly. Jessica's father occasionally was physically abusive toward Jessica when she was oppositional. Child Protective Services had been involved. Her parents had a tumultuous relationship and were also in therapy with me to improve their parenting skills and to work on repairing their relationship. Jessica was very angry and attacked her mother frequently. While I was seeing the parents in my private office, Jessica and her older brother, Gregory, had an altercation in my waiting room. Ironically, I had just explained to the parents about how a modulated voice and a calm facial expression would enhance a connection with their children when they are misbehaving. Jessica's mother responded, "I just don't think I know how to do that."

I asked Jessica's parents to observe me. We walked into the waiting room and I sat down on the floor next to Jessica, who was crying because her brother had poked her. I looked at her with a calm, gentle facial expression and in an almost whispering tone of voice empathized with her about how it must have felt being poked. I softly said, "Jessica, I can see that you are very sad. I imagine you might also feel mad too." She nodded her head in agreement as she glanced up at me. I asked her what transpired prior to Gregory poking her. She responded that her brother had taken her building blocks and she took them back. Gregory then poked her. At this point, Gregory ran to the couch, lay down, and hid his face. I said in a calm, empathic voice to Gregory, "I see that you are hiding your face. I wonder if you might feel sad and ashamed for poking your sister." Gregory did not respond immediately but later said that Jessica was hogging the blocks. I said that he must have felt very mad at her. I asked Jessica what she could do differently; she stood up, went to the almost-full container of blocks, and softly said that she could give Gregory more blocks. I praised her while maintaining my quiet, modulated voice. I said that I hoped that they would apologize to each other, then explained that I needed to do more work with their parents, and promised that we would join them shortly.

The parents and I went back to my office to discuss what transpired. The parents were amazed when they did not hear any more noise coming from their children in my waiting room. About 10 minutes later, we went into the waiting room and Jessica was quietly coloring while Gregory was playing with the blocks. They told us that they had apologized to each other. I praised them and noted how well they were behaving. I sat down next to Jessica to inquire about her coloring. I was astonished when she responded in a whisper as she described what she was coloring in the coloring book. After this brief intervention, Jessica continued to mirror my quiet voice; I actually could barely hear her! This example demonstrates how malleable a child's brain is and how using empathetic and soothing facial expressions and modulated vocal tones can facilitate a connection with the child. This, in turn, strengthened Jessica's ability to calm herself and mirror me.

However, building a relationship with Jessica did not happen overnight. When I first began treating Jessica, she would not even look at me. Over time, she began to glance at me and then at times would lean up against me and give me a hug on departing. Jessica slowly began to build an attachment to me that I hoped would transfer to her parents as they learned to respond in a calm way to her oppositional behavior.

Children who are verbally abused or grow up in chaotic, noisy, and threatening environments, as Jessica had, will shut down their ability to listen to me even when I talk to them in a normal tone. I have a soft voice and often people tell me to speak up. So it is quite remarkable that children will tune me out even when I am talking in my normally quiet voice. What I have learned to do is to talk even more quietly (almost in a whisper); to slow down the rhythm of my voice and pace what I am saying. Suddenly, children who were averting their eyes and were unresponsive will pause from playing to look at me. I look back at them, confirming my acceptance of them. As I continue talking in a slow, whispering voice, children eventually will begin responding. Only after their brains register that I am not a threat, they will begin to connect with me. Once children begin to engage with me, I slowly increase the loudness of my voice to my normal level. In most cases, children maintain their engagement with me. By varying the sound of my voice from a whisper to a normal level, these children will expand their auditory window of tolerance without resorting to dissociation.

I recall the wisdom of a wise pediatrician, Dr. Richard Silberg, who told me that when small children are having meltdowns in his office, he advises their parents to pick them up and in a whispering voice tell them a story (personal communication, July 30, 2010). He reported that the children will immediately stop crying and listen intently. This technique helps the parents calm their hyperaroused child.

To teach parents the power of vocal inflections, I play them the 1951 Stan Freberg hit radio program, "John and Marsha," a humorous depiction that consists of a couple—John and Marsha—repeating each other's name with different inflections for 2½ minutes.[1] Freberg explained that he wanted to see whether he could cover all the various emotions that the early radio soap operas covered without all the verbiage (Steward, 1999). During the program, John and Marsha express multiple emotions, including sadness, joy, astonishment, and passion, by only varying the tone of their voices while saying the other's name. The recording provides an entertaining example of mirroring emotions through vocal inflections.

I played this radio program to Jessica and Gregory's parents. At the end, both of them were smiling and had greater awareness of how different tones of voice impacted interactions with their children. This simple, humorous clip adds levity to the session while helping parents develop self-awareness of their voice inflections and become effective co-regulators of their children's affect.

COMPLEXITY OF ATTACHMENT WITH YOUTH WITH DISSOCIATION

There are a number of complex and interrelated factors to consider when building attachment with dissociative children. These factors include: the presence of self-states and how they influence the child's attachment behavior; a self-states relationship to past parental figures and awareness of present caretakers; and how much past relational experiences interfere with a self-state's ability to develop an attachment to the child's current parents. The therapist needs to explore these factors with the child in coordination with the parents, as the parents can provide additional information regarding their child's attachment behavior and can provide important clues regarding whether a self-state is involved. As noted in Chapter 3, dissociative children may appear to have reactive attachment disorder (RAD), but vacillation from avoidance to closeness is often the result of shifting self-states who have divergent feelings toward their parents.

Parents as well as teachers are often the best informants of children's behavior, particularly children who exhibit perplexing mood and behavior switches that impair attachment. Parents and teachers often notice the nuances of patterned fluctuations in their child's voice, mannerisms, and memory abilities; however, they usually do not understand what these changes mean. For example, parents may experience incongruent patterns of attachment behavior by the child, ranging from closeness, rejection, avoidance, withdrawal, and aggression. These dramatic shifts understandably place much stress on parents who may feel threatened, rejected, or confused and may withdraw from their child. During these turbulent periods, it is critical that parents maintain their calm while pursuing what is "underlying" the contradictory behavior.

Providing ongoing psychoeducation to parents about why one minute the child loves them and the next minute the child rejects them with little provocation can help sustain parental involvement (see the section on psychoeducation in Chapter 5). There are a number of self-state dynamics that present challenges to dissociative children's ability to attach to their parents. One of the most basic reasons for attachment problems is that the child has a self-state who still believes that he or she is living in the past traumatic environment and is not aware of the child's current caretakers. In many cases, these self-states were created to contain a specific traumatic event, affect, behavior, and/or sensation and, consequently, did not have knowledge or understanding about relationships. They are fearful of getting close to others and need much orientation and guidance about relationships. When I encounter children with such self-states, I encourage the self-states to learn from observing and experiencing through the child's senses (e.g., eyes, ears, touch) about how to relate to parents and others and to distinguish the past from the present. Parents can encourage their child to explore within his or her mind to see whether parts of the self are aware of the here and now and whether they know their current caregivers. Self-states can also be encouraged to look at their body to see how their body has grown, and to look at a calendar to recognize the passage of time. Simple orienting techniques such as these can help bridge the gulf between the past and the present. I will discuss more specific techniques that you can teach parents in Chapters 7 and 8 on stabilization.

Another reason that a child may have difficulties with attachment is because of the presence of self-states who are protective of other parts of the self, and who have assumed a parental role that is in direct competition with that of the parents. Parental self-states can be very resistant when the child is asked to comply with certain rules. It is critical that the parents understand, empathize, and respect the self-state's protective role in order to gain the self-state's trust and cooperation. Eventually, these parental self-states will be encouraged to engage in fun, developmentally appropriate activities with the child and relinquish their "responsibilities" to care for the child, as with the case of Lisa, who was introduced in Chapter 4 and whose case will be discussed further in Chapter 7.

Attachment difficulties can also be caused by angry self-states who are hypervigilant and extremely distrusting. They keep their distance from others and may even attack when people get too close. Parents need to respect the self-states' need for distance while demonstrating that they are nonthreatening to these angry protectors. Over time, these angry protectors will cooperate with the parents if they are respected for what they had to do to stay safe and do not see the parents as a threat.

When feasible, I often include parents in the therapy sessions so they can learn firsthand how to employ attachment strategies and learn modified therapeutic interventions for home use. Many examples of teaching parents these various skills are provided throughout this book.

Special Parenting Strategies for Use With Children Who Have Self-States

Connecting Before Correcting

An important principle for parenting traumatized children is connecting before correcting (Hughes & Baylin, 2012; Siegel & Payne Bryson, 2014). For example, when Jessica acted out in the waiting room during her parents' therapy session, I first attempted to connect with her by "empathizing" with what she was feeling. I, therefore, was able to engage with her and she did not feel threatened by me. She was then able to come up with a solution and maintain a calm demeanor for the remainder of her parent's session.

When children are dyregulated, parents need to view their children as *in distress* rather than in opposition to them. This perspective helps to avoid triggering an escalating fight for power and control between the parent and the child. When the parent views the child in distress, it is natural for the parent to connect with the child and seek to *understand what is motivating* the child. The parent is then in a better position to determine effective correction through mutual problem solving. Moreover, *it is only after connection that the child will be able to listen and learn from the parent's correction.* Although traumatized children may not always be able to come up with solutions, if parents give them a list of several alternatives regarding consequences, the traumatized child can have some control over what correction they receive. Engaging the child in finding solutions to their behavior will lead to less power struggles while helping the child to "save face" and maintain some dignity and sense of power. Allowing them to retain some sense of power helps children remain engaged with their parents. The connection is initially established by the parent speaking in a soothing voice and gazing at the child with eyes that convey care and understanding.

Promoting Acceptance Between the Children's Self-States and Parents

For a dissociative child to develop a firm and secure attachment, all parts of the child will need to accept the parent as well as feel that the parent accepts them. *Acceptance of each other is a beginning step toward building attachment between the parent and the whole child.* This will minimize various self-states feeling threatened by the parents and interfering in the child's ability to connect.

"Adoption Ceremony"

"Adoption ceremonies" between children's self-states and their parents can be helpful to solidify the child's recognition and acceptance that the parents accept *all of the child.* They can also help self-states formally accept the parents as their parents too. This can be a simple recognition in the therapy session of self-states agreeing to accept the parents, and of the parents accepting all parts of the child. A hug between the parents and the child with the parents saying, "I love all of you and accept all of you as my child" and the child saying, "I and all my parts accept you as my mom and dad" can be a powerful moment. Afterward, the child and parents can be encouraged to discuss how they were able to arrive at this point and how they can continue to enhance their relationship. They can then celebrate by going out to lunch or spending time together in a special activity that the child chooses.

Keeping a Journal

I ask parents to keep a journal of their child's shifting behaviors and affect. This helps the parents and clinician identify patterns associated with traumatic triggers and behavioral and affective shifts related to the influence of a self-state. Triggers may be environmental, such as a location, smell, toy, or sudden noise that was associated with their child's past trauma. A trigger may also be relational, such as a family member's facial expressions, vocal tone, or physical touch. For example, Doug, a 9-year-old boy who was anally penetrated by an adolescent, was lying on the couch when his mother sat down next to him and lightly brushed his buttocks. Doug suddenly began screaming and became enraged at his mother. He later explained, "I felt my butt was splitting in two with electrifying pain." Although he had a conscious memory of the penetration, he had never remembered the extreme pain caused by the rape until he experienced this unexpected touch. Doug identified a self-state he called the Angry One, who felt like killing his mom; however, another self-state, the Nice One, kept telling him not to do so. Previously, Doug and I had practiced deep breathing and removing himself from situations until he could calm down enough to manage his explosions. Using this technique, he was able to go to his room, sufficiently calm down, and then reveal to his mother this painful sensory memory. His mom held and comforted him.

Fostering Internal Awareness

Because children with self-states can suddenly shift from being loving to their parents to being angry and rejecting, it is very difficult for parents to stay calm. I advise parents that these shifts can offer important information about what is causing their child's disruptive behavior. I also teach parents to handle sudden shifts by acknowledging the sudden change in their child's feelings while communicating concern for their child's distress and expressing curiosity as to what has changed. The parent can ask the child to go inside of her mind to figure out what happened just moments before he or she became so upset. The focus is on trying to understand and guide the child to learn what triggered the sudden change in behavior. This approach places the responsibility on the whole child to sort out what transpired in order to take control over the part that is causing disruption. The child will still have to take responsibility for the behavior, but the main focus is *less on punishment and more on helping the child gain better internal awareness, cooperation and mastery over the shifting states*. If the child checks inside but is unable to articulate what transpired, the parent can express empathy, noting how confusing that must be for the child to not know, and then engage with the child on possible triggers and to determine a reasonable consequence. Children who experience amnesia for disruptive behavior often feel that it is unfair that they must experience consequences. I counsel parents to provide the child with reasonable consequences for misbehavior that are short term—for example, not letting the child continue to play a video game after he threw the remote control.

Modified Stabilization Techniques

Modified therapeutic stabilization techniques (particularly those highlighted in Chapters 7 and 8) can be used at home for the child to safely discharge negative affect and to minimize escalating, negative behaviors. Some are code words and hand signals that alert the child to self-reflect on behavior and regain self-control.

To promote release of anger, the parent can encourage the child to hit a pillow, throw tennis balls at trees (or snowballs during the winter), jump up and down on a trampoline, or play basketball. The child can also be encouraged to listen to music or cuddle with his or her favorite stuffed animal, write, or draw pictures of his or her feelings or traumatic memories in a journal. Most importantly, by discussing with the child his or her feelings and praising the child for utilizing healthy techniques, positive behavior can be reinforced. In addition, parents can contract with the child for rewards when the child accepts discipline, takes responsibility for behaviors, and initiates self-regulatory techniques when hyperaroused (Waters, 1998a). *The most desirable rewards are those in which the parent engages in an activity with the child, as this helps build attachment between the child and parent.* However, children can also be rewarded with extra time on their electronics, be allowed to invite a friend over to their house, earn a toy, and so forth. An even greater reward can be offered when the child is able to stop himself (or a part of himself) from acting out and uses a stabilization technique before his caregiver has to step in.

Case Example of Peter: The "Unattached Teen"

The most disturbing problem for parents is the child or adolescent who is detached toward them. It is extremely challenging for parents to continue to provide care for a youth who does not demonstrate the capacity to connect. Parents understandably become depleted, resentful, and finally rejecting toward their child. They give and give over the years with the hope that the child will be able to reciprocate and express genuine feelings. The following example is that of Peter, an adolescent, who was not attached to his parents, who struggle to parent him.

Outwardly, Peter was a pleasant, cooperative, respectful, and handsome 14-year-old Hispanic American. However, he was devoid of genuine emotions. He communicated politely with me and talked about his behavior in a matter-of-fact way. He was currently in the ninth grade. He enjoyed reading, sports, and video games. He exhibited minimal acting-out behavior compared with other emotionally impaired teens because his style was passive resistant. He was likable, but his adoptive parents were despondent that Peter did not thank them for what they did for him or show reciprocity. His parents indicated that he lied about doing chores and his homework. He had been stealing their money and candy for a long time. Sometimes, he denied or did not recall doing these behaviors. They desperately wanted him to communicate with them and to be honest.

Peter's early life was chaotic. His biological parents neglected him due to drugs and alcohol abuse. He bounced back and forth between his biological parents and relatives numerous times until he was placed in several foster homes when he was between 3 and 5 years old. Then, he and his younger brother were placed in his current adoptive home. Peter's parents described him as highly intelligent, but underperforming in school. Peter described both past and present memory disturbances. He did not recall any of his teachers until he was in the third grade. He also did not recall his early childhood and some recent incidents of lying and stealing.

Peter's parents brought him to see me after an incident that resulted in Peter having complete amnesia. He and his mother had an altercation over him eating her chocolates. She accused him of lying and slapped him. After he completed a chore, he said he felt paranoid that someone or a presence was watching him. He ran out of the house very frightened and began walking. His parents discovered the family dog was dead and thought Peter was responsible for its death and that was why he left.

There was a severe snowstorm and as nightfall approached, their anxiety heightened. They notified the police. Four hours later, the police spotted Peter. He told me, "I don't remember walking. I came to when I heard the sirens. I was kind of sleepwalking." He had walked 12 miles in a brutal snowstorm! His parents rushed him to the hospital due to his fugue experience. He was admitted to the youth psychiatric unit for the night for an evaluation; however, he was dismissed the next day, as he did not exhibit any ongoing memory problems.

When Peter's parents found a note that said, "I'm sorry," they thought he had written it because he was apologizing for killing the dog by feeding it chocolate, which can be poisonous to dogs. Peter indicated that he had written the apology note because of his disrespect toward his mom when they had argued. Peter admitted to abusing their dog several years ago, but adamantly denied that he had abused and killed this dog that he "really liked." He explained that he had left home because he was frightened and felt someone watching him.

Peter recalled feeling this "presence" earlier when he was 7 years old and when he was alone. He was administered the Adolescent Dissociative Experiences Scale (A-DES) and scored a 2.53—well below the significant range for dissociation. He did rate a 5 or above on the following items: People telling him he says or does things he does not remember; feeling in a fog or spaced out and things around seeming unreal; confused whether he has done something or only thought about doing it; finding himself doing something that he knows is wrong, even when he does not want to do it; others telling him he acts so differently that he seems a different person; doing something when he knows it is wrong; and his past is a puzzle with pieces missing. He denied auditory or visual hallucinations. Peter also indicated that he would change suddenly and become angry with others. He was accused of lying about not doing his chores and stealing money from his parents. Sometimes, he would know when he had stolen something, but other times he had no memory of it. He was perplexed when he stole money, saying, "I wanted to have money, but not to spend. It was a dumb thing to do because it is not mine."

Peter was disconnected from understanding how his parents felt. Peter said, "I never really had parents before or know how to deal with it. It is hard to accept them as parents. They don't look like me at all and they are not really my family." When I asked him whether he wished he were with his birth family, he replied, "I don't care at all that I am not with my birth family. I am better off with these sets of parents than with my birth family."

Peter did not recall his biological parents, and only had few memories of his early childhood. He recalled an early memory in an emotionless way. He saw an image of himself in his mind at age 3 sitting on his bed in a foster home hearing screaming in the next room. Then, he indicated, "This person came into my room and started beating me with a belt all over my body." He described in detail what the large man looked like. I asked his adoptive father to join us so that Peter could describe this memory to him. Though his father questioned him about feeling angry about the severe beating, Peter showed no affect, stating, "I can't do anything about it." Another memory he had was that of hiding under a bed when it was time to leave his biological mother. He could not tell me what he felt, but when I asked him to check inside of his mind, he said, "One part said I was crying and another part said I just accepted it." However, he could not elaborate on what he meant by parts. Remarkably, he could not recall what his mother looked like.

Peter had moved back and forth between his birth parents' and relatives' homes until he was eventually placed in his adoptive home. Based on his history, I suspected his attachment impairments and dissociative symptoms were related to early neglect, alternating placements and the beating incident. I began to work with Peter two to three times a week in individual and in family therapy. An early goal was to help Peter acquire emotional literacy and to connect with his affect. I showed him feeling words as we talked about his current and past life. He was articulate and open with me, but again in a dispassionate way. He described having persistent thoughts of how to get away with committing the perfect crime without being caught and would go through various scenarios in his mind. He once took a drill bit out of his carpentry class without being caught, but then returned it. He denied being motivated by anger, revenge, power, or control. He said, "I think it is filling a hole inside of me. I don't know what it is." I asked whether it might have to do with his early, unpredictable life. He said, "I didn't have a place to be." I asked him what he felt. He looked at the feeling words and stated, "I felt lonely, exhausted, discouraged, rejected, frightened, nervous, anxious, worried and disappointed that no one could care for me." He talked about frequent placements and having "no friends or good parents" to care for him. In a detached manner, Peter talked about how exhausted he felt and how the hole inside him got bigger with each move. He said, "I didn't know how to fill up that hole." I suspected his stealing food and money probably was his attempt to fill the empty place within.

I encouraged Peter to connect with the feeling of emptiness and to see whether there was a little part of him that may have something to do with those feelings. He closed his eyes and when he opened them, he said, "I see the little boy. He seems so far away." Peter described the little boy who looked similar to him at age 3 sitting on the edge of his bed in a barren room with white walls. I wondered whether that was the part of him that he remembered sitting on the edge of the bed when the man came in the room and beat him. I began to feel hopeful that Peter was connecting with the little part of himself that appeared to hold pain and despondency. If so, his healing could now begin.

It was a slow, tedious, and methodical process to help Peter connect with this part of himself. Peter would close his eyes and enter the world of the little part of him. I had Peter introduce himself to his little part and explain that he was a part of him that resided inside of Peter. I encouraged that part to look through Peter's eyes and listen with Peter's ears to learn about the present environment. I explained who I was. I asked Peter to check on the little part daily and to build a relationship with him.

During the follow-up session, Peter closed his eyes and connected with his little part, but the little one was still unresponsive. I was disturbed by the bleakness of his surroundings and asked Peter to put him in a more cheerful room with yellow walls and sunlight streaming in a window. Peter added stuffed toys and art supplies to the room. I suggested that he put his adoptive parents in the room and introduce them to the little boy with the hope that his parents could begin to nurture this part. Using his imagination, Peter introduced the boy to his parents.

At the follow-up appointment, Peter told me that the little boy returned to the barren room, because he "did not know who those people were." I realized that I was reacting to my need to rescue this little boy from such a barren existence! In ongoing sessions, Peter made more attempts to connect with the despondent part of himself, but struggled with how to do so. I then asked Peter to bring in storybooks and art supplies to engage the little boy, but he still would not talk to Peter. The more Peter encouraged him to interact, the more the little boy gave Peter irritated looks, turned away, and lay down on the bed. I suggested that Peter bring in a ball to play catch with him. Peter complied but said that the boy could not catch the ball. I asked Peter to move closer to him. They tossed the ball back and forth a few times, and then the little boy sat down on the bed again. Peter and I were struggling to find something that would bring the little boy out of his lonely shell. Because dogs can be great companions, I suggested that Peter put a dog in the room in the hope that it would comfort the little boy. Peter did so, but the little boy did not respond. However, the next time Peter checked on him, the little boy was sleeping with the dog. Both of us felt relieved. I asked Peter to play with the little boy and the dog with the ball. There was more interaction with the little boy, but he remained unexpressive. Attempts to talk with this part about feelings toward his birth parents, the beating, multiple moves, and multiple losses were unsuccessful. He simply looked away in silence.

Although Peter did not seem to have a bond to his birth parents, I asked Peter whether he had a picture of them that he could put in the room. Peter replied that he neither had any pictures nor could remember what they looked like. His part was again mute when asked how he felt about his birth parents. I was determined to find a meaningful question that would help Peter's little part open up. I asked Peter whether he had a relative or family member who he felt close to. He responded in a strong, clear, voice, "Yes."

Peter told me about a great aunt who loved him and favored him over his younger brother, because he carried his birth father's name. His aunt even visited him after he was adopted. However, unfortunately his parents and his aunt had a falling out and she died a few years back. I expressed sadness that this had happened and noted how important she was to him, and he to her. I asked him whether he recalled what she looked like. He did. I asked him to put a picture of her in the room. As soon as he brought the picture to the little boy, he immediately grasped and hugged the picture! That was the first sign of positive affect that the little boy had demonstrated. Peter talked to the little boy about his aunt and how much she loved him. Connecting the little boy with the great aunt's memory and her love of him was the linchpin that helped the little boy to begin to process his loss and grief of his aunt, as well as his other losses. It became clear that the little boy needed to process his grief of his great aunt's loss before he could again experience the capacity to connect and express positive emotions. The little boy's self-state appeared to hold the key for Peter to connect with his adoptive parents.

Peter put his arm around the little part of him as they grieved their loss. I asked Peter to talk to his little part about whether he could transfer the affection he felt for his aunt to his adoptive parents. Peter agreed. His little boy listened but was silent. To assure Peter that his adoptive parents would accept the little part, I set up a family session and his adoptive parents expressed affection and a desire to be parents to Peter's little part. Over time, the little boy began to smile and engage more with Peter, who visited him daily. He still would not talk to Peter about their traumatic past, but there was an immense improvement in his countenance.

Peter transformed as well. He began to engage in reciprocity with his parents and was more open, honest, and communicative with them—a sign that his little boy had accepted Peter's parents. They were elated.

It was apparent that the little boy, who held the key for emotional expression, was directly influencing Peter's capacity for experiencing affect. After Peter's little part grieved the loss of his great aunt, Peter was finally able to experience genuine feelings. Soon afterward, Peter's little boy self-state began to grow up to be Peter's age with hypnotic suggestions and he spontaneously integrated with Peter.

Shortly thereafter, Peter and his family moved away. Months later, I received a phone call from his father, saying, "Peter is doing wonderfully. His grades are excellent and he has made good friends who come to our house. He couldn't be doing any better!" According to Damásio (1994), emotions are not a luxury but are a complex aid in the fight for existence. This was truly the case with Peter!

SUMMARY

Peter, Martha, Jamie, and Miranda exemplify how trauma and dissociation can affect attachment behavior and place stress on parents' ability to connect with and manage their child. Children need to grieve their earlier relational losses—some contained in self-states—to open the door to attach to their current caretakers. Parents bring their own traumatic losses into the next generation. Their acknowledgment of and willingness to grieve their losses and be mindful of their traumatic triggers will help them be better able to attend to their child's struggles. At the same time, parents' ability to modulate their vocal and facial expressions can help their child to more appropriately respond and maintain a sense of connection with them even when their child is upset. Providing a calm, safe environment can facilitate a traumatized child's capacity to express feelings, to differentiate between past and present parental figures, to resolve issues related to loss and grief, and to develop an attachment to their current caregivers "across all parts of the self." In doing so, the child will come to recognize that this is their final home, as noted in the refrain of Martha's poignant song, "I guess they're going to keep me. I tried everything . . ."

NOTE

1. Available at www.last.fm/music/Stan+Freberg/_/John+and+Marsha.

7

"My Invisible Team"
Identifying and Stabilizing Self-States

Rudy looked down and in a quiet voice told his dad, "My invisible team told me to do it." Rudy had suddenly lunged at his sister, tackled her, and choked her with his arm. Just moments before, he was sitting quietly on his dad's lap watching a family television series. There was no visible provocation that caused Rudy to leap off of the security of his dad's lap, run after his sister, grab her around her neck, and choke her.

In Chapter 1, I described in my Star Theoretical Model the powerful influence that significant others have on children's perceptions, identification, intentions, affect, beliefs, and behaviors. In my model, I explained how Bowlby's (1980, 1982a) internal working model helps our understanding about the importance of attachment to parents, and how the development of mental representations within children guides their interactions with others throughout the rest of their life. Internal representations of significant figures can be either positive or negative depending on the child's experiences with his or her caretakers. When children have been neglected or maltreated, these representations can develop into self-states that replicate the child's abusers by mirroring their affect and actions. Other self-states can identify with people in the child's life who have positive qualities, such as a caring nonabusive parent or admired hero figures. However, when children are brought for therapy, the self-states that draw the most attention are those that are aggressive, destructive, and/or suicidal. I begin my chapter by focusing on the most challenging self-states because of their impact on the child's overall functioning. Often, it is advisable to address and engage these self-states early in treatment to reframe their roles in a positive way, as this will help stabilize the child.

TAMING THE LIONS: IDENTIFYING
PERPETRATOR STATES

When traumatized children do not learn from past actions and repeatedly engage in destructive behaviors, it is a signal that something is amiss, and it would be wise to explore whether there are any dissociated parts that are contributing to, or responsible for, their behavior. Unless those parts are accessed, any form of discipline will have little, if any, effect. This is a critical task of stabilization. Although self-states may not be known to the child initially, it is important to inquire about the presence of any self-states, especially any threatening voices or images that the child experiences. If self-states are identified, the clinician should explore their connection to the child's ineffectual responses to interventions.

Self-states (a child's "invisible team," as aptly described by Rudy) are initially developed to help traumatized children survive. They can contain various degrees of traumatic memories, roles, affect, sensations, and behaviors that the child was unable to manage alone at the time of trauma. Sequestering traumatic responses is an adaptive survival mechanism that is used to protect the child when he feels helpless and overwhelmed with negative affect, such as rage that is unable to be expressed for fear of retribution. The child may view self-states based on the emotions they carry. For example, a child may refer to a self-state holding negative affect as "the angry part," "the devil," or "the monster," or call the self-state by the name of the abuser, as Kaitlyn did when she referred to Charlie, the inside voice of her abuser in Chapter 1.

Vogt (2012) describes perpetrator introjects as complex psychological models that were formed when the child was forced to manage boundary violations by an aggressor, and unconsciously internalized the toxic information contained in the violent scene. His edited book provides an extensive discussion on perpetrator introjects, which includes classifications and treatment approaches. Regarding treatment approaches, Twombly (2012) points out, "Being aware that all parts are performing in scripted ways that helps the patient survive their childhood, helps the therapist maintain curiosity and compassion in the face of situations that ordinarily might inspire horror and dismay" (p. 135). With these words of wisdom, let us examine a number of classifications of perpetrating self-states in dissociative children. Potgieter-Marks (2012) identified four types of perpetrator introjects (self-states): (a) the violent introject; (b) the sexualized perpetrator introject; (c) the controlling perpetrator introject; and (d) the self-harming introject.

The violent introject can lash out at a child or an adult without remorse or awareness of the impact of such behavior. Violence usually increases if this introject is not identified and dealt with. The sexualized perpetrator introject is more devious and grooms other children to engage in sexual acts. The number of victims and types of perpetration can vary. I see these introjects as identifying with their own sexual perpetrators and reenacting their own trauma to gain mastery over their victimization. Close to the sexualized perpetrator introject is the sexually obsessive self-state (Waters & Silberg, 1998b), as both have a compulsive aspect. The sexually obsessive self-state can engage in sexually compulsive masturbation or other sexual acts that result in self-harm, as well as engage in sexually reactive behaviors with peers. I treated a sexually abused 2-year-old boy who would go into a trance state and compulsively masturbate during the entire hour-long children's program, causing him soreness.

According to Potgieter-Marks (2012), the third type of perpetrator introject—the controlling perpetrator—uses intense temper tantrums to control caregivers who, ultimately, give in to the child. Consequently, these self-states are often able to control the whole family. The final type of perpetrator introject described by Potgieter-Marks is the self-harming introject who tries to hurt or kill the child through constant commands to physically harm the body. This type of self-state often has early traumatic experiences rooted in unresolved near-death experiences or had a parent who wished the infant was dead or attempted to kill the infant (Kahr, 2007, as cited in Potgieter-Marks, 2012).

I believe that similar dynamics are involved in each type of perpetrator introjects, as all of them appear to be projective identifications with abusers and/or reenactments of violence they experienced. In the dissociative children who I have treated, perpetrating introjects have often experienced and hold memories of the worst aspects of the trauma. These introjects strive to feel powerful due to their fear of being weak and helpless. Perpetrator introjects are often disconnected from the emotional and physical pain that was experienced during the abuse; instead, the emotions are transformed into pure rage. The helpless affect or victim identity is "transferred" to another self-state. Consequently, the perpetrating introject can taunt the helpless part, as it reflects the perpetrator's deepest fear of helplessness and victimhood.

These dissociated perpetrating states can appear formidable. However, once recognized and redefined (the younger the age when treated, the more promising the outcome), they can be transformed into a healthy ally for the child (this process is described in Chapter 8). Left unattended, however, these states can be dangerous, resulting in eventual incarceration when the child gets older. Consequently, it is crucial to uncover the underlying operating dynamics that ignite the perpetrating introject and to learn the purpose that these introjects serve.

In addition to perpetrators, other types of self-states may be formed depending on the nature of the traumatic events and the psychological impact on the child. Some of the more common self-states are helpers/rescuers or hero figures, maternal figues, babies, affective states (e.g., laughing or scared), or a beloved pet that was killed by the abuser (Waters & Silberg, 1998b).

Karpman's Drama Triangle Model[1] graphically displays the dynamics between persecutor, rescuer, and victim. This model is useful when describing the intense interactions that can exist between self-states, and also between patient and therapist (Lowenstein & Brand, 2014). The Drama Triangle is illustrated by an inverted triangle with the victim at the bottom in "a down position." The victim self-state feels helpless, hopeless, and ashamed about his or her victimization. The "up position" of the persecutor can be synonymous with perpetrating self-states, which are symbolically referred to as "lion" states that blame and attack the victim. The last corner of the up position of the triangle is that of the rescuer. A rescuer self-state feels guilty about whether he or she is not able to rescue the victim. The rescuer keeps the focus on the victim rather than on dealing with his or her own issues and anxieties. The rescuer also keeps the victim dependent and in a position of failure.

The Drama Triangle is useful, as it helps us to be aware of how various self-states play out traumatic scripts that keep the child in internal conflict and impede the child's recovery. Intervention techniques focus on exploring the underlying role that each self-state serves and how they communicate with each other internally. It is important to negotiate for constructive roles with each of these states, and to promote healthy internal dialogue. Let us examine further the underlying dynamics of "lion" states.

A "lion" state can be activated by minor stimuli, and the defensive response can be very powerful. While under the influence of such, the child may become fast and agile "like a roaring lion attacking its prey."

The child can engage in aggressive and destructive behavior for which he or she has no control or conscious memory. These states can also turn on the child—despising the child's weakness. The child's lack of control over aggressive states can also be misconstrued as a lack of care. When activated by a threat, the aggressive part takes control and is in the driver's seat. Because this part was formed to often carry the child's rage, and did not have attachment-building experiences with caregivers, its sole aim is self-protection and retribution. This part has not developed the capacity to empathize with others or to be concerned about the harm he or she may have inflicted. Often, this part does not even know what a relationship is. Although the perpetrating state may not exhibit concern for the harm it causes, often, another state, perhaps the victim, does care and feels remorse and shame. After a perpetrator state emerges, a rescuer or helper self-state may take over to comfort the child. The therapeutic task is to connect with the perpetrator state, express empathy for the original survival role that the self-state played for the child, and negotiate a safe release of this state's rage. This will encourage the self-state to develop a positive transference toward the therapist and parents that will encourage self-state's willingness to learn about healthy relationships.

Furthermore, although angry self-states can be intimidating and disruptive, I have found that the hidden motive underlying their aggressive behavior is to protect the hurt child or the little ones inside. At the same time, the perpetrating state can be angry over having to handle the worst part of the abuse and/or the child's rage, and this state seeks revenge by attacking the child for his or her weakness. Because children are intimidated by their perpetrating self-states' power and strength, they often perceive these parts as adults. However, the perpetrating parts themselves may be young children. They camouflaged their identity by behaving similar to "fierce lions" to defend themselves through intimidating and threatening behaviors. These "lion parts" are determined to not let anyone hurt them or the younger parts again.

One 8-year-old girl with DID called her self-states "Mr. and Mrs. Crush Brains." They represented her severely abusive parents and she perceived them as a 1,000 years old. The child saw them as so powerful that she ascribed such an age to them, but in reality they were young child states simulating their abusive parents and had actually taken the worst of their parents' abuse. While perpetrating states can be dangerous, they view their motives as rational but, in reality, their motives are based on cognitive distortions derived from their aversive experiences. An example of this is provided later in the chapter when Rudy describes why his "invisible team" tried to strangle his sister.

Because dissociative children often display sudden extreme emotions and behaviors, and often fail to respond to consequences, they are often diagnosed with intermittent explosive disorder, oppositional-defiant disorder, bipolar disorder, or conduct disorder. Although traumatized children often exhibit destructive patterns, it should not be assumed that the child is evil, trying to get attention, or a sociopath (as some traumatized children have been labeled). Nor should it be decided that the child is beyond help because of multiple treatment failures that unfortunately occur because of lack of recognition of such states who are responsible for such aggressive behaviors.

Because therapists can be intimidated by perpetrating self-states, when I conduct trainings, I usually show a slide of a fierce hairy monster's face growling with sharp teeth to represent the perpetrating self-state. I explain that this part may seek to protect itself and/or a vulnerable child state by acting aggressively in order to scare people away. The next slide I show is that of a cute puppy sitting calmly in an oversized dog dish with the word "Killer" printed on the dog dish. It is clear that there is a misnomer between the word "Killer" and such a cute little puppy. The little dog slide may provide a more accurate image of the perpetrator who puffs up and growls for protection, but beneath the surface, it is a puppy. The "monster" is actually a frightened child covering up fear with intimation. I have found these images to be an effective way to help therapists and parents better understand intimidating self-states and not take them at "face value," but rather to consider what motive may be underlying the child's "monstrous" behavior. This perspective can help parents remain calm in the midst of the "roar," and to search with the child and therapist for the purpose that these destructive states serve.

The following are questions that can help analyze the presence and types of self-states in dissociative children.

Questions to Explore the Presence of Perpetrator and Other Self-States

In Chapter 4 on assessment, I provided a list of questions that are used to assess for dissociation in children and adolescents. The following are questions designed to build on previous assessment questions, in order to assess for the presence of self-states. *It is important to consider the child's responses to these questions within the framework of earlier discussions of dissociative symptoms, such as memory problems, trance behaviors, hallucinations, extreme switching of affect and behavior, and so forth, as these questions will not be repeated.* Rather, the questions provided in this chapter are specifically tailored to consider the impact of trauma exposure and its relevance to the types or roles of self-states that subsequently may have developed. These questions focus on learning about the circumstances of the child's trauma exposure, the impact of the traumatic relationship on the child's identity, and the developmental and psychological impact on the child. They are questions for therapists to consider and to explore with the parent and the child. Some of the questions overlap with one another.

1. What types of trauma were experienced (e.g., emotional, physical, and/or sexual abuse, physical and emotional neglect or deprivation, witnessing domestic violence or war, medical trauma, peer bullying)? How often was the child exposed to the trauma? Does the child reenact the trauma on self or others?

2. Even if the child did not visually witness the trauma, did the child experience frightening and startling noises (e.g., shouting, swearing, loud crashes, gun shots, glass breaking, sirens)? Did the child see the physical aftermath of the violence (e.g., broken glass, house in disarray, parent with black eyes and bruises, dead bodies)?

3. Who was the perpetrator(s) of the trauma and what was his or her relationship to the child? Was the child dependent on the perpetrator for survival? Did the child witness the perpetrator harm other family members? Does the child sometimes mirror the perpetrator's affect and behavior?

4. What was the child's age(s) at the time of the trauma(s), including prebirth, and how has it disrupted the child's development and ability to master the relevant psychosocial stage? Is there evidence in the child's behavior that suggests that there is a part that remains developmentally stuck at the age of the trauma? For example, are there times when the child becomes mute and curls up in a fetal position? Could there be a nonverbal, infant self-state? Does the older child sometimes act as though he or she is still the age they were when they were traumatized (e.g., a toddler state who engages in smearing feces, baby talk, and/or biting)? At times, does the older

child display symptoms of encopresis or enuresis? Or does the child act similar to a pseudo-adult or a parent who could represent an adult or parental self-state?

5. What emotional toll did the trauma have on the child? Did the child experience the loss of, or separation from, a parent, caretaker, or close family member due to hospitalization, incarceration, jail, or death? Did the child experience a parent becoming emotionally unavailable due to depression, traumatic reactions, financial hardships, or other reasons? What impact did this have on the child's ability to form a healthy attachment and identity? Does the child have a self-state that mirrors the depressed, ineffectual caretaker? Does the child develop a caretaker self-state to cope with an unavailable parent? Does the child have a self-state that is detached and/or identifies with the perpetrator? Does the child have a self-state that mirrors the emotional and behavioral dysregulation and unpredictable behavior of the perpetrator? Does the child have affective self-states that hold emotions such as fear, anger, anxiety, depression, or shame? Does the child have a self-state that acts similar to a helpless, frozen victim who is unable to defend the self? Does the child have a rescuer/helper self-state?

6. Do the child's symptoms signify reactions to traumatic exposures? For example, does the physically abused child attack when accidently bumped into or have a startle reaction to any touch? Does the child become highly dysregulated when exposed to loud noises or shouting because of verbal abuse? Does the neglected child hoard food because of the fear of experiencing hunger again? Does the sexually abused child sexually act out to gain mastery and control over the trauma through reenactment? Does the child display self-states that contain these symptoms?

7. Does the child experience periodic, nonorganic somatic disturbances, such as loss of sensation, inability to walk, and/or pain in extremities (e.g., legs and arms)? Is there a self-state that carries these somatic disturbances (i.e., somatic issues only occur when this self-state is activated)?

These questions help the clinician to begin to understand the internal mechanisms operating when a child develops an "invisible team" to rescue her or him from terrifying events. For example, imagine a young girl whose father enters her room every night, places his gun on her night stand, and tells her not to say anything as she looks at his gun. He then begins to touch her and his touching becomes more intrusive with each visit. He puts his hand firmly over her mouth when she cries so she cannot be heard, thereby obstructing her breathing. How did this child cope with this horror? Did she develop various self-states to take specific parts of the trauma and the myriad trauma-related thoughts, emotions, sensations, and beliefs? This actually happened to a child whom I treated and who developed numerous self-states to manage such horrific abuse.

I have treated many children who were sexually, physically, and emotionally abused, if not daily, multiple times a week by their caregivers. There was no escape from the terror, and seeing their caregivers each day was an ongoing trigger that caused increasing fear and paralysis, resulting in dissociation. Their abuse often began in infancy and continued until their removal, sometimes not until they were adolescents. As Putnam (1997) indicated in his discrete behavioral states theory, chronically abused children do not have restorative and protective barriers, and thus have no other recourse but to further compartmentalize their emotions in separate self-states for self-protection from the terrifying moment-to-moment traumatic exposure and reminders. It would simply be too overwhelming for a child to face such intense affect without creating internal barriers. Some of these children have drawn pictures of dozens of self-states. I asked them how they know there are so many self-states and they tell me, "I know. I see them and I count them." Fortunately, most of the self-states were undeveloped fragments that held one specific affect or behavior. However, others were more differentiated with more characteristics of a separate self, particularly those who were perpetrating introjects.

The Purpose of Rudy's "Invisible Team"

Six-year-old Rudy, who was introduced in Chapter 4 and mentioned at the beginning of this chapter, revealed self-states during treatment for aggression, enuresis, and encopresis. After uncovering a baby self-state, I provided Rudy a doll to represent this internal baby. Rudy was encouraged to rock the doll daily as a way to help him learn to soothe his internal baby self-state. I let him take the doll home, and he was very conscientious about taking good care of the doll. He kept the doll on his bed, except once when he left the doll on the floor. When his mother, Carol, reminded him, Rudy quickly ran into his room, carefully picked up the doll, and placed it on his bed. In the follow-up session when I asked how he and his internal baby part were feeling, he responded, "They are loving each other." I asked whether he could say more about how he felt when he was rocking the baby part of him. He responded, "I feel happy. I'm starting to feel more comfortable inside. The little part is already 1-year-old!" Rudy's mother, who was in the session, said that she noticed that Rudy was acting more relaxed. When Rudy got agitated and acted mean to his sister, his mom told him to get the doll and rock it. He complied and immediately calmed down.

However, Rudy continued with soiling accidents and lacked sensory awareness of the accidents until his mother brought them to his attention. Because Rudy's first 18 months of life were in an orphanage, I wondered whether his physical needs were not immediately attended to when he soiled himself. This may have resulted in a painful diaper rash, and it explained why he numbed himself to this area of his body. The early physical and emotional deprivation could also account for his depersonalization and the development of a self-state to manage the pain.

While Rudy sat politely next to his mother as she discussed his progress, his eyes glazed and he appeared unaware of our discussion. I had to gently call his name several times to bring him back. It was apparent that there was still much going on within him. I explained to Rudy that perhaps the soiling accidents were a result of his 1-year-old part not yet being connected to his body. I encouraged Rudy and his self-state to share somatic sensations. Rudy indicated that the baby was now 3 years old. I suggested that it was time to toilet train this part. I asked whether Rudy could help that part learn how to use the toilet with the use of his doll. Rudy enthusiastically agreed, and we set up a makeshift toilet with a plastic tub in my office. Rudy proceeded to show the doll how to use the toilet. To reinforce shared somatic awareness between Rudy and the 3-year-old part, I stressed that they were joining together to feel the body's need to go to the bathroom with an awareness of stomach pains and pressure in Rudy's lower abdomen.

Rudy's mother also brought up Rudy's violent temper: Rudy had threatened to shoot the family when asked to clean up his toys. I asked Rudy what was going on inside of himself during these episodes. Rudy responded, "I get mad inside a lot." I asked whether he had an angry part inside and he said he did have one. With the help of action toys, I helped him talk to that angry part and explain to that part that his mother's request was reasonable. I also asked Rudy whether he would help that part to agree to pick up the toys and be nice to his mother. Rudy agreed to do so. I suspected that this angry part was emotionally detached from his mother. The source of his rage was yet to be discovered.

A week later, Rudy leaped from his dad's lap and lunged at his sister, choking her. When Rudy explained why he choked Katrina, he said to his dad, "Me and my invisible team wanted to get some meat. The invisible team no one can see. I was trying to kill Katrina to get some meat because my team didn't have any food." This was an unfathomable motive that seemed to be rooted in his invisible team's hunger, and it propelled him to want to kill his sister! I wondered whether this was also his motive when he stabbed and choked some children at school.

Rudy sat calmly next to his mother holding the doll I gave him. I began to talk to Rudy about this incident and his invisible team.

Rudy stated matter-of-factly, "Nobody can see them but I can. I can see them because they gave me special eyes to see them because they are invisible. They have eyes to see me too and mom."

Therapist: "Do they seem real to you?"

Rudy: "Yes. They are real. They don't have a skinny body, but they have the same body with skinny arms. They look the same as me. They're 12 years old."

Therapist: "How long has your invisible team been around?"

Rudy answered calmly, "They've been there a long time. They've been living in mom and dad's closet but mom and dad didn't see them. [*I am always amazed how dissociative children's creative minds can accommodate a living space for their self-states.*] They've been sneaking food off the table but they didn't get much food. I got them more food (in the past) and choked Katrina."

Therapist: "Why would they eat people?"

Rudy: "They're hungry. They don't mind if they eat people, but they don't eat me 'cause I'm their partner. They eat other people."

Therapist: "Do they know that they are not to eat people?"

Rudy: He put his hands over his eyes to check inside of his head and answered, "No."

Therapist: "Do they know that you live with your mom and dad and not in the orphanage?"

Rudy: He paused for a moment and said, "They know my mom and dad but think they live far away in another house." He paused again and said, "Mom and dad might not know who my team is."

Therapist: "It would be very important for your mom and dad to know your invisible team. Do they know that your mom and dad have plenty of food for them to eat?"

Rudy: He covered his eyes again with his hands while checking inside and then removed his hands, saying, "No. I will tell them in my head right now." When he took his hands off of his eyes again, he simply said, "They said, 'Okay.'" Rudy added, "They get really hungry and I get them food."

Therapist: "Do you remember being hungry in the orphanage?"

Rudy: "Yes."

Therapist: "How did you feel?"

Rudy: "I was angry 'cause I didn't get any food. I just was mad all the time in the orphanage. The ladies were feeding us a little."

Therapist: "How long have you known the invisible team?"

Rudy: "When I was 6 years old, I met the invisible team at my birthday in my head."

Therapist: "Ask them if they were around when you were in the orphanage."

Rudy covered his eyes again, saying, "I'll ask them in my head." Rudy uncovered his eyes and reported, "They said, 'Yes.' They helped me when I was hungry. They didn't have hunger 'cause they had food but I didn't. They forgot about giving me food."

Therapist: "Did they have to steal food?"

Rudy: "They didn't steal food. They bought food."

Therapist: "Okay. Do they know that they are not to eat dead people?"

Rudy: "No. They didn't know that they didn't have to eat dead people. I will tell them in my head that they don't have to kill people to get food."

Therapist: "Thank you Rudy for helping them understand. When you eat, can they feel it, taste it, smell it and get full?"

Rudy: "No." He thought for a moment and said, "They don't make me poop. But they poop their pants too."

Therapist: "What part of you poops their pants?"

Rudy: "There is a 2-year-old that is a part of the invisible team and three 3-year-olds. All of the other ages are 4. Four of them are 4 years old. That's all of them."

Therapist: "Do you recall that you told me they were a different age?"
Rudy: "Yes, but they have magic and can change their ages."

I was amused by Rudy's answer. Perhaps Rudy was thinking they were older and when he checked internally, he learned they were younger. However, this is typical of young children with self-states that are less developed and can rapidly change in ages and numbers depending on their functions or situations. Nevertheless, the most important intervention was to stop the assaultive behavior by ensuring that Rudy's invisible team do not experience hunger and can somatically share the experience of eating with Rudy. I continued to talk to Rudy.

Therapist: "Rudy, when you eat, can you make sure that all parts of you are present and tasting the food, smelling the food, noticing the texture of the food?"
Rudy: "Sure."
Therapist: "Thank you, Rudy. Sounds like you and they can be a good team and you can help them not be hungry by sharing the experience of eating, and letting them know there is plenty of food."

Rudy smiled and nodded his head. I asked Rudy's mom to bring his favorite snack for the next session so that he could practice sharing the experience of eating with his invisible team.

Rudy drew a picture of his invisible team. It is a simple drawing of five figures with little detail or differentiation. All of them are smiling now that they are assured that they will not experience starvation and can share Rudy's experience of eating. One of them does not have arms, which may depict the sense of helplessness that Rudy may have felt when he was hungry (Figure 7.1).

Analysis of Rudy

One of the principles mentioned in Chapter 5 is that every behavior has meaning. Based on this principle, I wondered about the following: When Rudy said his invisible team bought food, did Rudy witness children bartering for food? When he attacked his sister and peers at school, did other children in the orphanage attack him for his food? Certainly, a toddler could not defend himself against older children grabbing his food. Did

Figure 7.1 *Rudy's "invisible team." (Used with permission.)*

other children threaten to eat him when they were hungry? We know that children often reenact what they see and what happened to them. Was Rudy's invisible team of perpetrators simply imitating what they witnessed or experienced? Was Rudy's aggressive behavior toward his sister and children at school a reenactment, driven by his invisible team, of what he experienced in the orphanage?

It is difficult to know what Rudy observed and experienced in the orphanage during the first 18 months of his life. As an infant and toddler, his brain stored information on a motor sensory level, which suggests that Rudy was trying to piece together what he experienced based on his primary senses. He did not have the cognitive capacity to make sense out of it. But, based on Rudy's disclosure, his invisible team was created to deal with his starvation and their solution was to kill humans and eat them. Because Rudy's invisible team was deprived of stable, nurturing care and did not develop an attachment to a caring person, they did not have the capacity to understand what it really meant to kill someone. To them, it was merely a means to eat.

Furthermore, Rudy seemed to be living in two worlds. His invisible team was stuck in experiencing starvation and in influencing Rudy to follow their orders. Rudy was aware of his current life, but he was under their tutelage even if their views did not fit present reality. Rudy's internal and external worlds crossed over at some juncture when Rudy was controlled by the strong urges of his invisible team and felt obligated to act out what they told him to do. These self-states were encapsulated within Rudy, reliving their starvation, and finding a solution, albeit a dangerous one. Their encapsulated environment within Rudy insulated them from the reality of Rudy's present life. The invisible team was not connected somatically to the experience of eating when Rudy ate. Although Rudy himself was aware that one does not eat humans, Rudy was part of a team and felt obligated to help them. On an internal, unconscious level, Rudy was also stuck in the past with the traumatic memory of starvation. Until all parts of Rudy resolved their feelings of deprivation, Rudy would not have complete control over his behavior and mood.

When looking at Rudy's disturbance from a different lens—one that fails to recognize the impact of trauma that can result in dissociation—Rudy's internal voices and their belief about eating humans most likely would have been attributed to a thought disorder, resulting in a diagnosis of psychosis. Rudy would have likely been placed on psychotropic medications. However, this treatment trajectory would not have addressed the source of Rudy's real problem—unresolved experiences of early deprivation contained in internal states that were driving Rudy's aggression. His invisible team would most likely have become more developed as time went on, resulting in continuous assaults on people to obtain "meat to eat." His homicidal and other destructive actions probably would have resulted in a life of repeated hospitalizations, residential treatment programs, and, eventually, incarceration.

Prior to this session, Rudy's parents had no idea what caused his spontaneous and often unprovoked aggression. Now that Rudy explained the reason for his homicidal behavior, all of Rudy could be included in his treatment, opening the door to helping him gain control over his behavior and resolve his early trauma.

The Internal World of Dissociative Children

Rudy's case provides an example of how self-states can be cut off from current reality, resulting in persistent and often retractable symptoms related to their early trauma. Dissociative children often have vivid internal lives that are completely incongruent with their external lives. These children rely on their imagination to create what they need in order to survive. Some children have developed internal imaginary rooms for each self-state. An important task of treatment is to learn about the internal world that dissociative children have developed, as their internal world can interfere with their ability to adapt to their current external world. However, ironically, both of these worlds may contribute to their safety and survival as well as to their disturbance. Because children are imaginative and creative, we can encourage them to use this skill to promote a healthy internal world that over time becomes more in synch with their external world.

The following are therapeutic interventions that will help children create an internal atmosphere that is coherent with external reality, and will decrease the child's reliance on dissociation so that all parts of the child are oriented to current time.

STABILIZATION TECHNIQUES

Stabilization techniques provide the foundation for dissociative children to begin the process of accepting, learning, and working with all parts of the self. These techniques are the building blocks toward integration and provide the structure for later safe processing of traumatic memories across all parts of the self while maintaining stability.

Promoting Self-Awareness and Developing Communication Channels

Removing boundaries between parts of the child and developing internal awareness is a critical step in stabilization. Impermeable boundaries can exist between self-states as a protection from traumatic memories, affect, sensations, and behaviors contained in different self-states. Impermeable boundaries between self-states are analogous to a house with many rooms but without doors or windows between them. It can take time to remove these barriers, but knowing all parts of the self and having the child "own them," as the child comes to terms with what the self-states contain, will bring the child closer to trauma resolution. Usually, these impermeable boundaries are not removed until the child has the strength to manage what is contained behind them.

Internal awareness of self-states can vary within the system. Knowledge can be unidirectional, through which one self-state knows about all or some of the other parts of the self, whereas other parts may have no knowledge that this particular self-state exists. Or internal awareness can be bidirectional, through which self-states have mutual knowledge of one another (self-states that share traumatic experiences are more likely to be aware of one another). It can be helpful to diagram the internal system, including their feelings, characteristics, roles, and thoughts, along with how they interact with each other. A circle can be drawn to represent each self-state with arrows that show awareness and communication patterns between them. Making this diagram with the child provides an opportunity to discuss how self-states dialogue with each other and to propose constructive communication characterized by respect and appreciation for what they each did to help the child survive.

Becoming familiar with how each of the self-states helped the child survive can be frightening for the child, particularly when dealing with self-states who intimidate and harass the child or contain traumatic memories and intense affect. I explain to children that together we can learn about how their parts helped them survive, and I assure them that I will provide tools to help them manage their feelings and memories. I attempt to normalize traumatic reactions by suggesting, for example, that perhaps the angry parts were created to help them by taking the anger that they could not express at the time of their trauma, or perhaps they took the really scary, bad aspects of their trauma and are now angry about it. This approach can decrease destructive self-states' or symptomatic states' (those who carry disturbing symptoms such as encopresis or an eating disorder) fear of being known and fear that others will try to "get rid of them," or blame them for misbehavior. These states may "eavesdrop" to learn whether caregivers or the therapist will be accepting of them.

An open and nonjudgmental attitude toward self-states will decrease their fears of rejection, criticism, or "extinction." They are a part of a child's mind and cannot be "extracted" or removed, as some professionals or parents may attempt to do so. However, if self-states feel threatened, they may temporarily go underground and appear to have disappeared only to resurface later to wreak havoc in the child's life. I reassure the child that in time we will learn more about what motivates different parts of the child, and work with the child to find more adaptive ways to manage disturbing feelings and memories. I emphasize that mutual respect and partnership will facilitate recovery. The motto that I want the child to adopt to promote internal cooperations is: "We do much better when we work together!" (Appendix D).

Rudy had no awareness of his self-states until his sixth birthday party—a time of celebration with special food that seemed to have been the catalyst for dissolving the amnestic barrier between Rudy and his invisible team. Until then, Rudy's invisible team had been causing his chronic soiling problems, feces smearing, and violent attacks on his sister and peers. It was puzzling and frustrating for Rudy to not have control over his behavior. Now that Rudy's parents and I were aware of his invisible team, they were really not "invisible" anymore and he was able to gain control over his behavior. His recovery was now on the horizon. More about Rudy's recovery and strategies for contracting with self-states for safe expression of feelings and behaviors are discussed in Chapter 8.

The Four Ls: Look, Learn, Listen, and Love

I developed the "Four Ls" when working with two siblings, 8-year-old Maggie and 6-year-old Michael, who had experienced early sexual and physical abuse by their father. Both Maggie and Michael had formed several self-states and frequently experienced complete amnesia surrounding triggering situations. One situation during which they were amnestic was a visit to their pediatrician. It was impossible for them to have a physical examination without dissociating, even with an empathetic staff and their mother present. They could tell me all of the details of what they did before entering the doctor's office and what they did afterward, but neither of them recalled the actual visit. Their performance in school was compromised as well, as they would "check out" and not be able to perform when under stress.

Michael, who was a very bright, articulate, and imaginative child, would fail math and spelling tests involving items answered correctly the previous day. Minor anxiety would cause a shift in Michael, and a toddler would take over. The teacher noted how his speech and mannerisms were often similar to those of a much younger child. I reminded Maggie and Michael about some stabilization and coconsciousness techniques that we had practiced. One of them was the "two Ls," look and listen, that referred to all parts of the self looking through their eyes and listening with their ears so that all parts of them were aware of the present moment. I would use hand signals to signify this by pointing to my eyes and ears. Since children may not hear what they are told when in a dissociative state, using nonverbal hand signals to bring them back to the present moment when they dissociate can be very helpful.

Maggie was also struggling in school but to a lesser degree than her brother. I thought of a third "L," and said to both of them, "I now have three L's instead of two." Can you tell me what the third "L" is? I could see that Maggie, a charming and engaging girl, was deep in thought. She exclaimed, "I know the third L! It is love!" I looked at her in amazement and said, "That is wonderful! That wasn't the one I was thinking of; so now there are four L's. That one is even better than the one I was thinking of. That is really a great one! Tell me more about what you mean by 'love.'" Maggie beamed with satisfaction as she said, "All parts need to love themselves and one another first, and then love the good people on the outside!" I responded, "Maggie that is brilliant! Yes, that is the most important one—to love yourself and all of your parts! They helped you in so many ways to get through all of the bad stuff that happened to you. It is also important to love all of those people in your life who care about you too!"

Since they were struggling to figure out the fourth "L," I told them that the fourth "L" stands for "learn." All parts of the self are to "learn" about each other and about what is occurring outside of themselves at school, home, and everywhere. Only through all parts of them learning will they do well at school and at other places. I then repeated the four Ls while adding new hand signals: pointing to my eyes for looking, my ears for listening, my forehead for learning, and my heart for loving—the most important one! I continue to be amazed at what I learn from severely traumatized children who endure so much at an early age, but who have such lovely spirits and much wisdom.

The adoptive mother of a severely traumatized 7-year-old girl, Tara (introduced in Chapter 2), composed a lovely song for her daughter about using the four Ls. She sang the song to Tara every morning before she left for school to reinforce that all parts of her look, listen, learn, and love during the school day. Tara's mother also made a healing shrine on a table and added significant pictures and objects to it, including Tara's adoption papers and life book. She also placed symbols on the shrine that signified Tara's growth. Tara placed a soiled, small teddy bear on the shrine; it was the only gift her birth mother had given her. Since Tara was easily hyperaroused, this visual reminder of her growth and her current life helped calm her. You will learn more about Tara in Chapter 10 on trauma processing. A handout on the four "Ls" is available in Appendix D.

Cue Words, Symbols, and Hand Signals for Stabilization

Besides engaging all parts of the self in the four Ls, I provide a variety of other cue words, symbols, and hand signals that are shortcuts to communicate what the child is experiencing or for others to communicate to the child (Waters & Silberg, 1998b). These can be helpful in promoting the child's ability to self-reflect and apply what they have learned in therapy. I have developed numerous simple visual and auditory interventions, but the child and the therapist can decide what cue words, hand signals, and symbols to use. Once the cue words and signals are developed, a comprehensive plan should be developed involving the child, the family, and school personnel, all of whom are taught to use these shortcuts with a reward system.

Reinforcing positive behavior is important for building the child's self-esteem and for working cooperatively with self-states. A hand signal of thumbs up to represent a "good job" can be used when the child and self-states cooperate, comply with requests, or do something positive. A cue word and a hand signal for kindness is developed so that the parents can reinforce this behavior with their child. The cue word for kindness can be "kind," and the hand signal can be patting the top of the hand with the other hand.

When children are feeling dysregulated, the hand signal of a peace sign and the word "peace" can be used as a reminder to seek peace when agitated. Cue words that denote that the child is experiencing intense, overwhelming emotions such as anger are helpful communication tools. For example, if the child feels as though he is going to burst like a bubble, the cue word "bubble" can be used. For flashbacks or memories, I offer the word "spike," signifying that flashbacks and traumatic memories are spiking or piercing the child's consciousness. Spike can be signaled by pointing the index finger upward. In therapy, these cue words are practiced with triggering situations so that the child can use these shortcuts to communicate what she or he is experiencing at the moment.

The therapist and the child can develop laminated cards with words or images signifying deep breathing, pictures of the child's hero figures that make them feel empowered, pictures of loved ones to help the child feel connected to them, and calming scenes or pictures of the child's safe place to remind the child to momentarily stay there until he calms down and can resume normal activities. At home, the child can also go to an actual "calm place" that is equipped with soothing objects such as soft pillows and calming music.

The child's teacher could be encouraged to use calming cards and positive words for the entire class, as they are nonintrusive and can benefit all children. If the child is unable to calm down in the classroom, an alternative plan can be in place for the child to talk to the counselor about the memories and feelings, or the child could be given permission to go to a quiet place and draw a picture of what is bothering him, or write in his journal about his feelings, thoughts, and memories. As a last resort, the parent would be notified to come and take the child home.

When the child is able to regain composure and resume school activities, the teacher can reward the child with special privileges, such as handing out papers for the teacher or receiving a star that can be used to earn an agreed-on reward. These techniques are also helpful at home where the reward may involve engaging in a fun activity with parents and friends, or extra time on the child's favorite game or electronic device.

It is preferred that the child initiates the use of these cue words and hand signals when he recognizes his distress. However, sometimes, this is not possible and the teacher or caretaker must initiate these shortcuts when they observe the child to be in distress. When the child is able to initiate the use of these techniques, then a greater reward should be provided to reinforce the child's ability to interrupt the triggering process and use self-control. The overall goal is to help the child self-reflect, communicate with others what he is feeling, and finally regain composure. The therapist and child, in cooperation with the child's internal system, can role-play different scenarios that occur at home and at school using these techniques. These techniques can also be instilled by using eye movement desensitization and reprocessing (EMDR; Chapter 12) or imagery.

Promoting Internal Cooperation and Appreciation

Metaphors That Symbolize Internal Cooperation and Appreciation

Metaphors that are familiar to children can powerfully convey messages that can be used throughout all phases of treatment. "The inside family" is an important metaphor that refers to all parts of the self as a family unit. This is an opportunity that is used to discuss the qualities of a healthy family, such as physical and psychological safety, collaboration, cooperation, respect, openness, and honesty, with the child. As reviewed in Chapter 6, I will engage children and their parents in a discussion about the qualities of a healthy external family that can be duplicated within the child's internal system. This discussion is part of an educational and stabilization component, because many traumatized children do not know what a healthy family entails.

There are many different creative, visual symbols to help dissociative children appreciate all aspects of the self. For example, Gomez (2013a) uses a rainbow in which the different colors signify different aspects of the self and together, they make a beautiful rainbow. I have used similar techniques by asking dissociative children to draw by using different self-states' favorite colors as a symbol of themselves. This exercise requires internal communication to learn about each self-state's favorite color. Various colors of clay have also been used to signify self-states. The different colors of clay can be blended to show closeness between the self-states, and then formed into a ball, or other shape they choose, to demonstrate cooperation and unity. Making crossword puzzles using self-states' names and/or qualities can also help children appreciate their self-states' connections to one another.

Gomez (2013a) also uses color-coded cards to represent a dissociative child's current level of awareness by using red, yellow, and green to signify completely dissociated, partially dissociated, and fully present, respectively. When children begin to dissociate, I use the cue phrase "get it together," while clasping my hands together to signify unity within all parts of the child. These cue words can also be used with the color-coded cards. Teachers have implemented these innocuous techniques at school with much success.

Silberg (2013) employs a hand puppet that has many little birds in a nest to denote self-states connecting and working together. I have used a marionette puppet to demonstrate internal cooperation. When the strings are in alignment, the puppet can move in a coordinated fashion to walk, dance, and so forth. I will then take one or two of the marionette strings, cross them over, and entangle them to show the child how this prevents the puppet from moving appropriately. This visual representation provides a demonstration of what it is like internally when the child and self-states are not working together and shows how this interferes in the child's ability to perform a task.

Another toy that I use to demonstrate the importance of cooperation is a windup caterpillar toy (Figure 7.2). This toy has moveable body parts that can be turned upside down. Each body part of the caterpillar represents a difficult feeling (e.g., sadness, anger, fear), and the head represents

Figure 7.2 *Caterpillar toy symbolizing internal cooperation.*

thoughts. When the feeling body parts are turned upside down, this represents the caterpillar's inability to manage those feelings. When the head is upside down, the caterpillar has disturbing thoughts. When the moveable parts are upside down and the caterpillar is wound up, it is unable to walk. I tell the child that "it cannot move to find a leaf, build a cocoon, and transform into a beautiful butterfly." I use this as a metaphor about how children can have overwhelming disturbing feelings and thoughts within parts of themselves, and how important it is to work in concert to resolve negative thoughts and feelings so they can grow up to become beautiful people.

Another metaphor that can symbolize the importance of internal coconsciousness, cooperation, and unity is the use of the child's favorite team activity. Every player on the team needs to attend to the rules of the game, do what he is expected to do, and coordinate with other team members in order to play the game successfully. I emphasize that these same principles apply to the child's internal team. The child can draw a picture of his or her self-states while cooperatively engaging in a favorite activity to instill a visual representation of internal teamwork (Waters, 2011).

The child's favorite dessert can also be used as a metaphor to symbolize equal respect, value, and unity between all parts of the child. For example, I explain that all of the ingredients in the cookie recipe are equally important and need to be blended together to make the cookie delicious. If one ingredient is left out, the cookie will not taste as good.

Eight-year-old Miranda chose pumpkin pie as her favorite dessert. Miranda had an internal state that was named Miranda Sue after her birth mom, Sue. Miranda Sue was still grieving the loss of her birth mom and resisted attachment to her adoptive mom. I suggested that Miranda make an audio recording of a farewell letter to her birth mother to help resolve her grief and loss. Miranda, speaking for Miranda Sue, said in her clear, sweet voice, "Mom Sue, I love you and missed you very much. I know you wanted to take care of me but you just couldn't do it because of your problems. When I get older I hope to see you." (As indicated in Chapter 6, she visited her birth mother when she was 16 years old.) Then, Miranda surprised me and said, "We are going to put extra pumpkin in the pie. Miranda Sue is the pumpkin in the pie and that means extra love!" I said, "Does that mean that she will accept your adoptive mom now?" Miranda smiled and with a lilt in her voice said, "Yes." Then, in a more serious tone, Miranda apologized to her adoptive mom, saying, "Mom, I am sorry for all of the times that I yelled at you and did not listen to you. Miranda Sue now accepts you and she is the pumpkin in the pie and she loves you now!" This simple exercise became a transformative moment.

Using Miranda's favorite dessert as a symbol for internal unity helped Miranda be able to express how important Miranda Sue was to Miranda's ability to attach to her adoptive mom. Miranda Sue represented the pumpkin in the pie. The pumpkin was the essential ingredient that symbolized love and, ultimately, her ability to transfer her attachment from her birth mom to her adoptive mother.

Equal Respect Among Self-States

An important principle for gaining cooperation among self-states is to show them "equal" respect and appreciation regardless of their roles and qualities. This includes even the most destructive ones, to gain their trust and cooperation and to encourage constructive roles and behavior, as occurred with Rudy. As stated earlier, it is natural to want to favor those parts of the child that are helpful, positive, and pleasant but this can create internal competition and jealousy, and resistance to comply with caregivers. Silberg (2013) encourages children to write a thank-you note to their self-states, even those who were initially viewed as threatening, a practice that I have also employed. Parents can also participate in this exercise.

A Collaborative Approach When Conducting an Intervention

Another important principle when working with dissociative children is to encourage a collaborative approach between children and their internal systems when conducting an intervention. Although some self-states may not be capable of participating in some of the exercises due to their age or lack of understanding, it is still important to have their awareness and acceptance so they will not sabotage the activity. For example, if a younger part is incapable of doing schoolwork or playing baseball, then that part should not be present during that activity. Instead, the younger part can be encouraged to stay inside and observe or be placed in an internal nursery until the self-state is old enough to participate. Some parts that are not directly involved in the activity can be "cheerleaders" supporting the child's performance.

Imaginative and simple interventions can be employed to help dissociative children not be influenced or disrupted by self-states. For example, I worked with an 8-year-old girl, Pamela, who had a baby state that would cry and interfere with Pamela's ability to pay attention in school. Pamela also had a self-state that acted as an internal mother. I suggested that Pamela create an internal nursery that was completely soundproof where the internal mother could care for the baby while Pamela was in school. Pamela was able to imagine this and create this nursery in her mind with the cooperation of the internal mother, who was pleased to help. After this simple intervention, Pamela's baby self-state no longer disturbed Pamela and her school performance improved.

Synchronization of Circadian Rhythms Across Self-States

When self-states are not synchronized with the child, persistent problems can occur with sleep, eating, and elimination. For example, I have encountered many children with self-states that are on opposite sleep cycles from the child. A child may think she is sleeping through the night, but a self-state may awaken and roam about unbeknownst to the child. Children have reported being so sleepy during the day that they have fallen asleep during class. It is also problematic to have self-states roaming around at night. These nocturnal self-states may engage in destructive behavior in the home or delinquent activities outside of the home without the youth's awareness or control. One 9-year-old girl's self-state got up in the middle of the night, went into the bathroom, and sprayed a caustic aerosol on her arms, burning them—an act committed by the child's perpetrating state. A 4-year-old boy's self-state would sneak out of his bed, go into the bathroom, squirt toothpaste on the sink and floor, break the toothbrushes, and spread hand cream on the wall—a symbolic reenactment of violence he witnessed in his home. An adolescent male's self-state broke into a house in the early morning hours to steal money to supply his drug habit. None of these children were aware that they had engaged in these destructive behaviors.

Having a child's self-states be aware of bodily functions related to eating and elimination can prevent serious health problems. If the child and self-states do not share physical sensations associated with these functions, the child can develop eating disorders or experience embarrassing episodes of soiling. I have had dissociative children either binge or starve themselves due to: (a) depersonalization—numbing of the body and unawareness of such harm; (b) a controlling influence of an infant or young self-states that were unable to eat much; (c) a controlling self-state that was unaware of the deleterious impact of restricting food (Waters, 2005); or (d) an unconscious motive related to some cognitive distortion that caused the self-state to binge or refuse to eat, such as with Sarah in Chapter 13.

Interventions to promote synchronization of daily rhythms with self-states should be geared toward identifying self-states that are impairing these rhythms to help them understand the seriousness of their behavior and enlist their cooperation. This entails *exploring with relevant self-states their underlying motivations* that can involve distorted cognitions and fears, nefarious activity, and avoidance of disturbing situations, traumatic triggers, and phobic reactions, that is, related to feeling the body that remind them of sexual and physical abuse. An agreement with those self-states to implement alternative, healthy responses is critical to achieving equilibrium with the child and preventing possible disastrous results. Sometimes, the reasons can be benign and involve self-states but disrupt the child's functioning. One such example is of Cathy's self-state, Little Sister, in Chapter 8.

BUILDING EMPOWERMENT

Dissociative children often feel defeated, helpless, and immobilized due to sensitization to minor triggers in their environment, increasing maladaptive patterns of behavior. Also self-states can experience much internal confusion affecting their perception of their environment, engaging them in dissociative behaviors that reinforce their feelings of helplessness, and placing them at risk for revictimization. It is important that this cycle be broken so that these children can feel present and empowered to assess their current environment accurately, vocalize their feelings and thoughts constructively, and engage in safe actions. Building a child's sense of self-efficacy with simple empowerment strategies that help the child stay present and feel strong can begin to break the automatic cycle of helplessness and increase assertiveness. Repetitive practice of these strategies will help create healthy neural networks (Perry, 2006) and enhance children's ability to use these strategies when under duress.

Principles for Using Empowerment Strategies

When treating dissociative children, special considerations, including presence of self-states, are needed for effectiveness of empowerment techniques to be achieved. The following are some principles to consider:

1. *Empowerment activities should be developmentally appropriate and encourage socialization.*
   Peer activities, such as organized sports and clubs (e.g., scouts, chess, Lego, forensics, drama), can motivate dissociative children to stay present, grounded, develop socialization skills, and learn teamwork. Peer activities can also help children learn problem solving and enhance their affective and cognitive skills. As traumatized children develop socialization skills and receive positive feedback, they will feel more empowered to manage conflicts without dissociating.
2. *Elicit cooperation from self-states before engaging in an activity to avoid a part of the child sabotaging the activity.*
   Ask the child to check inside to see whether all parts agree and can participate in a particular empowerment strategy. If there is a part that is not in favor of it, or unable to participate due to a younger age, then negotiate with the part to not interfere and instead to use

the four Ls, or go to an internal safe room while the child is engaged in the activity. In return, the child can offer the nonparticipating part to have time in an activity that he or she enjoys. For example, if a teenager likes to write poetry to express feelings when stressed, but another part of the self would rather work out, then they can negotiate to alternate these activities.

3. *Use people who the child admires, including hero figures, role models, or spiritual figures who the child can draw strength from when anxious or facing new challenges.*

First, discuss with the child the qualities the child likes in a role model. The child can draw a picture of the figure and/or himself or herself having these qualities, and make up a story or poem about how the child will use the qualities to help deal with stress. These hero figures can later be used when processing traumatic events. Ryan, an 8-year-old sexually abused boy with DID first introduced in Chapter 2, and his self-states had Superman as their hero figure (Waters, 2015). When Ryan had to have surgery, he was given permission to wear a T-shirt with the Superman emblem on it under his hospital gown to help him feel strong. Many of his drawings included the Superman emblem. He also had an internal helper, "Super Ryan," who combined Superman's qualities with Native American clothing. See Figure 7.3 of Super Ryan's drawing with lots of "S" emblems, a colorful cape, and a feathered headdress.

Eddie, an 8-year-old boy with OSDD who was sexually abused by his stepbrother, was a frail, frightened child when I first met him. He incorporated within himself the cartoon hero figure, Bettle Borg, a strong, brave character that regularly faces his archenemies. Eddie drew himself very large with Bettle Borg in the upper left corner infusing power throughout Eddie's body. Eddie wrote, "The Bettle Borgs are giving me power to be strong" (Figure 7.4). In trauma processing, Eddie continued to use the image of Bettle Borg to give him the courage he needed to express his rage toward his stepbrother during EMDR therapy (use of EMDR is discussed in Chapter 12).

4. *Involve as many senses as possible in empowerment activities.*

The more sensory domains are involved, the more neurological connections are made. These connections can strengthen children's ability to use what they have learned in other activities. For example, movement combined with music, such as marching and singing a song of empowerment that the child composed, is one way to engage

Figure 7.3 *Ryan as Super Ryan modeling Superman's powers. (Used with permission.)*

multiple senses. I will ask the child and parents to work together to compose a poem or song about the child's positive qualities and their bright future. We will then march and sing the song, as the child drums or shakes a rattle or tambourine. This fun activity is repeated often to help overcome traumatized children's dismal belief system about themselves and their future, and to instill hope. Any activity that engages the child's entire body, is playful, and engenders laughter

The Bettle Borgs are giving me power to be strong

Figure 7.4 *Eddie's cartoon hero Bettle Borg infusing him with power. (Used with permission.)*

and the opportunity to look into one another's eyes will build attachment between all involved—the child, parents, and the therapist.

Another activity that can be helpful is to have children role-play themselves as hero figures expressing positive feelings and thoughts about themselves and how strong the self was to survive the traumatic events they experienced. Again, it is important to engage all parts of the child in these activities. Creating empowerment activities that the child enjoys will enhance self-efficacy while at the same time preparing the child to master difficult situations, including trauma processing, while staying present.

5. *Practice these activities regularly.*

Encourage children to practice empowerment strategies at home and to engage regularly in organized peer activities. It is through repetition that the child begins to reframe himself from a victim to a survivor. Repetition is how healthy neural connections are formed, making it easier for the child to retain the positive feelings of empowerment elicited by these strategies.

6. *Support the child's progress in gaining competency in self-expression and mastery over negative affect with rewards, particularly those that engage the child and parents in playful activities to build attachment.*

I work closely with parents and encourage the use of modified therapeutic techniques for safe discharge of affect at home with rewards. Many of these activities can also promote integration. For example, the child can draw a picture of the person with whom the child is angry and discuss the drawing with his or her parents, instead of becoming destructive. They then celebrate this achievement with a fun activity that the child chooses. Blaustein and Kinniburgh (2010) outline a number of activities that the parents can do with their children to foster attachment, self-regulation, and competency.

CASE EXAMPLES

Lisa's Stabilization

When she was 5, Lisa collapsed after a temper tantrum and wailed that she missed her birth mother. She often exhibited contradictory emotions and behaviors toward her adoptive mom that were characteristic of a disorganized attachment style. For example, Lisa would attack her mother, who would withdraw, and then Lisa would run to her mom wailing for her not to leave her! Her mother would approach her and Lisa would become immobilized or strike out again. Given Lisa's contradictory attachment behavior directed only at her adoptive mother, I wondered whether her foster mother, whom she lived with since birth until adopted, was responsible for Lisa's oral trauma. Lisa's attachment disturbances, including deep-seated grief surrounding the loss of her birth mother, her oral trauma present when adopted, and subsequent posttraumatic stress disorder (PTSD) and dissociation, would need to be resolved before she could accept her adoptive mother and gain control over her affect and behavior.

Lisa's Self-States

Lisa exhibited severe memory problems, such as an inability to immediately recognize her parents and sisters, and amnesia for her disruptive behavior and completed homework. In therapy, Lisa began to disclose internal auditory and visual hallucinations. She described hearing a baby crying who she called "Mary." She also identified two other self-states: Helper, a maternal figure that cared for the baby, and Shadow, who held her feelings of helplessness, fear, hurt, loss, and abandonment. When Lisa would explode and later have little or no memory of her behavior, she learned that an angry self-state "Cindy" was present at that time. Lisa's erratic behavior began to make sense as we learned more about the presence of these self-states that frequently appeared and disappeared.

When Lisa decompensated and screamed that she wanted to be left alone, her mother would leave. When her mom walked away, Mary, the baby state, wailed and Lisa would run after her mother begging her not to go away. When her mother walked back toward her to comfort her, Lisa switched to angry Cindy, who would strike out at her mother and run away again. Switching from one state to another was accompanied with significant amnesia, resulting in a confusing, chaotic life that adversely affected her ability to attach to her mother. Lisa felt much despondency and finally run to her room sobbing that she wanted to die or kill her parents. This pattern was repeated throughout her life, until we learned what really was behind these extreme behavioral shifts.

When Lisa first reported that she had a baby inside of her, I wanted to reassure Lisa's baby part, Mary, that she is safe now. Lisa gave a startling response, "Baby felt like it was going to die." I asked Lisa how she knew that. She simply responded, "'Cause I feel it." I asked her where she felt it and she responded, "I felt it in my heart." Lisa seemed to be reporting an implicit memory that most likely pertained to her oral trauma. I suspected that the original part of her, Mary, had experienced this trauma and felt as though she was going to die.

A startling revelation occurred from an independent evaluator who was unaware of Lisa's dissociation and baby self-state, Mary. After 4 months of treating Lisa, her mother brought her to see a chiropractor because of her poor fine motor coordination and inability to properly manipulate a fork and knife. The chiropractor discovered that Lisa had retained a primitive infant reflex called the asymmetrical tonic neck reflex (ATNR), which infants display until they are 6 months old when it normally vanishes. The reflex causes the arm and leg to turn and extend in the same direction that the head turns. The chiropractor prescribed a series of daily exercises for Lisa to train her brain to cross over the midline by having her perform alternate bilateral movements with her body. Although Lisa practiced these exercises at home, she had difficulty mastering them. I suggested that Lisa help Mary and together they would participate in these exercises that occurred. I then began to age progress Mary by having Lisa hold and rock a doll representing Mary. During this intervention, I emphasized that Mary was safe and loved and could grow. Lisa quickly "outgrew" this primitive reflex. The chiropractor was intrigued to learn that Lisa's abnormal neurological symptoms were rooted in a dissociated baby state.

All parts of Lisa were oriented to her present reality by looking through Lisa's eyes and noticing that they were a part of Lisa's body and were now living in a loving home. The cue phrase "Get it together" was often used to increase internal cooperation. Lisa agreed to create an internal nursery for Mary where she could feel safe and Helper was enlisted to care for her. The nursery was supplied with stuffed animals, music, television, crackers, milk, a crib, a ball, a bathtub, dolls, and a rocking chair so that Mary could be rocked. However, when Lisa's mother, Sandy, wanted to hold Lisa, she threw a fit and disclosed that it was Mary who did not want to be held. Lisa was asked to reassure Mary that her mother would not hurt her and that the rocking would help Mary grow up feeling loved and positive about herself. After this information was shared internally, Mary became more receptive to being held by Lisa's mother.

Lisa's angry self-state, Cindy, agreed to release her rage in an internal, soundproof anger room in which she could draw pictures of her anger, and yell and scream. Lisa learned from Helper and Shadow that they became scared when Lisa watched television. As a solution, they agreed to go to their own internal shielded rooms whenever Lisa watched television. (Although Helper and Shadow portrayed adult roles, it is clear they were really children.) When Lisa, herself, felt as though she was going to explode, the word "bubble" was used to cue her to take deep breaths, and then to go to her room to read or play her flute. With these interventions, conflicts between Lisa and her self-states, and between Lisa and her mother, lessened. However, further stabilization could only be achieved when Lisa and all her internal parts attached to her adoptive mother. Helping Lisa to process the loss of her biological mother was the next step in achieving this goal. Lisa's case is continued in Chapter 10 on trauma processing.

Cathy's Stabilization

Cathy's words "I had to zone out everything. That's the way I lived" described how she survived her nightmarish childhood. Cathy, initially described in Chapter 4, used dissociation as her primary means of coping. As Cathy got older, her dissociative symptoms were intruding more and more on her ability to function and threatened her safety. Cathy had a reduced awareness of her environment, placing her in danger. For instance, Cathy went to the beach with some friends and walked into a beach fire, burning her foot.

In a family session, Cathy's mother, Jane, reported that Cathy was dissociating frequently and was unable to recall a sequence of chores that she had given her. Her mother reported that she would have to ask Cathy to do one chore at a time; otherwise, Cathy could not recall what she was supposed to do. Even then, Cathy would often forget what she was doing and just stand there staring. Cathy tearfully told her mother how she got really scared, because she lost awareness even when she walked from the table to the sink. Cathy told her mother, "I feel weird—not right." Cathy, a very bright, articulate girl, pithily explained the gravity of her dissociation, "When I lived with dad, I had to zone everything out. That's the way I lived. Now, it's dangerous. It became a habit. It was a good habit back then because I could zone out and forget about what was going on. Now, it is a bad habit. Now, I have to think about what's going on around me."

I became concerned that Cathy's dissociation was more severe than what I had originally thought it was when her mother complained that the dog was missing for hours, and Cathy had no memory of letting the dog out when she was alone in the house for the day. I began to explore more about her memory problems and she revealed seeing flashing lights.

Cathy's Flashing Lights

Therapist: "Cathy please go inside of your mind and see if you can figure out what happened that might account for your memory problems."

Cathy: *(closing her eyes)* "I hear voices in my head. Sometimes I hear my dad and it throws me off and I don't remember what I am doing."

Therapist: "Do you know what the voices sound like and what they say?"

Cathy: "They tell me that I am worthless and I don't belong here. I see something there and then it's not there all of a sudden. Then I see a flash of light."

Therapist: "Can you tell me more about what that is like?"

Cathy: *(in a solemn voice)* "The voices are there one moment and I stare off and then I am back (to the present). It's like I am in a whole different world. I hear a kid's voice that sounds like Justin [her brother] and I hear a little kid's voice screaming, 'I need help!'"

Therapist: "How often do you hear these voices?"

Cathy: "I hear them almost daily. Sometimes when I am out [in a different world], I get a headache. When I'm starting to come back to reality, I have these flashes of light and I'm back in this world."

Therapist: "Is there something that happens before you go to this other world?"

Cathy: "If a person is going to pick on me, I go back there and they (internal voices) tell me, 'It's going to be okay.' I think they want to talk. Do you think they have problems too? One of them is my dad. He's not a helper."

I indicated that it does appear that the voices have problems too. I proposed that they may have taken some of the abuse to help her, have lots of mixed-up feelings and thoughts about it, and need help to deal with it. I suggested that sometimes the ones who sound really angry and say mean things to her may have taken the worst of her dad's abuse; they may have so much anger that they do not know how to manage it. I reassured her that we would work together to get to know all parts of her and to understand them. I stressed that her mind created these parts to help her when she had no one to rescue her, and noted how scared and helpless she must have felt. I concluded that we would work together to figure out what the voices did to help her, and see whether we could help all parts of her so that all of them can get along. Cathy listened intently and then breathed a deep sigh of relief with a slight smile on her face. I could see her shoulders start to relax.

In our next session, Cathy revealed more about her self-states:

Therapist: "Can you tell me what you noticed about what's going on inside of your mind?"

In a quiet, thoughtful tone, Cathy began to tell me her internal experiences.

Cathy: "One sounds like my dad. He's not nice. The others are nice. There's a little kid that sounds like me when I was smaller. One sounds like my mom trying to save me."

Therapist: "What do you make of those voices?"

Cathy: "I think the one that sounds like my dad took the most [abuse], and the one that sounds like my brother took the least. One that sounds like me took the second most. One that sounds like my mom got me out of the stuff. She helped me." She paused and thought for a moment and then resumed speaking, "Is it possible that the little girl that's screaming is feeling things?"

Therapist: "Yes, I think she may be feeling afraid."

Cathy said in a plaintive voice, "I think she might not know we're out of it. That it's over."

Therapist: "Yes, I think you may be right. Sometimes, they can still be stuck in the moment of when it happened. Have you told all parts of your mind about the here and now and that the abuse is over?"

Cathy: "I tried, but it seems like they're sleeping. Can they sleep?"

Therapist: "That's possible. What makes you think they're sleeping?"

Cathy chuckled and with a twinkle in her eye, she said, "I hear snoring and they don't seem to be there."

I smiled, admiring Cathy's reflective abilities. She could articulate what she was experiencing internally, while relating to me her knowledge and impressions. I responded by telling her how important it was for all parts of her to be awake when she was awake, and asleep when she was asleep. This will help them to understand about the difference between the past and the present, and to learn along with her about this life. I asked her whether she could wake them up. She said she would and proceeded to close her eyes to ask them to wake up. She laughed and said, "That was Little Brother who was snoring. He didn't want to wake up but the others were awake." I encouraged her to try and wake him and she smiled, reporting, "Little Brother agreed to get up."

She resumed describing the flashing of light she sometimes saw:

Cathy: "Before I go into it, before I go into my mind, I am aware of the flashing of light. It flashes six times or once." She paused and corrected herself, saying, "Once, it didn't flash at all."

Therapist: "What is it like when you get into it?"

Cathy: "It is dark for a second. Then a light goes on or I see pictures of these people in my head or figures, but not like people, like I see you and me." She paused and in a quiet, drawn-out voice, said, "Like shadows."

Therapist: "You see shadows and then what do you experience?"

Cathy: "I jump back in my mind 'cause they get really close all of a sudden. Someone stops them from touching me."

Cathy described her dad's voice screaming at her, telling her she was worthless and her brother's voice in the background telling her dad's voice to stop screaming. Cathy continued, "Then I hear my mom saying, 'I'm here for you. I will always be there for you.' My mom is the helper. My dad's voice doesn't seem like a helper, but I think he was a big helper." She paused a moment and resumed, "I remember going away in my mind a long time ago. I saw flashes of light and heard the voice of my dad. He seemed nice then. After that, he seemed to get mean. He was yelling at me, like he had taken too much. He didn't understand. He couldn't control it. He had been there, through too much, and he became like a bully. He had to take it out on somebody else, and that somebody happened to be me."

I suggested that Cathy ask the dad's voice whether he had taken the bad stuff. She checked and reported that the dad's voice confirmed that he had done so. I then asked Cathy to thank him for helping her, which she willingly did. She said, "He said, 'It's alright,' and he seemed a little better." She began to refer to him as "The Dad," her internalized dad. He told her that he also helped her with the bullying, which surprised and pleased her. When Cathy expressed appreciation for The Dad, it was a turning point in their relationship. He became more supportive of her.

Cathy's Mind and Dual Awareness

Cathy asked in a contemplative tone, "Is it possible the voices might have their own minds?"

> **Therapist:** "What makes you wonder that?"
> **Cathy:** "They seem like when they go away, they're not there; like they're somewhere else, not in my mind. Sometimes I feel that I am there and here. I can do something while I'm in my mind, and hear the voices while I'm still here. But other times, I'm fully away. Sometimes, it's dark in the room. Sometimes it's light in the room, but before I can see I'm back."
> **Therapist:** "How long does it last when you go away?"
> **Cathy:** "The shortest is 10 seconds and the longest is about 5 minutes. It's really weird."

Sometimes, Cathy experienced dual awareness, which is a positive step toward reaching constant coconsciousness. I was amazed at Cathy's ability to quickly shift from fear to understanding and appreciation for The Dad. I asked her to tell me more about what the other parts may feel and think. She then glanced over at the chair where a special dissociative doll was sitting with little feeling dolls (see Figure 4.1 in Chapter 4 for a picture of this doll). Cathy politely asked whether she could use the doll to explain about her internal voices. I smiled at her and said, "Sure." She reached inside the pocket of the doll's head and picked out the tiny dolls. In a quiet, measured voice, Cathy explained that her internal self-states were a replica of her own family, with the addition of a 7-year-old part that she called "Little Sister," and another one called "Crystal," who was Cathy's age. She quickly identified the angry doll as The Dad. The "Inside Mom" was represented by a doll with a smile on her face. The doll with a sad expression represented "The Brother," and the doll that was in a fetal position, looking scared was named "Little Sister." The surprised doll represented Crystal who was closely connected with the Inside Mom. Cathy said that Crystal developed the Inside Mom, and both of them were helpers. She went on to explain that when her dad yelled at her, her Inside Mom would tell Little Sister, "It will be alright." Inside Mom was a replacement for her supportive mom who had been denied visitation by her adoptive father for several years. Cathy had creatively found another way to get her needs met by duplicating her mother inside of herself.

Analysis of Cathy's Self-States

It appears that Cathy created the Brother self-state to deal with the trauma of her father forcing her brother and her to fight each other. The internal brother allowed her to maintain her attachment to her actual brother through this ordeal. Little Sister was a part of Cathy that separated when she was 7 years old and was placed in the sole custody of her abusive, adoptive father. Little Sister was still living the trauma and was filled with fear, depression, and grief over the loss of her mother. Sometimes, Little Sister would appear to be Cathy's current age and other times, she would remain 7 years old. Cathy reported that she created Crystal to help her deal with the abuse, and then Crystal created Inside Mom to also help provide comfort to Cathy and Little Sister. Crystal and Inside Mom were very closely connected, and sometimes Cathy could not discern Crystal from Inside Mom. Cathy's internal system was developed to replicate her "lost" family in order to meet her emotional needs when living with her abusive father.

Cathy's Stabilization Begins

Now that I was aware of all of Cathy's self-system, the stabilization process was able to begin. Orienting all parts of Cathy, particularly Little Sister, to the current environment was critical to slowing down the flashbacks and decreasing Cathy's reliance on dissociation. Cathy and her self-states agreed to develop imaginary safe places to help them calm down. Each of them developed their own special rooms to meet their own specific desires and needs. Since it was important that communication and internal awareness occur across all of Cathy's internal parts, each of the rooms had doors to afford access between them.

To further enhance coconsciousness, I taught Cathy and her parts the two Ls—look and listen (the other two Ls had not yet been developed)—along with the corresponding hand signals to remind them to be mindful of the present. We practiced this regularly with scenarios that triggered Cathy to dissociate (e.g., teasing by peers), to build neural connections in the brain to help her stay present. I consulted with Cathy's teacher and taught her the hand signals along with the phrase "Get it together," which she could say to Cathy when she was zoning out. This proved to be effective in increasing her attentiveness at school. Her self-regulation also improved.

In Chapter 8, more stabilization techniques are described, which include contracting between self-states for safe discharge of affect, managing triggers, and further techniques to calm an overactive stress-response system.

A TEEN'S POEM

Because poetry can beautifully express feelings and add meaning in one's life, an adolescent with DID composed this eloquent poem describing the meaning of her "inside family." I conclude this chapter with this poem, which may be inspirational to other dissociative children in appreciating their internal states.

My Inside Family[2]

The darkness surrounds me
But the light still shines
Down.
The far seems farther away.
But there they are.
My friends, My family,
Held together. We, the moon
in the sky.
Though something connects
Our hearts,
It's something that can't
Be explained.

NOTES

1. See www.karpmandramatriangle.com
2. Poem is printed with permission.

8

Calming the Stress-Response System and Managing Triggers

There is no place of safety if the child is flooded with reminders
every day, or even every hour, of his or her life.
—Gaensbauer (1996, p. 19)

THE BIGGEST CHALLENGE IN STABILIZING children with complex trauma is dampening their stress-response system, which includes managing traumatic reminders. As Gaensbauer (1996) so aptly stated, these children do not feel safe when flooded with traumatic reminders even if in reality they are safe!

In Chapter 7, empowerment techniques were discussed to stabilize and build a sense of efficacy in children with dissociation. This chapter focuses on helping children to further develop their skills in self-reflection, mindfulness, and somatic awareness, along with managing triggers and learning calming techniques. This chapter also discusses contracting with self-states for new responses or roles that enhance mastery of daily skills. These techniques will improve the child's overall functioning—an integral step toward stabilizing the child for trauma processing. The ability to calm oneself in the "midst of a storm" enhances the child's sense of empowerment and will help prevent abreactions during trauma processing.

SELF-REFLECTION AND BEING GROUNDED TO THE "EARTH"

There are many mindfulness practices that can help dissociative children become more aware of their internal and external worlds—an important step in gaining mastery over their arousal. Mindfulness techniques help children calm their stress-response system when triggered. They are then able to stand back and witness what is occurring by using "higher-order" brain functions such as language and information processing.

I often talk to children about imagining that they have an extra pair of eyes looking at them to help them develop self-reflection and self-awareness of what they are "feeling in their body," what they are "noticing in their mind," and what they are "noticing around" them. For example, I ask them what the extra pair of eyes sees when they look at themselves. I use the acronym of EARTH: The E stands for an extra pair of "eyes" looking back at one's self; ARTH stand for noticing one's "affect" and "reflecting" on "thoughts" that the child is experiencing in the "here" and now. Simply put, EARTH is a shortcut word that signifies being grounded to the earth in the present moment across all sensory domains. With dissociative children, this also includes the child's internal state—the self-states—so that self-reflection is inclusive of all parts of the child.

Baita (2007, 2011) developed the Inside–Outside Technique, which involves teaching duel awareness. Children are asked to make a self-reflective drawing by using two circles. In the first circle, the child is asked to draw what others see when they look at the child. This involves the external demeanor of the child, for example, the child's behavior and affect (e.g., head down and crying). In the second circle, the child is asked to draw what she is actually experiencing "inside" of herself—the inside feelings that explain why she is crying. Baita explains that the child is the only one who knows why she is crying and it is her choice whether to disclose what is going on inside of herself. This gives the traumatized child a sense of control over what she reveals to others. When the child has known self-states, the therapist can also inquire about what the self-states are experiencing internally. This technique has been instrumental in developing reflection, including revealing the presence of self-states, finding out whether the self-states are aware of and communicate with each other and the child, and how a self-state may be impacting the child's feelings and behavior.

Awakening Bodily Sensations and Building Mindfulness Across Self-States

A dissociative child's mind can operate in two incongruent worlds—the internal world and the external world—impairing mindfulness, as highlighted with Rudy and Cathy in Chapter 7. The inner world of self-states can be highly sensitive to sensory cues, which can cause the child to become depersonalized or hypersensitive to physical sensations, as reactions of these states are often based on fear and the need for survival. When self-states are triggered, children can react in an unpredictable and often apparently bizarre manner, even though the trauma has long passed. Those in the outer world (e.g., family, teachers, peers) are often perplexed by the child's seemingly irrational reactions. When bodily sensations intrude on and disrupt the child's focus on the present moment, it is impossible for a child to be mindful of the here and now.

Connecting with bodily sensations associated with trauma is an essential portal for healing (van der Kolk, 2014). The skill of perceiving the physiological condition of the body, including muscle sensations, signals from the heart and intestines, and sensory cues in the environment, is called *interoception* (Siegel, 2010). When building mindfulness, the first task is to help the child—across all self-states—to identify somatic sensations that have been warded off and then to learn to master disturbing sensations. It is a team process of engaging self-states that contain disturbing sensations and including them in mindfulness techniques to ensure effectiveness. Building somatic literacy is needed with dissociative children so they can begin to understand and express what they are feeling.

Building Somatic Literacy

One way to build somatic literacy is through the use of flashcards depicting various emotions and scenarios to increase children's awareness of their feelings and bodily sensations, as well as the feelings and behaviors in others (Blaustein & Kinniburgh, 2010). These flashcards can be used with various self-states as well. Wieland (2008) described taking pieces of felt cloth that have the words for various bodily sensations written on them, such as *pain, cold, squeezing,* and *burning,* and asking the child to choose what he is feeling in his body. I have expanded this idea and cut a piece of fabric in the shape of the child's body. The child is then asked to place the pieces of felt representing different body sensations on the area of the fabric where the child is feeling a sensation. I have also outlined the child's body on a large piece of paper and have the child color sections of the paper to signify where the child felt the bodily sensations. The different sensations can be represented by different colors. A modified version is to have the child draw a symbolic representation of his body and fill in where he feels different emotions and sensations with words or colors that signify those emotions or sensations. During these exercises, identifying different self-states that have these body sensations and noting them can help the clinician to engage them later in exercises to master disturbing sensations.

A female adolescent with two different states painted a picture that showed a split within herself. She showed that one side of her held rage by using black and purple for head and body with a red eye and red, sharp teeth. She colored the other side of her body with blue to signify the depression she felt. She also seemed to have some feeling of hope as she made the top of her head yellow with a yellow sun above her, countering the dark purple and black moon on the other side (Figure 8.1).

Ryan (Waters, 2015), a sexually abused 9-year-old boy with DID, was asked to draw colored shapes to represent his feelings about his sexual abuse. At 9 years old, Ryan did not have conscious memory of the anal

Figure 8.1 *Adolescent's painting of her two self-states. (Used with permission.)*

penetration that he had reported to me when he was 3 during his earlier episode of treatment. However, unconsciously he drew a symbolic figure of a human body representing himself with different shapes and colors related to what he felt in his body. He wrote the feeling that each colored shape represented. His mother and I looked on in amazement as these interlocking shapes portrayed his anal penetration by a stick. Significantly, a rectangular shape in the genital area signified the stick that was inserted that he labeled feeling "pane" (pain), and below that was a figure of a stop sign that he labeled "scareding" (scared). Ryan narrated what had transpired and his desire for it to stop. The round shape that would symbolize his face was colored black, indicating that he felt "imbarst" (embarrassed). The heart-shaped figure represented his heart that felt "hart" (hurt). From the top to bottom of his symbolic self, he listed his feelings as bad, sad, embarrassed, angry, ashamed, hurt, pain, and scared (Figure 8.2).

After the child draws a symbolic representation of what he is feeling in his body, you can ask him to role-play events that trigger these disturbing feelings and somatic reactions along a continuum of least to

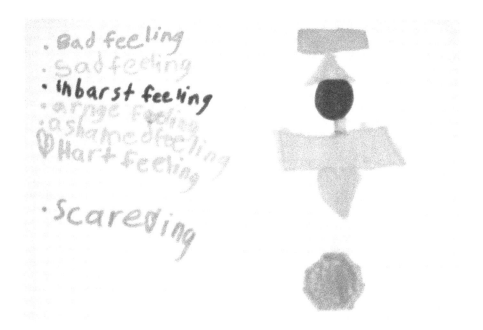

Figure 8.2 *Ryan's drawing of his feelings about his sexual abuse. (Used with permission.)*

the most intense to expand his window of tolerance for emotions and sensations. During the role-play, the child is asked to be aware of where he notices feelings in his body. Once he is in touch with what he is feeling, the next step is to expand the child's window of tolerance for feelings and sensations.

Expanding the Window of Tolerance

Siegel (1999, 2010) discusses the "window of tolerance," a state in which a person can manage sensory arousal effectively. At the outside of one side of the window of tolerance, the child experiences high arousal and is overwhelmed and flooded with affect. At the outside of the other side of the window, the child has low levels of arousal and is numb or dissociates.

Children with complex trauma can rapidly move out of their window of tolerance, vacillating between being flooded with affect and being shut down and numb. When one moves toward the outer edge of the window of tolerance, one moves closer to chaos or rigidity, resulting in a loss of a sense of balance and harmonious functioning. Teaching children calming and mindfulness techniques as they begin to move out of their window of tolerance is critical for returning to homeostasis, as well as for preventing future destabilization. Connecting with his or her body can be triggering, as even pleasant sensations can be threatening to a traumatized child. Thus, moving cautiously is recommended. Struik (2014) provides a worksheet for children to list the things that take them outside of their window of tolerance, and once outside of their window of tolerance, what helps them calm down. A number of clinicians (Levine, 2010; Ogden & Fisher, 2015; Ogden, Minton, & Pain, 2006; Siegel, 2010) encourage clients to move beyond the center (a comfortable physiological state) of their window of tolerance to gain mastery over uncomfortable levels of arousal, which are often associated with a traumatic event. Levine, Ogden and Fisher, and Ogden et al. recommend a technique called *pendulation* or *oscillation* in sensorimotor psychotherapy. In this technique, clients move back and forth in increments from the center of their window of tolerance while focusing on the sequence of minute physiological reactions that elicit a mild to an increased level of disturbing sensations as they move toward the edges of their tolerance and back to the center. Based on the individual's movements, the therapist may ask the client to expand a movement to notice what the body wants to release that was aborted during the traumatic event, that is, the need to push the perpetrator away. This helps them master their arousal and achieve reorganization. The body becomes the portal for healing the traumatic event thus releasing tension and completing the act of self-defense; this is better than a top-down approach using cognitive therapy to talk about the event (van der Kolk, 2014).

Siegel (2010) created a mindfulness exercise in which clients are asked to alternate back and forth between focusing on their breath and noticing their bodily sensations and external stimuli. Similar techniques include the "affect dial" that has been used with eye movement desensitization and reprocessing (EMDR) therapy (Chapter 12). The affect dial can be imagined as the on/off button on a television remote control. This can be utilized by the child and self-states to manage in increments with the on/off buttons the levels of disturbing images, thoughts, and emotions (Forgash & Copeley, 2008; Kluft, 1993). Daitch (2007) describes numerous hypnotic interventions for developing mindfulness, increasing sensory awareness, and dialing down reactivity, all of which are adaptable to children and adolescents with complex trauma.

I combine many of the techniques mentioned earlier with the concept of EARTH. I have children initially focus on pleasant sensations to help them feel more comfortable in their bodies as they move to feeling more difficult sensations. With EARTH, after the child describes the sensations, the child is asked to describe any thoughts associated with the sensations. This provides the opportunity to help children with any distortions they may have about their self and their body. The key is to practice these exercises along the continuum from pleasant to more aversive sensations and engage relevant self-states by using different scenarios that elicit these sensations. In these exercises, children learn to step back and witness what they are experiencing rather than becoming immersed and overwhelmed by it. This helps children widen their window of tolerance while also providing the opportunity to reframe any cognitive distortions they may have about their body and themselves. Through repetition, the window of tolerance expands and the child learns to become mindful without becoming numb or hyperaroused.

This practice can be employed with different modalities such as play therapy, imagery, hypnosis, and EMDR. Figure 8.3 is a symbolic facial representation that depicts expanding the window of tolerance and combining the acronym EARTH (also reproduced in Appendix D).

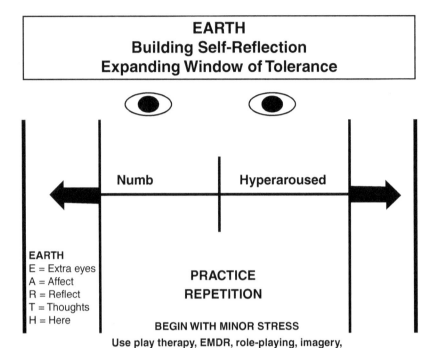

Figure 8.3 *EARTH: Building self-reflection and expanding window of tolerance.*
© Waters, F. 2015.

Incorporating Physical Exercise for Regulating Affect and Increasing Mindfulness

Incorporating physical exercise to build affect regulation, increase mindfulness, and also expand window of tolerance is essential for calming down the overactive stress response system. Intense aerobic exercise that involves balance, coordination, and major muscle groups can raise endorphins and helps severely traumatized, dissociative children become more connected to their body. Tara (introduced in Chapter 3) who drew the sexualized picture of herself with large, vacant eyes was one of the most highly dysregulated children I have ever treated. Every sound she heard caused her to jump, and it was nearly impossible to calm her enough to participate in therapy. Tara went to respite care several times a week to give her adoptive mother, a single parent, a break. The respite parents had just bought a trampoline and Tara bounced on it for 2 hours! When the respite care father came home, he did not think Tara was still there because she would typically be "bouncing in his face," but instead was calmly sitting watching television, something she had never been able to do earlier! This intense exercise increased her endorphins and helped her release tension. It also helped her to be aware of her body so that she could balance herself and master gymnastic movements on the trampoline. Because of its calming effect, Tara's adoptive mother bought her a trampoline and she jumped on it before and after school, even during the winter with her coat and boots on. Her mother gladly shoveled the snow off the trampoline! Tara's window of tolerance expanded. She calmed down considerably and was able to participate in therapy—a major achievement for her, as previously she was literally "bouncing off the walls."

Yoga has recently received much acclaim for calming the stress-response system in traumatized individuals (Danylchuk, 2015; van der Kolk, 2014). Martial arts also helps clients to connect with the body and to build a sense of empowerment, as this was beneficial to Briana, highlighted throughout this book, and helped her become centered.

There are a number of other techniques that can help the child self-regulate. Sensory motor affect regulation therapy (SMART; Warner, Cook, Westcott, & Koomar, 2011) combines a variety of therapeutic approaches, including trauma-focused sensorimotor and family psychotherapy by using props such as mini-trampolines, large foam pillows, and weighted blankets, to help children self-regulate and experience comfort. Anne Schmitter-Boeckelmann has a hammock in her office to rock and calm highly disorganized, dissociative children (personal communication, March 15, 2013). When possible, she has the parent rock the child to enhance attachment.

Instead of a typical time-out, I have asked parents to provide a "comfort corner" where their traumatized child can retreat. I instruct parents to outfit the comfort corner with soft pillows and blankets, music, and drawing supplies to provide a soothing sensory experience to help calm the child. In sessions, I offer children squishy toys to play with when they are anxious in the sessions and have them focus on the sensations of manipulating them.

Case Example: Cathy

Cathy, whose case was discussed in Chapter 7, had depersonalized as a result of aversive assaults to her body (e.g., forced to take cold showers, made to sleep in wet clothes, being placed for hours in an unheated storage room, being beaten and screamed at frequently). Her self-states developed different roles to manage these traumatic events, and their participation in mindfulness techniques was critical to Cathy's ability to avoid depersonalization and hyperarousal. Because much of Cathy's sensory disturbances were contained in Little Sister, engaging Little Sister with Cathy in the techniques was paramount to their effectiveness. The other self-states agreed to cheer them on during the exercise and comfort Little Sister. With all parts of Cathy onboard, sensory techniques were practiced during therapy sessions and at home. The exercises focused initially on pleasant sensations in the "here" and "now" to awaken Little Sister's somatic senses. After this was mastered, the pendulation technique was used in therapy. Cathy and Little Sister, with support of the other self-states, moved back and forth from pleasant to distressing sensory stimuli while noticing bodily sensations.

Because Cathy had experienced years of her father incessantly screaming in her face, Cathy and Little Sister would blank out visually when an angry person came close to Cathy or yelled at her. Cathy needed to overcome this automatic defense response and "reawaken" her visual and auditory skills. To encourage this process, Cathy and Little Sister practiced listening to music they enjoyed and identifying the lyrics and musical instruments involved. Cathy was a gifted singer and enjoyed singing along as well. To work on improving visual mindfulness, we would look outside of my office windows and observe the forest with its sloping hillside and creek. I asked Cathy to describe what she saw. She described how sunlight and shadows played on the trees; she noted the shapes and colors of the leaves, the wildflowers on the hillside, and the sounds of the creek, birds, and squirrels. We would use pleasant activities such as these to build her auditory and visual awareness. I then moved to having her imagine angry people shouting at her from a distance and then in close proximity.

To help Cathy reconnect to her physical self, I asked her to close her eyes as I placed objects with different textures, shapes, and temperatures in her hands, on her arms and on her face, and asked her to identify their characteristics. When she was able to feel these objects, I had her imagine someone suddenly touching her shoulders (a reminder of her father shaking her) with her and Little Sister staying present while tracking bodily sensations. Cathy enjoyed the challenge. Using the pendulation technique and shifting her focus back and forth from pleasant to trauma-related sensations, Cathy began to master troubling sensory triggers. She and Little

Sister began to gain mastery over their traumatic sensory experiences, and Cathy's window of tolerance increased without her becoming hyper-aroused or numb.

Incorporating Music and Psychodrama for Regulating Affect and Increasing Mindfulness

Music and psychodrama can be a highly effective way to calm hyper-aroused and fearful children, and increase mindfulness and feeling of empowerment to help them to overcome their fears. Since Cathy enjoyed singing, using music and drama to regulate affect and increase mindfulness was helpful. One technique I used to help her regulate emotions was employing musical instruments that were played softly and loudly as a gauge for Cathy to determine the level of emotions she felt about current stressful and nonstressful events. She played the drum with degrees of loudness and rhythmic intensity that represented degrees and types of emotions she felt, such as happy, sad, angry, hurt, scared, and ashamed. She would beat the drum while depicting how her various self-states felt as well. It was an engaging and entertaining activity that increased sensitivity and awareness across all her parts, while widening her window of tolerance to stressful situations.

In addition, we talked about what she and her self-states needed to decrease negative emotions and increase positive emotions to better manage triggers. Cathy and her self-states agreed that they would each go to their safe place (each went to their internal bedrooms) in combination with deep breathing for a few seconds, instead of dissociating when she felt hurt and anxious due to being teased. We then practiced her doing this while she imagined being teased so that Cathy could remain present and calm.

Psychodrama in which children tell their stories by acting them out is another sensorimotor technique that can be very healing and empowering (Palidofsky & Stolbach, 2012). Rewriting a script of a desired outcome can also be healing. Psychodrama described in Chapter 6 on Rudy's family was very effective in resolving conflicts and installing new ways to behave, particularly around mealtimes.

A person who inspired me in my work was an Israeli art teacher, Shachar Bar, who works at a Kubbutz in Israel. Shachar Bar became concerned after children in her class were showing signs of posttraumatic stress during the Kassame rocket attacks. Shachar Bar observed, "They were getting hysterical when the alarm sounded—some freezing in place, unable to seek cover" (HaLevi, 2008). She composed a marching song that integrated forms of sensorimotor psychotherapy, mindfulness therapy, and bilateral stimulation from EMDR therapy to help the children feel empowered. In the beginning of the song, the children mimicked the sounds of the alarm system. They then moved to recognizing their physiological reactions while they sought shelter under the tables and chairs while singing.

> *My heart is pounding, boom, ba-ba, boom, boom, boom,*
> *My body is shaking, doom, da-da, doom, doom, doom.*

The children ended the song, allowing their bodies to shake and release the built-up tension while standing and singing:

> *Our body we shake, shake, shake,*
> *Our legs we loosen, loosen, loosen.*
> *Breathe deep, blow far,*
> *Breathe deep, now we can laugh.*

By facing and mastering their terror of the bombings, and then physiologically releasing bodily tension, the children were able to seek cover and their posttraumatic stress disorder (PTSD) symptoms subsided.

I used a marching song to help Maggie and Michael, who were introduced in Chapter 7 when discussing the 4 Ls. Both Maggie and Michael suffered severe dissociative symptoms as a result of significant abuse by their father beginning in infancy. Many times a day, they would freeze, lose time, become combative, or scream in terror, even though they had been protected from their abuser for several years. Their highly sensitized arousal systems were constantly activated, impairing their ability to perform basic self-care such as dressing. Their mother and I composed a marching song that contained the elements of their trauma, the emotions that were held in their parts, their physiological reactions, and their present safety. I gave both of them drums to use while all of us marched around my office and sang the song.

In the beginning, Maggie would hardly move and only whispered the words. We repeated the march on a regular basis. After several weeks, the transformation with Maggie was profound. She marched with vigor, sang loudly, and drummed with emotion. Maggie and Michael would take turns standing on my footstool while proclaiming their feelings in strong, loud voices. They would then laugh with a sense of empowerment. When fear can be replaced with laughter and relaxation, then the stress-response system becomes more regulated and children can think better and are less sensitized to triggers. Over time, Maggie and Michael's highly reactive systems began to become less reactive and they were able to better master their fears. They also dissociated less, felt more empowered, and tolerated being around strangers when their mother was not at their side—a major accomplishment for them!

Let us examine how to help dissociative children to increase their capacity to manage traumatic triggers.

MANAGING TRAUMATIC TRIGGERS
AND THE ROLE OF SELF-STATES

When working with dissociative children, it is critical to not only know what the trigger was but also what part or parts of the self may have been triggered, along with the part's connection to the original trauma(s).

As described in Chapter 7, Rudy looked down and in a quiet voice told his father, "My invisible team told me to do it." Rudy had suddenly lunged at his sister, tackled her, and choked her. What prompted Rudy to suddenly leap from the comfort of his father's lap and attack his sister? He and his family had just finished watching a classic, endearing American family television program, *The Waltons*, about a family who homesteaded in the mountains of Virginia during the depression and World War II. In the episode they had just watched, the father hunted and killed an animal to feed his family. This innocuous scene triggered Rudy's hungry invisible team to want to kill his sister for "meat." As previously noted, once the motivation of his self-states was understood, I had Rudy tell his invisible team that there was plenty of food for them to eat in their adoptive home and ask them to share in the gustatory experience of eating with him at home. Rudy's mother brought snacks to the session and Rudy and his invisible team shared eating the snack, which satisfied their hunger. This ended their "homicidal behaviors." These simple but powerful interventions brought Rudy and his invisible team in alignment with current reality and in partnership with each other—an important first step toward integration. Knowing the underlying motivations of a dissociative child's triggered behavior is the key to finding effective resolutions.

Gaining Control Over Triggers

Gaining control over a triggering event involves eight main overlapping tasks: (a) exploring what the child (and/or self-state) felt in his body that informs him that he was distressed; (b) exploring what the trigger was in the environment that elicited strong reactions by examining sensory cues; (c) exploring the influence of any self-states that may have been triggered by the sensory cues; (d) exploring how the trigger relates to the original trauma, and what the self-state's "underlying motive" was for the strong reaction; (e) orienting the child and the self-state to present reality; (f) negotiating with the child and the self-state for safe alternative solutions to manage the "underlying motive" and provide them with comfort; (g) practicing deep breathing and containment exercises; and (h) practicing alternative solutions with the participation of the relevant self-state.

Determining what in the environment may be triggering the child can be a challenging task. Often, dissociative children do not have a clear understanding of the triggering process and may lack conscious awareness of internal states that may become activated. Children may even lack knowledge of the original traumatic episode, because it may have been laid down in the preverbal or sensory motor memory system, or the information may be contained in a self-state of which the child is unaware. The child may simply report suddenly feeling propelled into the survival mode. When in a state of high arousal, the higher brain centers are deactivated and the sympathetic and parasympathetic anatomical nervous systems are activated in the fight, fight or freeze stress response (Chapter 1). When this happens, children are unable to self-reflect and discern whether their concerns are reality based. Instead, dissociative children often resort to maladaptive survival behaviors that often appear bizarre and confusing to others.

It is critical to methodically inquire about the triggering event and the associated sensory cues—sights, sounds, touches, and smells—along with any internal feelings. It is also important to inquire about the influence of self-states who may be involved in the defensive reaction. Once these are known, the therapist can begin to work with the child and self-states to "break" the chain reaction of the automatic defensive response that occurs with exposure to triggers.

Determining what has triggered the child often entails a meticulous exploration of what transpired just "seconds" before the shift (Silberg, 2013).

Children usually will not be able to tell you; so, tenacious probing may be necessary. For example, the clinician may need to ask different versions of the same question in the hope that one may open the child's mind to find the answer. A sensitive inquiry of "when," "where," "what," and "how" questions, along with questions about sensory cues, can begin to illuminate connections between triggering events and the child's traumatic past. Playing a therapeutic detective role with the child's assistance is a helpful analogy to uncovering traumatic reminders (Silberg, 2013). Questions related to what transpired within the child's mind such as auditory and visual hallucinations, internal conflicts, disturbing bodily sensations and thoughts, or any upsetting environmental reminders will provide valuable information about what instigates these shifts. For example, simply asking the child to notice any sensory reminders and exploring the inside of her mind for any internal influences, or parts, affected by the sensory stimulus may recapture what happened moments before the child reacted to the trigger and perhaps shifted into another self-state. Sometimes, I ask the child to draw the scene of what transpired just before she acted out, as this visual depiction can facilitate a recall of the traumatic trigger.

If the child identifies a self-state that was triggered, it is important to explore the self-state's awareness of present reality, as that part may still be "living" in the traumatic environment. If that is the case, the state will need to be "relocated" from the traumatic scene to the current safe environment and, if need be, placed in an imaginary internal safe room for security. The dissociative child or adolescent along with his or her caretaker can then be taught to comfort and educate self-states and reassure them about the safety of their current environment, as described with Rudy's invisible team and baby state (described in Chapters 4 and 7). Interventions that meet the safety needs of the child and self-states will minimize or eliminate triggers.

In Cathy's case, she was triggered by touch, particularly rough and unexpected touch, and loud voices due to physical and emotional abuse by her adoptive father. When he noticed that Cathy had zoned out, Cathy reported that he would shake her "to get me out of it." Her adoptive father did not tolerate her dissociating. There was no escape for Cathy when he was present. A different part, Little Sister, would surface during these traumatic episodes and so was triggered by similar stimuli. For example, Cathy was triggered when her new stepfather yelled at her to do chores. When he recognized that she was frozen, he stopped yelling and talked to her calmly. He told me what happened, saying, "She lost it, crying, freaking out, and covering her face. It took a long time, a few hours, before she came out of it. She had a flashback." Little Sister felt terrified and helpless. She released a flood of tears that she was unable to safely express when residing with her adoptive father. Her mother and stepfather were able to comfort Cathy though, at the time, they were unaware that it was Little Sister who was in distress.

When Little Sister became known, I helped Cathy move Little Sister out of the traumatic scene with her abusive father and into a safe room. When I told her about safe rooms, Cathy and all of her self-states wanted to develop their own individualized ones. Little Sister's safe room was furnished with lots of stuffed animals, books, and art supplies. Cathy's Inside Mom agreed to help Cathy comfort Little Sister.

Strategies for Containment and Alternative Safe Release of Affect

A crucial task for managing traumatic triggers is to help the child develop containment strategies and practice alternative ways of responding to triggers. In addition to what was presented in Chapter 7, stabilizing techniques such as safe containers, protective shields, and safe place imagery have been proved helpful with dissociative children. These techniques can be installed with EMDR therapy (Chapter 12), hypnosis, or play therapy. Struik (2014) provides worksheets to help children evaluate and manage their difficult emotions.

Safe Containers

One way to help children manage traumatic material is to teach them to use containers to hold charged feelings and traumatic memories until they are ready to process them. An actual box can be used and decorated by the child. The box is then kept in the therapist's office. The safe container can provide an emotional respite from being bombarded with unwanted material. O'Shea (2009) has a protocol using EMDR principles and bilateral stimulation in the form of tapping to help a child develop an imaginary container with a lock to hold negative material, including "everything that has yet to be learned from or sorted through including past, present and future material" (K. O'Shea, personal communication, November 12, 2013). This information can be reviewed when the child is ready to do so. The child develops a cue word to automatically place material in the container.

I have successfully used this protocol for making safe containers with many traumatized children. For example, Steward a 9-year-old boy who was sexually abused by a babysitter, built an elaborate cave out of seashells, blocks, and rocks. He placed a locked door on the cave. The cave was surrounded by a wall and lookout towers to alert him of anyone approaching his cave. His mother tapped alternately on each of his shoulders as he put his traumatic material and unwanted thoughts and feelings into the cave. The material stayed there until he was ready to review it with me in therapy. Steward picked the cue word "rocks" to signify his cave and moved unwanted material into the cave whenever upsetting events triggered him. A picture was taken of his locked cave and placed on his I-Pod as a visual reminder (Figure 8.4).

Figure 8.4 *Steward's safe container. (Used with permission.)*

Protective Shields

Imaginary protective shields can be used to help "inoculate" the child when exposed to stressful people or triggering events such as peer teasing, or when exposed to people who remind the child of past abusers. For example, the child can imagine that he (and the self-states) has been sprayed with a bug repellant that protects the child from absorbing the "sting" of offensive things that others say and do.

The child can act out, spraying himself with bug spray to instill this imagery prior to being around a person who he fears. Or he can imagine that he is wearing a plexiglass shield that completely covers and protects him, while also allowing him to see and hear what is occurring around him without absorbing the negative message and becoming hurt by it.

Safe Place or Safe State Imagery

Another technique asks children to imagine a safe place (either real or made up) that provides a sanctuary for the child to go to in his or her mind when he or she feels threatened or experiences a flashback. I ask children to describe in great detail the place that they imagine, including the majority of their senses—sight, sound, smell, and kinesthetic. I then make a recording describing this place and ask the child to listen to this daily. If the child feels anxious at nighttime and has difficulty sleeping, I ask the child to listen to the recording before going to bed. Children often come up with creative safe places such as a Ferris wheel, a beach, an island, a boat, or a mountaintop. A cue word can be developed to quickly access this safe place imagery.

Some children are unable to imagine a place where they could feel safe. For these children, I ask them to imagine a time when they felt safe—"a safe state"—such as cuddling with a supportive person or reading a book. I then have them use this feeling of safety as a place to retreat to when they are anxious or fearful. O'Shea (2009) explains to the child that the amygdala (emotional center of the brain that is alert to danger) is operating 24/7 to warn the child of danger and it instinctively knows what to do. This information can help reassure children that it is all right to relax since another part of their brain will remain watchful. Then, the child is asked to notice what it feels like to be in this "safe state" of relaxed awareness.

As with the container exercise, incorporating a cue word to immediately access the feeling of safety is an important shortcut. If the child agrees, parents and teachers can be taught to use the cue word to help the child go to the place or feeling of safety when upset. Therapists can have the child practice using the cue word and then help the child access the place or state of safety to enhance his or her ability to use these techniques whenever needed.

Internal Rooms for Safe Affect Release

Madison, who had a "dad" voice that harassed her into stealing articles in the girl's locker room at school and the neighbor's mail, was introduced in Chapter 3. Madison was terrified by this voice, as it threatened to hurt her if she did not comply with his commands. Through this voice, Madison was reliving the presence of her father, who had abused her. Although she no longer was in contact with her father, she felt helpless and compelled to comply with the voice's commands. As a result, she had been suspended from school for multiple incidents of larceny and was currently on probation. Madison's mother called me, desperate to get Madison some help.

When I saw Madison, she was a pleasant, petite 13-year-old who reported hearing two voices in her head: a good voice that was the voice of her mother and a bad voice that was the voice of her biological father, who had yelled at her and beat her when she was a toddler. The voice of her father emerged a couple of months earlier when her mother was suspected of having a terminal illness. Madison's security was threatened and she feared being placed with her father even though his paternal rights had been terminated when she was 5. Madison wanted to know more about her father and had talked to her mother about him. Madison reported that the dad's voice was listening and then began talking to her. Madison reported, "The bad voice told me to do bad things, to steal and not help mom. I did what he said. He had so much power over me. He yelled at me. He was so much bigger and in control. I felt scared and nervous. I was thinking that he would stop yelling at me if I did what he told me to do. I felt too scared to reason with him even though he's not here."

When Madison did what he told her to, he demanded that she steal even more. I suggested to Madison that perhaps the dad voice had helped her in some way with scary things. I suggested that he was similar to "a helper with her mind," and maybe he took the abuse for her and was really angry about it. I asked her to check inside of her mind to see whether anything I said resonated. She closed her eyes and when she opened them, she matter-of-factly said, "He said he's not trying to help me."

Madison was my last client of the day and I was tired. I let out a deep sigh wondering how I was going to connect with the dad voice. I validated how strong and powerful he was and then explained to the dad voice that Madison was unable to attend school due to her stealing from the school lockers and was placed on probation. I asked Madison, "Would he be willing to use his strength and power in a different way so you wouldn't get in trouble anymore?" She moved her eyes upward and to the side, as she went inside to see what he would say. She paused and then looked at me and responded simply, "He didn't come here to help me. He makes me do bad things or he will leave." In reality, he could not go anywhere else, because she created him and he was a part of her. If I agreed that he should leave, he would think that I was trying to get rid of him and he would be angry at me and even angrier at her. This would impair any chance to positively influence his behavior. Furthermore, he might go "underground" and later reappear to wreak havoc by having her engage in more delinquent behavior. He could also become more resistant to cooperating. I did not want to battle with him. So, I replied that he was an important part of her and had done so much to help her that I did not want him to get into trouble or get hurt either. My hope was that his defenses would be lessened by my demonstrating respect for him.

Madison again rolled her eyes upward, listened to what he said, and responded, "Nobody could hurt him 'cause nobody can see him. He doesn't live inside of my body." I asked whether he was a part of her and whether he shared her body. She replied with some confusion in her voice, "He said that he's not a part of me. He's himself. He thinks he has a separate body." She continued to say, "He sounds like my dad because he wants me to be afraid of him so he can be in control." I asked whether he was mad. She said, "He's always mad." I asked why and she replied, "That's the way he's always been." That was an important piece of information. It appeared that he was created to hold her anger.

I tried another angle, suggesting whether it was possible that when she was mad at her dad, she could not show these feelings. She agreed that her dad would hit her if she showed anger. I asked whether the dad voice held her anger, because she could not express it. She again checked inside and replied, "He took my mad feelings so I would not overpower him." This part seemed to believe that anger meant power—most likely her dad's anger engendered much power over her mother and their children. Again, I did not want to do battle with him and replied, "He did you a favor. He took your anger. He wants to be powerful to protect himself from getting hurt." She responded, "Another reason he wants to be powerful is to make me do bad things. No one can hurt him and I can't control him." I said, "He did you a favor by taking your mad feelings but in exchange he took over your behavior. I wonder if he would contract with you to cooperate in a different way and still be strong." Madison checked inside with same eye roll, and responded that he refused to cooperate.

Madison reported that he wanted to get her in trouble or just leave. I did not want to argue with the dad voice or take his "bait," so I ignored that comment. I said, "He did you a favor by taking your bad feelings. Is he mad for taking your angry feelings 'cause it's hard to have fun when you're mad?" Madison replied, "No, he doesn't want to have fun. All he wants to do is get people in trouble." I said, "Does he know that he's hurting lots of people." Madison said, "He knows but he doesn't care."

I glanced out the window. It was getting late and growing dark outside. I felt increasingly desperate to find a way to reach the dad voice. As the light faded, so did my energy. I breathed another deep sigh. I was really struggling to find a doorway to reach the dad voice. It was clear that no amount of reasoning or contracting for desirable behavior was going to work. Then, it struck me that since he carried the rage that Madison could not handle, maybe I could give him an option to deal with the rage. An idea came to me—one last-ditch proposal. I said, "I wonder if he could find a special room inside to release all of the mad feelings. He could have a punching bag, balls and other things he could use to get out all of that anger. Carrying around all of that anger makes it hard for him to have fun. I would like him to have fun." Although he only knew anger, I was introducing the enticement of having fun—an emotion that was foreign to him, but important for him to experience. Madison again checked inside and opened her eyes, saying, "He said he can find a place. He will go there to get away and not have to listen to this anymore!" I chuckled to myself but still was not going to be baited.

However, a tremendous sense of relief came over me. It was totally dark outside and I now felt a glimmer of hope. I said, "What would he like in that room? I would like it to be a room with things that he wants to have in it to help him get all of that anger out that he took for you. He really did you a favor." She checked inside and listed the following: "pillows, punching bag, bean bag, television, couch, food, candy, and junk food"—in that order. I suggested a sauna to help him relax. Madison responded, "He's already too hot." I chuckled to myself, agreeing that he was too hot with anger. Her eyes again turned upward to the right as she listened to him in her head. She lowered her eyes, looking at me and saying with a smile, "He wants a swimming pool." I said, "Oh, that's great!" as I now knew he was onboard! Madison added that he would like a slide in the swimming pool. I said that was even better and how much fun he was going to have! She said, "He wants to go there now to get away from all of this." I again was amused, responded that this was a great idea, and expressed how much I appreciated that he was going to work on getting out all of the anger that he took for her. I asked whether he would tell her what the anger was from. Madison said with a surprise, "He won't tell me. He just wants to work it out on his own." I noted how helpful and protective he was of her and asked her what she would like to say to him. She thanked him. Then, she said, "He said that he is thankful to you and to me too!" I was astounded to hear this from the angry dad voice. She then said, "He is going there now with the good voice, the mom." (Madison had also reported earlier hearing the mom voice who assumed the identity of her mother.) Before he went to his room, I quickly asked whether he could change his name, because "dad voice" did not fit him anymore. He decided to be called "Helper!"

There was a complete turnaround when I provided a vehicle for the dad voice to discharge his rage. Moreover, he did not see me as a threat, as I had shown him that I had no intention of getting rid of him or criticizing him for getting Madison in trouble. I provided a nonjudgmental approach and did not argue with him. Furthermore, it was clear that the dad voice was not a man representing Madison's dad but an angry child disguised as the abusive father in order to gain power and control. He appeared to have taken on the identity of her dad for his own protection. His true identity was revealed when he said he wanted junk food and a swimming pool with a slide. As I previously noted, many children's angry self-states portray themselves as abusive grown-ups and inevitably are disguised as recalcitrant children acting big to scare people away. After this intervention, the dad voice/Helper did not harass Madison to steal things and there were no further delinquent behaviors.

I have also successfully used internal anger rooms for affect release with dissociative teens who had extensive problems with substance abuse and delinquency, along with considerable affective and behavioral dysregulation. Since the intervention described earlier, I have suggested an adjoining "comfort room" that angry self-states retreat to for relaxation. Typically, dissociative children's angry parts will initially only agree to go into the anger room to discharge their rage; however, in the follow-up session, they will usually agree to go into the comfort room. Since angry self-states are often created to only carry rage, the idea of a place of comfort is completely foreign to them. They may only be able to imagine a comfort room after they are able to discharge some of their rage. The comfort rooms usually are furnished with food, couches, pillows, books, and electronic equipment. One teen included a dance floor with flashing lights with his favorite songs playing. Once the child has outfitted the room, I will also suggest including funny movies and entertaining activities, as I want them to begin to "blend" their emotional state of anger or rage with happiness, fun, and relaxation. This is an integrating step toward experiencing a full range of emotions within a window of tolerance that is necessary for successful affect modulation.

Dissociative youth tend to be very imaginative and creative, and different internal rooms can be developed to deal with a range of problems. I treated a female college student Sarah, who was diagnosed with DID and had several self-states. Sarah was included in the study on dissociative youth and was diagnosed with obsessive-compulsive disorder (OCD), which was discussed in Chapter 3 on differential diagnoses. One of Sarah's compulsions was to rub something silky, which she literally did all day long! She was unconscious of it most of the time. Sarah was also dissociating during one of her college classes and was completely amnestic during the professor's lectures. We explored what could be triggering her during this particular class. After discussing the male professor's looks, size, and voice, Sarah recalled that his voice sounded similar to that of her abusive father. Sarah herself was able to distinguish between the professor and her father, but Sarah revealed with some embarrassment that she had a baby self-state that was terrified when hearing the professor's voice, causing Sarah to dissociate and to rub the silky lining of her purse. This baby state was highly anxious and would soothe herself by rubbing anything silky, even her pet dog's ear. She had done this since birth when she would rub her blanket's satiny edging when her father screamed at her. This state did not know that Sarah was now 19 years old and was no longer living with her father. With my help, Sarah oriented the baby state to current reality and reassured her that she was safe. To ensure that this state would not be activated when Sarah attended college, Sarah placed her in a soundproof nursery prior to going to class. Consequently, Sarah no longer dissociated during class. Moreover, when the baby self-state was in her nursery, Sarah's compulsive behavior of rubbing silky textures ceased.

CONTRACTING WITH SELF-STATES FOR NEW ROLES

Cathy

Cathy's mom complained that rather than sleeping, Cathy was roaming the house at night. Cathy insisted that she was sleeping. However, on several occasions, Cathy, a seventh grader, fell asleep at her desk and her teacher was unable to awaken her. Cathy's mom was called to pick her up to take her home many times. Then, Cathy began to engage in bizarre behavior at school. She got up in the middle of class, twirled around, and sang. Cathy had no memory of this behavior. Unfortunately, this only increased her being teased by her classmates. Cathy sat in my office bewildered by her behavior. I asked her to go inside of her mind to see whether she could figure out what might be causing this unusual behavior. She closed her eyes. Twenty seconds later, she opened them and exclaimed, "Oh my, it was Little Sister!" She went on to explain that Little Sister admitted to doing this to help Cathy not fall asleep in class! Cathy had been sleepwalking and had entered her sibling's room making an embarrassing comment. Little Sister decided to stay awake at nighttime to prevent Cathy from sleepwalking and embarrassing herself again. Little Sister was tired in the morning and thought if she stood, twirled, and sang in the classroom, she could keep herself and Cathy awake. I thanked Little Sister for her creative efforts but explained that all parts of Cathy were to sleep when Cathy went to bed. They agreed and there were no further problems with sleeping (or twirling and singing) in school.

Although dissociative children can engage in peculiar behavior, when you assess the child's inner world, all of it begins to make sense. We simply cannot make assumptions about what is driving traumatized children's aberrant behaviors. We need to carefully explore what is going on internally with them.

Briana

Briana's treatment was marked by several tumultuous starts and stops with multiple placements. Briana was also a part of the study on OCD that was referenced in Chapter 3 on differential diagnoses. She was addicted to drugs, alcohol, sex, cleaning, and food. I initially treated Briana when she was 7 years old for sexual abuse by several older boys in her neighborhood.

Briana also suffered physical and emotional abuse by her father and older siblings. Briana's mother referred her to me again when she was 13 after she refused to continue seeing her current therapist. Briana was on juvenile probation and was ordered to receive therapy after she assaulted a boy who had made sexual slurs toward her. She gave the boy a concussion, was temporarily placed in juvenile detention, and was then returned to her mother's care. Briana's behavior had begun to deteriorate around age 12. She disclosed to me that her stepfather's brother had sexually abused her on a number of occasions when she was 12. I reported it to the authorities; fortunately, he admitted what he had done and was incarcerated.

Briana would rapidly vacillate from depression to rage. When she was 15, Briana was admitted to the children's psychiatric/substance abuse facility for major depression and substance abuse. Unfortunately, her insurance would only pay for a week of treatment despite my protests. On release, Briana refused to return to therapy, indicating that I "was too nice" and she did not want to be forced to attend therapy. Her probation officer agreed despite her serious emotional and behavioral disturbances. After quitting therapy, Briana quickly deteriorated and her compulsions escalated, as did her aggression toward her family and peers. Briana's eating disorder cycled from anorexia to bingeing and purging coupled with excessive exercise. She was sexually promiscuous and her alcohol and drug addictions worsened. She was suspended from school for altercations with teachers and peers and for truancy.

A year and half later, Briana called me, requesting an emergency session. She was highly anxious and depressed when she disclosed that beginning on her 16th birthday she was sexually abused and given cocaine by an older man. The abuse lasted several months. Because the state law held that a 16-year-old can consent to sex, no charges were filed. The authorities were also unable to prosecute the man on any drug charges due to a lack of evidence.

In therapy, Briana began to deal with her traumatic past. She drew a picture of her sadness (Figure 8.5).

Unfortunately, Briana's substance abuse was a major obstacle to her recovery. She refused to go to an inpatient program, and her probation officer and the court refused to order her into treatment. Her behavior worsened and she threatened to kill her mother and stepfather. Briana was escorted by the police to the psychiatric hospital and shortly thereafter was transferred to the 30-day inpatient substance abuse program. On her admission, I called Briana to express my concern for her. She responded

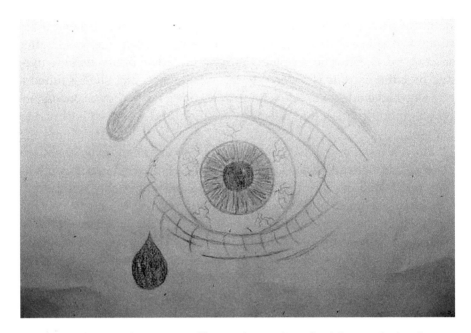

Figure 8.5 *Briana's picture of her sadness. (Used with permission.)*

with a two-word profanity, "Fuck off." I immediately hung up the phone, as I needed to set firm boundaries with her and set an example by not tolerating any abuse from her.

Three months later, Briana called me, sincerely apologized, and in a humble voice asked whether I would see her again. I agreed, as I was committed to her and knew that there was a connection between us. I understood that her severe attachment impairment, extreme distrust of adults, and fear of closeness had interfered in her ability to maintain a consistent therapeutic relationship. On returning, the first question I asked Briana was why she wanted to see me again. Briana simply said, "You're the only one who knows what's inside of me." And so, our work truly began.

Briana had much to process. She grew up in a chaotic, volatile home environment characterized by domestic violence by her father toward her mother, a contentious divorce, and three older siblings who also had labile moods and behavior problems. Briana had been physically and emotionally abused by her father and older siblings throughout her childhood.

Briana responded to therapy and began to make positive changes. Briana's head was clearing after abstaining from alcohol and drugs. She was very intelligent and insightful as to what she needed. She recognized that she could not return to school but was motivated to complete high school. She enrolled in a home schooling program and worked independently and diligently to catch up academically. She attended Alcoholics Anonymous (AA) support groups several times a week. She participated in individual therapy several times a week and kept all of her appointments. She often rode her bike to our appointments. Her mother, Rita, continued to be involved in collateral and family sessions with Briana to repair their attachment. Rita received individual psychotherapy for her own trauma and dissociation, and couples therapy with her second husband while focusing on child management and communication. Slowly, the home environment began to stabilize.

Several stabilization interventions with Briana were instituted. I made several recordings for Briana to listen to with the aim of helping calm her stress-response system. Briana had a desperate need for spiritual growth, as she felt spiritually depleted and despondent. Several resources and books on spirituality were provided to her and she "devoured" them. She began to feel a sense of hope both in herself and for the future.

After Briana developed some ego strength and stability, she was able to more deeply explore her dissociative symptoms. She had intense affect and behavioral switches that were beyond her control. She reported voices in her head but was unclear about them. She reported memory problems when highly aroused or agitated. Otherwise, she felt numb and depersonalized. Her lack of control over her obsessions and compulsions plagued her daily. We began to explore what was going on within her and how her voices might play a role in the compulsions that were endangering her health.

Briana's Self-States

It was a bright, sunny August day. Briana sat on my couch smiling. She felt good about riding her bike to our session. She was ready to tackle her obsessions and compulsions. There were no signs of resistance, shutdown, or attempts to provoke me, as she had demonstrated during the prior 3 years. She closed her eyes to see what she could learn from her internal world regarding her obsessions and compulsions.

Briana opened her eyes after 30 seconds and said in a quiet voice, "I have three distinct personalities. The Little Girl who feels vulnerable. She took the trauma. The Angry Part who covers up the little girl's pain through compulsions or anger—through anything that would avoid confronting feelings. The Angry Part uses abuse as the main cover up—abuse of others, self, drugs, sex, cleaning. Then there is the Intuitive Part that is helpful."

> **Therapist:** "Can you tell me what you notice when you begin to feel anger."
>
> **Briana:** "A black cloud comes over me. I feel the Angry Part. Then the compulsions come over me. I don't know why that happens."
>
> **Therapist:** I validated the discovery of her different parts and asked, "What do you feel at that time?"
>
> **Briana:** "I feel shame. Then the cycle happens again."
>
> **Therapist:** "Tell me more about the cycle."
>
> **Briana:** "The black cloud is the detached feeling of not being in touch with myself. Then the compulsions set in. Before I am in a detached state and then go into the compulsions, I can be feeling good and happy, or think of the past and maybe might want to cry. I might feel spiritually close to God. Then the detached state comes in. The Angry Part takes over. (She paused again in contemplation and then continued.) The Angry Part holds all the compulsions, the addictions, the negativity."
>
> **Therapist:** "Is it difficult to express anger in other ways?"

Briana paused and then quietly said, "It's not anger. It's just pain. The pain is held in the Little Girl."

This was a major breakthrough. Briana began to understand how her Angry Part was using compulsive behavior to cover up the pain felt by the Little Girl. The Angry Part was the key to remedying her compulsions. To do this, it was critical that we reframe his role. I pointed out how Angry Part was trying to protect the little girl and how important that was for her to have him. I asked whether Angry Part could use his strength and protection in another way rather than through compulsions, as they were hurting Briana.

Briana quickly responded, "Definitely. I don't feel that I have to be angry anymore or have to defeat myself. Angry Part is willing to drop negativity, drop old ways of protecting the Little Girl. Compulsions don't have to be there anymore." She paused for a few seconds and then added, "I just feel safe and don't have to do compulsions like overeating and exercising."

Therapist: "You're feeling safe. Tell me more about that."

Briana: "When I feel safe, I don't have to have any part of me storm through and take care of me 'cause I feel safe . . . I feel in touch when I feel safe. I feel in touch with things going around me, my spirit, my body. I feel in control of myself and I don't need to use compulsions. When I am in touch with my body, it is easier for me to learn. When I notice feelings in my body it helps me to realize things that I feel on the inside. My body and mind are then connected."

I was amazed with her insight and clarity. However, I wanted to make sure that Angry Part was on board with letting go of his role, because parts that have prominent roles are often reluctant to relinquish their functions and assume new roles. Briana checked inside again and replied, "Angry Part is defensive about having to let go of the compulsions. I feel apprehensive myself. I know it is a self-defeating behavior, but it is a safe one that I've used so long."

I indicated that Angry Part was a survival part that she needed. There is strength in anger and anger is not bad. But knowing how to express anger in a way that is not self-defeating can be more powerful. I explained that controlling anger takes more power than indiscriminately letting it out. I asked whether Angry Part could express anger by helping her verbalize when she is angry—by speaking up when she is upset. Briana looked away and then turned to face me. She told me that she had suddenly recalled when she was young that once when she was in church, someone was crying and her biological father had pointed out that crying is a form of weakness. Briana told me that her father would make fun of her when she cried. (It occurred to me that Angry Part seemed to have identified with her father in not allowing Briana or the Little Girl to express pain and sadness.) Briana went on to state that while growing up she felt that femininity was a sign of weakness rather than of strength, but now she saw it as more of a strength than a weakness. She surprised me when she added, "You have a strong femininity. You don't let my bad attitude affect you. You find positive ways to deal with it. I am beginning to see femininity as good."

I chuckled to myself and thought, "Well after firing me two times in the past 2 years, she finally formed a positive transference to me!" Briana had tested me but I did not let myself be baited. I set limits with her, but

I did not reject her. She recognized this and was able to form a positive identification and a secure attachment with me. Healing was very possible for her.

To help Angry Part feel appreciated, I asked Briana to thank him for all he had done and to thank him for his willingness to use his strength in a new way. His rage was understandable given the years of chronic and multiple forms of trauma. Although there was much processing to be done, I reassured her and all her self-states that we would take things slowly, and help Little Girl feel safe and comforted as we carefully processed her trauma. After this intervention, Angry Part seemed less resistant. Briana's Intuitive Part, who contained her wisdom, agreed to assist. It was clear that her Intuitive Part was working "behind the scenes," as Briana expressed herself with such insight and sensitivity. Finally, all parts of Briana were onboard and able to cooperate as a team. Angry Part agreed to work with Intuitive Part to find new ways to manage feelings.

Briana's severe behavior and emotional disturbances could have been perceived as borderline personality disorder with a completely different treatment trajectory. She could have easily followed the path of ongoing addictions and compulsions with eventual incarceration. However, borderline features are often a result of severe attachment impairment, trauma, and dissociation. Exploring the underlying causes of her acting-out behavior was essential to her recovering. It took patience, belief in her recovery, and "accepting Briana as a worthwhile person" without judgment that created the atmosphere for her to return to me again and again. She was finally able to trust me enough to begin to explore her internal life of chaos and dissociation. Once Briana obtained internal cooperation, she began to gain control over her compulsions. She was now ready to process her traumatic memories. This process is described in Chapter 10.

In summary, the key to healing dissociative children is seeing beyond the triggers and acting-out behavior and discovering the true source of the child's impairment—the fractured mind that drives the behavior. This then allows light to shine on the hidden self so that it can be healed.

9

Medication as an Intervention in the Treatment of Dissociative Disorders and Complex Trauma With Children and Adolescents

With Adrian J. Stierum

THE DESCRIBED PSYCHOPHARMACOLOGICAL INTERVENTIONS ARE brief overviews and are thus far from complete. They contain important information on treating children and adolescents with dissociative disorders that are rarely described in the mainstream literature. For more extensive information, refer to the *Clinical Manual of Child and Adolescent Psychopharmacology*, second edition, edited by McVoy and Findling (2013), which constitutes the official American Psychiatric Association (APA) guidelines, or *Psychofarmaca in de KJP, Formularium voor de Kinder- en Jeugdpsychiatrische Praktijk*, edited by Dieleman, Dierckx, and Hofstra (2011), which is the Dutch standard on practical psychopharmaca. All of the dosages discussed in this chapter are derived from APA guidelines. It is advisable to consult with a children's physician regarding any medication concerns.

INTRODUCTION

This chapter describes the essential aspects of using psychopharmacological interventions and medication in the treatment of children with dissociative disorders and complex traumatization. There is no specific medication that addresses dissociative symptoms. In addition, there is virtually no scientific research on psychopharmacological interventions for children and adolescents with dissociative disorders or complex trauma. At the same time, clinical observation suggests that children and adolescents with dissociative disorders use more medication than children and adolescents with other psychiatric disorders, but often with poor efficacy.

PSYCHOPHARMACOLOGICAL INTERVENTIONS WITH CHILDREN AND ADOLESCENTS

In the Netherlands, the prescription of psychiatric medication to children and adolescents has been increasing since the early 1990s, in particular for methylphenidate, a common medicine for attention deficit hyperactivity disorder (ADHD). However, in 2012, there was a decrease in methylphenidate prescriptions for children less than 12 years of age. This suggests a growing awareness about the risks of psychiatric medication in early childhood (Griens, Jansen, Kroon, Lukaart, & Van der Vaart, 2014).

In 2013, the United States' National Health Interview Survey showed that one in 13 children and adolescents younger than 18 are prescribed medication for emotional and/or behavioral problems (Centers for Disease Control and Prevention [CDC], 2013). In addition, 7.5% of all children and adolescents between 6 and 17 years (9.7% of boys and 5.2% of girls) of age are on psychotropic medications (CDC, 2013). It is estimated that 7.5% (in the United States) and 3% (in the Netherlands) of all children and adolescents use some kind of psychiatric medication. In the Netherlands, many children use one type of medication; whereas in the United States, combinations of different drugs are more common. In addition, in the United States, the use of anticonvulsant and antipsychotic medication is more common. In the United States, 55% of parents or caregivers think that the medication has positive efficacy, 26% believe that the medication helps somewhat, and 19% see no effect at all.

Compared with their counterparts, adults who have experienced stressful childhood experiences require a higher dose of every sort of psychiatric medication for the same effect (Brenner, Southerland, Burns, Wagner, & Farmer, 2014; Schneeberger, Muenzenmaier, Castille, Battaglia, & Link, 2014). Foster children are prescribed more psychiatric medication in comparison with the entire population (Hulette, Freyd, & Fisher, 2011). Therefore, the clinical observation that children and adolescents with dissociative disorders and complex trauma use more psychiatric medication is understandable given their aversive childhoods and high level of comorbidity.

Research on Psychopharmacology With Children

Research data on adults cannot be applied to adolescents and children (Costello, Long, Wong, Tuleu, & Yeung, 2007). Children and adolescents have different pharmacological dynamics than adults, because their developing bodies and brains work differently. Therefore, the neurological effects, including adverse and side effects, and their efficacy differ from those found in adults. This presents a serious problem, because nearly all of the research on psychopharmacological interventions for dissociative disorders and posttraumatic stress disorder (PTSD) is done on adults. There are only case reports of the use of medication for dissociative disorders with children. So, no systematic clinical research is available to guide practitioners.

Doing empirical research on children and adolescents is difficult. The health risks, more specifically the risks of effects on the developing brain and body, are unknown, and there are more ethical objections to doing randomized controlled trials (RCTs). Furthermore, it is virtually impossible to do research on a group of children or adolescents with dissociative disorders that is large enough to have sufficient statistical power. Many research papers have a poor design, are only on short-term effects, have a poor effect size, or work with groups that are changed to improve the outcome (Marcovitch, 2007).

Pharmaceutical industries play a dubious role in promoting medications. These industries finance research only when it is profitable. Doing pharmacological research on dissociative disorders with children and adolescents is not a priority for these companies because of the small group size compared with that of other psychiatric disorders. Most of the pharmaceutical industries spend more money on marketing and advertising than on research (Anderson, 2014). The pharmacological research that is sponsored by the pharmaceutical industries is not always reliable because of their conflict of interest. The results are often overly positive and found to be less so when the research is duplicated. If results are unfavorable for the pharmaceutical industries, the research is sometimes withheld from publication (Gray, 2013). Therefore, we suggest that for the treatment of dissociative disorders, medical doctors should not rely on medical representatives of the pharmaceutical industries and should instead base their treatment on professional guidelines and peer-reviewed research that are not sponsored by pharmacological companies.

Efficacy and Adherence of Psychopharmacology

The effect of a psychopharmacological agent is determined by both specific and nonspecific factors. The most important specific factor is the biochemical effect of the agent. Nonspecific factors include the following: the faith of the medical doctor in the agent, the working alliance with the patients and their parents or caregivers, and the placebo effect. Although these nonspecific factors are often underestimated, they can influence the efficacy of the agent in as much as 50% of cases. The adherence to a prescribed drug regimen is influenced heavily by the working alliance between the physician and the patient and his or her parents or caregivers (Moore, 2007; Sanders-Woudstra, 1978). General research on medication adherence reveals that only 50% of all patients use their medication as prescribed (Hov, Bjartnes, Slordal, & Spigset, 2012).

General indications for psychopharmacotherapy with children and adolescents include the following: to improve the therapeutic alliance and the therapy, attention, and concentration and learning (cognitive development); to give extra support in a stressful period or during a crisis; and to reduce chronic symptoms. It is important to keep in mind that the prescribed medication should always support the child's development and ability to perform age-appropriate activities; a sedated child can neither learn nor play. Medication should always be one of a number of interventions or therapies. It should never the first and only intervention to be considered with children with emotional and behavioral problems. Rather, it should be used as part of a comprehensive treatment plan. Medication should only be prescribed after a thorough diagnostic process, as presented in this book and described by the International Society for the Study of Dissociation (ISSD) in its Child and Adolescent Treatment Guidelines (ISSD Task Force on Children and Adolescents, 2004). In addition, a careful evaluation of the long-term safety of the prescribed medicine should occur before prescribing the medicine to children. Finally, other alternatives to medication, such as increasing the number of therapy sessions, exploring what self-states may be contributing to a child's disruptive behavior, examining environmental/family factors, and applying stabilization techniques, are advisable, as described in this book and elsewhere (Silberg, 2013; Wieland, 2011).

MEDICATION FOR CHILDREN AND ADOLESCENTS WITH COMPLEX TRAUMA AND DISSOCIATIVE DISORDER

Since children and adolescents with dissociative disorders and complex trauma suffer from many disabling symptoms, there is great urgency and necessity to relieve these symptoms, encourage normal development, and support their treatment. Severely traumatized children often have many previous diagnoses and have been prescribed numerous medications with little efficacy. Most of the time, children with a dissociative disorder present with a complex picture of high comorbidity that is often changeable depending on what self-state is activated. Differentiation between the intrinsic symptoms of a dissociative disorder and other psychiatric disorders is difficult and often not possible due to overlapping symptoms and a misunderstanding of the child's dissociative responses. Because of the severity of the symptoms and their disabling side effects on functioning, there is a great need for rational and, as much as possible, evidence-based guidelines for using medication in these children.

Research on the Use of Medications With Youth With Complex Trauma and Dissociation Disorders

There is no known medicine for the core symptoms of dissociative disorder (e.g., amnesia, depersonalization, derealization, presence of self-states, and hallucinations derived from self-states). Furthermore, there are no specific research data or RCTs on the treatment of children and adolescents with dissociative disorders with psychiatric medication (Stamatakos & Campo, 2010a, 2010b; Strawn, Keeshin, DelBello, Geracioto, & Putnam, 2010). Instead, most research comprises case histories reported by clinicians. There are also limited research data on the treatment of children and adolescents with PTSD with psychiatric medication. Research suggests that up to 80% of the children and adolescents with dissociative disorders have comorbid PTSD and up to 90% suffer from hypervigilance, traumatic nightmares, and intrusions. In addition, it is estimated that at least 70% of children with dissociative disorders also exhibit ADHD or ADHD-like symptoms (Strawn et al., 2010). Virtually, all child and adolescent psychiatric diagnoses can coexist with a dissociative disorder (Chapter 3).

Because most of the prescribed medication for children and adolescents with dissociative disorders and complex trauma is not registered for treatment of these disorders, they are prescribed as off-label use. Off-label use is relatively common in child and adolescent psychiatry because of the absence of pharmacological research in children with mental health problems. Off-label use means that medical doctors can prescribe medication that is registered and tested for the treatment of other diagnoses or age groups to children and adolescents who have a dissociative disorder. The prescription is tolerated when there is some clinical evidence or consensus among professionals regarding the efficacy of the medication (McVoy & Findling, 2013). The children's parents or caregivers must give informed consent for the medication. They should be provided extensive information about the purpose of the medication, possible adverse effects, and its off-label use. There should be a time-limited trial followed by an evaluation of the efficacy of the medication by using measurable variables, so a decision can be made to either continue or stop the medication.

There are special complications that arise when treating children and adolescents with dissociative disorders with medications. These complications are related to the survival strategies that these children and adolescents have developed. First, they often have an extreme fear of loss of control. Dissociative children have a need for control given that they have experienced trauma and their survival was threatened. These children often think that medications will change them, causing them to lose control. Therefore, it is important to provide them with clear and honest information about the medication and its effects. Patients need to know that medication will not control their way of thinking and will only help them change if they want to do so themselves. Moreover, medication can help them cope with some disabling symptoms such as anxiety, depression, and extreme mood changes and it can improve their concentration and functioning at school (Nemzer, 1998).

Dissociative patients are also very sensitive to adverse effects of medication. Again, clear and honest information about the possible side effects of medication and what to do if they experience them will help patients accept the medication and will also help prevent reactions based on fear if a side effect does occur. The prescribing doctor can reassure the child and parents by saying, "If you experience side effects, don't hesitate to call or come to the office. We can discuss them, and see if we can do something to make them go away. I like it better when you call me often, rather than be worried or afraid. If the side effects do not stop, and the good effects of the medicine do not compensate for them, we will stop the medication."

A major challenge in treating dissociative clients with psychotropic medications is the possibility of different side effects and adverse reactions related to different self-states. It is important to be aware that some self-states can be amnestic for what happens in other self-states and can react with fear or anger when they are suddenly influenced by a medication. Whenever possible, the prescribing doctor and the therapist should collaborate closely about the medication and its impact on self-states so that all of them are informed about what to expect. When dissociative children's self-states agree to take the medication, there could be an increase in the success of the medication (Silberg, 1998, 2013).

Case Study: Dylan

Dylan, a 9-year-old boy, was referred for a consultation. His therapist requested medication for ADHD. The diagnosis was a dissociative disorder, PTSD, and ADHD. Dylan had multiple self-states, some of which were destructive and aggressive. He had severe behavior problems at school, where he could not sit still. He would not listen to the teacher's instructions, was spaced out often, and could not concentrate. He often hit other children and the teacher and sometimes ran away from school without remembering why or where he went. His parents had good parenting skills and trauma therapy was intensive but had little effect. The teacher warned Dylan's parents that Dylan could not continue in school if he did not change his behavior quickly, and she suggested medication.

After consultation, we decided to prescribe methylphenidate for Dylan. First, Dylan's self-states were consulted and all agreed to the plan. The target symptoms were poor concentration, impulsivity, and hyperactivity. After beginning therapy, Dylan's hyperactivity diminished, but his concentration did not improve and he remained highly impulsive. In fact, these symptoms were more prominent, because Dylan was more spaced out and was switching self-states more often and faster with less control over switching. When the methylphenidate was stopped, the switching of personality states returned to normal but the ADHD-like symptoms remained.

Dylan related that the angry one and the little one (self-states) became sad and angry when using the medication and that they wanted to play boss all the time and did not listen to him anymore. This is an example of serious side effects (sad mood and agitation) that were only present in two of Dylan's many self-states. However, these side effects resulted in a worsening of Dylan's dissociative symptoms and threatened his entire ability to function. The next intervention was intensifying the trauma therapy, which included specialized treatment for his dissociation. Dylan was referred to a therapeutic day-care center. His treatment remained a challenge for a while, but was eventually completed successfully.

As in Dylan's case, the effect of medication in the treatment of dissociative disorders in children and adolescents is unpredictable, because early traumatization leads to distinct anatomical changes in the brain. These include dilatation of the ventricles and reduction of the hypothalamus mass, leading to altered neurobiological functioning (Bremner, 2002; National Scientific Council on the Developing Child, 2014; Perry, Pollard, Blakely, Baker, & Vigilante, 1995; Vermetten, Schmahl, Lindner, Loewenstein, & Bremner, 2006; Shin et al., 1999; Twardosz & Lutzker, 2010; Vermetten, Schmahl, Lindner, Loewenstein, & Bremner, 2006). These neurological changes can lead to unpredictable responses to medication. In adult patients with PTSD, the structural neuroanatomical anomalies caused by trauma may be reduced by psychopharmacological treatment (Thomaes et al., 2014).

Because of the neurobiological and anatomical changes in dissociative patients, there are many possibilities of how a dissociative patient may respond. These neurobiological and anatomical changes are not measurable in individual patients, the effects of these changes are not clear, and reactions to medication are less predictable. For example, most of the time, the effect of a specific drug is the same as in nontraumatized, nondissociative patients; however, sometimes, a drug may have no effect at all or the child may experience more side effects and adverse reactions than expected. Also, the dosage in which the drug should be administered to achieve a therapeutic result can vary. Consequently, adjusting the dosage to a higher or a lower level is often necessary in dissociative youth. It is recommended to start with a relatively low dosage and increase it slowly, while carefully monitoring for possible side effects.

Another complication, which unfortunately is scarcely researched and often unknown by medical doctors, is that medication can worsen the dissociation (as with Dylan's two self-states that became sad and angry). Many prescribed medications cause sedation, including benzodiazepines, antidepressants, antipsychotics, and antiepileptics. Methylphenidate, the most prescribed drug for ADHD, can also cause sedation when prescribed in high doses (Putnam, 1997). Sedation can lead to a loss of control and can cause a child to dissociate more frequently. Methylphenidate can even cause children with ADHD to dissociate while learning (Johnson et al., 2008).

Another factor to consider when prescribing medication is the child's environment. The efficacy of medication will be severely compromised if the child or adolescent is not safe and continues to be abused. Medication is best used as an adjunctive intervention in all treatment phases after safety is achieved and traumatization has stopped.

Case Study: Latifa

Latifa was a 16-year-old female with drug-resistant schizophrenia, cannabis abuse, and behavioral problems who was referred to a clinic. She was suffering from hallucinations and paranoid ideations. For 3 years, she was plagued with feelings of persecution by a group of men who belonged to a motorcycle club. She was prescribed huge doses of three different antipsychotics, which had little effect on her paranoia and hallucinations. The medications left her very sedated, and she reported that she felt similar to a zombie. Unfortunately, because of her hallucinations and paranoid psychosis, a trauma history was never properly explored.

Latifa's first admission to a psychiatric hospital occurred when she became psychotic after cannabis abuse. During this admission, two patients sexually abused her. This trauma reactivated the trauma of her strict upbringing, which included physical abuse by her father. After suffering sexual abuse, she began having feelings of persecution.

By lowering the dose and prescribing only one type of antipsychotic medication, she was better able to talk about her traumas and revealed dissociative states that had contributed to her destabilization. Latifa's self-states self-mutilated heavily and attempted suicide on numerous occasions. Eventually, Latifa was provided eye movement desensitization and reprocessing (EMDR) therapy and she integrated her dissociative states. She stabilized and was no longer flooded with traumatic memories on a daily basis. Her feelings of persecution were also reduced. Although the final diagnosis is not yet clear, a psychotic disorder and a dissociative disorder are reasonable provisional diagnoses.

Comorbidity

Many dissociative children and adolescents have symptoms mimicking other psychiatric diagnoses such as ADHD (Harrison & Wilson, 2005; Wozniak et al., 1999), psychosis (Foot & Park, 2008; Read, van Os, Morrison, & Ross, 2005), depression, and bipolar disorder (Waters, Laddis, Soderstrom, & Yehuda, 2007). It is very difficult to prove whether these symptoms originate from the dissociative disorder or from a comorbid psychiatric disorder (Hornstein & Putnam, 1992).

When a history of trauma is present and a child or adolescent meets the criteria for a dissociative disorder, the discussion about whether symptoms originate from the dissociative disorder or from a comorbid psychiatric disorder is not always helpful. It is more important to determine whether a symptom is interfering with the development of the patient or impeding the treatment of the dissociative disorder. If so, the symptom should be viewed as a target symptom and psychopharmacological intervention should be considered. Pharmacological intervention should address the most disabling symptom first. It is recommended to target one symptom at a time, using one type of medication at a time, to make a clear evaluation possible. When using more than one agent at a time, it is not possible to evaluate the effects of the medication properly. Moreover, there is an increased risk of side effects or adverse effects when using multiple medications (Hilt et al., 2014). When a symptom improves, additional medication can be prescribed to address any remaining symptoms.

For example, a dissociative child may have ADHD-like symptoms such as a lack of concentration, impulsivity, and hyperactivity that are interfering with the child's cognitive development and schoolwork. If methylphenidate is prescribed and the child's hyperactivity decreases and his or her concentration improves, then learning at school is possible again. Moreover, behavior in class is improved and therapy is enhanced. When trauma therapy is complete, the medication can be stopped. If the ADHD-like symptoms continue, then the child is likely to have a comorbid ADHD and may need ongoing treatment. If the ADHD-like symptoms stop after successful trauma therapy, it is likely that the symptoms originated from the dissociative disorder and further intervention is not needed.

Medication for the Treatment of PTSD in Children and Adolescents

Data supporting the use of medication in the treatment of PTSD in children and adolescents are limited (Stamatakos et al., 2010a). Strawn et al. (2010) did an extensive literature search and a data analysis on the pharmacological treatment of PTSD in children and adolescents. In approximately 80% of cases, children and adolescents diagnosed with a dissociative disorder had comorbid PTSD, and about 90% of these children displayed symptoms of PTSD, such as hypervigilance, traumatic nightmares, and intrusions. Therefore, medication targeted to symptoms of PTSD with dissociative children can play an important role in the psychopharmacological treatment of these patients. Strawn et al. concluded that there is no support for using antidepressants and benzodiazepines as treatments for PTSD in children and adolescents. However, there is limited evidence that the brief use of some antiadrenergic agents, antipsychotics, and mood stabilizers may improve some PTSD symptoms in youth. Controlled trials of these agents in children and adolescents are needed to confirm this. Table 9.1 summarizes medications used to treat PTSD symptoms along with the level of supporting evidence for the main symptoms researched.

Because the level of evidence for treating PTSD in children and adolescents with medication is very limited, pharmaceutical companies tend to advise the use of medication that has been well researched in adults and found to be effective. However, this approach does not take into account the different physiological functioning with children and adolescents and the potential for toxicity with long-term exposure. When treating PTSD in children and adolescents, a symptom-orientated psychopharmacological approach is required (Huemer, Erhart, & Steiner, 2010).

MEDICATION AS AN INTERVENTION IN THE TREATMENT OF DISSOCIATIVE DISORDERS AND COMPLEX TRAUMATIZATION

Because there is no research supporting an evidence-based psychopharmacological treatment of dissociative disorders in children and adolescents, psychopharmacological interventions are currently based solely on clinical experience. Far too often, children with a dissociative disorder are

Table 9.1 *Level of Evidence for Various Psychopharmacological Treatments for Children and Adolescents With PTSD Symptoms*

Medication	Level of Evidence	Symptoms That Improved
ANTIADRENERGICS		
Prazosine	Case study	Intrusive/hyperarousal
Clonidine	Case study	Reenactment
Guanfacine	Case study	Intrusive
Propranolol	Case study Negative RCT	Hyperarousal
ANTIPSYCHOTICS		
Quetiapine	Case study	TSCC scores: anxiety, depression, and anger
Risperidone	Case study	Intrusive/hyperarousal
ANTIDEPRESSANTS		
Sertraline	Two negative RCTs	None
Citalopram	Case study and open-label study	CAPS scores: reexperiencing, avoidance, and hyperarousal
MOOD STABILIZERS		
Carbamazepine	Case study	
Divalproex	Case study	
BENZODIAZEPINES		
	No evidence to support use	None

Adapted from Strawn et al. (2010).

CAPS, clinician-administered PTSD scale; PTSD, posttraumatic stress disorder; RCT, randomized controlled trial; TSCC, Trauma Symptom Checklist for Children.

treated with multiple medications—one for every symptom—often with unclear or absent results. The only effect that is clearly observable may be sedation. Sedation is sometimes needed for a brief period in a crisis situation. However, most of the time, sedation is counterproductive in the treatment of a dissociative disorder. Sedated children and adolescents cannot profit from psychotherapy; they cannot fulfil their developmental tasks, and their dissociation often worsens. Sedation also interferes with learning and functioning at school. Recommendations provided by Elaine D. Nemzer in her chapter "Psychopharmacologic Interventions for Children and Adolescents with Dissociative Disorders" are still relevant. The chapter can be found in *The Dissociative Child*, the first complete book about children with dissociative disorders, edited by Silberg (1998). Nemzer advocates a cautious and practical, symptom-based approach when treating dissociative youth. Table 9.2 provides practical and, as much as possible, evidence-based recommendations for treating children and adolescents with dissociative disorders. The table summarizes some of the most common and disturbing symptoms found in children and adolescents with dissociative disorders, along with some clinical remarks and the suggested psychopharmacological interventions.

Stimulants

Of the stimulant drugs, only methylphenidate (brand names Concerta, Methylin, Medikinet, and Ritalin, among others) is discussed, because methylphenidate is the most often used and its impact is the best known and the most predictable. Methylphenidate has been studied and researched for decades and has a very good efficacy and safety record for the treatment of ADHD. Other stimulants such as dexmethylphenidate, dextroamphetamine, and amphetamine have slightly different pharmacological working mechanisms, but generally have the same effect and efficacy. Also, the adverse effects and side effects are the same as for methylphenidate (National Institutes of Health [NIH], 2000).

Methylphenidate

Methylphenidate is a central nervous system (CNS) stimulant that acts mainly on the noradrenergic and dopaminergic systems. Absorption into the systematic circulation and the brain is rapid, and effects on behavior can be seen within 30 minutes. Plasma concentration reaches a peak by 90 minutes, with a mean half-life time of about 3 hours and a 3- to 5-hour duration of action (McVoy & Findling, 2013).

Table 9.2 *Psychopharmacological Treatments for Children and Adolescents With a Dissociative Disorder and/or Complex Trauma*

Target Symptoms	Clinical Remarks		Preferred Medication[a]
Sleeping problems	Worsen dissociative symptoms	Initial insomnia	1. Melatonin, high dose 2. Clonidine
		Nightmares	1. Clonidine
		Adolescents > 15 years	1. Mirtazepine
Attention and concentration	School therapy	Spaced out	1. Methylphenidate 2. Clonidine
Impulsivity and aggression			1. Methylphenidate 2. Risperidone
		Explosive	1. Valproate
Hyperarousal and anxiety		Children Adolescents > 15 years	1. Clonidine 2. SSRI
Intrusions		Adolescents > 15 years	1. Mirtazepine
Psychosis[b]	Antipsychotics may increase thought disorders and dissociation		1. Risperidone 2. Aripiprazole
Depression	Irritability	Adolescents > 15 years	1. SSRI

[a]The numbers denote first- and second-choice agents. [b]Hearing voices from self-states is not considered psychosis.

SSRI, selective serotonin reuptake inhibitor.

The MTA Cooperative Group (Multimedia Treatment of Attention Deficit Hyperactive Disorder Study) (1999) makes the following recommendations:

1. Start with immediate-release methylphenidate with a low initial dose: 0.5 mg/kg/d

2. Carefully titrate the doses up to adequate levels: 1 mg/kg/d. Do not prescribe more than 2 mg/kg/d.
3. Dose three times a day initially, switch to long(er) working methylphenidate after evaluation of the effect. Do not give this after 4 p.m. because of the potential for initial insomnia.
4. Monitor for side effects.
5. Provide close follow-up.

Contraindications for prescribing methylphenidate include the following: hypertension, glaucoma, hyperthyroidism, and cardiovascular abnormalities. Before starting methylphenidate, a cardiac family history should be done (Cooper et al., 2011). If there is a family history of sudden deaths before 40 years of age and/or cardiac arrhythmias in the first line of the family or if this is unknown, which is often the case with adopted and foster children and children of dissociating mothers, an EKG should be done to exclude cardiac abnormalities. The blood pressure should be taken before administering methylphenidate to rule out hypertension. In one out of 100,000 cases, the child may become hypertensive, which is fully reversible by discontinuing the medication. In the first month of treatment, the blood pressure should be taken at least twice. After every dosage increase, the blood pressure should be monitored as described earlier. The blood pressure is not expected to rise after 1 month of a steady dosage. Also, the heart rate should be monitored, as well as the height and weight of the patient. A growth curve should be kept as well (American Academy of Child and Adolescent Psychiatry, 1997; Dieleman et al., 2011; Preston, O'Neal, & Talaga, 2010). After the patient is adequately dosed, examinations can be decreased to every 6 months.

Methylphenidate has few interactions with other medications, as it is metabolized extrahepatically. When used together with anticonvulsants, theophylline, diuretics, tricyclic antidepressants, or monoamine oxidase (MAO) inhibitors, consultation with a pharmacist is advisable. Because vegetarian patients have slower excretion, they may require a lower dose (Dieleman et al., 2011).

Case Study: Dani

Dani is a 10-year-old boy who was referred with serious behavioral problems. He lived with his grandmother, because his mother could not handle him anymore. He did not listen. He was oppositional and was hitting other children, his mother, and the teacher. He could not accept rules or regulations. At school, he could not sit still, concentrate, and maintain attention, and was always interrupting. His mother did not remember most of his developmental milestones clearly. She was crying and reliving her own traumas while Dani's history was being taken.

Dani witnessed a lot of domestic violence. His father used to abuse his mother physically and sexually. When a family cardiac history was taken, his mother said that there were no sudden death and no heart problems known in her family. Dani was diagnosed with an attachment disorder, PTSD, ADHD, and oppositional defiant disorder (ODD) like comorbid symptoms originating from the first two diagnoses. The father, mother, and a couple of nephews had also been diagnosed with ADHD.

Because his scholastic performance was poor, Dani was medicated with methylphenidate to help him concentrate, maintain attention, and reduce his behavioral problems at school. He also received trauma therapy. His mother and grandmother participated in family therapy with Dani, at which time it became clear that the mother was dissociating frequently and switching between different self-states, without awareness.

Dani and his mother did not keep their appointments, preventing regular medication reviews. After 3 weeks, Dani collapsed while playing soccer and experienced serious cardiac arrhythmias. The cardiologist determined that the arrhythmia was exacerbated by the methylphenidate. The next time we saw Dani's mother she remembered the sudden death of a nephew and a paternal history of blood pressure and heart problems, including arrhythmias. The methylphenidate was discontinued immediately. Dani had no permanent heart damage.

This case illustrates that it is very important to be extra careful when prescribing medication to children of traumatized and dissociative mothers who may have trauma-related amnesia and are therefore unable to provide adequate family medical history. When in doubt, order an EKG before starting methylphenidate or antipsychotic medication to rule out arrhythmias and other heart diseases.

Discontinuation

Methylphenidate can be started and stopped without tapering. So during periods when the child does not need the medication, the child can have a medication break, for instance, during summer holidays when learning in school and increased attention is not required. However, if the medication is being used to control other symptoms such as impulsivity and aggression, it might be wise to continue it during holidays.

The effect of long-term use (years) of methylphenidate is delayed length growth, which is not a problem most of the time. When a child is very small and has loss of appetite and weight loss while using methylphenidate, a careful approach and consultation with a pediatrician is advisable. There are no other known long-term effects (Farrone, Biederman, Morley, & Spencer, 2008).

Side Effects

The side effects of methylphenidate are well known and predictable. Frequent but often mild effects include the following: loss of appetite sometimes with nausea and stomachache, initial insomnia (problems falling asleep), sedation, dizziness, weight loss, mild dysphoria (irritability, crying, and dreariness), and headache.

Table 9.3 *Recommendations for Dealing With Side Effects of Methylphenidate*

Side Effect	Solution
Insomnia	Try earlier dosing Add melatonin Switch to clonidine
Reduced appetite/ weight loss	Breakfast within 30 minutes after administration Healthy snack before bedtime Switch to extended release Switch to clonidine
Stomachache	Give medication with food
Sedation/more spaced out	Reduce dose Switch to clonidine
Headache	Reduce dose Change to a different stimulant
Rebound	Additional low dose at the end of the afternoon or in the beginning of the evening
Mild dysphoria	Change to a different stimulant
Anxiety	Lower dose

Less likely side effects include the following: rebound when the dose wears off (e.g., restlessness and disinhibition), confusion, and anxiety. Rare effects include the following: palpitations, mild elevation of the blood pressure and pulse, rash, and accommodation disorder of the eye. The side effects of methylphenidate and suggestions on how to handle them are outlined in Table 9.3.

Methylphenidate can improve cognitive abilities. Positive effects include the following: enhanced attention and concentration, improved memory for information taught at school, reduction in chaotic thinking and better focus, and decreased impulsivity and hyperactivity. It should be noted also that methylphenidate may have a slight effect on decreasing aggression. These improvements create the opportunity for social and cognitive development and may indirectly lead to increased self-esteem, because fewer corrections are needed.

The following are some statements by dissociative patients regarding their experience with taking methylphenidate:

- *I can pay attention better now, I have much better grades, the teacher is not angry at me all the time anymore.*
- *My voices are nicer to each other; they don't fight that often anymore.*
- *I don't forget things and remember what I should do.*
- *I can talk with my therapist without thinking hundred things at the same time.*
- *It's like my inner people are helping me now; they talk one at a time.*
- *I think now before I do something stupid. I first listen to my voices and don't just do what they say without thinking about it first.*
- *My others are leaving me alone now when I want to listen to the teacher or read something.*

Case Study: Marissa

Marissa was a 6-year-old girl who resided in a foster home. She was referred to Adrian J. Stierum by a trauma therapist for a psychiatric consultation. She was diagnosed with an attachment disorder, PTSD, and a dissociative disorder. Marissa was sexually abused by three of her older brothers for more than 3 years in her strict religious family. Her foster parents noted that she was hyperactive, hypervigilant, easily frightened, and spaced out. She had tantrums and aggressive behavior that she later did not remember. At school, she was performing poorly in reading and writing and the teacher thought she was mentally challenged. She could not concentrate, could not sit still, and was daydreaming away her days. She was also impulsive, unable to follow instructions, and did not complete tasks. In therapy, she was very restless, hyperactive, and sometimes aggressive, peevish, and sad. She was unable to establish a therapeutic relationship with the therapist and was failing to make any progress. Because of her disequilibrium, IQ testing was unable to be administered. There was a suspicion of multiple self-states. The symptoms that interfered with her cognitive development were ADHD-like hyperactivity, daydreaming, physical restlessness, impulsivity, and lack of concentration. These symptoms also interfered with her developing relationships with her teacher, foster parents, and therapist.

Marissa was started on methylphenidate. Target symptoms were concentration, impulsivity, hyperactivity, and restlessness. Marissa continued with trauma therapy and family therapy with her foster family. The foster parents were provided extensive psychoeducation on trauma. After a couple of days, Marissa's teacher called to relate that Marissa was concentrating better, listening well, and able to follow instructions for the first time. A month later, Marissa's reading and writing skills began to develop; 6 months later, Marissa's cognitive skills were improving. After a year, her IQ was tested and was found to be in the normal range.

In therapy, the therapeutic relationship developed quickly. EMDR therapy was utilized, and Marissa disclosed multiple self-states. Trauma therapy progressed well and after 18 months, Marissa's self-states integrated and her aggressive behavior and amnesia disappeared. Six months after integration, methylphenidate was discontinued because Marissa was functioning well both in school and at home. Because ADHD-like symptoms did not return after the discontinuation of the medication, we concluded that they were part of the dissociative disorder and the PTSD.

Case Study: Valery

Valery, similar to Marissa, was a sexually abused girl of about the same age and exhibited many of the same ADHD-like symptoms. Her symptoms were impairing her progress in school and hindering her trauma therapy and her relationship with her foster parents. Valery was diagnosed with a dissociative disorder and PTSD, and she was prescribed methylphenidate with positive results. After finishing trauma therapy and functioning well for 6 months at school and in the foster family, the medication was discontinued. However, Valery's ADHD-like symptoms instantly reappeared. She was hyperactive, impulsive, and could not concentrate. When methylphenidate was resumed, Valery began functioning well again. We changed the diagnosis to dissociative disorder and PTSD, both in remission, complicated with ADHD of the combined type.

Antipsychotics

Antipsychotics should be used with caution in dissociative children and adolescents. Auditory hallucinations should not be treated with antipsychotics. The voices are derived from self-states formed as a result of trauma, and therefore, by definition, are not psychotic hallucinations. Antipsychotics will not make the voices accompanying a dissociative disorder go away, and the sedation caused by high doses of antipsychotic drugs can even worsen traumatic voices. They can also cause a loss of control over dissociative processes, less control over switching between self-states, and more difficulty in regulating the self-states.

Because many children and adolescents with dissociative disorders are misdiagnosed with a psychotic disorder, a trauma therapist can expect to be confronted with this problem regularly (Moskowitz, 2011; Sar & Oztürk, 2009). Consultation with the prescribing doctor to explain concerns about this medication is advisable. Discontinuation of the antipsychotic medication is also often advisable. There are, however, some cases in which antipsychotic medications may be useful.

Indicators of Limited Use of Antipsychotic Drugs With Children and Adolescents With Dissociative Disorders

1. Impulsivity and aggression, but only when methylphenidate has no effect (risperidone) (Buckley, 1999)
2. Traumatic nightmares; use only when melatonin and clonidine have no effect (quetiapine low dose)
3. In a crisis situation, for temporary sedation (risperidone)
4. In the rare case of a comorbid psychotic disorder (risperidone or aripiprazole)

Currently, it is recommended to use atypical or second-generation anti-psychotic drugs with children and adolescents (McVoy & Findling, 2013), as these drugs have milder side effects.

It should be noted that antipsychotic medications are linked to various serious health risks and side effects such as weight gain, which causes a higher risk for type 2 diabetes, and cardiovascular disease (McVoy & Findling, 2013). Because of the potential for adverse effects, prescription of antipsychotic drugs should be avoided when possible. When prescribed, a rigorous follow-up trajectory has to be planned.

Monitoring Antipsychotics

Before starting antipsychotic medication, a family history of heart problems should be taken. If there are sudden deaths before 40 years of age and/or cardiac arrhythmias in the first line of the family, or if this is unknown, which is often the case with adopted and foster children and children of dissociating mothers, an EKG should be done before starting to exclude cardiac abnormalities (Corell et al., 2009).

The following blood work should also be done: prolactin, liver function, kidney functioning fasting glucose, glucose tolerance, fasting total cholesterol, high-density lipoprotein (HDL), low-density lipoprotein (LDL), and triglycerides. Weight, abdominal circumference, height, and blood pressure should be monitored. The recommended pattern of blood work and physical examinations are as follows: prior to starting; 1, 3, and 6 months; and then once every year. Every 6 months, the patient should be checked for tardive dyskinesias (Fedorowicz & Fombonne, 2005). Please bear in mind that this regime is time consuming and invasive for the patient.

Contraindications for Use of Antipsychotics

Antipsychotics cannot be used by patients with serious heart, kidney, or liver disorders, patients with bone marrow depression, and patients who are using other sedative medications. When a patient is suffering from epilepsy or has organic cerebral damage, a neurologist should be consulted (Preston et al., 2010).

Side Effects of Antipsychotics

Most side effects of antipsychotic medications are caused by the medication's blocking of a specific receptor system. Antidopaminergic, anticholinergic, antiadrenergic, and metabolic side effects appear within the first few days of the treatment or when the dose is increased. Young children are more sensitive to extrapyramidal side effects. Adolescents are more sensitive to weight gain. Young men have a higher risk of developing acute dystonia (Preston et al., 2010). The second generation of antipsychotics described here generally have mild side effects. When using them with children or adolescents with a dissociative disorder, a high dose is rarely necessary, which means that most side effects are milder. However, this does not mean that the health risks described earlier are lower. Table 9.4 outlines the main side effects of antipsychotics and provides recommendations on how to handle them.

Health Risks of Use of Antipsychotics

Weight gain is a serious side effect of all antipsychotic agents. It is associated with hyperlipidemia and hyperglycemia (high levels of fat and sugar in the blood), which can lead to higher risks for type 2 diabetes and cardiovascular disease when older. When there is weight gain of more than 11 pounds (5 kg), one should either change to another antipsychotic or discontinue antipsychotics altogether. While treating a patient with antipsychotics, information should be provided on maintaining a healthy diet, and participation in healthy exercise and sports should be promoted (Dieleman et al., 2011; Findling et al., 2008).

Neuroleptic Malignant Syndrome

Neuroleptic malignant syndrome is a very rare but potentially life-threatening complication of antipsychotics. It typically arises in the early stages of treatment. Symptoms include: muscle rigidity, severe extrapyramidal symptoms (i.e., dystonia, akathisia, and tremor), delirium, and autonomic instability—such as high or fluctuating temperature and blood pressure. Laboratory findings include elevated creatine kinase and leukocytosis. The patient has to go to an intensive care unit immediately and must be treated with bromocriptine 5 mg, three times daily. Sometimes,

Table 9.4 *Strategies to Deal With Main Side Effects of Antipsychotic Medication*

	Side Effect	Solution
Antidopaminergic (EPSE)	Parkinsonian: slowed movements, decreased facial expression, resting tremor, shuffling gait	Lower dose Switch antipsychotics Add biperiden
	Dystonic symptoms: muscle spasms mostly of neck and shoulders	Biperiden IM or IV When biperiden is not stopped, add lorazepam IM or IV
	Akathisia: intense feeling of restlessness	Lower dose Add benzodiazepine or propranolol
	Hyperprolactinemia with galactorrhea	Lower dose Switch antipsychotics
Anticholinergic	Dry mouth and eyes Blurred vision Constipation Urination problems Confusion Cognitive impairment	Lower dose
Antiadrenergic	Orthostatic hypotension[a] Sedation	Psychoeducation Lower dose
Metabolic	Weight gain Alteration of lipid and carbohydrate metabolism	Dietary advice Exercise If > 5 kg weight gain, switch antipsychotics
Heart	Prolonged QT interval	—
Tardive dyskinesia	Involuntary movements, mostly of the face. Appears late in treatment or when dose is reduced or discontinued	Stop anticholinergics Switch antipsychotics Discontinue antipsychotics

[a]A blood pressure drop immediately on standing. Can lead to dizziness and possible falling.

EPSE, extrapyramidal side effects; IM, intramuscularly; IV, intravenously.

electroconvulsive therapy is needed (Caroff, Mann, & Campbell, 2000; Silva, Munoz, Alpert, Perlmutter, & Diaz, 1999).

Discontinuation

Antipsychotic medication cannot be stopped all at once, because of the likelihood of the patient experiencing anticholinergic withdrawal symptoms (also known as anticholinergic rebound effect). Rather, the dose should be lowered gradually over at least 2 weeks; a month is recommended.

Risperidone

Risperidone (trade name Risperdal; generics also available) may at times be helpful for treating hyperarousal and aggression in children and adolescents with a dissociative disorder. It is only indicated when methylphenidate does not work. The medication is given once or twice daily. The APA advises a dosage of 1 to 4 mg daily when treating aggression (McVoy & Findling, 2013). In children, start with 0.25 mg and build up to a maximum of 1 mg daily with the dosage being increased at 2-week intervals while monitoring the effect. In adolescents, start with 0.5 mg and build up to a maximum of 2 mg daily. As with younger children, increase the dose at 2-week intervals while monitoring the effect.

In the rare case of a dissociative disorder with comorbid psychosis, risperidone is the drug of first choice (Pae et al., 2008). The treatment of psychosis is not covered in this chapter.

Aripiprazole

Aripiprazole (brand names Abilify, Aripiprex) is a relatively new antipsychotic with milder side effects and good efficacy (Findling et al., 2008). In the rare case of dissociation and comorbid psychosis, aripiprazole is a second-choice drug after risperidone. Furthermore, aripiprazole is a good second choice for children or adolescents who gain weight or have other disabling side effects of risperidone or other antipsychotics. The dosage with children has not yet been properly researched. Aripiprazole is administered once daily. In children, start with a low dose such as 1 mg and build up to a maximum of 5 mg. In adolescents, start with 2.5 mg and build up to a maximum of 10 mg (Dieleman et al., 2011). The maximum approved adult dosage is 30 mg/d (McVoy & Findling, 2013).

Case Study: Peter

Peter was a 15-year-old boy when he came to my office with severe behavioral problems such as truancy, lying, running away from home, having unprotected sex with older men, and refusing to follow any rules. He was referred by a child protection organization. Nobody asked him about possible trauma; instead, his therapists focused on his many behavioral problems. Peter's parents wanted him to be a normal and heterosexual son. Peter was diagnosed with a conduct disorder and was developing an antisocial personality disorder. His general practitioner prescribed him a high dose (600 mg) of the antipsychotic quetiapine so his parents and his therapist could better control him. As a result, Peter was very sedated; he talked and moved very slowly. Making eye contact with him was very difficult. He dozed and fell asleep often. In addition, it seemed that he did not listen. He was forgetful, often did not seem to know where he was, and was at times amnestic for what he had said or done. The first intervention was gradually reducing the dose of the antipsychotic. The sedation disappeared. This allowed improved interaction with Peter and he was able to talk about his trauma history.

Peter's history consisted of severe rejection by his stepfather in his early childhood, his parents not accepting his homosexuality at the age of 12, and sexual abuse by older men from the age of 12 onward. The destructive, unprotected, and sometimes paid-for sexual contacts with older men happened in a certain self-state, a 12-year-old boy, who did not care about anything. Another self-state was an angry 9-year-old who was aggressive and mean. The diagnosis was changed to a dissociative disorder and PTSD. The antipsychotic activated the presence of the self-state of the 12-year-old boy who did not care about anything and wanted to punish himself for being different—a homosexual. Impulse control and control over which self-state was present increased when the medication was stopped and adequate dissociative therapy was begun. Peter was treated with EMDR and integrative psychotherapy. His mother and stepfather attended family therapy with Peter and were eventually able to accept his homosexuality. After more than 2 years, Peter's self-states integrated and he became a conscientious adolescent who could experiment with sex and relationships in an age-appropriate way, without hurting himself. Peter moved out of his parents' home, returned to school, and later graduated.

Selective Serotonin Reuptake Inhibitors

Selective serotonin reuptake inhibitors (SSRIs) are antidepressants that elevate the serotonin level in the synapse by inhibiting its reuptake. SSRIs are proved to be effective in anxiety disorders and depression in adolescents and adults. Research indicates that SSRIs are less effective and cause more side effects (noted next) in children and adolescents younger than the age of 16 (Bridge et al., 2007; Hetrick, McKenzie, Cox, Simmons, & Merry, 2012). Thus, SSRIs should be avoided with patients younger than 16 years of age.

For youth with a dissociative disorder, it is recommended to prescribe an SSRI with no or small sedative effects (sertraline), because sedation could promote dissociation. The main effects of SSRIs are fading of depressive symptoms and lowering of the anxiety level. These effects are often not spectacular but they can help to make living more bearable. Indirectly, attention and concentration can improve, which promotes cognitive development. Clinical observation suggests that the use of an SSRI also has a light mood-stabilizing effect. Evaluation of the antidepressive and antianxiety effects of an SSRI can take place after 4 to 6 weeks; the effect usually starts within 2 weeks. An exception is the hypnosedative effect, which starts straightaway.

Because SSRIs are metabolized in the liver by the cytochrome P450 system, which is also used by many other medicines, the chance of interaction influencing the blood level of the SSRI and/or other medicines in either way is possible. Consequently, mono pharmacotherapy is preferred when prescribing an SSRI (Leonard, March, Rickler, & Allen, 1997).

Contraindications of SSRIs

SSRIs are contraindicated for those with a serious heart, kidney, or liver disease. Do not combine with MAO inhibitors and pimozide.

Side Effects of SSRIs

Most of the time, SSRIs are tolerated well in children and adolescents. The most frequent side effects are gastrointestinal complaints, such as nausea and stomachaches, that can be avoided by administering the SSRI with some food. In the beginning of the treatment, there can be a transient rise of the anxiety level and agitation. Other side effects include diarrhea, vomiting, headache, tremor, insomnia, sedation, loss of appetite, constipation, visual complaints, perspiration, dry mouth, and palpitations. Sexual side effects, such as loss of libido, delayed ejaculation, and erection problems, are also associated with SSRIs and can be particularly distressing for adolescent boys (Leonard et al., 1997).

The patient should be monitored for signs of restlessness, agitation, insomnia, and/or disinhibition, as SSRIs may precipitate a manic episode in some patients (Hairmann & March, 1996). Other important side effects to monitor are suicidal thoughts or intentions. Patients and parents should be instructed on how to respond if these arise (Bridge et al., 2007; Cooper et al., 2014). Clinical follow-up is recommended weekly in the first month of treatment, biweekly in the second month, and then every 3 months thereafter (McVoy & Findling, 2013).

Discontinuation Strategy for SSRIs

Because of withdrawal symptoms (cholinergic rebound syndrome) that consist of gastrointestinal complaints, headache, insomnia, and general malaise (flu-like symptoms), SSRIs cannot be stopped instantly. Rather, the dose should be lowered gradually over at least 2 weeks; a month is recommended.

Common SSRIs Used in Children and Adolescents

Fluoxetine

Fluoxetine (also known by the trade names Prozac and Sarafem, among others) is the most extensively researched SSRI in children and adolescents. Research has shown fluoxetine to be effective in adolescents with depression and anxiety disorders (Leonard et al., 1997). Fluxetine can be useful for the treatment of depression, anxiety, and hyperarousal in children and adolescents with dissociative disorders, because it has mild side effects with little sedation so that dissociation will not worsen. However, fluoxetine has slightly more interactions with other medicines than other SSRIs.

The starting dose is 2.5 mg for children less than 30 kg and 5 mg for children greater than 30 kg. The dose should be built up slowly over 3 weeks to 20 mg daily; then, the dosage should be increased, guided by the effect to a maximum of 40 mg daily. The starting dose for adolescents is 5 mg. The dose is increased slowly over 3 weeks to 20 mg daily. Then, the dosage is increased, guided by the effect to a maximum of 60 mg daily. Usually, a dose of 20 mg daily is effective (Dieleman et al., 2011; McVoy & Findling, 2013).

Sertraline

Sertraline (trade names Zoloft and Lustral) has been found to be effective in treating adolescents with depression and anxiety disorders (Robb, Cueva, Sporn, Yang, & Vanderburg, 2010; Rynn, Siqueland, & Rickels, 2001). Sertraline has mild side effects with barely any sedation, so dissociation will not worsen in children and adolescents with a dissociative disorder. Sertaline is the preferred agent for treating depression, anxiety, and hyperarousal in children and adolescents with dissociative disorders, because it has fewer interactions with other medicines than other SSRIs.

The starting dose for children is 25 mg. The daily dose varies from 25 mg to a maximum of 200 mg a day. The starting dose for adolescents is 50 mg a day. The daily dose for adolescents varies from 50 mg to a maximum of 200 mg; usually, 100 mg daily is effective. The dose should be administered once daily in the morning, around breakfast. Children and adolescents sometimes need a higher daily dose than adults as a result of their faster metabolisms (Dieleman et al., 2011). The highest dosage recommended by the APA is 300 mg (McVoy & Findling, 2013).

Atypical Antidepressants

Tricyclic antidepressants are not included in this chapter, because they are not considered to be effective in children and adolescents and have dangerous cardiotoxic side effects (Clark, Jansen, & Cloy, 2012). Similarly, the use of benzodiazepines in children and adolescents with a dissociative disorder is obsolete because of the high risk of addiction, serious adverse reactions with aggression, and worsening of dissociative symptoms.

Mirtazapine

Mirtazapine (brand names Avanza, Axit, Mirtaz, Mirtazon, Remeron, and Zispin) is a drug with both serotonergic and noradrenergic properties. Side effects are mild and similar to those of the SSRIs. Because of its strong hypnosedative effect, mirtazapine can be used with adolescents with sleeping problems, especially those caused by traumatic nightmares. The risk of addiction is negligible (Wang, Li, Li, & Hao, 2014). The dosage is 15 to 30 mg daily, 30 minutes before sleeping (Preston et al., 2010).

Melatonin

Melatonin is a neurohormone produced in the pituitary gland that influences the sleep–wake cycle. It is available over the counter. There are no known serious side effects, but there is not enough knowledge about the long-term effects of chronic use and the effect on pubertal development. Research on small groups suggests a positive effect of melatonin on the length of the sleeping period and the time needed to fall asleep. Melatonin has no effect on nightmares. Caution should be used when prescribing it to children with a history of epilepsy, as melatonin can be epileptogenic.

Children and adolescents with a dissociative disorder often suffer from initial insomnia, and they have difficulty falling asleep. Too little sleep can lead to worsening of dissociative symptoms and irritability. When administered at around 6 to 7 p.m., a "low dose" (< 1 mg) of melatonin resets the sleep–wake cycle (chronobiotical effect) so that the time to fall asleep is earlier and the normal sleep–wake cycle is restored. Melatonin has a sleep initiating effect when given in a "high dose" 1 hour before sleeping. To treat initial insomnia in children, start with 1 mg 1 hour before sleep. Increase as needed to a maximum of 5 mg. For adolescents, start with 3 mg and increase as needed to a maximum of 5 mg (Dieleman et al., 2011; Smits et al., 2003; Van der Heijden, Smits, Van Someren, Ridderinkhof, & Gunning, 2007).

The effect of melatonin should be clear within a week of daily use. When the maximum dose does not work within a week, melatonin should be stopped, which can be done immediately. There is no risk of dependence or addiction (Dodge & Wilson, 2001; Smits et al., 2003; Van der Heijden et al., 2007).

Adrenergic Agonists

Adrenergic agonists are antihypertensive medicines when used in a normal dose. When used in a low dose, there is also an effect on ADHD (enhances attention and concentration and decreases hyperactivity), tics, and sleeping disorders. Clonidine and guanfacine are the only adrenergic agonists that are regularly used in the treatment of child and adolescent psychiatric disorders. We focus on clonidine in this chapter, because there is more and better research suggesting the efficacy of clonidine in the treatment of ADHD, tics, and sleeping disorders (Connor, Fletcher, & Swanson, 1999).

Clonidine

Clonidine (trade names Catapres, Kapvay, Nexiclon, Clophelin, and others) is the only adrenergic agonist regularly used in treating children and adolescents with psychiatric disorders. There is some research that indicates efficacy in the treatment of ADHD, tics, and sleeping disorders. Clonidine is prescribed for children and adolescents with ADHD who have a comorbid tic disorder, or if methylphenidate is not tolerated well. For children and adolescents with dissociative disorders, clonidine can be used to treat insomnia caused by traumatic nightmares. Clonidine is also used to treat hyperarousal and anxiety. However, when a child with hyperarousal and anxiety is older than 15 years of age, an SSRI is the first-choice medication to treat these symptoms. Because of the antihypertensive effect, blood pressure should be monitored prior to initiating treatment, every week in the first month of treatment, and every 3 to 6 months thereafter (Connor, Grasso, Slivinsky, Pearson, & Banga, 2013; Harmon & Riggs, 1996; Jain, Segal, Kollins, & Khayrallah, 2011; Porter & Bell, 1999).

Before starting clonidine, a cardiac family history should be done. If there are sudden deaths before 40 years of age and/or cardiac arrhythmias in the first line of the family, or if this is unknown—which is often the case with adopted and foster children and children of dissociating mothers—consultation with a cardiologist should be done before prescribing the medication. In addition, prior to starting clonidine, an EKG should be done to exclude cardiac abnormalities. The EKG should be repeated once the desired dose is reached.

Dosage of Clonidine

When treating hyperarousal and anxiety, clonidine should be dosed at 0.004 mg/kg daily, starting with 0.025 mg at night, and building up to three times a day (8 a.m., 12 p.m., and 6 p.m.). The dose can be increased every 3 days by 0.025 mg until the desired dose is reached. The effect can be evaluated after 4 to 6 weeks of the desired dose. When treating insomnia due to traumatic nightmares, the child should be given 0.025 to 0.075 mg 2 hours before going to bed. This dose range is sufficient most of the time. The effect can be evaluated after 2 weeks (Dieleman et al., 2011; McVoy & Findling, 2013).

Clonidine cannot be stopped immediately because of the potential for dangerous rebound effects, including increased blood pressure, palpitations, insomnia, and increased arousal. Instead, the dose should be slowly tapered over the course of a month (Dieleman et al., 2011).

Side Effects of Clonidine
In general, clonidine is tolerated well. Sedation is the most prominent side effect when clonidine is dosed for hyperarousal and anxiety. Most of the time, the sedation is transitory and after 2 weeks, it is manageable by the child. Sometimes, clonidine causes dizziness and orthostatic hypotension. Less frequent side effects include irritability, headache, weight gain, and constipation. Clonidine can also potentiate the effect of sleeping pills and alcohol (Connor et al., 1999).

Anticonvulsants

Anticonvulsants are medications that help prevent seizures. Psychiatry has adopted a number of anticonvulsants to treat psychiatric conditions and there is some evidence that they are helpful in PTSD and dissociative disorders in adults, by interfering with kindling and quenching in the context of stress exposure. Anticonvulsants are used in child and adolescent psychiatry as mood stabilizers for children with bipolar disorder (Huemer, Erhart, & Steiner, 2010).

Anticonvulsants are used to treat explosive aggression in children and adolescents with dissociative disorders. Valproate and carbamazepine are the drugs most commonly used. Valproate (brand names include Convulex, Depakote, Epilim, Valparin, Valpro, Vilapro, and Stavzor) is considered the drug of choice, because carbamazepine has dangerous interactions with antipsychotics, antidepressants, and antibiotics. Valproate is an anticonvulsant with an unknown working mechanism. Because it is metabolized in the liver, contraindications include serious liver disease, the use of alcohol, and the use of benzodiazepines (Looff, Grimley, Kuller, Martin, & Shonfield, 1995).

Side Effects of Valproate

The side effects of valproate are generally mild. Sedation and gastrointestinal complaints are common but usually transitory and respond to lowering the dose. A more serious side effect, hepatic dysfunction, is more common in young children. Intoxication causes liver failure with increasing sedation, which can ultimately result in a coma. Before starting valproate, liver disease should be ruled out. Blood work should include liver function tests (ASAT, ALAT, AF, and gamma-GT) and hematological tests (platelets, leucocytes, and leucocyte differentiation) before starting the medication, after 1 month, and then every 6 months.

Blood serum levels of valproate should be monitored. An adequate level is 60 mg/L to 80 mg/L (Dieleman et al., 2011; McVoy & Findling, 2013). Serum levels should be done every week in the first month and then every 6 months. The blood levels of other anticonvulsants and tricyclic antidepressants are elevated by valproate. Fluoxetine, aspirin, and diazepam can elevate the blood level of valproate (McVoy & Findling).

CONCLUSION

On the surface, it is difficult to differentiate between a dissociative disorder and other diagnoses because of overlapping symptoms. A dissociative disorder has many symptoms mimicking many other diagnoses with a high level of comorbidity. With children who have early, severe, and chronic trauma, a comprehensive evaluation, including valid and normative checklists for dissociative disorders, will help to reveal the origin of symptoms (Chapters 2, 3, and 4).

Psychopharmacological interventions in the treatment of dissociative disorders in children and adolescents should be avoided when possible but are sometimes necessary. Children's and adolescents' brains and bodies are developing, and the long-term effects of most of the medicines used in child and adolescent psychiatry are unknown and insufficiently researched. Increasing therapy sessions and using stabilization techniques that include symptomatic self-states may effectively calm the child. When this does not work, then medication may be needed to stabilize the child enough to benefit from therapy.

Rather than be for or against medicalization, we need to get better at distinguishing between good and bad forms of medicalization (Parens & Johnston, 2008). The therapeutic relationship plays an essential role in prescribing medication. Without a strong working alliance with the child and parents or caregivers, medication is likely doomed to fail with negative consequences, particularly when there are aversive side effects. However,

Table 9.5 *General Rules for Prescribing Medication to Dissociative Youth*

Intensify other interventions first
Temporary pharmacotherapy
Mono-pharmacotherapy
Clear and measurable target symptoms
Patient chooses the most disabling target symptom
Invest in therapeutic relationships with the patient, parents, and caregivers
Invest in a working alliance with your team or cotherapist
Recognize specific issues with different self-states
Use drugs for which you can predict the effect and the side effects
Start with a low dose, build up slowly, until you obtain the desired effect
Give extensive psychoeducation about the medication for the patient, parents, or caregivers, and the cotherapist and/or team

when a child or adolescent is relieved of a disabling symptom, the overall therapy is enhanced and the therapeutic relationship may be strengthened. Pharmacological interventions should begin by targeting the most disturbing symptom. The youth can participate in choosing this target symptom, preferably by consulting with known self-states and parents or caregivers. The predicted effect should be measurable and is best evaluated by prescribing only one psychopharmacological agent at one time. If the intervention is not working, another one can be tried. It should be noted that most pharmacologic interventions can be discontinued when the trauma is worked through and the dissociative disorder is resolved in the therapy.

Table 9.5 provides general guidelines for prescribing medications to dissociative youth.

MASTERING TRAUMATIC MEMORIES

When I think of the bad stuff, I don't feel bad anymore.
—Dissociative child after treatment

THIS QUOTE IS ONE THAT I have heard repeatedly from traumatized children after they have successfully processed their trauma. I usually ask the dissociative child, "Does that mean that all parts of you don't feel bad anymore?" And when the child smiles, nods, and says, "Yes," then I know the child has mastered the traumatic memories. This is a significant milestone, as it means the child is no longer "ruled" by the horrors of the past. The past is now truly in the past!

Mastering memories can be viewed as the capacity to choose not to avoid but instead to confront adverse memories, recall them fully, and process and reconstruct them. According to Ford (2009), "The true antithesis to intrusive re-experiencing is not freedom from trauma memories or trauma-related distress, but the capacity to choose whether, when, and how to recall and make sense of (i.e., emotionally and cognitively finding meaning in) those memories" (p. 52).

This is the goal of our work with children. In the previous chapters, we discussed techniques for stabilization and building family support. These pave the way for trauma processing—the second phase of my three-phase treatment model. This chapter covers guidelines and interventions for trauma processing with the goal of helping children become "masters" over the trauma, rather than being "mastered" by it.

Many children whom I have treated have spontaneously disclosed traumatic experiences in the first session after I explain that I work with children who have had bad things happen to them, and it is okay to talk to me about any of those things, so that I can help them feel better. Disclosing traumatic experiences is an initial step, but it is not the same as trauma processing. Trauma processing is integrating the experience, including all parts of the self across all domains—somatically, emotionally, cognitively, behaviorally, socially, and spiritually. It involves self-reflective abilities as strong affect is expressed and painful realities are faced. It can precipitate an existential examination of the meaning of life and help the child recognize there is a future. We often do not think that children wonder about the meaning of their lives because they cannot express it in ways we understand; however, traumatized children often feel demoralized and despondent. They express these deeply masked feelings with defensive reactions. Our work with them is to instill hope for their future and belief in themselves. Knowing that there is a worthwhile future ahead for them fortifies them to face the nightmares of their past.

When children disclose trauma early in the treatment, it usually is a sign that they feel a sense of safety and want to share their disturbing memories with someone who conveys resonance and attunement with them. When children receive empathy, it can lead to trauma processing, as the therapist engages with the child about his experience. A child's early disclosure, in itself, can be a form of stabilization, particularly when the child's symptoms originate from the trauma he or she reveals. I will therefore begin to interweave some stabilization techniques to prevent or minimize the child from becoming hyperaroused or dissociated. However, if this does occur, it can be diagnostic and lead to exploring posttraumatic symptoms and dissociative responses.

Although trauma processing is considered phase two of trauma treatment after stabilization with adult clients (Chu, 1998; Howell, 2011; International Society for the Study of Trauma and Dissociation, 2011), as indicated earlier, there is variability with children. Clinical judgment is important in determining how to proceed with children's disclosures in the early phase of treatment. Because children may have not yet utilized years of self-defensive dissociative behaviors, their dissociative systems are often more flexible than those of adults. Consequently, they may be more capable of processing their traumatic events earlier in treatment (Marks, 2011; Silberg, 2013; Waters, 2005). Silberg, Marks, and I have had success in working with dissociative children and adolescents in intensive short-term therapy. Short-term therapy requires sensitivity to the needs of the child and careful pacing so that the child can integrate the traumatic experiences without becoming either hyperaroused or hypoaroused.

I saw Johnny, a severely traumatized 9-year-old boy who came to the initial session with his computer tablet. He lived alone with his single mother. He had been sexually abused by his grandfather who had not been allowed to have visits with him for some time. In our initial session, Johnny wanted to show me an application on his tablet, a drawing program that also contained numerous images that could be used with the program. To my surprise, Johnny immediately began to process his feelings toward his grandfather with this application. He wanted to show me how he felt about "all the bad things he did to me," as he skillfully clicked from one picture icon to another.

Johnny started with the whole screen covered with crying faces accompanied by the sound of crying babies. I sat quietly looking at the entire screen filled with crying faces and listening to the cacophony of their cries. It was intense and truly depicted his deep grief. Then, Johnny swiftly went from one image to another, showing me spider webs, bats, ghosts, skulls, and tombstones—each filling the entire screen, one image at a time. While displaying these images, Johnny told me how he was afraid of his grandfather, how these figures represented his grandfather, and what he would like to see happen to him. I empathized with how hard it must have been for him to have his grandfather hurt him. For the next several sessions, Johnny brought in his computer tablet, showed me the same images, and expressed the same feelings. Each time, after he was done, he would breathe a sigh of relief as he sat back and relaxed his shoulders. Then, he no longer brought the computer tablet to the sessions. He had expressed what he needed to express. Over time, we talked about the details of what his grandfather did to him while he depicted his trauma through drawing and the use of clay.

I interspersed a combination of stabilization techniques and interweaved many positive cognitions, such as telling Johnny that the abuse was not his fault. Johnny was relieved to hear this, as he had blamed himself for his grandfather's abuse. We talked about what he felt in his body as well. Interestingly, later on, Johnny did not feel the need to do any more traumatic processing, as he felt he had worked it through.

Johnny then disclosed numerous "imaginary friends" that were friendly. However, he identified one that was different than the others and was called "Killer Johnny." This one felt Johnny deserved the abuse and tried to get him to cut himself or jump in front of a car. Killer Johnny identified with Johnny's grandfather. I explained to Johnny's mother how important it was to accept all parts of Johnny in order to gain Killer Johnny's cooperation. The aim was to work constructively with Killer Johnny and to reframe his negative role into a positive one. I also explained to Johnny's mother how important it was for her to build an attachment with Killer Johnny. I stressed that over time he might come to identify more with her rather than with Johnny's grandfather.

Johnny's mother accepted Killer Johnny and began to show him affection. For example, when she hugged Johnny, she told him that she was hugging Killer Johnny too. Killer Johnny would "flee" during those times. Initially, Killer Johnny was resistant to thinking that Johnny did not deserve to be abused, denied he helped Johnny to survive, and was standoffish to Johnny's mother's kindness and "hugs." I would talk to Killer Johnny through Johnny showing respect for him and made suggestions for how he could handle his behavior differently. Johnny would report that Killer Johnny would leave, because he thought what I said was stupid and he was bored. Interestingly, over time, Killer Johnny became less menacing to Johnny, and his presence was infrequent.

Later, Johnny reported that Killer Johnny "was back" and was listening when Johnny and I talked about his grandfather. Killer Johnny appeared to be clandestinely scrutinizing what was occurring at Johnny's home and in therapy, because to my astonishment, Johnny reported that Killer Johnny decided to not be like his grandfather; instead, he wanted to go to college to learn how to help children who are orphans!

I think the critical factors for Killer Johnny's identity alteration involved the following: our nonjudgmental and accepting approach toward him as a part of Johnny who helped in some way (even though Killer Johnny denied it); our encouragement for Killer Johnny to deal with his feelings in a constructive way; and, most importantly, Johnny's mother's consistent acceptance and "nurturing," which seemed to break though Killer Johnny's armor. When she demonstrated care for him, his identity shifted to modeling her kindness and not his grandfather's cruelty. I encouraged a name change as well, but Killer Johnny prosaically said that it was just a name that he had "all of his life" and he did not feel a need to change it. I expressed concern about the connotation of "killer" and how that was not such a nice connotation given how Killer Johnny had changed so much and wanted to help children, but Johnny again said in a matter-of-fact way, "No. It is just a name to him." I smiled as I thought to myself, "Well, it was hard to argue with that!"

Although this process was a bit backward from the usual way of processing trauma, it worked for this child. I provide this example to show that as clinicians we need to be sensitive to where the child is at and follow his or her lead. At the same time, we need to use our intuition and skills to help the child maintain stability while moving forward in processing his or her trauma. It is important to note that Johnny's case differs from those of most children I see, as Johnny felt secure in his attachment with his mother and felt safe due to cessation of all contact with his grandfather. These provided him with the reassurance and comfort necessary to tell me what he felt and experienced, along with the ego strength to manage the process. These were critical conditions that promoted stabilization and made early traumatic processing successful.

Let us examine some guidelines for trauma processing that can further elucidate the timing of and conditions for trauma processing.

GUIDELINES FOR TRAUMA PROCESSING

I have developed nine guidelines for trauma processing in dissociative children. These guidelines are not necessarily sequential, and many of these guidelines overlap with each other to influence the child's ability to successfully process memories without abreacting or dissociating.

1. Therapist Readiness

It is critical that therapists be aware of their own feelings and thoughts to avoid any negative transference or inability to manage strong affect and disturbing content that the child expresses. Children are very sensitive to our degree of comfort with the material, and our acceptance of them and what they say. The *therapist's attunement* to the child will encourage the child to be open and will facilitate confidence and trust in the child that what he says will be accepted and managed by the therapist. Blaustein and Kinniburgh (2010) aptly describe the interplay and dynamics in the therapeutic relationship when a traumatized child discloses trauma:

> Bearing witness is rarely a completely disconnected process. Although most professionals learn the skills to maintain a reasonably comfortable objectivity and distance, empathic work requires, to some degree, the capacity to resonate with and respond to the affect, relational dynamics, thoughts, systems of meaning, and physiological energy of our clients. Just as attachment is a dyadic, rather than a one-sided, process, therapeutic work happens in the context of a relationship, and these relational connections have an impact on both the child client and the helping professional. (p. 212)

Having a positive relationship with the child is a prerequisite for providing the structure for trauma processing. When the therapist has the capacity to "hold" the child's intense affect, validate the child's suffering, and help the child manage it, the child builds the confidence to revisit the horrors of the past.

2. Assess the Dissociative Child's Internal and External Levels of Safety

Assessing a dissociative state's readiness for disclosure is important to avoid a self-state becoming angry at the child for telling the "secret." A self-state may resist disclosure out of a fear of retribution or because of loyalty to the perpetrator. Premature disclosure could instigate an internal "warfare" in which a self-state that is loyal to the perpetrator may try to harm the child for disclosure. The child is less likely to experience internal turmoil or threatening harassment after disclosure, if early groundwork has been completed in which internal cooperation and agreement among self-states are achieved. However, this may not always be possible, as the child may not be aware of hidden parts of the self that are fearful of being known. If the child shows signs of deterioration during trauma processing, it would be wise to explore what the child is experiencing internally as well as any environmental factors that may contribute to the deterioration. Adolescents who have a high degree of self-abusive behaviors or well-developed self-states who identify with perpetrators may be particularly resistant to trauma processing without necessary groundwork.

It is also necessary to assess the child's outer world for physical and emotional safety prior to doing trauma processing. Evaluation of family support is critical for successful memory retrieval and trauma processing. Children may recant their traumatic experiences if they feel blamed for disrupting the family structure. The optimal situation for trauma processing is when the child resides in a safe and secure home with an "attachment anchor"—most likely a committed parent. The continuity of an attachment figure during treatment will greatly enhance the success of the treatment (Struik, 2014), especially during trauma processing. Therapeutic focus on building attachment between the child and caregivers prior to trauma processing can provide this attachment anchor. Johnny's mother was Johnny's anchor and eventually became Killer Johnny's anchor as well.

Children who reside in an unsafe environment will need to disclose the trauma in order to become safe, but they are often faced with a difficult decision. Although disclosure may ensure their safety, it can cause them to be removed or ostracized by their family. Therapists need to work closely with protective systems to ensure that the child is safe and that the therapeutic treatment is also supported. Silberg (2013) emphasizes how critical it is to communicate with the various systems that exert control over the child, and that therapeutic interventions need to be reinforced throughout the many milieus where the child lives, learns, and plays.

When there is no attachment anchor for the child at home, the therapist can become this anchor, as demonstrated in the clinical case of Briana. Although her mother was concerned about her, Briana's attachment to her mother was disorganized due to her mother's own traumatic reactions to triggers precipitated by Briana. Briana, therefore, could not expect a consistent response from her mother. After several tumultuous years of treatment, including my being fired twice, I became the attachment anchor that provided Briana the ability to disclose extensive sexual abuse by multiple perpetrators.

3. Assess the Child's Comorbidity

As previously noted, dissociative children often have high rates of comorbid disorders. Consequently, it can be a struggle to determine what needs to be worked on first to help stabilize the child. Often, the source of the child's pathology is his or her history of chronic trauma and unrecognized dissociative defenses. Tackling the trauma experience helps to ameliorate comorbid symptoms. A two-prong approach is often needed when dealing with multiple disorders. With this approach, the clinician deals with the most debilitating symptom while also addressing the source of the symptoms—the trauma and dissociative reactions. For example, for adolescents who have complex trauma and substance abuse addictions, a coordinated dual treatment approach of a residential substance abuse recovery program that also incorporates treatment for trauma and dissociation has a more promising outcome for recovery. This dual approach promotes adolescents to begin to remove their dissociative barriers and process their traumatic experiences while in a safe, drug-free environment. (More information about working with dissociative adolescents in substance abuse recovery is provided in Chapter 11.)

4. Evaluate the Meaning of Implicit Memories

Early traumatic memories are often stored in the implicit memory system—the nonconscious or nondeclarative memory—rather than in the explicit memory system in which conscious recall of symbols or images is available (Lyons-Ruth, 1999; Stern et al., 1990). The implicit memory system is presumed to be present at birth and operating without conscious awareness (Cordón, Pipe, Sayfan, Melinder, & Goodman, 2004). Graf and Masson (1993) noted, ". . . explicit memory is only a small part—the conscious tip of the iceberg—of how memory for recent events and experiences influences us in our daily lives. The submerged and much larger part of the iceberg is the domain of implicit memory" (as cited by Cordón et al., 2004, p. 103). Cordón et al. added, "We have little idea of the extent of the 'submerged' part of the iceberg, with respect to memory for trauma specifically, although there is good reason to think that it is likely to be far from negligible . . ." (p. 103). Implicit memories are often reenacted (Terr, 1990) both at home and during therapy sessions with traumatized children.

Dissociative children (particularly infants or toddlers, but also older children) often express their trauma in symbolic or encoded behaviors that are held in their implicit memory system. Their bodies carry disturbing somatic memories and they respond to sensory cues that remind them of their trauma with a defensive response of fight, flight, or freeze. They reenact their trauma in interactions at home, school, and therapeutic milieus in encoded ways. This was evident in the earlier case description of Lisa, described in Chapter 4, who was adopted when she was 4 months old and who had a swollen gum of an unknown traumatic origin. It was apparent that she suffered excruciating pain as she resisted anyone and anything that came close to her face and mouth, including food, even when she was starving.

I have treated a number of preschoolers who suffered significant pain during infancy as the result of birth traumas, a botched circumcision, and brain surgery. These young children were emotionally and behaviorally dysregulated and exhibited significant sensory disturbances. Prior interventions that focused on trying to cure their symptoms with medications and behavioral strategies were ineffective. Conversely, processing their early trauma in therapy resulted in positive outcomes.

As therapists, we need to recognize that although children often cannot verbalize traumatic experiences held in the implicit memory system, we need to be able to explore whether their behavioral reenactments and somatic disturbances originated in their early trauma. Designing creative techniques that target implicit memories can pave the way for effective trauma processing. This task can be particularly challenging with cross-cultural adoptions in which there is often a paucity of information provided regarding traumatic experiences, as with Lisa. Nevertheless, we need to recognize that *all children's behavior has meaning,* be it hidden or symbolic, and we need to formulate interventions that access its core meaning. You will learn more about therapeutic techniques I designed to deal with Lisa's oral trauma later in this chapter.

5. Validating the Child's Survival

It is important to validate children's survival skills. Simply reminding children that they survived tremendous adversity by their own inner strength (including help from self-states) can in itself be empowering. The very fact that children are present to narrate what happened to them is an indicator that they did exactly what they needed to do to survive! Although this validation usually occurs during the early phase of treatment, it is particularly important to reemphasize it during trauma processing, referencing all parts of the child. During trauma processing, feelings of helplessness, shame, weakness, and immobilization, along with thoughts of self-blame and worthlessness are likely to be rekindled. It is important to remind the child about the physiological self-defense system of immobilization that is "involuntary" in mammals when facing terror (Porges, 2011). This can help mitigate feelings of guilt, shame, and self-blame based on the fact that children often cannot fight back or disclose immediately.

6. Utilizing Stabilization Techniques to Stay Present

The stabilization techniques that the child previously learned, including symbols and cue words, EARTH, 4 L's, mindfulness of bodily sensations, feelings, and thoughts, are employed during the trauma processing stage to help the child stay grounded and discern differences between the past and the present. Staying grounded in the present helps the child to express the trauma from a safe distance rather than reliving the trauma. The child can express intense affect but not feel as though the event is occurring now. The stabilization techniques that were practiced earlier should have expanded the child's window of tolerance, allowing the child to process intense feelings, thoughts, and sensations without becoming completely overwhelmed. The ability to face the past without disintegrating can result in a sense of empowerment and overall well-being.

Tara, the 8-year-old girl with DID described in Chapters 2 and 7 who drew the haunting sexualized picture of her face with large red lips and vacant eyes, did intense trauma processing that depicted her sexual abuse through the use of anatomically correct dolls. Tara expressed outrage toward her biological mother, who abused and prostituted her, and her mother's boyfriends and their party friends who also sexually abused her. She repeatedly threw the adult male and female dolls representing her abusers on the floor, as she expressed her rage for what they did to her. Tara was able to release pent-up emotions while remaining oriented to the here and now the entire time. She would smile at times at her ability to tell her abusers how she felt.

Tara became breathless at one point and her adoptive mother, who was present during the session, reminded her to take deep breaths. Her adoptive mother also used hand signals to signify to Tara that she and her self-states should work together as a team during the processing. Afterward, Tara's adoptive mother held Tara on her lap in the rocking chair. Tara and her mother looked into each other's eyes while her mother comforted and reassured Tara in a soft, soothing voice, telling her that it was not her fault and remarking on how brave and strong Tara and her parts were to survive. Tara's adoptive mother, a single parent, was very committed to Tara and was engaged throughout her treatment. Strengthening the attachment between Tara and her mother was an integral factor that facilitated Tara's ability to face the terror of her past and process her traumatic memories.

7. Process Trauma Across Self-States

Cooperation and teamwork across all parts of the self are keys for complete processing of traumatic experiences. Trauma processing should include relevant self-states that were involved in the particular traumatic event (Waters & Silberg, 1997). Discussing and defining the child's self-states' roles in regard to what, when, and how they will process their traumatic experiences shows them respect and minimizes sabotage. Special arrangements can be made for those who were not directly involved in a specific trauma by placing them in a safe room or enlisting their support. During processing, the use of hand signals and cue words that signify internal cooperation can be helpful reminders, as with Tara. Tara's parts that were not involved in the sexual abuse were enlisted to be her "cheerleaders" and "coaches," and the others were placed in a safe room so they were not impacted.

8. Telling the Traumatic Narrative Across Modes of Expression

A variety of interventions can be employed to help children process their trauma. These interventions can be tailored to the youth's interests. Puppets, drawings, clay, dollhouses, sand trays, journaling, and computer tools can assist in helping children tell their stories along with specific treatment modalities, such as eye movement desensitization and reprocessing (EMDR) therapy (Adler-Tapia, 2012; Adler-Tapia & Settle, 2008; Gomez, 2013b), ego state therapy (Watkins, 1988), sensorimotor psychotherapy (Levine, 2010, Levine & Kline, 2007; Ogden, Minton, & Pain, 2006), and hypnosis or guided imagery (Daitch, 2007). I often use many different tools and treatment modalities in the course of trauma processing. (Chapters 11 and 12 discuss art and EMDR therapies.)

Telling the traumatic narrative may occur in stages as dissociative children gain the strength and knowledge necessary to manage traumatic aspects, and self-states are ready to process their material. As a result, a child's trauma narrative may not be coherent and sequential until later in the trauma processing stage. For example, during processing, a new self-state may surface that contains information that the child was previously unaware of. Children need to be heard and understood from the perspective of a fractured mind trying desperately to piece together fragments of memories composed of images, sensations, and feelings. During processing, the child is reorganizing and assimilating the traumatic material from different aspects of the self, eventually leading to a more cohesive narrative.

Having the youth process across sensory domains—visual, auditory, olfactory, kinesthetic, and somatic—is critical to comprehensive processing. There has been much written about the body being a portal of trauma processing (e.g., Levine, 2010; Ogden et al., 2006; van der Kolk, 2014). Levine and Kline (2007) noted, *"trauma is not in the event itself; rather, trauma resides in the nervous system"* (p. 4, emphasis in original). A somatic approach entails observing minute body and facial movements while the child is processing the trauma. These subtle movements arise from the sensory motor memory system and convey more than words can about what the body is carrying. The bodily movements are often unconscious expressions that communicate where the traumatic memory is stored and the body's signal of needing to release the frozen or thwarted traumatic experience. For example, the child may have frozen during the abuse and while immobilized, the body was unable to complete the desired movement to resist or seek safety. As a result, during trauma processing, the body may exhibit a stunted attempt to do so (Levine, 2010; Ogden et al., 2006). Encouraging the child to move the body to successfully complete the aborted act to defend himself or herself helps to physically release the pent-up energy stored in the nervous system.

Lisa, whose history is detailed in Chapter 4, displayed symptoms of somatoform dissociation. She had numerous somatic disturbances ranging from constant numbness around her mouth and arms when eating to periodic pain in her arms and legs. She was also highly sensitive to her hair touching her neck and had difficulty tolerating her hair being combed. She also complained of stomachaches after she ate and had frequent headaches. Lisa's somatoform symptoms appear to be the result of an unknown oral trauma (diagnosed by a pediatric dentist) that she suffered prior to being adopted at 4 months. On her placement in her adoptive home, she was immediately highly defensive to anyone or anything that came near her face or mouth.

A therapeutic goal was to help Lisa find meaning in her persistent somatic disturbances, some of which appeared to relate to aborted attempts to escape when orally traumatized as an infant. A number of sensorimotor interventions were developed to help Lisa complete self-protective actions and regain mastery over her body. These techniques resulted in a cessation of her somatic disturbances, as you will learn later.

9. Grieve the Loss of the Idealized Childhood and Past Attachment Figures

A critical and often the most difficult part of interpersonal trauma is grieving the loss of the child's first attachment figure and the idealized parent. However, unless traumatized children face their pain, they will have difficulty attaching to their current caregivers. In order for children to grieve and experience their deep pain, they have to become vulnerable—a formidable task for well-defended children. The pain caused by being abused by a parent can be described as feeling as though their heart was repeatedly stabbed with a serrated knife. In addition, these children often are in conflict with competing emotions of love and hate, and thoughts of "I am no good; I am bad; it was my fault; they were mean; I love them; they didn't love me." Even among children who were horribly abused, there is often a part of them that still has an attachment to their abusive parents. Miranda, described in Chapters 6 and 7, had a self-state, Miranda Sue, who was named after her birth mother. This part had not been abused and had a favorable view of her mother, who had been nice to her.

This grief work is often the last component of trauma processing. It is the raw, penetrating pain of rejection coupled with self-loathing. There is much confusion to process with lots of "whys" regarding their abuse. Traumatized children often need a secure or stable attachment figure to do this work, yet their fear of rejection and negative transference to their current caregivers can cause them to reject support and be stuck alone in their grief. It is important to help their current caregivers understand their paramount role in holding the child while the child grieves the loss of his or her biological and/or ideal parents. This will help to provide an empathic and comforting atmosphere for the child to release the deep pain. However, this can be a difficult task for some adoptive parents who have been repeatedly rejected by the child. To repair the relationship between adoptive parents and a rejecting child, it is important to help the parents understand the child's negative transference and reenactment of rage on them, while working with the child on appropriately directing his or her rage, pain, and grief toward the abusers. Once the child is able to grieve the loss of the idealized parent, this can pave the way for the child to build attachment to the present caregivers.

Supportive caregivers of young children can be directly involved in the therapy to bear witness to their child's trauma processing and to provide nurturing. After teens have processed traumatic events, inviting their parents to the session to provide understanding and empathy to their child can be helpful in building attachment.

CLINICAL EXAMPLES OF TRAUMA PROCESSING

Lisa Processes Her Maternal Loss and Grief

Lisa, who was introduced in Chapter 4, was removed from her Asian biological mother at birth and placed in a foster home until she was adopted
at 4 months of age. Lisa arrived in the United States with a painful swollen gum that the pediatric dentist ruled was from an unknown trauma.
She was highly dysregulated and Lisa's adoptive parents, Sandy and Joe,
had first sought professional help for Lisa when she was 18 months old.
Lisa's adoptive parents had secure attachment with their own parents and
a healthy marriage that provided a solid foundation to endure 9 difficult
years of trying to contain Lisa. Although Lisa's parents were depleted,
they did not have any unresolved childhood issues that triggered them.
They were steadfast and committed to helping their child. Sandy worked
at home and devoted her life to finding solutions to Lisa's problems and
managing her two sons.

Sandy was eager to soak up any knowledge that might help Lisa and
was willing to follow my directions. She became an integral part of her
daughter's healing, as I taught Sandy about the facets of complex trauma
and dissociation, including dysregulated affect and behavior, along with
attachment, attention, somatic, and memory disturbances. I explained that
even though on the surface Lisa's difficult behavior did not make sense,
there was hidden meaning to it. To understand it, we needed to recognize
what triggers ignited Lisa and explore how these connected to her early
trauma.

Since she was a small child, Lisa's themes in her play were loss
and abandonment due to parents who were absent, hurt, disabled, or
deceased. I encouraged Sandy to begin to talk to Lisa about her feelings
regarding her birth mother to provide Lisa an opportunity to express
her grief. Sandy used Lisa's favorite stuffed animal to mirror what Lisa
often demonstrated in her play about lost or disabled parents. Sandy then
inquired about Lisa's feelings toward her birth mother. Lisa immediately
opened up about her sadness and how much she missed her birth mom.
Lisa reminded her adoptive mother about how she had previously discouraged Lisa from talking about her feelings. Her adoptive mother
reported that previous clinicians had told her to only focus on Lisa's behavior and not her feelings. Sandy apologized to Lisa, telling her that she

now realized how unhelpful this had been. Lisa was then able to express mourning over the loss of her birth mother with Sandy resonating with her. Lisa's severe temper tantrums immediately began to subside and she became more tolerant of minor frustrations. It was as though a balloon that had been stretched to the breaking point was finally able to release some air.

During the follow-up session, Lisa told me that her self-state, Mary, missed her birth mom. Lisa picked a gorilla hand puppet to represent her birth mother and a baby puppet to symbolize Mary. Lisa's choice of the gorilla puppet from the array of puppets in my office suggested to me that she viewed her birth mother as powerful and strong. Lisa sat in her adoptive mother's lap holding the gorilla puppet that, in turn, held the baby puppet. Sandy began to rock Lisa while the gorilla puppet simultaneously rocked the baby puppet. Sandy and I talked to Lisa in soft tones about Mary's sadness over her birth mother's inability to care for her, and her long voyage to the United States to be adopted. Sandy reassured Lisa that when she became an adult, she would help locate her birth mother. Lisa's large almond eyes filled with tears as her mother continued to gaze into her eyes and comfort her. Sandy explained that her birth mother was unable to financially care for her but that she loved her and wanted Lisa to be happy. Then, Sandy asked whether Lisa and Mary would accept her love. I explained that through their adoptive mother's love, they could heal from their losses and the Mary part of her could grow up to be Lisa's age. Lisa and Mary readily agreed. As with Rudy (Chapter 4), this intervention was also repeated at home.

As Lisa began to open up, we found that Lisa blamed herself for leaving her birth mother. She told her adoptive mother that she broke her own heart, because she had left her birth mother. Sandy further explained to Lisa how her biological grandparents could not provide for both her and her mother. Mary appeared and sobbed, saying, "I want Mamma." Sandy again reassured her that she would help Lisa find her birth mother when she grew up. Sandy suggested that she pretend that she is the birth mother. Lisa agreed and Sandy portraying Lisa's birth mother told her how pleased she was that Lisa found a new mother. She told Lisa how pretty she was and asked why Lisa looked so sad. She then said that she was sorry that she had placed her for adoption but could not keep Lisa because she did not have a house or food. She reiterated that she was glad that Lisa found a new mommy who took good care of her. Lisa calmed down and seemed accepting of what was being said. The intervention seemed to work, as

Lisa began to demonstrate more attachment behavior toward her adoptive mother by initiating closeness with her and actually hugging her. Through Sandra's nurturing of Mary, the infant self-state spontaneously age progressed to Lisa's current age of 9.

Although considerable trauma resolution and attachment work had occurred, we felt that a memorial service in honor of her birth mother would help finalize Lisa's mourning process. On a bright, sunny fall day when the trees were at their peak of color, Lisa, Sandy, and I climbed a rocky cliff that overlooks the city of Marquette, Michigan—the rural town where I practice that is nestled in a forest that borders Lake Superior—to perform a farewell ritual for her birth mother. Lisa gathered some stones to form a small shrine. She wrote a note to her birth mother, telling her that she loved her and hoped to see her when she grew up. She tucked the note under the shrine as her adoptive mother resonated with her feelings. This ceremony provided Lisa the final closure for her maternal loss and strengthened Lisa's attachment to her adoptive mother.

After Lisa grieved the loss of her birth mother, she told her adoptive mom that Mary missed her foster father, who fed and played with her. Sandy again comforted Lisa over her loss. Although there were concerns because Lisa had been injured while in the foster home, Mary seemed to be attached to her foster father and did not show any fear toward him. This made me suspicious that her foster mother was responsible for the oral injury. Because of Lisa's positive experience with her foster father, she had transferred those feelings to her adoptive father, with whom she demonstrated a close relationship. He periodically attended the sessions to strengthen their relationship and to actively support Lisa's healing.

However, attachment building still needed to occur with Lisa's other self-states, angry Cindy, and the two adult protector states, Shadow and Helper. Sandy praised them all for how they helped Lisa in various ways. She noted that Lisa could not have handled all of her anger without Cindy's help. Cindy agreed to comply with our request that she use the various calming techniques I had taught her and to visit the internal anger room rather than explode outwardly. Sandy asked Shadow and Helper whether they would work as a team with her to care for Lisa, as working together would allow them more time to relax. They agreed.

As Lisa's internal life stabilized, she managed transitions much better and was not as easily triggered. She was calmer and more self-regulated. Her rages were bimonthly instead of daily. Lisa became more coordinated and was finally able to hold and use silverware. Significantly, after 3 months of intensive therapy consisting of 2-hour sessions twice a week, Lisa was able to begin attending school full time—something she had been unable to manage since kindergarten.

Lisa Processes the Oral Injury: Untangling the Implicit Memory

Overall, Lisa was doing much better; however, she began to report sensory disturbances, such as tasting blood when she ate, getting nauseous, and feeling as though she was going to regurgitate while eating.

One day at home, Lisa was cutting a peach and was complaining that her stomach hurt. Lisa's former behavior returned and she screamed at every attempt her adoptive mother made to comfort her. When Lisa calmed down, she revealed to her mother that there was a scared baby inside her. Sandy asked her why the baby was scared and Lisa replied, "I don't know why." Sandy told Lisa that she wanted to find out what happened so that she could do something to fix whatever was troubling her. Lisa replied, "The baby was afraid you were going to hurt her." Sandy explained, "There was a mother that hurt her, but you came to us, and even though you are afraid you are going to get hurt, you are safe." I suspected that Lisa had an implicit memory of the oral trauma that was triggered when she cut the peach. The baby self-state's fear of being hurt (later identified as Tommy) had been generalized to Lisa's adoptive mother. The rest of the week, Lisa was irritable and easily angered with her mother.

Shortly thereafter, Lisa had a flashback and ran to her mother trembling. She reported seeing a woman with dark hair and dark skin cut her gum with a piece of glass or a knife. She could taste the blood in her mouth and was choking. Tommy was then identified as an infant state that was formed at the time of the traumatic event. As she connected with Tommy, Lisa felt his terror. This was a major breakthrough. Her sensory disturbances and fear were now comprehensible to her, as well to her mother and me. Lisa's inexplicable statement to me earlier, "Baby felt like it was going to die . . . I felt it in my heart," now made sense. The implicit memory was now in her conscious memory system where it could be processed. Lisa's history of head and face banging resulting in nosebleeds appeared to be a reenactment of this trauma. Her infantile oral defensiveness, intense fear of anyone approaching her, numbness in her face, mouth, and extremities when eating, and her development of dissociative states appeared to be derived from this oral trauma that she likely incurred at the hands of her foster mother.

After this flashback, Lisa's stomachaches decreased and she and Tommy were receptive to affection from her adoptive mother. Helper agreed to watch and comfort Tommy in the nursery so that he would feel safe. Shadow agreed to block out internal distractions so that Lisa could pay attention at school, and Cindy again agreed to use the anger room to manage her anger. With these interventions, Lisa was able to maintain her stability at school; as well, her mood and behavior improved at home.

Healing Lisa's Somatic Disturbances

As previously noted, Lisa had many nonorganic somatic complaints, including pain in her legs, arms, head, and neck. She was also hypersensitive to touch and would cry when her hair was gently combed. Based on the principles of somatoform dissociation (Nijenhuis, 2004) and the effects of cumulative trauma on the body (van der Kolk, 2014), I hypothesized that Lisa's somatic disturbances were related to her body being immobilized with fear—unable to fight or flee when Lisa was abused. Lisa needed to release the pent-up tension held in her nervous system not only psychically but also physically (Levine & Kline, 2007; Ogden et al., 2006; Schauer & Elbert, 2010). An important step toward healing her somatic problems involved helping Lisa's body to move from a passive/frozen state to an active state of doing whatever the body wished it could have done to defend herself at the time of the trauma.

Because Lisa had revealed that both Tommy and Mary held feelings related to her early trauma, it was important to include them in the intervention. I asked Lisa whether it would help to be able to release the pain in her arms and legs by moving them in such a way to defend herself from the oral injury—something she had been too small to do when she was injured. Lisa indicated that she would like to push, hit, and kick her foster mother (the various behaviors she had exhibited toward her adoptive mother). I held a pillow and encouraged Lisa, along with Tommy and Mary, to vigorously kick and punch the pillow in defense of the assault by her foster mother. As Lisa released pent-up energy, she expressed anger, hurt, and sadness. When she finished, Lisa expressed a great deal of relief and empowerment. Sandy wanted to aid in Lisa's recovery by repeating this technique at home. However, I did not want Lisa's adoptive mother to hold the pillow, as I did not want her in any way to be associated with the foster mother. Sandy then suggested that Lisa could kick an old piece of furniture. I agreed, and Lisa was encouraged to kick a stuffed chair. Before the next session, Lisa vigorously kicked the chair multiple times, while her adoptive mother observed, praised, and comforted her. Many of Lisa's somatic symptoms ceased.

Rewriting Lisa's Traumatic Script

Another therapeutic intervention used to resolve Lisa's trauma involved rewriting the traumatic script with a positive ending. A sand tray with various animal and hero figures was used to stage a symbolic traumatic reenactment with a rescue scenario. Lisa used a nanny goat to represent her foster mother and a baby goat to represent Tommy. The nanny goat hurt the baby goat. However, this time, her adoptive mom played the hero. Lisa picked a male action figure to represent her adoptive mother, who along with her adoptive father (represented by a police figure) rescued Tommy and took the nanny goat to jail. Other animals were picked to represent Lisa's adoptive siblings and grandparents. All of them were present to witness the rescue. During the sand play, Lisa expressed her sadness and fear of being hurt, and her relief when being rescued. This was important, because Lisa had many lingering fears of being hurt again and had generalized these fears to her adoptive mother. This rescue scenario symbolically represented what the adoptive parents had actually done when adopting Lisa. This intervention increased Lisa's sense of security and safety with her adoptive parents (Figure 10.1).

Increasing Lisa's Sensory Awareness

Although Lisa's behavioral and attachment problems were resolving, Lisa still experienced depersonalization when eating. This was one of the last major issues left to tackle. As previously noted, Lisa had no sensory awareness of the taste, smell, or texture of food in her mouth or on her body, resulting in food dripping on her when she ate. Sandy agreed to bring a hamburger to our next session for Lisa to eat. As expected, Lisa ate the hamburger without any awareness of the food and condiments dripping from her mouth onto her chin, arms, and clothing. While she ate, I gently directed Lisa to notice any sensations on her face and body and to look at her arms and clothing. I gave her a mirror to look at her face. She expressed surprise at seeing the food smeared on her face. To address

Figure 10.1 *Lisa's sand tray—rewriting the script with a rescue scenario. (Used with permission.)*

Lisa's depersonalization, I developed several interventions. The first was a healing ceremony for the part of Lisa who had been injured.

A Healing Ceremony for Lisa's Injured Self-State

Since Lisa identified Tommy as the part who incurred the physical trauma to the gum, I suggested a healing ceremony by using dolls and applying a "magic cream" to heal the gum injury. I explained to Lisa and her adoptive mother, Sandy, what each of their roles would be during the ceremony. We began by using the dolls to reenact what likely transpired when Tommy's foster mom cut his gum. Lisa played Tommy and I played the foster mother by using dolls to reenact the trauma. Lisa expressed Tommy's pain and fear at being cut. Sandy played herself by using a mother doll and did the reparative work of comforting Tommy. The mother doll administered the "magic cream" on the Tommy doll's gum to soothe and heal it. While administering the cream, Sandy empathized with Tommy, saying how much that must have hurt and how sad she felt for Tommy and Lisa.

Lisa held the Tommy doll, expressing her fear, pain, and sadness. Then, I suggested that Sandy pretend to put some of the imaginary magic cream on Lisa's gum. Lisa opened her mouth and when her mother put her finger close to Lisa's mouth, Lisa suddenly put her lips over her mother's finger and began to suck it. It was apparent that Tommy, an infantile state, was briefly present. Sandy indicated that the magic cream was healing Lisa's gum, and Tommy was safe now. Not only was this a healing experience for Lisa, but it also increased the attachment between Tommy and their adoptive mother.

Repairing Lisa's Traumatic Connections With Eating

The final piece was to assist Lisa to somatically repair her traumatic connections with eating so she could experience pleasant sensations associated with eating. It was important to enlist not only Tommy but also all parts of Lisa in reconnecting across sensory domains, because, to some degree, all of them were involved either directly or tangentially. All parts of Lisa agreed to be present and work as a team. I explained that it was safe now to connect across all sensory domains while eating and to notice the experience. To help Lisa focus on the kinesthetic, olfactory, and gustatory experience, she and her parts agreed that her adoptive mother would place a bandana over Lisa's eyes, as I would place food on her face for her to smell, feel, and finally, taste. Lisa described the feel, smell, and taste of the food while blindfolded. Then, the bandana was removed and we added vision to the sensory experience of eating. At home, Sandy repeated this exercise several times. Lisa found it to be a fun activity and she enjoyed the challenge.

To test the efficacy of these interventions, I asked Sandy to bring another hamburger to our next session. Sandy added extra ketchup, mustard, and mayonnaise to the hamburger. Lisa ate the hamburger and when a small piece of food got on the corner of her mouth, she immediately felt it and wiped it off! While eating, she maintained awareness across all sensory domains. Lisa was careful to keep the sandwich juices from dripping down her arms; however, because there were so many condiments on the sandwich, some landed on her lap. Amazingly, Lisa noticed the fact that the food had dripped on her immediately. All of us laughed. Sandy and I praised all parts of Lisa for eating with complete sensory awareness. It was another major milestone toward Lisa's ultimate integration, which is described in Chapter 13.

Rudy's Trauma Processing

Rudy, whose case was first introduced in Chapter 4 and continued in Chapters 6, 7, and 8, was adopted with his sister from an orphanage in Eastern Europe when he was 18 months old. Rudy had a history of serious aggression at home and in kindergarten, resulting in a school suspension for 45 days. As noted in Chapter 7, Rudy and his mother rocked and comforted Rudy's internal baby part to heal his early deprivation. Rudy's baby part began to age progress and within a few weeks, the baby part was Rudy's current age of 6. When Rudy's "invisible team" became known, they were oriented to their current reality of living in a loving adoptive home with ample food, and they were asked to share the full sensory experience of eating. After this, Rudy's aggression toward his sister around mealtimes subsided. His invisible team learned that they do not have to kill people to eat. Rudy also learned that his invisible team had helped him obtain food and took his hunger away so that he did not feel hunger when he lived in the orphanage. Rudy thanked them, and they cooperated fully with Rudy, his adoptive mother, and me. They now understood they were a part of Rudy and were happy to live in an attentive home that took care of their needs.

Unfortunately, Rudy continued to display aggression toward his sister, Katrina, by grabbing toys from her. Rudy explained that his invisible team did not have toys to play with when living in the orphanage. A simple intervention to resolve this early deprivation was to suggest that when Rudy played, they would share the experience with him. The invisible team stopped attacking Katrina, as their needs were being met.

Rudy, however, still suffered from difficulty controlling his bladder and bowels. Although Rudy's baby state likely contributed to his encopresis and enuresis, Rudy was also depersonalized from his body, most likely as a reaction to a lack of timely attention when he soiled his diapers in the orphanage. Rudy expressed the physical discomfort of soiled diapers while his mother held him, explaining how hard that was for him to endure. I stressed that it was safe to now feel that part of his body. Rudy's invisible team agreed to help Rudy and his baby self-state become aware of their bodily needs and to alert Rudy when he needed to go to the bathroom. Figure 10.2 is a picture that Rudy drew of himself and a toilet with a message from his invisible team, saying, "I will help you to go to the bathroom."

Rudy struggled getting himself ready for school. He hated dressing in the morning, because it took too much time. His invisible team agreed

Figure 10.2 *Rudy's invisible team agrees to help him with his toileting issues. (Used with permission.)*

to help Rudy quickly get dressed in the morning for school by imagining that they were firefighters responding to a fire alarm. They also supported him in doing his homework and chores. With their cooperation, Rudy displayed better self-control at school and was able to manage staying at school for longer periods.

Unfortunately, a few weeks later, Rudy's behavior regressed. Rudy resumed his unprovoked hitting of his sister. When reprimanded, Rudy became agitated. When exploring what accounted for his actions, he revealed, "The Devil told me to do that. I heard it from my brain in my mind. It is different from the invisible team because its voice is different." Rudy also indicated that he saw the Devil in his mind. Knowing that self-states were formed to help in some way, it was important to reframe the Devil self-state as a positive part before it wreaked havoc on Rudy's progress. I asked Rudy to check inside to see whether the Devil may have helped him in some way. Rudy said, "People were being mean to me. That Devil took it." During this discussion, Rudy began to stare off and almost fell asleep. I had to repeat my questions several times and reorient him to the present moment. I suggested that this part did not resemble a Devil, because he tried to help him, but needed help to safely work through his anger over what he took for Rudy. I proposed that Rudy and his invisible team could help the Devil to express his anger appropriately. They agreed. Rudy surprisingly said that the Devil had a "sensor" that would alert Rudy to behave well when around his sister but the sensor's battery was bad. I asked Rudy what he thought could be done about that. Rudy indicated that the Devil immediately replaced the battery! I was pleased by Rudy's imagination, creativity, and willingness to tackle this problem. I suggested that Rudy change the Devil's name, since he was really a helper. Rudy renamed him Angel and Rudy's aggression toward his sister abated.

Many of Rudy's behavioral problems appeared on the surface to be very disturbing and resistant to typical child management techniques. But knowing the root of his problems—self-states' unresolved trauma, insufficient understanding of how to behave, and lack of current reality—simple interventions that were tailored to correct these problems resulted in Rudy responding well. In addition, family therapy sessions (Chapter 6) to repair some inappropriate treatment by Rudy's adoptive mother enhanced a positive, secure attachment. Soon, Rudy was attending school full time and was successfully riding the school bus without exhibiting any aggressive behaviors. His integration was well within reach, as you will learn in Chapter 13 on integration.

Cathy's Trauma Processing

Cathy, whose case was first introduced in Chapter 4 and continued in Chapters 7 and 8, experienced sadistic abuse at the hands of her adopted father after being sent to live with him when her mother had been seriously injured in an automobile accident. Cathy had depersonalized as a result of her father's abuse (e.g., forced to take cold showers, made to sleep with wet clothes on, placed for hours in an unheated storage room, and beatings and screaming in her face). As previously noted in Chapter 7, the stabilization phase of Cathy's treatment was focused on helping her reconnect with her body and empowering her. However, the relational component of loss, abandonment, and grief still needed to be processed.

Cathy wanted answers from her mother regarding why she was placed with her adoptive father from age 6 until she was 11, as she felt abandoned by her mother. In a family therapy session, Cathy's mom, Jane, explained that when she, Cathy, and Justin were in a serious car accident, Jane was disabled and required months of rehabilitation. Fortunately, the children were unharmed but she was unable to care for them. Even though Jane had reported her now ex-husband, Ken, for abusing their children when they were toddlers, they were, nevertheless, placed with him. When Jane began to receive secret phone calls from Cathy about her and Justin's recurring abuse by their father, Jane made numerous child protective services (CPS) calls. It took many investigations before CPS confirmed that Ken was indeed abusing Cathy and her brother. Jane explained how she went to court numerous times to regain custody of her children, but was unable to do so until their father was found to have abused them. Jane comforted Cathy and apologized for the abuse that Cathy had been forced to endure. This helped Cathy resolve her feeling of maternal loss and abandonment.

However, Cathy continued to be plagued with nightmares of being abducted, injured, and killed. These dreams were associated with her persistent fears about her adoptive father's abuse and fear of him hurting her again, even though she was not having visits with him. Cathy, along with the participation of her self-states, chose to use the dollhouse dolls to reenact her abuse and express her intense feelings, particularly anger and fear. Cathy depicted her adoptive father hitting her, shouting at her, forcing her and her brother to fight each other, putting her in a hot storage room, and throwing her in a cold shower. Her internal parts also used their internal anger room to express their anger. In follow-up sessions, EMDR therapy in the form of drumming was used to provide bilateral stimulation of her brain while we processed her feelings. Prior to trauma processing, Cathy's fear was 10 out of 10 and her anger was 8 out of 10 on subjective units of distress (SUD). With this intervention, both feelings were reduced to zero. Cathy and her parts also achieved the positive belief that they were now safe and that the abuse was not their fault.

After Cathy processed her fear and anger, we processed her sadness, pain, loss, and grief over her dad's maltreatment. These feelings were triggered when her dog died. We discussed her feelings of grief and Cathy sobbed as she drummed. After she released and processed her grief, Cathy was able to achieve the positive cognition that she was worthy and lovable. Cathy reported that she felt that she had resolved her trauma. The integration phase of her treatment is discussed in Chapter 13.

Briana's Trauma Processing

Briana, whose case was first introduced in Chapter 2 and continued in Chapters 3, 4, 6, and 8, suffered considerable trauma encompassing witnessing domestic violence, and emotional, sexual, and physical abuse by multiple perpetrators from an early age until she was 16. The abuse started when Briana was a toddler; as a result, she was not able to master any of Erikson's psychosocial stages (Chapter 1), leaving her impaired in areas of trust, autonomy, self-esteem, identity, and intimacy.

Briana was numb to her body and her feelings, and she abused alcohol and drugs. When Briana was almost 17 years old, she began to make significant gains in stabilizing. She maintained her sobriety, attended Alcoholics Anonymous (AA) support groups, and ceased association with peers who were using drugs and alcohol. Briana struggled with choosing healthy male relationships and recognized that a self-state she called Little Girl tried to fill her need for attention by engaging in sexualized behaviors. Briana's tenacity, intelligence, and desire to lead a healthy life were her greatest assets in facing her traumatic life. She agreed to participate in therapy sessions several times a week and kept her appointments. She was pleasant, open, and cooperative.

Although Briana had tested me over the 3 turbulent years, she finally trusted that I was not going to abandon her or pass judgment on her, in spite of her frequent attempts to incite such from me. I cannot emphasize enough the need for consistency and tenacity when working with chronically abused adolescents. If the therapist can demonstrate genuine empathy, patience, and belief in the adolescent's recovery, the distraught, fearful, and distrusting adolescent can, over time, begin to develop a positive transference. There were many times that I wondered whether I would even see Briana again, but she kept coming back. Eventually, I became the attachment anchor that provided her the stability to face her traumatic past and move toward recovery.

Themes of rage, pain, loss, abandonment, and grief were central to processing Briana's chronic physical, sexual, and emotional abuse as she struggled with her poor self-esteem, identity, and relational issues. Briana particularly struggled with reframing cognitive errors about herself. To help Briana process her trauma, I took a multimodal approach by using the following interventions: ego state therapy, gestalt therapy (Perls, Hefferline, & Goodman, 1951), art therapy (Cox & Cohen, 2005, Sobol & Schneider, 1998), EMDR therapy, hypnosis, and family therapy (Satir, 1983).

Briana's self-states, Little Girl, Angry, and Intuitive, were engaged at different junctures in the trauma processing. Briana was diligent in writing daily in her journal on specific therapeutic assignments that correlated with the issues that we were working on. Briana gained much relief and understanding as she processed her chronic trauma. The following are some of the interventions that were the most helpful in her recovery.

Spiritual Meaning as Briana's Anchor in Trauma Processing

Briana searched for spiritual meaning in her life. She said that she had a "broken spirit" and felt that a spiritual foundation would give her the strength to face the past. She said, "I'm trying to build up my spirit to take control of my life." She insightfully stated, "Once I bring out feelings in me, this will allow acceptance and forgiveness."

Briana's faith was Christian based and she read the Bible daily to provide her solace. It anchored her life while dealing with traumatic memories and feelings. Because traumatized children feel despair, it is important to support their religious orientation or spiritual beliefs. I provided CDs and books that helped her in being hopeful as well as self-forgiving to overcome her guilt and shame over her past behaviors.

Briana's Face Numbness

Briana felt much despondency that she did not feel anything, as she had numbed herself and was numb toward others for most of her life. She indicated, "I shut off my feelings so that I could endure what I put myself through." I asked her whether she knew what those feelings might be. She responded, "Pure pain." I asked her whether she could describe her pain more. She paused and said, "The pain is jealousy, anger . . ." and after a short pause, she added, ". . . total hurt." I asked, "Can you say more about the hurt and pain?" Briana looked away briefly and turned to me with sorrowful eyes. She softly replied, "That's all it comes down to—protection from feeling the pure pain."

Briana was artistic and often drew while we talked. I asked her to draw her pain. She drew a black tulip shedding red tears in a glass jar. She stated that she was the tulip, and she wrote, "hidden" at the top over curly lines and "imprisonment" below. These words described her hidden states and feelings, and the imprisonment of utter despair (Figure 10.3).

Figure 10.3 *Briana's hidden, imprisoned feelings of despair and pain. (Used with permission.)*

Briana Connects With Mind and Body

As described in Chapter 8 on calming the stress response, Angry agreed to allow Little Girl to begin to feel her trauma a little bit at a time with Angry giving her the strength to manage it. Briana agreed to use EMDR and rated her numbness at 8 out of 10 on SUD. She understood that she could stop at any time or retreat to her imaginary safe place when she needed a break. After a couple of sets of EMDR (Chapter 12), Briana looked at me with sadness and in that all-too-familiar despondent tone said, "I can't feel the pain in my body. I shut down. I am numb." Briana had separated from her body again. Being connected with the feelings and sensations in one's body is similar to having an alarm system that tells one about dangerous situations. To heal, Briana needed this alarm system to work. I wondered what dynamics were obstructing Briana from feeling her bodily sensations and emotions at this time. I asked her what she thought was keeping her from feeling her body. She said, "My mind won't let me feel the sensations in my body." I reassured her that it was the best to experience strong feelings a little bit at a time by using the analogy of a dripping faucet (Kluft, 1990). According to this analogy, her mind would allow her body to feel a little bit at a time, so that feelings would be released very slowly as she gained the ability to tolerate them.

Since Briana referenced her mind not letting her body feel sensations, I thought that ego state therapy might help. I suggested that her "body" talk to her "mind" by using an empty chair to represent the location of her mind and the couch to represent the location of her body. Briana, who sat on the couch, looked at the empty chair; she took a deep breath and began talking to her mind. Briana then moved from the couch to the chair so she could answer as though she was the mind. Moving back and forth, her mind and body had a conversation with one another. I guided her in the process while encouraging her to show appreciation for the wisdom of both her mind and body. I praised their willingness to participate and expressed my belief that they could work together in harmony.

The following is a dialogue between Briana's body and mind.

Body: "I can't feel. I know it is your way to protect me from the trauma, but I really want to feel and work it through."

Mind: "I know you want to feel your body because you think of it a lot. I will give you small portions of it at a time."

Body: "I am glad that I can trust that you will give me small portions because it is overwhelming. I don't want to go through my life not feeling. I don't want to go through my life being two instead of one. I do appreciate all that you have done to protect me. I am willing to share the knowledge that I have gained from these experiences with you. I hope you will let me feel."

Briana paused and looked at me, saying contemplatively, "This is the best thing I could do, right?" I asked her how she felt, as that would let her know. She said, "I feel good. I came in here kind of edgy and now I'm . . . It's like I just stepped on the meaning of life! I have a warm fuzzy feeling. It's just a warm fuzzy feeling!" She recognized that connecting to her body was integral to perceiving life. She resumed.

> **Body:** "I really appreciate your willingness to trust me, and your willingness to share things you've kept from me so long. I've wanted this for a long time." *(Briana switched to the chair again, paused a second in thought before responding.)*
>
> **Mind:** "I'm content. I'm a little bit nervous with letting you feel. Not nervous that you're going to feel, but that I'm not going to totally connect with you." *(Pause)* "I'm sure we will. It will be hard. It's good I'm giving it to you in small doses. Better than any drug you've had. I mean sex too, 'cause sex is a drug too. Will you let me know if you are overwhelmed, overburdened? I can take the feeling away."
>
> **Body:** "Yeah. I have good gut instincts."

Since Mind was hesitant to let Body feel, I interjected that if Mind could develop a trusting relationship with Body, knowing that each contributes different skills, this would promote Briana's healing. I asked Mind to talk to Body about this.

> **Mind:** "I want to develop a good trusting relationship with you because in the past I have always ignored your gut instincts and that has gotten me into trouble. I don't want to wipe the slate clean, but work through what we went through together."
>
> **Body:** "Yeah, it really pisses me off when you've ignored my gut instinct."
>
> **Mind:** "I am sorry I did that. I am willing to develop a good trusting relationship with you. This is going to be the hardest thing we will ever do in our entire life but the most rewarding. I'm glad we came to this understanding of working together."

This was a pivotal moment in Briana's healing. In working with somatic disturbances, I felt that it was critical to access the unconscious process that was thwarting her somatic awareness. Without this dialogue, she may never have been able to feel her body. Instead, she most likely would have resorted to her compulsions. This direct communication between her Mind and Body allowed them to form a partnership, which laid the groundwork for Briana to be able to process her traumatic experiences.

In the next session, Briana reported that she was not edgy and she felt totally content. She was able to self-reflect and take responsibility for her negative behaviors. She said, "I feel changes in a subtle way, little changes. I'm getting a clearer picture in the mirror. I see myself for what I am now. I can see my problem areas. My listening has improved. I am able to focus on things with more clarity."

The Mind–Body exercise appeared to create integrative shifts within her as her visual and auditory senses improved, along with her reflective abilities. She reported that she had not engaged in compulsive cleaning or exercising. Excited by the changes she was experiencing, Briana wanted to continue this ego state exercise. The following is an excerpt of another conversation between Mind and Body.

Body: "I really appreciate you letting me see, hear, and listen with more clarity everything that is going on around me. This is the beginning for both of us. It's a good beginning. We still have a long way to go. I would like to be able to be at the point of seeing myself on the inside and outside. That's when I'll know we will be one."

Mind: "I appreciate you thanking me, but as I told you before I would give you small doses so you will not be overwhelmed. We are two different separate persons and have a long way to go. I appreciate you're not putting me through the hell of exercising. You haven't been overeating or undereating. You exercise when you feel the need. I'm getting a good night sleep 'cause you've resumed taking your meds."

Mind was certainly stating her mind! Briana had resumed taking her antidepressant. I was surprised by Mind's statement that they were "two different separate persons." However, I am less concerned with the degree of separateness as long as there is internal communication, cooperation, and problem solving that enhances her recovery. I just silently noted it.

Briana resumed communicating between Mind and Body, wanting to explore hip and back pain that came on at nighttime.

Body: "I want to know if you have any memories that are connected with pain that I have in my hip and back."

Briana paused and then turned to me, saying, "I'm starting to get spacey." She paused again and said, "I know why. I don't want to deal with the feelings coming up. It is hard to deal with them." I asked her what the feelings were and she responded, "It's the pain and fear." I redirected her to explore this with her mind.

Body: "I know there is pain and fear and I hope you'll work with me on that."

Mind: "I know it's important for us to work together on this. I know you're scared to know the reason for the pain. Your God wouldn't give you something you couldn't handle. We'll handle it together."

Although Briana wanted to know the origin of the pain, her dissociating was a sign that she was not ready to deal with the specific traumatic memory. Body carried the somatic trauma, but Mind held the memory. Briana needed Mind's cooperation in order to understand and heal her pain. I felt that it would help Briana to express that somatic pain, even though she did not have a specific memory associated with it. I asked Briana to draw a picture of what the pain resembled. She drew a ball of pain that she described as "pointy, sharp and dark" (Figure 10.4).

In a follow-up session, Briana reported that she was beginning to experience some of the pain without being overwhelmed. She drew another picture of the pain. It was similar to the first drawing except that the pain was no longer "pointy and sharp"; the pain had lessened and now had rounded edges (Figure 10.5).

I recommended that Briana join a self-defense class to help her develop awareness of her body and to feel strong and centered. After several classes, she reported that she was learning about balance. She stated, "The midsection is the center of weight—the center of it all. The more I get in touch with my midsection, the more I get in touch with myself." I wanted to move her to a deeper understanding of being centered and responded, "Paradoxically, as you become more centered within yourself, and learn who you are, you are actually less centered on yourself and more on other people." Once again, Briana's response showed her depth, "Not I, but we."

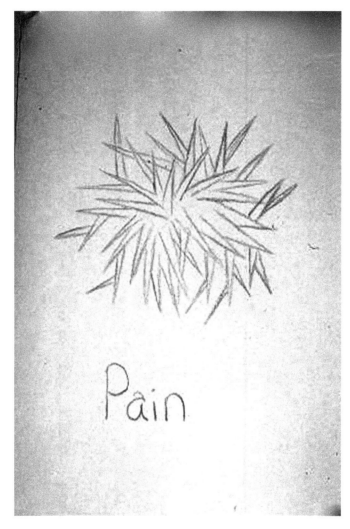

Figure 10.4 *Briana's pain with pointy edges. (Used with permission.)*

Dealing With Briana's Distorted Beliefs

Briana indicated that she did not have control over herself, particularly during arguments with her mother. During these arguments, Briana felt attacked and cornered, which activated the helpless child within. Briana would then become numb and verbally attack her mother. She said that she had no control over what she said and did. She realized that Angry was in charge at those times. Briana recounted, "Every time I was attacked

Figure 10.5 *Briana's pain with rounded edges. (Used with permission.)*

or abused, I felt trapped in a corner. I felt confused, scared, angry, ashamed, and didn't know why this was happening to me. I felt I was under siege. I was always wrong; wrong and bad all the time. That's when I developed personalities." Briana relied on her creative mind to help her escape but now it was time to find another way to deal with triggering moments when she felt trapped.

I facilitated another ego state exercise in which Briana talked to Angry who she viewed as male. Angry recounted that when she was young, Briana's father had told her that it was a sign of weakness to show feelings. He told her that she should "stand up and look like a man." She had to be powerful and not weak. Briana told Angry that what her dad said was ". . . totally wrong and he should not have instilled that in you. By not feeling, you're not able to be responsible and feel out the whole situation of what is going on. I understand that if you don't experience feelings, things can't hurt you. But I think it is important that everyone show feelings. That's being human. It's more a man and human to show emotions. The belief that was instilled in you was not right."

Angry surprisingly agreed with Briana and said that one of his big goals was to be able to cry. He said, "You and I haven't been able to do that. I will cry for the pain my family has felt, and not just me. We will walk hand in hand." Briana responded, "I hope you will cry and I will help you. I'm glad we will walk hand in hand. I will also pass on my knowledge of the good coping mechanisms to you so that we can work together. We both need to use the good coping mechanisms."

Parental messages that are relayed to children can powerfully thwart a child's ability to express vulnerable feelings. Angry, who staunchly protected Little Girl, carried an erroneous belief instilled by Briana's father. This belief had to be cleared in order for Angry to face painful affect, distinguish the difference between strength and aggression, and use more self-control and assertiveness. Angry was renamed Advisor when he agreed to assume this new role. It was now time to heal the Little Girl.

Little Girl's Trauma Processing

Briana's self-states (Mind, Body, Angry/Advisor, and Intuitive) agreed it was time to help the Little Girl face her traumas. Briana and I discussed what she needed when she was little, and explored what she could currently provide to Little Girl. Briana recognized that Little Girl needed to be held, comforted, and loved. Briana said she was willing to provide this to her. Initially, Briana did a writing exercise in which she and Little Girl wrote to each other to establish a connection and to provide support and understanding to Little Girl for the abuse she took for Briana. Then, I again facilitated Ego State Therapy. Briana picked out one of my dolls to represent Little Girl and held her in her arms. Briana assumed a maternal, protective role with Little Girl.

With her eyes closed, Briana comforted her Little Girl as both of them grieved their early and chronic abuse. Tears flowed down Briana's face as she softly talked to her Little Girl, explaining that although she learned at an early age to flirt with males and to comply with their wishes, it was not Little Girl's fault and the shame she felt was unwarranted. She told Little Girl that she was not protected and never taught what it felt like to be treated well. She did not understand what was happening to her. Briana further explained that Little Girl deserved to be treated with respect, kindness, and love for who she was, and not for what she could do to please men.

Since behaving differently was foreign to Little Girl, Briana vowed to be a model so that Little Girl could learn how to protect and value herself. Briana explained to Little Girl that with the help of Advisor, Intuitive,

Mind, and Body, Briana would be more assertive with others, set better boundaries, take better care of herself, and protect Little Girl from ever being abused again. Briana explained that she was noticing more about how her body felt and was following her intuition and gut instincts. Little Girl agreed to learn from Briana's modeling and promised she would not come out when Briana was around men. Briana asked Little Girl to stay in her safe room and watch from the window to learn how to be respected. Little Girl agreed. Briana agreed to visit and comfort Little Girl daily. Briana reported feeling peaceful after this intervention.

Briana's Grieving Traumatic Memories and Losses

Briana's grieving continued as more memories were recalled. One day, Briana watched a movie in which someone was dying and suddenly began to sob uncontrollably. She recognized that her own slow death and loss of herself were heightened by her utter betrayal and sexual abuse by an older man who had exerted immense power over her. She disclosed the details of his horrific abuse of power in which she was lured into having sex with him numerous times by him providing her with cigarettes, drugs, and alcohol. These had served to further numb her and make her compliant with his sexual demands. On one occasion, she almost died from a cocaine overdose. Her heart was racing and she passed out for more than an hour. When she returned to normal, the narcissistic abuser simply remarked, "You got me worried. You did enough cocaine to kill a horse." She expressed rage over her degradation while I listened silently, feeling my own rage for what had been done to her.

The physical and emotional pain Briana felt regarding the older man's abuse triggered previously dissociated memories of her father's abuse. She recalled that her father showered with her until she was 10 years old and insisted on washing between her legs with a washcloth. Briana said, "It was painful. I felt dirty and degraded." She went on to recount numerous other traumatic incidents at the hands of her father when she was young. When she was 5, he forced her to sit at the table until she ate a whole bowl of oatmeal that she had initially refused. She reflected back to that time and recalled hearing Angry's voice for the first time. Angry said, "Just eat it. It'll be fine. Just do it." Her dissociative defenses increased when her father, who hated cats, shot the neighbor's kittens—kittens that Briana had loved and played with. After recovering these memories, Briana limited her contact with her father, as she recognized she was reenacting their relationship with other abusive males.

Summary of Briana's Trauma Processing

Briana's journal was her silent, loyal friend with whom she shared her pain, grief, rage, confusion, and shame, as she detailed her extensive trauma. I became her witness and active listener as she shared her painful journey. EMDR, hypnosis, and Ego State Therapy were used to help Briana process her abuse. Through these interventions, Briana learned to value herself and set boundaries with others. She also gained insight into her self-destructive patterns and assumed more responsibility for her actions.

Although her home environment was stressful and often triggering, Briana came to recognize that when she raged at her mother, she was really mad at her mother's inability to protect her from the abuse. At one point, Anger/Advisor took over to protect Briana from experiencing the pain when an altercation with her mother triggered memories of sexual abuse. Briana asked Advisor to comfort her when she felt pain instead of masking it. When she connected with her pain, she realized that she felt horrible about herself and that this had led her into a cycle of bodily abuse involving exercise, sex, drugs, and food in order to mask her pain. After significant trauma processing, Briana reported, "I'm beginning to come to terms with a lot of things and I'm forgiving myself." She was more self-reflective and less reactive. Regarding the extensive trauma she incurred by the older abusive man, she remarkably said, "I don't hate him. I feel sadness and pity for him."

In summary, Briana's case highlights the intricate interplay between her powerful dissociative states and their roles in causing her behavioral problems and later in helping her recover. This case highlights the importance of pursuing the underlying dynamics related to self-states when there is a block to trauma processing. During the stabilization phase, Angry agreed to relinquish the compulsions and to instead provide Little Girl the strength to manage her painful feelings; however, until he could reframe his cognitive distortions and not see feelings as a form of weakness, Angry would not allow Little Girl and Briana to experience their vulnerable feelings. Just as Briana was ready to process her painful feelings associated with traumatic memories with the use of EMDR, she suddenly became numb. Another layer of dissociative states, Mind and Body, had to communicate with each other and come to an agreement so that Briana could begin to feel her body. After Briana got in touch with her body, she and Little Girl were able to process their pain.

As Briana developed a more internal awareness of her self-states, she eloquently said, "The beginning of liberation is the personalities listening to each other instead of being separate." I asked her what she felt. She responded, "I feel liberated. My mind is not racing. I feel calm and peaceful now. I am remembering lots of incidents that caused me bad energy." Although Briana remembered her abuse, these memories were no longer consuming her. Briana now had the internal cooperation and strength to be able to move forward in her life.

Briana did tremendous work on processing her trauma. She stabilized significantly and maintained her sobriety. Her compulsions ceased. She and her self-states worked in concert for effective problem solving. During the latter stages of her treatment, Briana and her family moved to another state. Briana was able to return for a couple of follow-up sessions to work toward integration. She recognized that she needed to move out of her mother and stepfather's home to maintain her growth and not revert to maladaptive behaviors due to triggering events in her family environment. She rented an apartment, got a full-time job, and finished her high school education online. She went on to attend college. Although she was not able to complete her treatment with me, Briana chose to work on her own rather than seeking out another therapist. While she may continue to face struggles, she appeared to have made significant gains in resolving much of her trauma.

11

HIDDEN VOICES
CREATIVE ART THERAPY INTERVENTIONS
FOR ADOLESCENTS WITH DISSOCIATION

With Diane Raven

JUSTIN WALKED FROM THE BATHROOM to the group room, where he sat at the table to work on his treatment assignments. Brie gasped, pointing at him. Justin appeared shocked as he wiped his hand across his bloodied throat. He seemed confused and unaware of the self-inflicted cuts. This was Diane Raven's (D.R.'s) third day working as an addiction therapist in a residential substance abuse treatment facility and her first clinical experience with self-injury and dissociation. Justin was taken to the local hospital where his wound was treated. When Justin returned, D.R. learned that he had neither been evaluated by nor referred to a professional who might address the underlying causes for his self-injury. He was simply treated for the wound and sent back to the facility.

That specific dissociative incident made an indelible impression on D.R. (Raven, 2004). At the time, the residential facility did not provide alternative coping strategies for nonsuicidal self-injury behaviors with approaches specially designed for traumatized and dissociative residents. She was motivated to design and direct a trauma-informed art program based on her current knowledge on the treatment for self-injury and dissociation.[1]

Most adolescents who D.R. treated for substance abuse problems were trauma survivors and almost 65% had clinically significant dissociation on Briere's (1996) Trauma Symptom Checklist for Children (TSCC; see Chapter 3 for more information about the results of the research on this population). However, few adolescents had made the connection among their trauma, their behavior, and their state of mental health. After years of listening to clients' heart-wrenching stories, and witnessing repeated self-destructive behavior, D.R. was convinced that the youth she was treating were doing their best just to survive a childhood of hurt and despair. There was no discerning between surviving and thriving. They were intervening on their own behalf by developing ad hoc coping strategies to salve their internal wounds (Grossman, 1997). However, healing was not occurring.

Some were ready to talk about their childhood traumatic experiences, whereas others found it impossible to verbally articulate the emotional and physical violations they endured. Many found it difficult to trust anyone with their secrets. For some, drugs and self-injury provided emotional numbing. For others, physical pain was familiar and comforting. Some shared the fact that drugs muffled internal voices and blocked flashbacks and nightmares. Many agreed that drugs and self-injury provided a sense of control over feelings of helplessness and hopelessness. For many adolescents, maladaptive strategies are more than behaviors; they assume the role of friends who can be counted on. Unfortunately, these "friends" often betray them, leaving them with feelings of shame and disgust. Adolescents who felt estranged found acceptance into a culture comprising others with similar experiences. Often, their self-destructive response to traumatic events trumped school, family, sports, and old friends. They hid behind the safety of an impenetrable wall, reassured that no one could get close. These adolescents were angry, anxious, depressed, confused, and frightened.

D.R. recognized that these adolescents required a comprehensive trauma-informed treatment plan so that they could stop their maladaptive use of drugs and alcohol and begin to face their pain. D.R. consulted with Frances Waters (F.W.) because of her specialty in the treatment of trauma and dissociation. After discussing the potential for a positive outcome with the adolescents and their parent(s), an appointment was scheduled with F.W. for further evaluation. Together, we offered a collaborative, coordinated, and comprehensive treatment program that provided evidence-based, best practices treatment that promoted self-awareness and therapeutic trust, which are two critical components of successful therapy (Castonguay et al., 2010).

If the adolescents and their family consented, we screened the adolescents for dissociation with Adolescent Dissociative Experiences Scale (A-DES) and Adolescent Multidimensional Inventory of Dissociation V.6.0 (A-MID) checklists and clinical interviews (Chapter 4). Those who met the criteria of posttraumatic stress disorder (PTSD) or dissociation were offered an intensive outpatient program along with intensive residential treatment for drug and alcohol addictions.

D.R. designed trauma-focused art therapy interventions. Most of the adolescents and their families had no idea that art therapy interventions could address their traumatic issues. The adolescents were initially suspicious of a process that suggested they could ease their emotional pain and help themselves regain balance in their life. No one had shared with them that their stress-response system had been compromised by their traumatic experience. They believed that their behavior defined who they were, rather than it reflecting their body/mind response to their traumatic experience. Many were under the impression that what happened to them was their fault and that they did not deserve happiness. Their reaction to the prospect of a healing process that encouraged them to revisit traumatic events ranged from caution to fear.

Since the adolescents were often from out of the area, F.W. provided two to three sessions a week of specialized treatment for trauma and dissociation. This intensive program provided a safe, supportive venue for the adolescents to begin to face the underlying issues of trauma and dissociation that were contributing to their substance abuse problems. When feasible, F.W. and D.R. conducted conjoint family therapy sessions with the adolescents with their parents and siblings. These sessions focused on psychoeducation about trauma and dissociation, updating the parents about their children's progress, and teaching strategies to correct maladaptive communication patterns between the parents and their adolescent children. Aftercare was also discussed to plan for how the adolescents would maintain their sobriety on discharge and continue to receive trauma treatment.

SPECIALLY DESIGNED ART INTERVENTIONS FOR TRAUMA AND DISSOCIATION

Art Expression: An Alternative Coping Strategy for Self-Injury

D.R. witnessed an alarming number of nonsuicidal self-injury incidents at the facility. Adolescents exhibiting dissociative symptoms cut and engaged in other self-injuring behaviors to mitigate posttraumatic stress symptoms after being activated by a sensory trigger (Nemzer, 1998). Many adolescents do not seem to feel pain when they harm themselves. Research suggests that reexposure to a traumatic stressor will precipitate opioid-mediated, stress-induced analgesia in people with PTSD (van der Kolk, Greenberg, Orr, & Pitman, 1989).

To help dissociative adolescents who engage in self-injury, D.R. developed an intervention called Art Expression: An Alternative Coping Strategy for Self-Injury (Raven, 2004), which was an integral part of their stabilization. Clients with a history of self-injury, or an interest in using the intervention, were provided with a satchel containing 5 × 7 inch canvases (the small size promotes containment of strong affect), nontoxic acrylic paints, and a palette trowel. The intervention entails seven steps:

1. Recognize signs of overwhelming emotions.
2. Identify and write the emotions on the back of the canvas.
3. Then, draw two lines (also on the back of the canvas) representing a pre- and postemotional severity scale from 1 to 5 (1 being the lowest).
4. Circle a number on the preemotional severity scale that best describes the intensity of the overwhelming emotion.
5. Using the trowel, paint their feelings on the front of the canvas.
6. Circle a number on the postemotional severity scale that best describes the level of the emotion after completing the painting.
7. Ask yourself "Does the emotion(s) feel less intense? Am I controlling the emotion?"

Adolescents are encouraged to use this intervention whenever they experience strong urges for self-injury. Over time, the intervention helps adolescents develop reflective abilities and gain mastery over negative affect rather than reverting to self-destructive behavior. The result is a body of work identifying "problematic" emotions. The intervention provides the opportunity to illustrate fragmented, chaotic, and often inaccessible emotional material and process it later during therapy. The intervention has also been useful in helping self-injuring adolescents recognize irrational thought patterns and gain insight into their origins.

This intervention was offered to 15-year-old Ian, whose trauma history included sexual molestation, emotional and physical abuse, and witnessing violent acts between his parents. Ian engaged in self-harm by burning, cutting, and punching himself in the face. Figure 11.1 depicts before and after ratings of his feelings of anxiety, hostility, and helplessness.

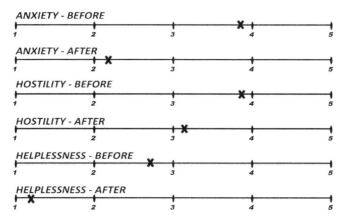

Figure 11.1 *Ian's pre- and postpainting emotional severity scale indicating a reduction in the intensity of negative affect after painting. (Used with permission.)*

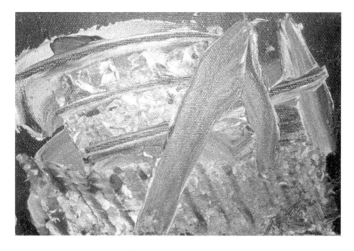

Figure 11.2 *Ian's painting of his emotional state. (Used with permission.)*

Figure 11.2 is Ian's painting of his feelings. The bold lines are symbolic of the slashing of his arms; however, there is yellow in the background, suggesting he feels some hope. Ian related the feelings that prompted his painting:

> *I was angry and sad today after listening to my dad tell me how worthless I am. I painted the whole canvas black with red. The row of lines toward*

the bottom represent the repetitive but contradictory thoughts of me being helpless but knowing I must have some power over what I do to myself. The anger started to leave as the colors mixed. Red became a pinkish gray. I could feel my heart calming down. Yellow always makes me feel good but I'm still cautious because I know I'm going to feel like this again when he talks to me like that. But today I didn't cut myself and I feel better about that.

Ian showed a decrease in all of the emotions, as he was able to safely release his anger at his father.

Nonverbal Expression: The Bridge Between Surviving and Thriving

Hidden Voices: Childhood Trauma

D.R. developed an art therapy intervention called Hidden Voices: Childhood Trauma. It is a three-phase creative process that helps uncover unconscious aspects of the self that hold traumatic material. This safe, nonverbal technique helps reveal hidden feelings, memories, and dissociated states, and it facilitates their expression. At times, youth are unconscious of what they are creating or do not recall what they have done, but feel a tremendous relief and connection to their work. This provides an avenue to safely explore memory disturbances related to self-states that are contributing to their problematic behaviors. This technique opens the door for self-discovery and provides participants with a greater understanding of the impact that trauma has on their fractured self. It provides an effective vehicle for discovering hidden voices of the unconscious (an important part of the early phase of treatment) and facilitates traumatic processing.

Hidden Voices: Childhood Trauma combines three forms of nonverbal expression: an abstract painting (16 × 16 inch canvas with acrylics using a palette trowel or brush); mask making; and a written interpretation. The intervention is phase oriented in that it provides emotional space among the three forms of expression. This process promotes cognitive processing of initially inaccessible emotional material while moving adolescents toward integrating dissociative aspects and traumatic material within their self.

In Phase 1, clients choose a significant or ongoing traumatic event that appears to be interfering with their ability to maintain emotional, mental, and/or physical control. It is particularly useful for clients who either are not ready to paint their trauma or do not remember it fully, as they can depict the trauma abstractly. This allows adolescents to explore disorganized emotions and fragmented memories while maintaining some distance from the traumatic event itself. This abstraction offers control of the seemingly uncontrollable (Betensky, 1977). It is an essential, nonthreatening step in the process of reframing unspeakable and unthinkable traumatic experiences that are stored implicitly in the brain through imagery.

In Phase 2, the youth creates a mask that serves as a metaphor of what the youth has been hiding about the self and the trauma. The color and design of the mask can reveal what was previously concealed. When the mask is completed, it is fastened to the abstract painting. It should be noted that the fastening of the mask to the canvas was client inspired. Earlier, in the use of the Hidden Voices intervention, a client asked, "Can we place our masks onto our canvases?" D.R. answered, "Yes, of course." When the two forms came together, a cohesive piece emerged. The connection between the hidden identity of the inner self depicted in the mask and unspeakable traumatic events (abstract painting) was undeniable. In fact, it was often visually shocking.

Phase 3 involves a written interpretation of the artwork. This phase is based, in part, on Betensky's work. According to Betensky (1977), ". . . sharing with or communicating to someone some inner experiences, known, vaguely sensed or just discovered, openly, angrily, fearfully or hopefully" is a basic human need (p. 179). The interpretation can be written in any form of narrative (i.e., poetry, story, or stream of consciousness).

Grace spoke in a self-assured voice as she interpreted her Hidden Voices piece (Figure 11.3),

I've felt split in half for a long time. My two parts, as I call them, feel and act opposite of each other, but both parts struggle for attention, especially the part of me depicted in the black mask. She has a lot of power! The black and purple square in the center means that my powerful anger, unhappiness, and resentment toward my mother are deeply hidden inside me. The orange mask represents the part of me that's more mature and has to get good grades and have fun. The gold peace signs in the center of both canvases mean that deep down I'm a good person. At least I want to be.

Figure 11.3 *Grace's Hidden Voices piece reveals two dissociative states. (Used with permission.)*

This intervention has had a profound impact on adolescents by illuminating their inner life. The process has helped them bring forth their hidden selves and honor them. It also helped them feel that healing was possible. After the narrative is shared, it is framed and placed next to the abstract painting with the attached mask in the art gallery of the residential facility.

"Stone Crazy" Images of Self

D.R. also developed an art therapy intervention called "Stone Crazy" Images of Self. This intervention was inspired by the creative work of artist and doll maker Gallup (2007). When D.R. saw Gallup's book cover, which contained an image of a clay figure embracing a stone, she imagined using clay and stone as an intervention for trauma victims struggling with a distorted self-image, low self-esteem, or a diminished sense of worthiness.

With this intervention, clients are invited to create three images of themselves: a baby/child self, a current self, and a future self. The clients are allowed to select the color of the clay and the size, shape, and type of the stone (e.g., sandstone, basalt, or granite). This part of the process has proved to be critical. The selections that the clients make are often done subconsciously and offer subtle clues about the self they are portraying. "Stone Crazy" Images of Self has been particularly therapeutic for clients presenting with dissociative symptomatology such as depersonalization and derealization. Dissociative clients often depict themselves in pieces: a headless clay body, the head in a hand, the head placed on a stone next to the clay body, a stone as the head, or stones protruding from a clay head. Working with clay provides a metaphoric means for adolescents to communicate their internal world.

Figure 11.4 is an example of one of the clay sculptures done by Kyra. The body is drawn tightly together and covered with snow. The sculpture appears to depict the "freeze" mode that Kyra experienced during her sexual molestation. It also shows an emotional and physical disconnect with the self and the world and a pervasive, unutterable numbness. The following is Kyra's interpretation of her sculpture:

Even though I am a light-skinned, blonde Native American, I feel if my skin and hair were darker, my feelings would match how I look. It would be better for me. This is me after I was raped. I felt numb and completely helpless. I drew my knees up and held myself for a long, long time. I don't remember a lot of what happened. I didn't want anyone to look at me or recognize me. I haven't talked about that night with anyone.

There is an innate sensory relationship between the mind and the body, so it is indicated with stone and clay. The relationship is a mingling of emotions and the unconscious. This sensorimotor process activates the right hemisphere of the brain where trauma images are stored, and the metaphor is understood (Elbrecht, 2012; Levine, 2010; Levine & Frederick, 1997; Pobric, Mashal, Faust, & Lavidor, 2008). The clients' efforts create a rite of passage through the chaos of wordless material. Creation of three images of the self allows youth to declare the past (baby/child self), confront the present (adolescent), and summon the courage to project images

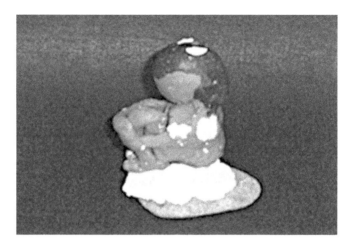

Figure 11.4 *Kyra's image depicting going into "freeze" mode when she was raped. (Used with permission.)*

of their potential self into the future. Similar to clay, the self is fragile, malleable, and always in flux. The inner and outer self is capable of being reshaped and restored (Larose, 1988). Franklin (1992) believes that clients' creations offer them an opportunity to confront and reabsorb the trauma in a redefined, "restructured form" without emotional backlash.

Similar to clinical cases discussed in *Trauma Healing at the Clay Fields: A Sensorimotor Art Therapy Approach* (Elbrecht, 2012), the dissociative adolescents participating in the "Stone Crazy" Images of Self intervention often created substitute figures such as animals. These were proxies that endured similar trauma, "carriers" of specific emotions, perceptions, or images of self-states. Both D.R.'s and Elbrecht's interventions are examples of the therapeutic efficacy of a body-focused approach that affords a safe emotional release, and movement toward internal resolution and the integration of self (van der Kolk, 2014).

The Fine Line Between Life and Death

The Fine Line Between Life and Death intervention is designed to help adolescents who are struggling with death or separation for safe processing of grief and loss. Many adolescents in residential substance abuse treatment have lost friends and family members to drug overdoses, car accidents, incarceration, homicides, or suicides. Others have experienced near-death experiences and subsequent resuscitation after overdosing or attempting suicide. Many live with the residue of divorce, removal from their parents or home, adoption, or separation from siblings. Some have experienced the death of a family member or the destruction of irreplaceable photographs and personal belongings in house fires. It might not seem plausible to ask adolescents in residential substance abuse treatment to think about and discuss their philosophy of life and death. However, after a thorough introduction to the intervention and one-on-one discussions, most feel comfortable embracing their own philosophy about life to help guide them through the process of healing.

Even though many of the clients found it difficult to express their cultural, spiritual, or religious views in a group setting—possibly because they feared criticism or were struggling with autonomy—all were able to express themselves by using paint. They applied acrylic paint (using fingers or brushes) on two rectangular canvases (size dependent on the size of the loss; see Steele & Raider, 2001) after preparation in individual sessions. For example, a traditional Native American philosophy of life and death might be informed by a cyclic view, whereas other religious or spiritual views might include heaven and hell, reincarnation, or simply a beginning and an end.

The Fine Line intervention evolved based on input from the traumatized youth we worked with. Adolescents asked questions, such as "Can we paint our emotional or spiritual death?" "Which comes first?" or "Can we combine our emotional or spiritual death with our physical death?" By feeling safe enough to be curious, they discovered the sublime connection between tapping into the appropriate type, or combination of types, of death and their own personal process of healing. Adolescents were intrigued with the idea of the Fine Line intervention and how an imperceptible temporal space had the power to hold them hostage—invisibly tethering them to helplessness. For some, the space between the two canvases represented the degree of the mind–body disconnect. For others, this disconnect emerged in colors, lines, or patterns while it still visually connected the canvases.

In Figure 11.5, a Native American boy, Robert, used the intervention to paint his grief over the suicide of his brother. He put his two canvases together, and one hung below the other. Robert explained his piece, saying,

I used strong cultural colors in both canvases. The lower canvas shows the rage, sadness, and depression I felt when he left me alone. The blues and

*violet colors are the colors of the setting sun in Anishinaabe culture, which
represents his passing. The yellow, full sun represents my brother and me
as one still. As you can see in the upper canvas, the connecting web of our
lives is still there between us; his spirit lives, but he's not tortured as I
depicted in the lower canvas with red and black colors.*

Robert's sun was completed by joining the two canvases, showing how
powerfully he and his brother continue to be connected. This was a powerful step in the healing of his loss.

Steele and Raider (2001) suggest that the integration of the cognitive
and sensory processes can enhance the healing of traumatized, grieving
children who are left feeling unsafe and helpless in their attempt to cope
with fear, anger, revenge, worry, and loneliness. By design, the Fine Line
intervention encourages self-awareness, reflection, and exploration into
how powerlessness can be transformed into strength and how power can
be restored to a compromised "organism" (Tippett, 2013).

Figure 11.5 *Fine Line Between Life and Death: A Native American boy
processes his brother's death. (Used with permission.)*

Missing Pieces

The Missing Pieces intervention is a sensory-based process that addresses incomplete narrative processing associated with traumatic events (White, 2007; Wigren, 1994). This intervention has been particularly helpful to victims of sexual violence in processing traumatic memories, understanding dissociation, and organizing a trauma narrative. The intervention has six steps. Clients are instructed to do the following:

1. Choose an unresolved traumatic event that continues to disrupt a sense of emotional, mental, or physical balance and emote it abstractly with paints (acrylics with palette trowel) on a 16×16 inch canvas.
2. Choose a universal symbol (e.g., heart, peace sign) or one that has personal meaning (e.g., basketball) and draw it on a piece of canvas similar in size to the abstract painting.
3. Cut the universal symbol into puzzle pieces of any design. These pieces represent parts of the trauma, such as secrets, unanswered questions, memory fragments, things that are confusing, and emotional or behavioral responses to the trauma—such as anger, guilt, numbness, detachment, disconnectedness, night terrors, or flashbacks.
4. Paint the pieces by using colors to add meaning.
5. Write parts of their trauma narrative on the painted puzzle pieces. The teen tells the traumatic narrative and visually sees how each puzzle size and color reflects meaning. Creating the pieces helps clients think about the trauma and its effects on them, including their feelings, thoughts, behaviors, and others' reactions (White, 2007; White & Epston, 1990). These pieces then provide a vehicle to assemble and attach meaning to aspects of the victim's life. Any of the following elements of the puzzle pieces can influence and inform the subsequent trauma narrative: size, color, placement (top, under, juxtaposition, etc.), distance between pieces, and blank or missing pieces. Any single element or combination has the potential to reveal crucial information, such as the degree of importance a specific puzzle piece might represent, difficulties caused by the traumatic event, fears associated with the traumatic event, traumatic memories, or posttraumatic growth.
6. Reassemble the puzzle pieces of the chosen universal symbol onto the canvas. This final step helps the client assemble their story on

the canvas as it reveals its meaning to them. It provides clarity and acceptance of the traumatic event.

D.R. offered Emily, a 15-year-old with an extensive trauma history, the Missing Pieces intervention as a way to help her process her trauma narrative. (Emily's case is presented in more detail in the following section.) For her universal symbol, Emily chose a heart shape (Figure 11.6). She interpreted her resulting picture, saying,

I painted my canvas with a lot of chaotic strokes because my life has been a mess. I used a lot of black and red to express the intenseness of my anger and rage over being abandoned and sexually molested, but also not being able to remember things that happened to me as a child. I think that's where the pink comes in. I chose the universal symbol of a heart because I want to be loved by my bio-mom and dad. My heart has been broken in a million pieces. As I confront each missing piece of my heart puzzle, I'm able to feel more whole and more loved.

Figure 11.6 *Emily's missing pieces. (Used with permission.)*

Emily had struggled all of her life over feelings of loss and abandonment by her birth parents and had difficulty feeling loved by her adoptive family. This intervention helped her voice these painful feelings.

Emily wrote the following on her various puzzle pieces:

Why did my mother want to abort me? What happened to me in my crib at 8 months? Why did my mother give me up for adoption? What did my mother do the night before she gave me away? I don't know my father's name. Why didn't my mother see me after my aunt adopted me? Why didn't my adoptive parents believe me when I told them Mark sexually molested me? I tried to kill myself. I'm afraid of older men. I don't trust some people. I like people to think I'm happy. I'm not as good as my adoptive sisters. Did my brother sexually molest me? Why can't I accept love from others?

These questions and statements provided rich material for trauma processing in her therapy sessions with D.R. and F.W.

The Missing Pieces intervention taps into both sensory and cognitive processing, identifying elusive parts in the trauma story that stymie coherence and continuity. The intervention has been particularly effective for trauma victims who have PTSD with dissociative symptoms. White (2007) noted that trauma victims with PTSD seem to have difficulty piecing together a complete and coherent story of the trauma. The self-narrative helps the client begin to sequence events (Omer & Alon, 1994; White, 2007), search for meaning by asking questions such as "Why me?" "Why now?" (Crossley, 2000; Davis, Nolen-Hoeksema, & Larson, 1998), and indulge in self-evaluation (e.g., guilt, responsibility, passivity, worthiness [Foa, Zinbarg, & Rothbaum, 1992; Steptoe, 2000]).

Providing opportunities to recover dissociated memories and sequence missing pieces are vital to the healing process (Kluft, 2013). White (2007) explains that "half memory" is always distressing and cannot be synthesized into a cohesive story; there is no beginning or end, just the response to the traumatic experience. A complete trauma narrative also helps clients understand how their traumatic experiences are related to problematic behaviors such as eating disorders, drug use, self-injury, promiscuity, dissociation, risk taking, suicidal feelings, depression, rage, and sleep problems.

Qualitative research by Tuval-Mashiach et al. (2004) found that guiding clients to share their trauma narrative is a valid and reliable intervention that promotes healing. They concluded that the natural process of story construction provides a pathway for understanding the traumatic event in the context of the victim's life rather than defining it. Deblinger, Mannarino, Cohen, Runyon, and Steer (2011) performed follow-up assessments of 210 children aged 4 to 11 years who had PTSD and a history of sexual abuse and who had been treated with Trauma-Focused Cognitive Behavioral Therapy (TF-CBT) with or without the inclusion of the trauma narrative treatment module. They found that the inclusion of the trauma narrative was "the most effective and efficient means of ameliorating parents' abuse-specific distress as well as children's abuse-related fear and general anxiety" (p. 67).

There are many examples in literature of trauma narratives. D.R. has found Barry Lopez's work exemplary, particularly his fictionalized narrative "Mortise and Tennon" from his collection of short stories, *Resistance* (Lopez, 2004). Lopez was 68 years old before he wrote a coherent, trauma narrative with continuity (see his memoir *Sliver of Sky: Confronting the Trauma of Sexual Abuse* [Lopez, 2013]). Emily found these stories inspirational, providing her hope for her own recovery. In a recent essay, Lopez (2010) emphasized the connection between narrative and healing for people who have been victimized:

> To my thinking, what finally proves important in our attempting to reconcile with the past is not necessarily the making of amends but our offering silenced parties the opportunity to tell their own stories without interruption, according to their own sense of timing, and without fear of refutation. For those in power simply to let what others say stand as their truth, and to go on from there, is a critical part of the healing . . . (pp. 382–383)

Residents' Art Gallery Depicting Their Healing Journey

Having a space to display the residents' healing journey serves many purposes individually and for the other residents. This phenomenological process empowers clients to take control and responsibility for their healing with help from the therapists, acknowledging that what happened to them was real and unfortunate, but does not necessarily have to destroy them or their hope for a happy, productive life. Betensky (1977) argued that a change in the client's perception occurs when self-discovery integrates their inner and outer reality. By openly displaying their artwork about their hidden voices, they overcome their shame and reclaim these hidden aspects of themselves.

The gallery provides a profound visual collage of the recovery process. It allows adolescents to step back and view their work as phenomenological observers—mentally distancing themselves while also recognizing their painful past, an important aspect of treatment noted by Betensky (1977). These separate but yet connected pieces of artwork in the gallery allow adolescents to truly fit together the missing pieces of their lives and, most importantly, of themselves. They share with each other similar yet unique stories, common struggles, and how they are coming to terms with what happened to them. Furthermore, sharing their story in a gallery removes their shame and need to hide both from themselves and the world.

Emily: Using Art to Process Trauma in Collaboration With Psychotherapy

Emily was 15 years old when she was admitted to residential treatment for abuse of alcohol, cocaine, marijuana, and prescription drugs. She obtained the substances by prostituting herself. Prior to this admission, Emily had been admitted to mental health facilities three times beginning at age 10. She had also been placed in a group home, and was incarcerated and put on probation due to delinquent behavior. Her adoptive parents were at their wits' end and said that they were unable to control her. Emily had been running away, using drugs, stealing her adoptive mother's car, committing fraud, and violating probation. She had been kicked out of the Great Lakes Recovery Center twice before: the first time for repeated truancy and the second time for assaulting a male resident who triggered memories of one of her sexual abusers. D.R. was assigned to Emily's case during her second admission and continued working with her throughout her third.

When D.R. read Emily's file for the first time, she asked herself the following questions: "Why would a 9-year-old want to kill herself? How did Emily get to be the way she is?" It took a collaborative effort between D.R. and F.W. to assess the damage caused by an unpredictable, inconsistent, abusive, and neglectful childhood, and to treat Emily after years of delayed, inappropriate, and unsuccessful mental health treatment.

Emily's History

Although Emily had a known, but inadequately documented, trauma history, her extensive symptoms and numerous diagnoses were not recognized as associated with her trauma until her current placement. Emily's early childhood trauma history encompassed the following: neglect by her birth mom; being told that her mother wanted to abort her and that her birth father attempted to suffocate her when she was 8 months old; witnessing her father's attempted murder of her mother; domestic violence between her birth mother and her boyfriend; physical and emotional abuse by her mother's boyfriend; attachment disruption; suspected sexual abuse at 8 months old by her birth father; and sexual abuse by her older biological brother, Jake, and brother-in-law, Mark, on multiple occasions between 5 and 14 years of age. Mark also stalked her and exposed himself to her on multiple occasions. Although Child Protective Services investigations were conducted, no charges were pressed against Mark who passed a polygraph. As a result, Emily's credibility was called into question. In addition, she had discovered the body of a man who had shot himself when she was 8 years old. Of all these traumatic events, Emily was the most disturbed that her adoptive parents did not believe that Mark had molested her, precipitating repeated attempts to hang herself while at home.

Emily fit the criteria for complex developmental trauma (Cook et al., 2005) with a myriad of trauma-related symptoms starting when she was very young. These included: trust and attachment problems, attention seeking, biting, an explosive temper, violent acts and threats (e.g., she chased her adoptive mother with a knife, kicked out windows with her feet, threatened to bring a gun to school, and slapped her adoptive mother), dissociative staring, memory impairment to traumatic and nontraumatic events, auditory and visual hallucinations (e.g., a figure with steel teeth and a depressed figure) beginning when she was 10, traumatic flashbacks, nightmares, low self-esteem, depression, isolation from others, somatic symptoms, eating disorders, sexual orientation issues, prostitution associated with drug use, self-injury, and multiple suicide attempts. During a prior admission for substance abuse treatment, she attempted suicide by hanging herself with a belt when a male resident triggered memories of her previous sexual abuse. She was discovered in a dissociated, hysterical state. She fled and the police were notified. D.R. caught her and they fell to the ground. As Emily lay in the driveway frightened and confused, the police tasered her.

Emily entered the facility with a number of diagnoses: initially bipolar (diagnosed at age 8 when she tried to kill herself), then attention deficit hyperactivity disorder (ADHD), reactive attachment disorder, oppositional defiant disorder, anorexia, and bulimia. While in residential substance abuse treatment and after returning from the local psychiatric unit for emotional stabilization, she was given the diagnostic impression of emerging cluster B borderline and histrionic personality traits. Over the course of her treatment for these various diagnoses, she was prescribed numerous antidepressants, medication for inattention problems, and mood stabilizers. Perry (2003) discussed the treatment ramifications of diagnosing traumatized children with bipolar disorder (BP),

> In the final analysis, what's the difference between diagnosing a child with seven core symptoms as suffering from bipolar disorder versus complex PTSD? It depends. At stake is the course of treatment. . . . drugs are the primary form of treatment for bipolar disorder. In contrast, when drugs are used to treat PTSD, they play an adjunctive role. (pp. 129–130)

While receiving pharmacological treatment for the various diagnoses she had been given, Emily's condition worsened. All of her medications had black box warnings, indicating a list of adverse side effects that required close monitoring. Pharmacological treatment was administered as early as age 8, after which Emily attempted suicide by hanging. She threatened to kill herself by drowning when she was 9. When she entered the residential substance abuse treatment center, she was experiencing severe psychotropic drug side effects (e.g., unable to stay awake during the day, rigid gait, depression, suicide ideation, headaches, agitation, and sleep problems) that left her unable to function.

In Emily's most recent admission at age 16, D.R. took a trauma history and recognized that Emily had significant trauma and dissociative symptoms. D.R. then contacted her adoptive parents to request their permission to refer Emily to F.W. for further evaluation and, if needed, specialized outpatient treatment. They agreed. F.W. administered the A-DES and the TSCC. Emily underrated herself on the A-DES, as well as on the TSCC, which was rendered invalid; however, her answers and scores remained relevant (underscoring can indicate fear, defensive, avoidant behavior, or feelings of mistrust and should be considered important information). Her endorsement of the following TSCC Critical Items deserved immediate attention: feeling scared of men, not trusting people because they might want sex, and getting into fights.

F.W. also administered the A-MID 6.0 (Dell, 2006), and Emily endorsed a number of items that were significant for dissociation and PTSD. For example, she endorsed: strong thoughts in your head that "come from out of nowhere; reliving a traumatic event so vividly that you totally lose contact with where you actually are (thinking you are 'back there and then'); feeling mad; strong feelings of emotional pain and hurt that come from out of nowhere; nobody caring about you; feeling empty and painfully alone; being angry that your life is ruined; being able to remember very little of your past; and wishing that someone would finally realize how much you hurt."

Emily also described significant trauma and dissociative symptoms in extensive interviewing by D.R. and F.W. It took Emily a while after becoming sober to actually become more conscious of traumatic and dissociative symptoms that drugs and alcohol had masked. F.W. diagnosed Emily with a primary diagnosis of dissociative disorder not otherwise specified (DDNOS) and PTSD. A number of treatment modalities were used to treat Emily. F.W. employed eye movement desensitization and reprocessing (EMDR), ego state therapy, art therapy, and family therapy. Art therapy was provided by D.R. in collaboration with the therapies provided by F.W. Emily was asked to express her trauma through drawing, painting, sculpting, and writing.

Emily's sexual molestations during her latency period seemed to mark a psychological turning point when she was cognizant of a dissociative state. She acknowledged that she was first aware of a self-state in the fifth grade at age 10. She described this dissociative part as "standing with black hair and metal teeth." Emily reported seeing this figure on the playground next to her teacher. Her parents and school officials assumed it was a predator loitering at the school, and they contacted the police who were unable to find the loiterer. However, Emily later realized that the figure was actually a projection of her inner self. In a therapy session with F.W., Emily reported that when she looked in the mirror, she saw a modified version of the figure that frightened her. She reported that it was still the same black figure, but now it had red teardrops and a red heart. Emily drew a picture of the self-state as she began to own this part of herself. She explained, "I was looking at myself in the mirror but I didn't see me at all. Instead, I saw this sad figure. I'm bleeding on the inside. My heart is pulsing out of my chest. I felt dirty. That's why it's black. The red around my head is anger."

Figure 11.7 is Emily's picture of what she saw when she looked in the mirror.

According to art therapists Cohen and Cox (1989), Emily's mirror image can be considered a "true switching picture" that could be used in combination with behavioral observations and dissociative assessment tools to diagnose a dissociative state. Interestingly, on the A-MID 6.0, Emily also endorsed the following item (with a rating of 5 on a scale of 0–10): looking in the mirror and seeing someone other than yourself. This self-state fluctuated from a small child to an adult size depending on her affect. Emily also explained, "The angrier she gets, the bigger she gets. The sadder she gets, the smaller she gets." Emily also experienced depersonalization in that she witnessed this girl looking at her from a distance, and also saw this girl at different spots in F.W.'s office. (Other dissociative

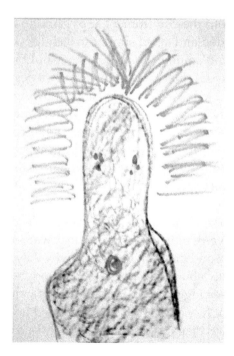

Figure 11.7 *What Emily sees when she looks in the mirror. (Used with permission.)*

youth have described similar experiences to F.W. of external visual hallu-cinations that appear to be a projection of a self-state that occurs during an episode of depersonalization.) It turned out that this self-state was not aware that she shared Emily's body. With F.W.'s encouragement, she looked through Emily's eyes for confirmation that she did share the body. This was a beginning step toward integration.

Although Emily, herself, did not express feelings of loss after being removed from her birth mother at age 3, the black self-state contained the sadness, fear, loneliness, and anger and seemed to be the original Emily. When Emily felt this self-state's despondency, she would become tearful and suicidal. Over time, Emily learned that this self-state was also protec-tive of her, as Emily felt "someone was holding me back from killing myself," and heard the words, "I won't let her die." Emily recognized that this came from the despondent figure in the mirror. Emily named this figure Angel for holding the early traumatic losses and stopping Emily from further suicidal attempts.

During residential placement, Emily was observed switching numer-ous times throughout the day from a happy child to a suicidal teenager. At times, she sounded and acted similar to a child, skipping around the facility, laughing, and smiling. Suddenly, she would switch to becoming depressed and suicidal. It appeared that Emily's despondent self-state, Angel, worked hard to mask her depression, knowing that Emily did not want to feel this way. Consequently, Emily would frequently pretend she was happy. Emily's need to hide her depression also showed up in her artwork. For example, at one point, Emily drew happy faces and painted the word, "Happy" on a canvas. It is common for children with complex trauma to spend a lot of energy trying to portray wishful feelings to avoid painful ones.

Emily also worked hard to mask her feelings of sadness and confusion toward her adoptive parents. She desperately wanted their acceptance, love, and protection, and did not understand why they did not believe that she had been sexually abused by Mark—a question she asked in her Miss-ing Pieces Puzzle (see Figure 11.6). Her adoptive parents told her that she was a sweet girl, but had a bad side, and reminded her that her biological father was violent and diagnosed as bipolar. Emily said that she was unable to remember some of the bad things her adoptive family said she did.

Emily's "Stone Crazy" Images of Self

Once the presence of Angel was revealed, F.W. began working with Emily on understanding Angel's role. Although F.W. had utilized early grounding and stabilization techniques with Emily, these techniques were now repeated to include Angel, who agreed to participate in therapy with Emily, F.W., and D.R. In art therapy, Emily sculpted her little self, Angel, lying on a stone clutching a ball. Emily explained, "I wanted to express how vulnerable and helpless I must have been as a baby." She sculpted her older self, playing her flute, a talent for which her adoptive parents praised her. Both of her selves were fashioned out of white clay, representing her purity and innocence (Figure 11.8).

As Emily explored Angel's role, Emily learned that Angel knew more of the details of the sexual abuse perpetrated by Emily's brother, Jake, and by her brother-in-law, Mark. Emily felt Angel's terror and F.W. immediately oriented Angel to the present environment, reassuring her that she was safe. Angel drew a picture of how much fear she had felt (Figure 11.9).

The distorted, ragged-shaped face with two asymmetrical eyes and a large sad mouth depicts Angel's terror, utter helplessness, and confusion. Emily wrote Angel's feelings on her face: "sad, lonely, hating, scared, guilty, and awkward" and added some small frowning faces next to the

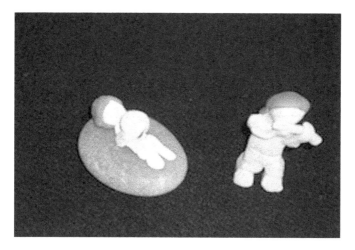

Figure 11.8 *Emily's depictions of her two selves. (Used with permission.)*

Figure 11.9 *A frightened self-state recalling her sexual abuse. (Used with permission.)*

words. On the outside of the face, she wrote the words that she had wanted to say to Mark and to herself at the time of the abuse but had not been able to, because she was frozen in terror. She wrote, "I don't want any hurt. Stay back! Don't get close! I can help myself." Emily comforted Angel as we helped Angel to begin to process the sexual abuse.

F.W. encouraged Emily to express more of her feelings about the sexual abuse by Mark, as it was more distressing to her than her abuse by her brother. She was instructed to draw Mark as an animal, another symbolic figure, or as he looked, and to express her feelings. She drew a picture of Mark as a Devil, carrying her limp, black body as flames engulfed them (Figure 11.10). Above them are lightning bolts and rain representing the terror she experienced during the abuse. In the center is a fiery sun over the Devil's head. Emily's limp body represents total immobilization or the freeze response that Nijenhuis (2004) and Porges (2011) describe as an instinctive, biological defensive reaction to overwhelming fear and helplessness. Emily's feelings of guilt over her immobilization when Mark abused her lifted when F.W. explained that her response was an inherent, neurobiological, and survival response to terror that she experienced.

Figure 11.10 *Emily's depiction of sexual abuse. (Used with permission.)*

Recognizing that the inclusion of a rescue scenario can empower survivors to complete processing of a traumatic memory, F.W. asked Emily to draw one. Because Emily (in collaboration with Angel) had a great need to have her adoptive parents believe and support her, she drew a wishful picture of her parents pulling her out of the fires of hell (Figure 11.11). Even though Mark was never prosecuted, she drew black bars in the upper corner that "lock him in jail forever." Behind the rescue scene is a large sun representing Emily's happiness. Interestingly, Emily did not put a head

Figure 11.11 *Emily's rescue fantasy. (Used with permission.)*

on herself. This appeared to represent her fractured self. This picture was primitive compared with Emily's earlier picture as Angel had drawn it. The drawing was later shown to Emily's parents to help them understand her need for their support.

As Emily and Angel worked together with F.W. and D.R. on the sexual abuse and feelings of abandonment, there was a significant shift in Emily; she felt hopeful and was better able to regulate her affect and behavior. Emily drew a picture signifying the positive union between Angel and herself (Figure 11.12). This picture is much more sophisticated than her earlier ones and shows signs of Emily's integration.

Emily again processed her feelings by writing what she felt on this picture: "I can love and I can allow myself to be loved. Happiness and joy. I can talk to people now. Better self-confidence. I can smile and mean it! Truest in the family! Inner peace." Beneath her beaming self-portrait, she drew a large happy face and wrote, "Angel and Emily = ME!" Next to it was a peace symbol that she had used in some of her other art. Emily felt united with Angel, recognizing that both of them were one person. She felt tranquil, authentic, and capable to express genuine feelings and socially engage in a healthy way. This was a major transformation!

Figure 11.12 *Emily depicts the positive effects of accepting Angel as a part of herself. (Used with permission.)*

Family Intervention With Emily

D.R. and F.W. had several family therapy sessions and phone calls with Emily and her parents in an effort to engage them as collaborators in Emily's treatment, and to eventually provide a safe and supportive environment upon her discharge. Ongoing psychoeducation about trauma and dissociation, and specialized therapeutic and behavior management strategies were provided with the ultimate goal of successful reunification. A major issue to resolve was why her parents disbelieved that Emily was molested by Mark—a question that Emily posed in her Missing Pieces artwork. Emily's parents explained that they did not believe that Mark had molested Emily due to her early contradictory statements about the abuse. Emily was able to provide further details to her parents that were garnered from Angel and explained that she had been afraid to tell them what happened for fear of retaliation. Emily's mother revealed that she too had been sexually abused as a child by a relative. This made it hard to believe her daughter, as she had not wanted anything similar to ever happen to Emily. She apologized to Emily for not believing her. Her parents then set boundaries to protect Emily from contact with Mark during family gatherings.

During another family therapy session, Emily recalled a sexual assault that occurred in the back of their garage on a winter day. She described the pink snow pants and white boots that she wore and the plaid shirt that her perpetrator wore. Prior to this session, her memory was fragmented and she suspected that it had been Mark who abused her. Her adoptive mother put the time in context and Emily realized that it was her brother, Jake, who molested her that day. This abuse had happened when she was 7 and Jake was 15. Ironically, her brother was incarcerated for sexual misconduct (unrelated to his abuse of Emily) while she was in treatment. In addition, it was discovered that Jake was sending Emily mail that included sexual references to his molestation of her as a child. Emily was embarrassed by the letters and said they made her feel "dirty."

Emily showed her artwork to her parents, explaining Angel's role in helping her cope with the abuse. Her parents were finally able to understand Emily's erratic behavior and accepted Angel. They praised both Emily and Angel for their courage to heal. They also expressed sadness over the abuse and love for Emily. Her parents were finally able to comfort her for all the abuse she had experienced. Emily said that the large hole inside of her was closing up and she was able to feel their love.

Emily's Missing Pieces artwork (see Figure 11.6) revealed unresolved attachment issues related to her birth parents. She had been removed from their care when she was 3. Many of her unanswered questions included in the puzzle pieces involved them. To heal from this early loss, she needed to understand what had happened when she was little and why they abandoned her. She needed to understand reports she had heard, such as that her birth mother wanted to abort her and that her birth father had tried to smother her as an infant. F.W. and D.R. arranged for Emily to call her birth mother during a therapy session.

Emily listened as her birth mother described an incident when Emily's father covered Emily's face with his hand to keep her from screaming when she was 8 months old and in her crib. Emily drew her legs up to her chest, covered her face with her hands, and cried. Emily resumed, listening intently on the phone as her birth mother expressed her suspicion that Emily's biological father had sexually abused her as an infant. At the time of the call, he was in prison for sexually abusing another child. Emily had no memories of him and had no contact with him since she was an infant. (F.W. wonders whether he molested his son who, in turn, molested Emily.) Emily's birth mother disclosed that she, herself, had been abused by Emily's father and felt despondent and overwhelmed, thus prompting her to consider an abortion. Her birth mother told Emily that she was glad that she did not have an abortion and told Emily that she loved her. However, because of her depression, she was unable to provide for Emily and thought that her relatives who had significant financial means could do so. Emily forgave her. Emily was coming to terms about her birth father as well. Her questions on her Missing Pieces art were now answered. She felt at peace.

Emily's Final Trauma Processing

After forgiving her birth mother and her adoptive parents, Emily needed to resolve her brother's molestation of her before her integration could be complete. Emily and Angel agreed that it was time to face Jake's molestation. Using EMDR, F.W. asked Emily to revisit the memory of being molested in the garage. Emily closed her eyes and pictured the shed. Her eyes filled with tears as she saw the face of her brother. She felt heartbroken as she processed the memory. It was the final trauma that needed resolution. Afterward, she reported that her brother's molestation was not on her mind and reported, "a weight has been lifted off me."

Emily's Integration

By combining psychotherapy and art therapy in safe and supportive therapeutic environments, Emily was able to reveal her dissociative self-state and begin to understand and manage her emotions, especially those associated with self-hatred. After 2 months of intensive outpatient treatment and 3 months of residential treatment, Emily and Angel indicated that they could now experience unpleasant feelings without going "berserk." Emily also realized that her ambivalence toward attaching to her adoptive parents was due to Angel, who was afraid that accepting the adoptive parents would betray her birth mother. Angel had wanted to be with her birth mother, whereas Emily had wanted to be with her adoptive mother. After talking to her birth mother, Angel no longer felt conflicted. Her birth mother's endorsement of her being parented by her adoptive parents allowed her to finally accept them. Angel was now willing to join Emily in attaching to their parents.

Emily had a brief moment of testing when another teen resident insulted her. Angel wanted to "stab her," but Emily took control and asked Angel to join her in an internal safe place, which had been developed during the stabilization phase of therapy. Emily felt proud of her ability to handle the situation, and her adoptive parents were pleased when Emily told them about what she had done. In processing the incident, Angel agreed to learn more constructive ways to deal with anger.

Emily and Angel were finally ready to integrate. As Emily drew two pictures to represent their integration, they spontaneously integrated. The first picture was of a diamond ring. Emily wrote, "We will/are successful. We are doing it!" Above the ring, she wrote, "We now shine together." Inside the ring band, she wrote. "We are one." On the back of this paper, she drew another symbolic picture of her integration (Figure 11.13). She repeated the heart shape that she had done in her Missing Pieces art; however, this heart was strikingly different. Inside the heart, she drew a treble clef and a peace sign. Her heart felt peace and joy!

To manage Emily's anxieties about returning home, we reviewed all that she had learned and she compiled a list of coping strategies. A referral to another therapist in her community was arranged. Emily also committed to attending Alcoholics Anonymous (AA) meetings.

After integration, there was a noticeable change in Emily's demeanor. She carried herself with self-assurance. She left feeling happy and confident to reintegrate into the community. She had an upbeat sound to her voice and her smile was now authentic.

After two previous failures, Emily's parents attended her final graduation from Great Lakes Recovery Center (GLRC). It was a proud day for her and her family as they witnessed her graduation ceremony. It was time for the last visit to the art gallery. Emily, as a curator of her own

Figure 11.13 *Emily's picture of integration. (Used with permission.)*

works, explained each piece representing her healing journey as her family proudly stood by her. She then wistfully took them down from the gallery to take home with her as reminders of her recovery. Emily is currently living independently and attending college. She continues to express herself with painting.

CONCLUSION

Unfortunately, similar to Emily, many dissociative children and adolescents are misdiagnosed and mismanaged. The current trend toward trauma-informed, sensory-based interventions, including art therapy, is promising.

However, as van der Kolk (1996) cautions, if service providers and therapists fail to look through a trauma lens, they are likely to misread the trauma victim's struggle with traumatic memory, revictimization, and self-destruction as merely behavioral problems or drug problems. Dissociative children require a comprehensive trauma-informed treatment plan. Art therapy designed to access trauma narratives can provide an important, adjunctive role in helping to reveal hidden feelings, memories, and dissociated states, and facilitate their expression in their healing.

NOTE

1. Great Lakes Recovery Center, Marquette, Michigan received an exemplary commendation from its accrediting agency for their art therapy program and recognized it for best practice within the behavioral health industry.

INTEGRATING DISSOCIATIVE TREATMENT AND EMDR THERAPY WITH CHILDREN WITH TRAUMA AND DISSOCIATION

FIVE-MONTH-OLD JAMAL WAS BROUGHT TO the hospital by his mother for swelling in his tiny legs. At the emergency department, the doctors discovered he had 28 fractures in various stages of healing. All of Jamal's toes had been broken. When he was discharged from the hospital 4 weeks later, Jamal was placed with a foster family.

Is it possible to help a traumatized infant from such horrendous abuse? Can eye movement desensitization and reprocessing (EMDR) therapy provide the vehicle for such healing? Read on to learn more about Jamal's healing.

EMDR THERAPY AND ADAPTIVE INFORMATION PROCESSING

In 1987, Shapiro (1995) developed EMDR to treat numerous physical and mental health symptoms. It is a comprehensive treatment that integrates cognitive, behavioral, psychodynamic, and body-oriented psychotherapies. Shapiro (2001) later developed adaptive information processing (AIP) theory, which provides the theoretical foundation for EMDR therapy and guides case conceptualization. AIP postulates that traumatic memories can be fragmented and dissociated in neural networks in which they remain in a raw, unprocessed form. Because they are unprocessed, they continue to be activated by triggers, including thoughts, emotions, and somatic sensations that remind the individual of the trauma. AIP theory postulates that for healing to take place, the information must be accessed, stimulated, and then moved toward adaptive resolution.

During EMDR treatment, the client attends to emotionally disturbing material in brief, sequential doses. The core of EMDR treatment involves activating components of the traumatic memory and pairing those components with alternating bilateral stimulation (BLS). BLS appears to activate both sides of the brain, which facilitates more complete processing of distressing events. Therapist-directed lateral eye movements were originally used (Shapiro, 1995); however, a variety of other bilateral stimuli are effective, including hand-tapping the child's hands, shoulders, or knees; NeuroTek Tac AudioScan ("buzzies"); visual lap scan devices (EMDR NeuroTek Machine)[1]; alternate drumming (Adler-Tapia & Settle, 2008); or the "butterfly hug" (Jarero, Artigas, Mauer, Alcala, & Lupez, 1999; children cross their arms and each hand taps the opposite shoulder).

Although EMDR therapy was originally created for the treatment of adult and adolescent clients, adaptation of the language and consideration of child developmental needs has made EMDR effective with children (e.g., Adler-Tapia, 2012; Adler-Tapia & Settle, 2008; Gomez, 2013b; Greenwald, 1999; Lovett, 1999). EMDR therapy can be used in conjunction with play, art sensorimotor therapy (Ogden & Gomez, 2013), and ego state therapy (Forgash & Knipe, 2008) techniques with dissociative children.

EMDR Therapy as Evidence-Based Practice With Traumatized Children

A number of peer-review studies show the efficacy of EMDR with children. Adler-Tapia and Settle (2009b) and Fleming (2012) examined extensive peer-review studies and found evidence for the effectiveness of EMDR therapy. Rodenburg, Benjamin, de Roos, Meijer, and Stams (2009) conducted a meta-analytical review of the efficacy of EMDR for the treatment of trauma in children compared with traditional cognitive behavioral therapy (CBT). They concluded that EMDR provides a small but significant incremental value over CBT. Based on the empirical support for EMDR, the World Health Organization, the National Registry of Evidence-Based Programs and Practices of the Substance Abuse and Mental Health Administration (NREPP/SAMHSA), the American Psychiatric Association (APA), and the National Institute of Clinical Excellence (NICE) have listed EMDR therapy as evidence-based practice.

Similarities Between AIP and Dissociative Theories

There are significant overlapping theoretical constructs between AIP (Shapiro, 2001; Solomon & Shapiro, 2008) and dissociative theories (Lanius, Paulsen, & Corrigan, 2014; Putnam, 1997; van der Hart, Nijenhuis, & Steele 2006; van der Kolk, 2014). The main goal of both dissociative and EMDR therapeutic modalities is to effectively and safely access and stimulate processing of traumatic events across all memory networks in order to achieve resolution and integration. Both recommend a phase-oriented healing process with emphasis on stabilization that promotes successful processing and reconsolidation of traumatic memories. For example, my three-phrase treatment model for children and adolescents with dissociation is complementary to the eight phases of EMDR therapy with similar goals and objectives (Waters, 1993; Waters & Adler-Tapia, 2009). Dissociative theory specifically focuses on specialized treatment of dissociation, whereas EMDR therapy interventions can be successful with dissociative children as long as it includes special preparation and intervention that incorporate dissociative defenses such as self-states.

INCORPORATING EIGHT PHASES OF EMDR TREATMENT WITH DISSOCIATIVE TREATMENT

This chapter offers guidance on integrating EMDR treatment and dissociative treatment phases of children with dissociation. Table 12.1 outlines how the eight phases of EMDR therapy correspond to the three phases of treatment of dissociative children. This chapter does not replace training in EMDR therapy; instead, it provides additional information about incorporating specialized treatment of dissociation and/or dissociative symptoms throughout EMDR therapy. There are eight phases in EMDR treatment, with specific goals, objectives, and procedural steps for each stage (Shapiro, 2001). The eight phases include: (1) history taking, case conceptualization, and treatment planning; (2) preparation; (3) assessment; (4) desensitization; (5) installation; (6) body scan; (7) closure; and (8) reevaluation. A brief explanation of these stages is provided next, incorporating specially designed interventions for dissociative children. In addition, play, art, and sensorimotor techniques are discussed in

Table 12.1 *Integrating EMDR and Dissociative Treatment Phases*

EMDR Treatment	Dissociative Treatment
Phase 1: History taking, case conceptualization, and treatment planning	Phase 1: Same as EMDR Phase 1 with special attention to: • Identify degree of dissociation and any self-states • Educate about dissociation • Assess internal and external safety
Phase 2: Preparation • Informed consent • Identify child's resources • Further assessment of the child's functioning • Teach mechanics of EMDR therapy • Teach safe/calm place and containment • Teach advanced resourcing skills for affect management	Phase 1: Additional preparation: • Engage relevant self-states in each step • Develop internal awareness and communication • Develop ego-strengthening and empowerment strategies • Include self-states in resource techniques
Phase 3: Assessment • Identify target • Floatback cognitive interweave • VoC set • SUD set	Phase 2: Trauma processing • Engage relevant self-states in EMDR steps • Any self-states not involved are put in safe internal rooms
Phase 4: Desensitization • Sets of BLS • Employ regulation strategies as needed • Goal is to desensitize target to SUD of 0	Phase 2: Trauma processing • Engage relevant self-states in each EMDR step
Phase 5: Installation • Goal is to install PC to VoC of 7	Phase 2: Trauma processing • Engage relevant self-states in VoC
Phase 6: Body scan • Goal is a clear body scan	Phase 2: Trauma processing • Engage relevant self-states in body scan

(*continued*)

Table 12.1 *Integrating EMDR and Dissociative Treatment Phases (continued)*

EMDR Treatment	Dissociative Treatment
Phase 7: Closure • Tools to debrief	Phase 2: Trauma processing • Engage relevant self-states in debrief
Phase 8: Reevaluation • Reevaluate treatment plan • Reevaluate treatment outcomes	Phases 2 and 3: Trauma processing and integration • Reevaluate across self-states • Integration of self-states

BLS, bilateral stimulation; EMDR, eye movement desensitization and reprocessing; PC, positive cognition; SUD, subjective units of distress; VoC, validity of the cognition.

combination with EMDR therapy to help traumatized children express themselves and resolve their traumatic experiences. Adler-Tapia (2012) and Gomez (2013b) provide a more thorough description of conducting EMDR therapy with children, as well as special preparation techniques for children with dissociation.

EMDR Therapy Phase 1: History Taking, Case Conceptualization, and Treatment Planning

Phase 1 of EMDR treatment includes history taking, case conceptualization, psychosocial education, and evaluation. This is consistent with Phase 1 of the traditional treatment of dissociative children, with an emphasis on evaluation of trauma and dissociation, and treatment planning incorporating any dissociative states. Refer to Chapters 2, 3, and 4 for a more thorough discussion of dissociative warning signs, differential diagnoses, assessment questions, and the use of trauma and dissociative checklists.

Because EMDR therapy provides the clinical tools for probing neural networks that may be linked to self-states, the clinician should explore for the presence of any self-states, their roles related to trauma, and survival functions (Chapters 4 and 7). Although it may not always be possible to identify self-states during the initial phase of treatment, the clinician's alertness to the signs of self-states and willingness to adapt EMDR therapy to include them will enhance stabilization and lead to successful trauma processing. Self-states can appear organically, as different interventions are employed and their appearance will then require some analysis before proceeding.

When analyzing for the presence of self-states, some questions to explore include: Could there be hidden self-states that are influencing the child's mood and behavior? If so, what role did the self-states originally play in the child's survival? What are their feelings, thoughts, behaviors, and current functions? Are they aware of the "here" and "now" or are they still living in their traumatic past? Do they identify with the abuser and hurt the child and others? Chapters 7 and 8 provide examples of working with self-states.

Case Study: Dexter

I treated a 4-year-old adopted boy, Dexter (introduced in Chapter 3), who was extremely destructive to personal property in his adoptive home. Dexter had a history of early, chronic physical and emotional neglect and multiple failed placements (including a previous adoptive placement) due to his destructive behaviors. These would occur during the night after everyone was asleep. Dexter's parents had to remove items from his room and put an alarm on his door so that they would know whether he left his room. Dexter had no awareness of these episodes.

I asked Dexter whether he could go inside of his mind to find out what might be contributing to these frequent destructive episodes. Dexter provided a detailed description of several self-states that assumed maternal and perpetrating roles. Two perpetrating parts assumed the identity of his biological father, who was a drug abuser and a violent man who had abused Dexter's mother and destroyed property. Dexter usually witnessed these violent episodes at nighttime. Dexter also had an attachment to his father, who played with him and took him places. As a result, the perpetrating parts assumed the birth father's identity and modeled his behavior, yet they also carried fear and anger toward Dexter's father. These parts would destroy personal items in Dexter's adoptive family's house just like Dexter's father had done. They appeared to be reenacting the trauma they experienced. This may have been Dexter's way to gain control over his trauma while also trying to maintain his attachment to his birth father.

Before Dexter could truly gain mastery over this destructive behavior, he and his parts had to agree on safe ways to express anger, such as hitting a pillow and expressing anger with words. After this was achieved, the next step was to help them begin to grieve the loss of Dexter's biological parents, and then process witnessing his father's violence as well as his fear and anger toward his father. EMDR therapy was used throughout the treatment by using bilateral tapping of his knees by his mother and father, who took turns, and with the handheld Tac scanner that emits alternate vibrations while he held one in each hand. Dexter's adoptive parents wrote and read to Dexter a traumatic script of what he experienced (Lovett, 1999) that included grieving his attachment losses of both of his birth parents and witnessing traumatic events.

Dexter's self-states, including the maternal one, were able to grieve their losses and effectively process their conflicted feelings. The maternal part was able to relinquish her maternal care of Dexter and accept Dexter's adoptive mom's love and nurturing. Once the perpetrating self-states resolved their traumatic attachment to his birth father, they were ready to attach to his adoptive father, from whom Dexter had been distant. Dexter was able to sit comfortably on his adoptive father's lap and engage in activities with him—activities that he had previously avoided. There were no further destructive incidents. Dexter reported, "I am all one now," and displayed normal behavior of a 4-year-old. It was clear that his previous diagnosis of reactive attachment disorder (RAD) was not the true diagnosis that impaired his attachment to his adoptive parents (see the section on RAD in Chapter 3 on differential diagnoses).

Phase 2: Preparation

Phase 2 of EMDR therapy is complementary to Phase 1 of dissociative treatment. This phase includes explaining the efficacy and mechanics of EMDR treatment, identifying the child's resources (including self-states), and expanding the child's repertoire of self-regulatory skills. Gomez's (2007) book *Dark, Bad Day . . . Go Away: A Book for Children about Trauma and EMDR* is a helpful, child-friendly resource for explaining EMDR therapy. Adler-Tapia (2009) created a coloring workbook—*My EMDR Workbook*—for working through the phases of EMDR therapy with children. These books can be adapted to include a child's self-states. Using reading and coloring books to explain EMDR therapy and dissociation can prepare dissociative children for treatment and help them better understand themselves.

AIP and dissociative theories suggest that for individuals with extensive abuse and neglect histories, it is advisable to install internal resources and positive experiences that can prepare them for trauma processing and adaptive resolution. Let us look at some strategies to prepare children who have self-states for trauma processing.

Connecting With the Self-States, Teamwork, and Present Orientation

In preparation to work with dissociative children, mapping the presence of self-states is important for thorough processing. Adler-Tapia (2012) asks children to draw a picture of their body or Adler-Tapia will draw an outline of their body. Then, the children are asked to show where their parts reside in their body (e.g., head, toes, stomach), what the functions of their parts are, how they communicate, any rules they adhere to, and where they may feel sick in their body. This exercise helps explore whether somatic disturbances may pertain to a somatic flashback, a physical ailment, or a self-state. I have developed a crossword puzzle for dissociative children with names and functions or qualities of the parts interlocking. This can help not only identify parts but also emphasize their connection to each other. These techniques also encourage internal awareness and communication.

Installing pictures that depict teamwork with BLS and cognitive interweave, such as, "We do much better when we work together," is helpful to encourage internal cooperation with dissociative children. Pictures of teamwork can be found on the Internet. These can be printed, laminated, and given to the child and the child's parents and teachers to be used at home and school. Different images and positive cognitions (PC) can be developed to fit the internal system of the child and environmental expectations. For example, if the child is in school or participating in an extracurricular activity, it is important that the other self-states do not interfere in the child's functioning, unless they are capable of participating appropriately. One way to help the child stay in charge is to have the child look at a picture of himself or herself or another child playing the sport combined with a cognition, such as "I stay out while my inside family agrees to look, listen, and learn." Baby self-states can be safely placed in an internal nursery that is soundproof with another older self-state, if available, to watch the baby while the child is in school. The therapist can show the child a picture of a baby in a nursery with a cognitive weave of "Baby part of me is safe in the nursery so that I can pay attention while I am at school." These techniques can then be installed with BLS. When creative resources are tailored to meet self-states' unique needs and varied ages, they can decrease dissociative switching, enhance healthy behavior, and affect regulation. For example, resource development designed to manage a frightened baby self-state will be different from one needed to manage an angry teen self-state.

Because there may be hidden states still frozen in the traumatic experience who are unaware of the passage of time and circumstantial changes, it is best to orient all parts of the child to the present reality. I will say, "I would like all parts of you, even those we may not know about, to look through your eyes and listen with your ears and know that you are in my office, and that I work with kids to help them feel better about the bad things that happened to them. I want all parts of you to feel better." BLS can be used to install this message. If hidden self-states become known later in the treatment process, it is important to assess their internal resources and awareness of earlier stabilization techniques that were installed. It may be necessary to reinstall these resources before proceeding any further with trauma processing.

Achieving stabilization is an ongoing process that unfolds throughout the treatment, as self-states become known. It is important to enlist parents to support the child in practicing stabilization techniques several times a week at home. This will increase the child's ability to employ them when triggered. When these stabilization techniques are mastered, trauma processing will be much more successful, as the child will be equipped with skills to manage the intense affect that may arise.

Reverse Protocol in Preparation Phase

EMDR therapy involves a three-pronged approach in which traumatic events from the past are processed before current triggers or future anxieties. However, this protocol in which the first and/or worst memories are processed may be too difficult without first installing in the client a future orientation for himself or herself and dealing with current triggers. This is often the case with children with complex trauma, attachment problems, a high level of comorbidity, and a dismal perception of their future. For these types of situations, Adler-Tapia (2012) developed a reverse protocol in which targets are reprocessed in reverse order— beginning with the future and ending with the past traumatic events. For clients who have a foreshortened sense of future, reprocessing negative beliefs about the future and installing hope while "containing" the present triggers and traumatic memories may help improve client stability and willingness to participate in treatment and process their traumatic memories.

Therefore, with resource installation, it is important to initially build on positive feelings and experiences before addressing negative ones. For example, focusing on the child's attributes, talents, and skills—such as kindness, musical abilities, or athletic skills—with a picture of the child involved in the activity in which he or she excels can increase feelings of confidence and empowerment that can later be used when processing traumatic memories. These resources can be installed by using slow BLS (Adler-Tapia & Settle, 2009a) and a cognitive interweave of positive attributes and skills. For a detailed description and script for the reverse protocol, see Adler-Tapia's book (2012, pp. 184–201). Some examples are provided later as well.

Future Orientation

Future orientation can be easily adapted to children with self-states. Questions adapted from Adler-Tapia (2012) include: "How do you and your parts want to be thinking, feeling, and behaving in the future?" "How do you and your parts see the future without these symptoms that brought you into treatment?" "What prevents you and your parts from accomplishing this future goal?" These questions can provide useful information about divergent thoughts and feelings among self-states that will need to be attended to before proceeding.

Another future-oriented exercise that Adler-Tapia (2012) developed is a targeted future positive scene. Adapted questions to ask include: "When you and your parts imagine your future, what do you think about?" (Clinicians may need to assist the child to identify a specific time or event in the future, such as a major birthday or social activity event in the client's life.) "What is it that you and your parts want to accomplish in the future?" "What dreams do you and your parts want to have (or had in the past) about the future?" "How are we going to know when we're done and you're ready to graduate from therapy?" The therapist can assist children to tease out a more realistic future by asking them about something they did well that made them feel proud. Then, this past "mastery experience" can be installed to help them feel positive about themselves in current time. Some parts may be unwilling to recognize a future because of guilt, shame, and despondency. If so, this will need to be further explored and resolved before proceeding.

Another technique that Adler-Tapia (2012) developed is "making the positive future real." Questions adapted for children with parts include asking the child and his or her self-states to pick a dream or goal and say, "Now pretend you are watching a video of yourself and your dream is coming true for all of you. Are you able to watch your dream? What's the positive thought you and your parts are all having?" Again, the therapist can help the child tease out a more realistic future by asking the child when the child felt proud of something he or she did well. There may be different dreams for the parts. It is important for the child to acknowledge these. As parts resolve their trauma and begin to integrate, a more unified dream can be installed.

When there are specific problem behaviors, the child can be asked, "What do you think you can try now?" This question was posed to a 13-year-old girl who had been reported to child protective services for sexually acting out against her 5-year-old sister. The adolescent had been sexually abused by her uncle when she was 5. Her sister turning 5 appeared to trigger her to offend against her sister. Adler-Tapia (2012) asked the client to say to herself, "When I feel those funny feelings in my body, I will not touch anybody else. I can learn to do something else until those feelings go away." By focusing on a positive future with replacement behaviors, the child was able to stop her offending behavior and no further child welfare reports were made against her. If a self-state is responsible for the problem behavior, it is important to elicit from that state what he or she could do differently with the support of other parts of the self.

Installing Attachment Resources

Because traumatized children often have been maltreated by their parents and have unresolved grief and loss, having a positive adult image as an alternative attachment figure can provide them with a way to meet their unmet needs. Adler-Tapia (2012) suggests that if a family member is unavailable, the therapist can ask the child about a close adult, caretaker, teacher, coach, or neighbor. If no one in the child's life is identified, the therapist can ask about a superhero or someone in the media whom the child admires. Using the reverse protocol, the therapist asks the child and self-states to visualize the future with this supportive person parenting them. The resource is installed by using slow BLS. Some self-states may have different supportive people who can be separately installed. In some instances, a child's self-states may need help with finding an appropriate attachment figure.

To build attachment between the child and a supportive parent, the parent can participate by alternately tapping each of the child's shoulders when installing a resource. The parent's participation also provides a psychological and physical anchor for the child that can be helpful in trauma processing later. The parent can also repeat the protocol when the child needs stabilization at home.

Case Study: Alex

Alex, a 14-year-old male adolescent with DID who was adopted from a European orphanage at age 4, had many unresolved attachment issues. When he was upset, he could escalate rapidly, ending in physical aggression. In a family therapy session with his adoptive parents, Alex became highly agitated when his father had to leave the session early to attend a meeting. Alex frantically begged his dad not to leave him. It was clear that he was being triggered with abandonment issues. Given that this reaction is atypical of an adolescent, who is often glad to have time without his parents, I asked Alex what was going on inside of himself. Alex related that he saw in his mind a baby self-state that was fearful of being left alone. I suggested that he put the baby state in a safe nursery and reassure that state that he would see their father in about an hour. Alex agreed. He pictured his baby-state in the safe nursery and focused on thinking that he could manage being separated for the time being from his adoptive dad. Three different BLS were administered to him simultaneously at his request. His mother tapped his shoulders in synchronicity with handheld "buzzies" (Tac scanner device that vibrates alternately left to right) as he listened to the audio scan. Within a few minutes, Alex calmed down and was able to finish the therapy session without any further incident.

Building Internal Resources for Stabilization

Adler-Tapia and Settle (2009a) adapted the use of resource development installation (RDI) from Korn and Leeds (2002) to help children manage intense affect and prepare for trauma processing. Cognitive and motor interweaves (installing positive thoughts with simultaneous movement) are more advanced resourcing skills used during preparation phase and trauma reprocessing. Advanced resourcing skills for children, including those with dissociation, can be found in books by Adler-Tapia (2012), Adler-Tapia and Settle (2008), and Gomez (2013a). These resources with cognitive interweaves can be installed with slow BLS.

Installing Empowerment Figures

Another resource technique involves encouraging children to create a picture of "a team of helpers" comprising real people in their life. Having this team can help them feel safe and supported (Adler-Tapia, 2012). Another technique is to create a bracelet or necklace from beads, with each bead representing one of the child's team of helpers. The child can wear this and touch each of the beads as a reminder of each of the helpers, especially at school when the helpers are unavailable (Adler-Tapia, 2012).

A variation of the technique just mentioned is the identification with a fictional hero figure. This can provide significant ego strengthening and help children to feel strong when managing past and present stressful events. A drawing or photo of the fictional hero figure can be used to install a sense of strength and safety within the child, along with BLS and a positive cognitive interweave. Ryan had Superman as his hero character (Waters, 2015). This played a significant role throughout his healing process. If possible, having a common hero figure across all self-states is preferred, although this is not always possible. In cases where it is not, one should respect self-states' different preferences, as the aim is to encourage stabilization and collaboration and avoid conflict.

Containment Strategies With Cue Words

Developing locked containers to hold traumatic memories and disturbing sensations, feelings, thoughts, or behaviors until they can be safely processed is an important containment strategy. Locked containers can also be used to place any residual emotions or incomplete trauma processing at the end of a session (Adler-Tapia, 2012; O'Shea, 2009). These containers can be imaginary, induced with hypnotic suggestions (Kluft, 1988), or actual boxes that are decorated by children (Adler-Tapia & Settle, 2008). Children can put pictures or notes to represent negative feelings, sensations, and thoughts in the container and then lock the box. A cue word can be installed with BLS to quickly insert unwanted material in the container. See Chapter 8 for a description of Steward's container and the cue word that all of his self-states used.

Adler-Tapia (2012) has developed other types of containers for use with her reverse protocol. A technique called "Launching Containers in the Future" was designed to hold memories, feelings, sensations, and thoughts until the child has the resources to deal with them. The child imagines or creates a time capsule that is sealed and can be opened in the future when the child is ready. The therapist asks the child, "When do you think you will be able to open this container?" "What resources do you need to acquire/learn so that we can empty this container in the future?" "What skills do you need to be able to deal with those issues in your container?" "How will you be thinking, feeling, and acting in the future when you have more confidence that we can open your container and clear out those things that seem overwhelming right now?" These questions imply that the therapist believes the client will have the competency to address the issue in the future and thus instills hope. These questions can be adapted to include self-states.

Another container technique that Adler-Tapia (2012) designed to manage negative feelings is a portable plastic container that the child decorates with stickers of symbols to remind the child of self-soothing techniques. The child places a mint in the container and puts a cue word on the container representing the aroma of the mint (i.e., pleasant, cool). When the child gets triggered or feels overwhelmed, the child eats the mint and puts any disturbing thoughts into the container. The container is then brought to the next session. The sensory experience of eating the mint is a clever way to shift focus from disturbing feelings to a pleasant experience.

Michaela, a very creative 17-year-old young woman with DID, created imaginary containers that all parts of her could use to place disturbing feelings, memories, sensations, and thoughts into until each of her parts was ready to deal with them. Michaela and her parts conferred and came up with color-coded pneumatic tubes representing each of the favorite colors of her 14 self-states. The imaginary containers would be dropped into a chute (like at a bank) and carried to a room with an area of matching color-coded space for each of the containers to be stored. When one of her parts is ready, he or she could then place the tube in the chute and sent it back to be processed. EMDR was used to install this. Michaela reported feeling much better after participating in this technique and no longer felt bombarded by her self-state's emotions and memories while at school.

Another form of containment that I use with very angry, destructive "perpetrator" self-states is an imaginary internal, locked room that provides an outlet for safe and appropriate expression of rage, as described in Chapter 8. The anger room is an "all around proof" (including soundproof) room that contains objects for safe discharge of feelings (e.g., exercise machines, balls). Adjoining the anger room is a comfort room filled with enjoyable activities where the angry part can relax after releasing his or her rage. The self-state is encouraged to equip the room with pleasant items, such as music, funny movies, food, and comfortable furniture. The use of these two rooms allows the blending of anger with pleasant feelings to mitigate the intense anger—a critical process that reduces acting out destructive behavior. These and other such techniques are installed by using BLS.

A television remote can be used to have children define stations for various resources, such as safe people, safe place imagery, and for traumatic memories (Adler-Tapia, 2012). A real remote can be used to show the children how they can switch the channel to a resource if a traumatic memory surfaces before they are ready to process it.

Increasing Mastery Over Disturbing Somatic Sensations

Dissociative children often have sensory disturbances and can depersonalize from their bodies, leaving them metaphorically suspended in time and place. Building resources to help these children reconnect with their bodies and register their somatic sensations provides a portal to reconnecting with themselves and their environment. It also grounds them to do the difficult work of processing traumatic memories.

Helping children to initially track their sensory sensations is referred to as bottom–up processing rather than top–down processing that involves starting at the cognitive level. Although EMDR therapy does involve recognizing distressing sensations in the body, along with affect and beliefs, there is increasing literature that emphasizes tracking of sensory awareness to increase mastery over unpleasant feelings and to enhance mindfulness prior to processing emotional and cognitive aspects of traumatic experiences (Knipe, 2008; Levin, 2010; Ogden & Fisher, 2015; Ogden & Gomez, 2013).

Developing Exteroceptive and Interoceptive Awareness

Exteroceptive awareness is the ability to actively perceive external stimuli. Knipe (2008) developed the method of Constant Installation of Present Orientation and Safety (CIPOS) to help clients build exteroceptive awareness of things in the current environment to maintain orientation to the present—for example, noticing a picture in the room or the sound of a car passing by. This present focus is paired with BLS. When the procedure is successful, the client will be increasingly able to be aware of present safety and past trauma simultaneously.

Lanius and Paulsen (2014) also recommended promoting mastery of being in the present moment before focusing on interoceptive awareness, such as somatic sensations of the body. To build mindfulness, Lanius and Paulsen suggested that the dissociative client should initially practice awareness of exteroceptive signals and then segue into examining bodily sensations while staying present. Practicing exteroceptive awareness helps clients connect with the self within the present environment. This enhances the individual's capacity to process past traumatic events as "memories" rather than as events presently occurring.

I use a similar technique. I have children hold their favorite puppet or doll and ask them to feel and describe it in detail. They then continue to hold this puppet as an anchor to keep them present as we talk about past nontraumatic events, and then later use the object when processing traumatic events. Other grounding techniques include touching their hair— something that is always available to help them stay present—or touching a necklace or ring they wear. Chinese meditation balls are also effective to increase a child's tactile and auditory awareness as the child rolls the balls in his or her hands while describing the sensations and sounds of the balls. Often, children report feeling calm and relaxed while doing this. Making sure that self-states are involved in these activities is critical to maintaining mindfulness. These can be installed with slow BLS.

Sensory input that develops both exteroceptive and interoceptive awareness includes the five senses (vision, touch, hearing, taste, and smell), with the latter being particularly powerful given that smells bypass the thalamus and travel directly to the limbic system and amygdala—the emotional center of the brain (Ogden, Minton, & Pain, 2006). Listening to nature sounds, looking at a color, or smelling a flower or essential oils (Adler-Tapia, 2012; Lanius & Paulsen, 2014) are examples of interventions that encourage exteroceptive awareness while also increasing interoceptive awareness. I teach children to identify enjoyable smells, such as those of flowers, food, essential oils, and scented markers, as a way to increase sensory mindfulness. The therapist can inquire whether the child has any associated body sensations or emotions and ask the child to track where in the body he or she experiences these pleasant sensations. If necessary, the therapist can provide different feeling words for the child to choose to describe the sensations.

If any memories associated with the sensations arise, ask the child to tuck them away for later processing and only focus on the sensations in his or her body. Observe any minor or subtle bodily movements, bring them to the child's awareness, and explore the sensations that the child feels with those movements. Ogden and Gomez (2013) provide numerous techniques for helping children focus on their bodily sensations by using playful metaphors such as "feeling detectors," "a body compass," or "an internal camera" that can zoom in and out. If the child identifies a smell that makes them feel particularly good, the child is asked to pick a cue word to quickly retrieve this aroma. The therapist can install the positive associations with short, slow sets (2–4) of BLS. The child can be reminded that the aroma can be used both inside and outside of therapy for self-soothing.

Practicing these exercises will increase awareness of positive bodily sensations that can later be used when titrating unpleasant sensations, particularly during trauma processing. It is important to ask the self-states that are engaged during these exercises to share these somatic sensations with the child.

Lotion exercises can be used for strengthening the attachment between parents and children. The child is asked to choose a lotion and then gently apply it to his or her mother's hands. Gomez (2013b) recommends an exercise to help a child whose hands and feet are numb. She asks children to apply lotion to their hands, then make a handprint on paper, and apply powder to the handprint to make it look more real. Because children naturally engage in tactile activities, such as playing with clay and the sand tray, any of these activities can be also used to draw the child's attention to the textures, temperature, and smells that the child experiences.

Children who have been verbally abused may automatically dissociate from hearing even under minor stress. When working with these types of children, I ask them to bring in their favorite music. We play the music, I ask them to identify the instruments in the music, and we sing along with the words to increase auditory skills. Short, slow sets of BLS can be used during this experience with headphones attached to the NeuroTek Tac audio scanner. The child can use this music both inside and outside of therapy sessions for self-soothing. Additionally, the therapist can record a relaxation exercise that guides the child and self-states to use self-soothing experiences outside of therapy.

Developing Exteroceptive and Proprioceptive Awareness

Children who are depersonalized are often unaware of their bodies. A technique that involves both exteroceptive and proprioceptive (awareness of the position of one's body) experience is physical activity. Children like to show their capabilities by hopping on one foot, doing somersaults, or sitting or stretching on a balance ball. Children can also be encouraged to go from being tense to being relaxed (e.g., lying down similar to uncooked spaghetti and then switching to cooked spaghetti) and describe how different their muscles feel (Gomez, 2013b). During these times, children can also be asked to focus on their breath and notice how their stomach and chest rise and fall. They can also practice lying still and then laughing to see how their breathing and body changes.

During these exercises, the focus is "only" on somatic processing to develop full awareness of bodily sensations. If cognitive thoughts come up, ask the child to tuck them away and return to just focusing on the body sensations. By connecting to the body, the child is learning how to stay present and grounded. Sets of slow BLS can be used with these techniques. If these activities provoke any triggering memories, gently and calmly bring the child back to present awareness by asking the child to walk around the office, drink a glass of water, or engage in an activity the child likes to do, for example, throwing a ball.

Practice Pendulation of Bodily Sensations

Levine (2010) and Ogden et al. (2006) recommend mastering unpleasant bodily sensations through a pendulation technique that involves moving back and forth from an uncomfortable sensation to a pleasant one or to a feeling of a safe state. Practicing this helps children expand their window of tolerance. For example, helping a child stay within his or her window of tolerance while noticing uncomfortable sensations in his or her body related to trauma can result in the child moving from feeling the sensations to smelling a scented marker or essential oil and oscillating back and forth between these two activities. Over time, this will increase this child's ability to tolerate more unpleasant sensations without dissociating.

An "affect dial" (Forgash, 2005; Kluft, 1993) or a gauge technique (Adler-Tapia & Settle, 2008) has been used to help clients titrate their level of affect or distance themselves from distressing stimuli. The gauge technique helps children initially identify degrees of positive affect (e.g., from happy to ecstatic), describe times when they experienced these emotions, and move to events involving unpleasant sensations. Titration can be explained by using a pool analogy (Gomez, 2013b) of acclimating to a cold swimming pool by going into the water a little bit at a time until the temperature feels comfortable. Again, these techniques can be installed with slow BLS.

Developing Safe Place Imagery or a Safe State With Cue Words

An important strategy to prepare children for trauma processing is helping them to be able to access a safe place or a feeling of safe-state within themselves (Chapter 8). A *safe state* refers to a time the child felt safe (O'Shea, 2009). It may be when the child was comforted or was read a bedtime story. This can be used when a child does not have a real safe place and is unable to develop an imaginary one. The child can draw either a picture (or cut one out of a magazine) that represents a time when the child felt safe or an image of what he or she imagines the safe place would look like. Pictures of safe place imagery can be duplicated and taped on the child's bedroom door or school desk as a reminder to help the child calm down when he or she becomes agitated. These techniques can be installed with BLS along with a cue word that the child selects to quickly remind him or her to go to the safe place or safe state when agitated. Visual reminders, such as hand signals, can also be installed with BLS for parents and teachers to use either in addition to cue words or instead of them. The child can also do BLS himself or herself (e.g., tap his or her knees or do the "butterfly hug") while imagining the safe place. Parents can also be taught to alternately tap the child's shoulders to help the child access his or her safe place or state.

If a child's self-states have different safe place imagery, all of them can be asked to picture them simultaneously while doing the BLS. If they cannot do so, then the technique will need to be repeated to accommodate their individual safe place imagery. As with any technique, children are encouraged to practice this between sessions by tapping their knees, for example, so that they are skilled enough to use it when they are upset. Parents should be encouraged to remind the child to practice this technique. Cathy, whose case has been previously discussed, had self-states that created separate decorated bedrooms as their safe place (Chapter 8). Using the EMDR protocol, they were able to simultaneously visualize their safe bedrooms while Cathy held the "buzzies" in her hand for installation.

One 5-year-old dissociative child, who had been subjected to chronic sexual abuse by her father, was taught to capture a sense of safe state when at school or during other activities. I taught her to use the "butterfly hug" with the positive thought of "I am safe now." She practiced this many times and was able to use it when she was triggered to help calm down and stay oriented to the present. For example, one day in gym class, her teacher asked the students to perform a high leaping movement while imagining they were leaping over the scariest thing they had ever experienced. She immediately pictured her abusive father. Instead of freezing, she managed to leap high, and then she did the butterfly hug immediately afterward. She explained to her gym teacher that she had pictured her dad who hurt her and proceeded to show her teacher the butterfly hug that helped her feel calm and strong. Afterward, she told me, "Me and my other self did the butterfly hug. It worked!" She demonstrated in my office how high she leaped and then she practiced stepping on her dad instead of leaping over him. Each time she stepped on him, she tapped her shoulders and felt very strong and brave!

Imaginary Protective Shield

The Imaginary Protective Shield technique is one I developed to help keep children from internalizing negative experiences from the environment. The child is asked to imagine a hero's protective shield that completely surrounds or covers the child and all self-states when they feel threatened. I tell the child that this protective shield keeps them from absorbing unwanted experiences while still being able to hear and see what is transpiring around them. This can be installed with BLS along with the PC "I only allow positive things inside of me." This shield has been particularly useful when children are teased at school.

Installing a Mastery Experience

Adler-Tapia (2012) adapted Korn and Leeds's (2002) Resource Development and Installation technique to install mastery experiences in children. The technique involves asking children to describe something good that happened to them or something they felt really proud about since the previous session. They are asked to draw a picture or imagine something that represents the best part of what happened, the best thought about themselves currently, their good feelings/emotions, and where they feel them in their bodies. Then, they hold that image, positive belief, feelings, and sensations while slow BLS is administered. Noting self-states' role in the child's positive experience will increase their continuing cooperation, as they feel appreciated and empowered as well.

EMDR Therapy Phases 3 to 7: Trauma Reprocessing: Assessment, Desensitization, Installation, Body Scan, and Closure

EMDR therapy Phases 3 through 7 includes: Assessment, Desensitization, Installation, Body Scan, and Closure. This correlates to Phase 2 of dissociative treatment that also involves trauma processing. Within these phases are procedural steps that include identifying a target (maladaptively encoded information that is theoretically driving the presenting symptoms), selecting the image that represents the worst part of the target, eliciting a negative cognition (NC) and PC, assessing the validity of the cognition (VoC) on a 7-point scale, identifying an emotion that is triggered by the target, rating the subjective units of distress (SUD) associated with the emotion on a 10-point scale, and identifying the body sensations and location of the disturbance in the body (Shapiro, 2001).

Possible targets can include abuse or other experiences that have caused distress that is identified by the child. Most young children can express what is bothering them. For those who do not have clear memories due to dissociation or those whose trauma is held in the sensory-motor memory system, Lovett (1999) has provided a model in which the parent provides a description of the child's trauma. An adapted use of Lovett's model occurred in the case of Jamal, who is described at the end of this chapter.

Paulsen (2009) developed client and therapist readiness checklists to determine whether dissociative clients and the therapist are prepared for trauma processing. I have adapted these checklists for use with dissociative children and adolescents to ensure that the necessary components are in place for safe trauma processing. This is reproduced in Appendix C.

Assessment Phase

The Assessment Phase of EMDR therapy starts with identifying a target for trauma reprocessing. Adler-Tapia and Settle (2008) indicated, "It is important for the therapist to recognize the relationship between current stimuli or triggers, manifestations of symptoms, and maladaptively stored memories to successfully identify targets for desensitization" (p. 102). It is recommended that the therapist identify the "touchstone event," which "is the original incident that has been maladaptively stored and is driving the current symptoms that brought the client into therapy" (p. 106). To find the original time that the symptom appeared, the "floatback" technique is used to probe for the first time the child felt or experienced this symptom. If the child is unable to identify the first time a symptom was felt, the parent can be asked to provide this information.

Adler-Tapia and Settle (2008) suggested that a target can be identified by having children draw a map of their biggest worries. Dissociative children can check internally with their parts on what their most disturbing worries are and then draw them. The child can insert a favorite hero character into the drawing to give them strength to handle their worries. The child can then rank how big those worries are with input from self-states to determine which target to work on first. The child ranks the SUD from 0 to 10 (0 being not at all upset and 10 being the most distressed) or shows with the hands apart or with a ruler how distressing a worry feels.

With dissociative children who have suffered chronic trauma, there may be many touchstone events that are contained in different self-states. Eliciting their participation to identify the first time that they experienced symptoms related to specific touchstone events and getting them to agree to work collaboratively with a specific target are advisable. If possible, have the child be a spokesperson for the whole system, as this can minimize any switching among states that could result in destabilization or disruption of the process. Self-states who are not involved with the target can be enlisted as "cheerleaders" to support the child or placed in internal, soundproof safe rooms, if it would be too disturbing to be exposed to the traumatic material.

Once the target has been identified, the clinician explores the NC that accompanies this event. The NC is discussed and then changed to a desirable, positive cognition or PC. To show appreciation for the self-state's survival roles, I suggest that the PC include reference to all self-states. For example, the child may say, "All parts of myself survived. We are now safe." After a PC is decided, the child is asked to hold that image and rate the VoC on a scale from 1 (completely false) to 7 (completely true). At different steps of this process, the therapist can ask the child to check inside with any self-states that were involved in the event to receive their input, for example, their ratings of SUD and VoCs. Self-states may have different ratings due to various levels or degrees of involvement, or some may have witnessed the event but were not directly involved. The important point is that they dialogue with and support each other, as they process their degree of involvement. Egli-Bernd (2011) recommends a "dialogue protocol" that elicits internal communication among self-states with emphasis on the complex emotional and cognitive processes related to the client's self-perception and self-evaluation, rather than focus on the traumatic event itself.

The final stage is to identify any body sensations that arise when the event is pictured. Children can be provided a list of somatic sensations to help them express what they are experiencing.

After the child decides on the target to reprocess, the therapist asks the child to identify the traumatic experience associated with the target. Then, the child (with the self-state's awareness and cooperation) can draw a picture of the event or use pictures from other sources or a sand tray to represent the event. Again, the child can continue to insert his or her hero character or other resources for strength.

Eight-year-old Eddie, diagnosed with other specified dissociative disorder (OSDD), was sexually abused by his adolescent stepbrother. He was very timid and fearful. He identified with Bettle Borgs, cartoon heroes that battle bad people. As Eddie struggled with his feelings of fear and powerlessness, I asked him to imagine that he was being infused with Bettle Borgs's powers to help him feel strong and brave. Eddie drew a very large picture of himself; in the upper corner of the picture, he drew a Bettle Borg and wrote, "Bettle Borgs are giving me power to be strong." I then did BLS with him holding the Tac scanner while focusing on this picture (Chapter 7, Figure 7.4).

Later, to prepare for trauma processing, and with agreement from his self-states, Eddie again drew a Bettle Borg in the top corner of his picture to give him strength to express his anger at his abuser. Although he was a nonviolent boy, Eddie drew a gun firing but not in the direction of his stepbrother. Instead, Eddie drew a long leg and a large foot getting ready to smash his abuser, who was so small that a magnifying glass had to be used to see him (Figure 12.1). On the picture, Eddie wrote, "Where are you?" Near the tiny representation of his stepbrother, he wrote, "Afraid to tell the truth." Eddie was able to recognize how his abuser was too weak and "small" to tell the truth of what he did to Eddie, whereas Eddie felt big for having the courage to tell the truth. His PC was, "I am strong. I told." His SUD of fear was 0 at the end of the processing.

Figure 12.1 *Eddie's use of a Bettle Borg (in upper left corner) to give him strength. (Used with permission.)*

Desensitization Phase

The goal of the Desensitization Phase of EMDR therapy is to assist the child in accessing the traumatic experience cognitively, somatically, and affectively in order to complete the reprocessing. This includes reviewing the SUD and VoC levels. Then, the child, in cooperation with the child's system, simultaneously holds the image, negative cognition, and the body sensation identified in the assessment phase while the therapist applies BLS.

Before beginning to process the traumatic event, it is important to remind the child and self-states of the *present time and place* while recalling memories of the past, and reinforce their internal cooperation as a team as they reprocess the memories. Also, let them know that they can stop at any time by saying "stop" or with a stop hand signal. They can go to the safe place or safe state if their feelings become too big to handle. When they are ready, they can resume picturing the upsetting experience. It is important that the traumatized child feels in charge of the process.

With severely traumatized, dissociative children and adolescents, it is important to utilize a variety of containment, titrating, and distancing techniques for safe processing. Numerous suggestive/hypnotic techniques can be incorporated into EMDR therapy for safe processing of traumatic memories. Kluft (2013) described fractionated techniques in which the trauma is broken up into segments to minimize the client from being overwhelmed. Adler-Tapia and Settle (2008) recommend a black-and-white movie screen for the child to watch the traumatic event and include, if need be, a trusted adult or super hero character to protect the child.

The child may demonstrate physiological and emotional signs, such as movements in body, face, breathing, and crying, that indicate that the target is accurate. During this process, it is important that the child is able to speak for the different self-states as they process along with the child. Sometimes, I will ask the child how self-states are feeling or what they are thinking so that I can verify that the child is processing across all the parts that were involved. Self-states may present during these times to report specific parts of the trauma. If a self-state emerges, it is advisable to continue the processing and to acknowledge their thoughts, feelings, and sensations. The therapist then will stop the BLS for a short period to ask the child to self-reflect on the process.

Because young children are creative and have a need to be rescued, their trauma narratives often include rescue fantasies. It is important to understand the psychological needs of a vulnerable child and allow the child to continue to tell the narrative. At times, I will ask whether this is what the child wished had happened. When the child affirms, then BLS is resumed with that wishful thought. Young children may find it helpful to use art therapy techniques or a sand tray to express their traumatic experience. The Desensitization Phase concludes when the client no longer identifies any disturbance (SUD of 0) associated with the targeted memory.

I have had dissociative children engage puppets and the dissociative doll with little feeling dolls (Chapter 4, Figure 4.1) to process their traumatic experiences while their parent tapped their shoulders. It is important to be flexible and allow the child to find creative and comfortable ways to process their memories with projective toys. Maggie and Michael, described in Chapter 7, liked to have the buzzies put in their socks. Initially, it would tickle, which reduced their anxiety and allowed them to then work on the sexual abuse by their father while they held puppets "who spoke for them."

Managing the Spontaneous Appearance of Self-States
Sometimes during processing, self-states will spontaneously appear who have been involved in a specific part of the memory or affect. It may be a new part that was previously unknown or it may be a part that is already known that was involved in the traumatic event and has a need to report something. I continue with the protocol and explore the self-state's feelings, thoughts, and any images that surface. The focus should be on completing the processing with the child's team. If the self-state is cooperating, then it is advisable to continue. However, if the self-state is unwilling to continue, then the clinician can gently ask this part whether he or she would be willing to work from inside with the team or to go to a safe room and let the main child return. If he or she does not want to do so, then processing will need to stop until this part's needs or motives have been further explored. Closing down the processing with the team by placing the memory in a safe container until it is later processed is recommended.

When a self-state disrupts the trauma processing, it is important to analyze what is motivating this part's action. There could be a myriad of underlying issues that are thwarting the child's ability to process the trauma. It could be a hidden state that was activated and is unaware of the therapy, a state that fears retaliation for reporting the event, one that is still attached to the perpetrator, or for some other reason that is unique to the case. Even with significant preparation to prevent any "sabotage" from within, sometimes internal resistance surfaces. There are many layers to the dissociative mind, and constant vigilance and adaptation is required by the therapist to see what may be blocking progress and to explore for the presence of unknown dissociative states. It is important to show respect for the self-state's needs, be willing to adjust therapeutic interventions, and later reestablish a contract for further processing.

Installation Phase

The Installation Phase of EMDR therapy begins with the therapist having the child, in cooperation with designated self-states, bring up the original target memory and ascertain whether the original PC still fits. If a new PC surfaced during reprocessing of the memory, then the therapist has the client hold the image of the original incident together with the new PC and assess the VoC. The therapist then uses BLS to strengthen the VoC until it is at a 7 (top of the scale).

Body Scan Phase

Somatically encoded memory networks that contain disturbing body sensations related to trauma are accessed, activated, and reprocessed with BLS during the body scan phase. Children—especially infants and toddlers—often process a memory almost entirely in their bodies. Because children experience life through sensory motor and emotional memories, it is important to have children spend time clearing any "owies" or places where their body feels bad or uncomfortable. Unfortunately, children with dissociation are often disconnected from their bodies. Therapists and parents may need to teach children about their bodies and bodily sensations before such processing can occur. Another obstacle to connecting to the body may be the presence of protective parts that prevent the child from feeling bodily disturbances. This will need to be addressed before proceeding. As children connect with their bodily sensations—possibly for the first time since the trauma—they may become more dysregulated as they "unthaw." Using calming techniques can mitigate the disturbing bodily sensations.

The body scan phase of trauma processing starts with asking children to hold the original target experience and the positive cognition together in their mind while scanning their body for any experiences of disturbance or discomfort. If any disturbance or discomfort is identified, the therapist has the child focus on the disturbance while continuing with the BLS. With young children, the therapist can ask them to notice how their bodies feel, instruct them to scan their bodies with the use of a toy, or identify their body sensations with a doll or drawing representing their body. Once the distressing and somatic memories are reprocessed, children often make significant developmental gains.

Closure

The Closure Phase of EMDR assesses the client's success, including the self-states that participated, at completing the targeted event or closing down the session for more processing later. At the end of the session, the therapist provides specific instructions to the child on using the stabilization techniques that have been taught, such as utilizing the safe place or safe state, containment, and self-soothing skills, if disturbing material surfaces. Parents are encouraged to use the cue word previously installed to remind their child to place any disturbing material in a container until it is safely processed in the child's therapy session. By teaching children the ability to use containers, children often feel more confident to manage intense affect and uncomfortable situations.

It is important to remind the child and parents to be alert to known triggers and to apply stabilization strategies by using BLS, such as the butterfly hug or parental tapping, before the next session. Teaching parents to reinforce the child's ability to master triggers can greatly improve the outcome of therapy.

Phase 8: Reevaluation

The Reevaluation Phase of EMDR therapy includes reviewing the treatment plan and planning for graduation from therapy. However, the term *reevaluation* is used in different ways through the eight phases of EMDR therapy. Reevaluation is a process in which the therapist evaluates the reprocessing of a specific target, the overall target plan, and, eventually, the overall treatment progress. Reevaluation also occurs at the beginning of every session in which the therapist assesses the client's current functioning and revises the treatment plan if necessary. When working with children, it is important to gather input from both the child and his or her caregivers. After processing a target, the therapist evaluates the effectiveness of the treatment to ensure that the traumatic memory is cleared to an SUD of 0; positive cognitions have a VoC of 7; and the client experiences a clear body scan.

Typically, the final phase of EMDR therapy also involves planning for graduation from therapy and suggesting future goals for the child and caregivers. However, with dissociative children, the final phase is usually not the conclusion of processing the targeted traumatic event(s), as integration will still need to occur, if spontaneous integration did not happen during treatment. EMDR therapy can be used to unite the child's self-states as one with the child, as the child pictures them coming together with all of their skills, talents, thoughts, and feelings that are integrated within the child. Refer to Chapter 13 for specific integration techniques that can be installed with EMDR therapy. As an integrated child, new problem-solving techniques may need to be learned and EMDR therapy can be helpful in this regard.

HEALING INFANT TRAUMA

Jamal, who I introduced in the beginning of this chapter, lived with his foster family (who later adopted him) and made significant progress; however, Jamal was significantly delayed in all areas of development, and there was a possibility he would need surgery. His adoptive mother had great concerns about him, because Jamal did not express distress when he had a double ear infection and often would not protest when he was uncomfortable. He did not seem to react to pain and had a significant startle response.

At 14 months of age, Jamal's mother held him and told his story while Adler-Tapia elicited various types of eye movements in Jamal by using puppets and other toys. She later used puppets to tap on all the "owies" on his body. Initially, Jamal appeared dissociated and had poor muscle tone as he sat on his mother's lap while she told about his trauma in a soothing voice. After about 30 minutes, Jamal began to arch his back and verbally protest in a sound similar to a growl. He appeared to finally release his anger over the severe abuse he had experienced and somatic stress held in his body. The therapist then stopped the trauma reprocessing and used soothing techniques to help Jamal become calmer. In the next session, Jamal's mother reported that he had tantrummed in a manner she had never witnessed. He again seemed to be releasing all the emotions held in his body that had been dissociated. Over the next 2 months, there were four sessions with Jamal and his mother. During this time, Jamal made significant developmental gains in speech, gross motor skills, and attachment. In the fourth session, Jamal tracked his mother with his eyes as she was leaving the office. He then walked after her, calling "Mum, Mum." In a follow-up, when he was 4 years old, Jamal appeared to be on target in all developmental areas.

Although infants cannot verbalize their trauma, it is captured in the sensory motor memory and can adversely affect the child's growth, attachment, and emotional and behavioral regulation. Based on AIP theory, one could hypothesize that the traumatic experiences had been maladaptively encoded in sensory motor memories in Jamal's memory networks. As the memories were accessed and activated by his mother telling his story, these traumatic memories were reprocessed to adaptive resolution and reconsolidated. The combination of EMDR therapy, a loving adoptive family, and brief physical and occupational therapy facilitated a significantly traumatized infant to develop into a normal and healthy child. Jamal was able to go on with his life, no longer weighed down by the severe trauma he experienced during infancy.

A similar example is described by Potgieter-Marks (Waters, Yehuda, & Potgieter-Marks, 2011), who used EMDR therapy with an infant who suffered a painful surgical procedure without anesthesia to clip her tongue-tie. Immediately afterward, the mother nursed the infant, who apparently linked the trauma with her mother. The infant, who previously demonstrated a secure attachment (looked at her mother and engaged in mirroring), immediately avoided complete eye contact with her mother. With the use of the buzzies inserted in the infant's socks, the mother held her baby and in soothing words talked to her about the traumatic ordeal. The infant only looked at the therapist until the therapist gradually moved to stand behind the mother. This facilitated the infant to gaze at her mother. The same strategy was repeated in two more sessions. In the last session, the infant had resumed consistently looking at her mother, who, in turn, continued to talk to her infant in a comforting way. The attachment was repaired.

These two examples demonstrate how important it is to process infant trauma to avoid longer term developmental and attachment disturbances. While the child may be too young to talk about the trauma, an infant's dissociated trauma can be processed with an attuned caregiver who can provide a script of the trauma (Lovett, 1999) and tell the child's story in a loving manner while BLS is provided.

SUMMARY

EMDR therapy is an evidence-based treatment that has proved to be effective in helping people overcome traumatic events. Over the years, its specialized techniques have been adapted to and successfully implemented with children and adolescents who have complex trauma and dissociation. Combining the theories and practices in the EMDR protocol with dissociative theory can enhance dissociative children's recovery. Both theories recognize dissociative defenses and the need to access memory networks held in self-states. Both adhere to safe processing of traumatic memories with installation of stabilization and ego-strengthening techniques. When combined, these two treatments can provide a pathway for children with complex trauma to heal, even young children who cannot communicate their pain. For more resources on EMDR, see Appendix A.

NOTE

1. Available from neurotekcorp.com

1 3

"It's Like You're in a New World"
Integrating the Fractured Child

After Martha, age 10, finished her grieving of the considerable violence and losses she experienced early in life (Chapter 6), I asked her whether she would be willing to audiotape what it was like now that she and all her parts were working together as one. Martha readily agreed. She made a dramatic physical transformation after integrating (upright posture, enthusiastic gait, glowing complexion, and bright eyes), and her voice went from a hesitant, sad-sounding voice to an upbeat and confident one. When, decades later, I listened to her recording for this book, it was clear that she had awakened into a new world. It still brought tears to my eyes.

Here is an excerpt of what Martha said about what it feels like when "everybody's working together."

> It feels fun. It's pretty nice because you have everybody working together and your mom and dad are giving you compliments. You have a nice feeling . . . But when everybody's not working together, it's blah! It's not very fun at all 'cause I can't get things done. It's pretty hard to do things when you only have one or two people working together . . . Everybody's saying, "Martha, Why aren't you paying attention, huh?"

Martha highlighted the problems she experienced prior to integration by mentioning an incident when another part of her took over when she was riding her horse. Her horse threw her off and almost trampled her. Martha concluded by saying,

> I don't blank out a lot because I don't need to do that anymore. I have a new home . . . It's like you're in a new world. I used to be all black. My eyes would be cloudy. My mom and dad would sense that

something's wrong. But now it's like you're in a new world and you
aren't cloudy. You're really happy and you laugh and play a lot. It's
like you're in a new world!

Martha eloquently described her transformation of moving from
a dissociative state of blackness and cloudiness to one of happiness and
clarity. Healing her fractured self truly brought her into a new world free
of confusion, a world where she could fully experience the joys that her
new life offered.

INTEGRATION BEGINS AT BEGINNING OF TREATMENT

Although integration is considered the final phase of treatment, it actually begins when the fractured child first steps into the therapist's office,
as noted earlier in this book. When we as clinicians show utmost respect
for all parts of the child, we begin to build an alliance with those parts.
This alliance can be shared internally as parts come to accept each other—
a first step toward integration! An acceptance and appreciation for parts
of the self create the necessary therapeutic climate that will pave the way
for integration to occur later.

The Star Theoretical Model brings together multiple therapeutic
interventions that simultaneously help the child with the following: to
release dissociative defenses, process traumatic experiences across all
self-states, resolve attachment dilemmas and foster the development of
healthy attachments, promote effective communication within and outside the family system, exhibit developmentally appropriate behavior,
and, finally, integrate. Throughout the treatment process, incorporation
of neurobiological principles into specialized therapeutic strategies will
promote integration. Consequently, the process of integration can often
be a smooth and seamless one, particularly with young children. Children are typically more adaptable and flexible, and less invested in maintaining separateness than their adult counterparts. Compared with older
adolescents and adults, children's self-states have had less time to develop
and to practice their survival roles. Given a safe and nurturing environment, the earlier children's dissociative defenses are identified, the less
invested they are in utilizing such defenses and the more willing they are
to integrate.

A final treatment principle (described in Chapter 5) is the development of the metacognitive capacity that leads to integration of memory, behavior, affect, and sensations across self-states, resulting in a unified self. With dissociative youth, this entails the ability to self-reflect—to think about one's thoughts and to recognize one's affect, sensations, and behaviors "across multiple states of consciousness." This is no small feat for a child who is plagued with harassing voices, frightening images, and memory lapses. However, kind, patient, and empathetic caregivers and therapists can provide role models for children to develop mental representations of supportive adults. These positive transferences enhance children's self-reflective abilities. In addition, a safe home and therapeutic environment provide the structure for children to face their internal life and to begin to make sense out of the chaos.

Specially designed intervention techniques to help the child examine the multiple realties of the self, with parental participation or support, is an initial step toward achieving a cohesive self. The process requires the child to break down amnestic barriers between self-states and develop internal awareness, appreciation, and cooperation—a self-reflective process. The child's ability to negotiate with self-states for successful management of negative affect and behavior requires calming down the stress-response system to enhance the thinking process. This is often an arduous process that requires achieving dual awareness of internal and external worlds—worlds that are often incongruent. By facing and understanding the discrepancy between those two worlds, the child can resolve the contradictory feelings, sensations, thoughts, and behaviors contained within self-states. This requires an ongoing process of mindfulness that aids the child in putting together the pieces of the puzzle of the child's internal life and identity. It also entails resolving attachment dilemmas so that healthy relationships can develop, and resolving past traumatic memories so that they are no longer impeding the child's current functioning. Through this integrative process, the child is able to learn problem-solving skills and developmentally appropriate behavior.

Throughout this book, interventions are described that promote self-reflection and resolution of traumatic events. At times, the use of these techniques results in spontaneous integration, as once traumatic experiences are resolved, the need for separateness within the self often is no longer necessary. Over time, this creates a "blending" of the parts within the child that leads to a final integration—an experience of oneness across all domains—cognitive, affective, sensation, behavior, and spiritual. Once this occurs, children are able to more fully focus on living in the here and now, because their attention is no longer consumed with managing traumatic triggers and coping with disunity within the self. The child's memories of the trauma may remain or fade with time; however, the impact of the trauma will no longer strangle the child's mind and spirit. When these children are asked whether all of the self-states are one, they will often indicate *We are all one* or *There is just me now*. At this point, no further techniques are then required to finalize integration among self-states. However, when integration does not occur spontaneously, there are specific interventions that can promote integration with children and adolescents.

SPECIFIC INTERVENTIONS PROMOTING INTEGRATION

Infants can be negatively impacted by a number of experiences such as birth trauma, painful medical procedures, early deprivation, physical, sexual, and emotional abuse, and disruption in attachment. I have used a variety of techniques to help children who were traumatized in infancy process their trauma and "re-parent" their infant self so that they can be able to master the psychosocial stage of infancy/toddlerhood and thus develop autonomy and the ability to trust others. These techniques have been very successful in helping children resolve histories of early deprivation and trauma that have led to the capacity to attach to their parents and achieve integration. Rudy, Lisa, and Martha along with Melissa and Ricky (introduced later) are examples of children who developed dissociation after being traumatized in infancy. Next, I describe the techniques used to help them integrate. One constant in the various integration techniques is the integration message that I convey to the child.

Integration Message

When using integration techniques, the central integration message that I provide is that all of a child's self-states' skills, talents, thoughts, feelings, and sensations—all their qualities—will be joined as one with the child, and *nothing of them will be lost*. Once self-states have received this message, they do not seem threatened by integration, as they recognize that they will be there in unity with the child. I emphasize that there is strength in unity rather than in working alone or being separate.

Rudy: Use of a Baby Doll

Rudy, whose case was first introduced in Chapter 4 and continued in Chapters 6, 7, 8, and 10, was adopted with his sister from an orphanage in Eastern Europe when he was 18 months old. Rudy's case provides an example of how even a young child can "re-parent" his infant state. Rudy was able to connect with this deprived baby state that accounted for his soiling problems and other infantile behaviors, as he held and rocked a baby doll. Rudy's mother rocked him as he held the doll. Thus, she supported Rudy and helped him nurture Rudy's baby state. In doing so, she increased both Rudy's attachment to his mother and his acceptance of the baby state within. Rudy also used the baby doll to teach the younger part of himself how to be toilet trained. These techniques proved to be integrative, as the little part of him was able to master the early developmental demands by having consistent parenting provided by Rudy and his mother. The young part then began to age progress to Rudy's age and spontaneously integrated.

Rudy's invisible team, who carried the trauma of starvation, also integrated spontaneously once they were acknowledged and able to share in the gustatory experience of eating with Rudy. They felt nourished physically and emotionally by Rudy's parents, who accepted them as well. Rudy's Angel (formerly Devil) felt appreciated for handling people who were mean to Rudy and joined with the others in integration. Because of early detection of Rudy's self-states, which were fortunately not well developed, and with interventions geared toward uncovering their underlying motives and resolving their maladaptive behaviors, there was no longer a need for separation. Treatment prevented further development of Rudy's self-states and fracturing of his self. Rudy did not exhibit any further assaultive behavior at home or at school and he was able to attend school full time. After integration, Rudy smiled often. His window of tolerance for frustration was widely expanded, and he exhibited a healthy attachment with his parents.

Melissa: Clay Sculpture Technique

Nine-year-old Melissa experienced considerable infant trauma that was characterized by neglect and attempted suffocation by her father when she cried in her crib. One day, her adoptive parents came to my office very frustrated with Melissa. They reported that during the past couple of weeks, Melissa began to walk on her toes, spit out her food, pick her ears and nose and eat their contents. Interestingly, in the previous session, Melissa revealed to me that she was aware of a 1-year-old baby within herself. I suspected this accounted for her developmentally "regressed" behavior. I then met with Melissa, who confirmed that this part was influencing her behavior.

I offered Melissa several options for healing her baby part. The first option was to have her adoptive mom come in and rock her, while accessing the baby part, to help her heal from the early abuse and neglect. Melissa did not want to do this, as her attachment with her adoptive mother was tenuous. She was also offered the options of using a doll, drawing a picture, or making a clay sculpture of her infant state. Melissa chose to work with clay. While she was molding the baby self-state from clay, I sculpted a mother figure and a rocking chair. After we completed our sculpting, I asked Melissa who she would like the mother sculpture to represent. I suggested that it could be her birth mother or her adoptive mother. Melissa said she wanted it to be her birth mother. I then had her place the clay baby figure in the arms of the mother figure sitting in the rocking chair (Figure 13.1).

I proceeded to explain that this part was safe now and I expressed how sorry I felt for all she had gone through. I indicated that rocking and loving the infant part would heal her from the scary things that happened to her, and feeling her birth mother's love would help the baby to grow up to be Melissa's age. I asked Melissa to hold the sculpture in her hand and rock it as she rocked in my rocking chair.

I again reiterated that this part was safe now and through loving and rocking, this part would grow up to be Melissa's age. I counted from 1 to 9 years old slowly to encourage the age progression of Melissa's infant state. Melissa was given the same instructions as Rudy was given with the baby doll: to bring this sculpture home, keep it safe, and rock it daily so that her little part could feel loved and begin to grow up. Melissa left my office and excitedly showed her adoptive parents the sculpture, pointing out how cute the baby was, and she showed them the baby's hair curl that she had meticulously made. She explained to her parents that she was to take the sculpture home, keep it safe, and rock it daily. This exercise allowed Melissa to begin the internal healing of her baby state.

The next week, Melissa proudly announced that her infant self-state had progressed to age 3. Her adoptive parents reported that the regressive

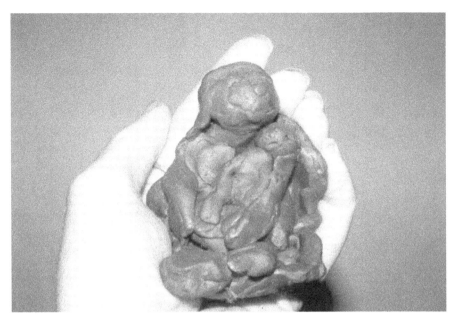

Figure 13.1 *Melissa's sculpture of her biological mom holding her baby self-state. (Used with permission.)*

behaviors Melissa had displayed ceased. I then suggested that Melissa sculpt her 3-year-old part as I again sculpted a mother in a rocking chair. I asked Melissa who she would like the mother to be, and she responded that she wanted it to be her adoptive mom. It was clear that Melissa needed to initially connect with her biological mother and resolve her loss of her biological mother before she could begin the attachment process with her adoptive mother. Figure 13.2 is a picture of Melissa's sculpture of her 3-year-old self-state being held by her adoptive mom.

Melissa rocked the sculpture as she sat in my rocking chair. I repeated that the 3-year-old was safe now and both Melissa and her adoptive mother were rocking her to help her receive their love so she could continue to grow. I again counted to encourage age progression; however, this time I started at age 3 and counted to 9. Melissa took the new sculpture home and continued to rock it daily. In her next session, Melissa reported that the part was now 9 years old. I asked her to create a new sculpture of the 9-year-old. Again, I sculpted the mother and rocking chair. Melissa again chose her adoptive mom to hold her—a sign of Melissa's desire to finalize the attachment process of this part with her adoptive mom (Figure 13.3).

Figure 13.2 *Melissa's sculpture of her adoptive mother holding her 3-year-old self-state. (Used with permission.)*

Figure 13.3 *Melissa's sculpture of her adopted mom holding her 9-year-old self-state. (Used with permission.)*

The next week, Melissa revealed that her self-state had attached to her adoptive mom. It was now time to integrate. I suggested that Melissa choose two colors of clay: one symbolizing herself and the other symbolizing the now 9-year-old self-state. She was instructed to join the two colors into a ball. As she formed the ball, I told her that all of Melissa and all of the 9-year-old self-state would come together to form one 9-year-old Melissa containing all of their thoughts, feelings, memories, and sensations in one self. Melissa then integrated. I have successfully used this integration technique many times with dissociative children.

Although the principles remain the same, many different methods can be used to help children achieve integration. For example, I have guided children to blend watercolors together to represent their self-states integrating within them. The following integration technique involved using the child's favorite stuffed animal, Pooh Bear.

Ricky: Healing Infant Birth Trauma With Pooh Bear's Help

Ricky's mother, Karen, came to my office desperate to get her 4-year-old son help. She tearfully detailed her son's history. Ricky's birth was traumatic and he entered this world with the umbilical cord wrapped around his neck and body several times. Later, Karen heard him screaming as she waited down the hall while he endured a botched circumcision, leaving him disfigured and in pain for months afterward.

From birth on, Ricky was an irritable and underweight child. At 2½ years of age, he only spoke 14 words. He was a very fussy eater and developed numerous food allergies. He also experienced chronic, severe constipation and was only able to have a bowel movement weekly at best. Behavioral therapy and mineral oil were ineffective. Meal times were extremely stressful for Ricky. He became highly agitated and would pace back and forth, anticipating that if he ate, he would need to defecate. He often avoided eating as long as he could in order to avoid needing to have a bowel movement, which was painful given his chronic constipation.

At 2 years of age, Ricky's mother took him to a pediatric urologist who recommended reparative cosmetic surgery on Ricky's circumcision to prevent later embarrassment due to his penile disfigurement. Ricky's severe constipation worsened after his reconstructive surgery. At one point, he was so miserable after not having a bowel movement for 2 weeks that his parents rushed him to the hospital emergency department where he was administered an adult enema, because the hospital did not have a child-sized one. He had to be held down during the administration of the enema and cried the entire time. He was given child-sized enemas several times after that. Although Ricky was aware when he needed to pass stool, he adamantly refused to use the toilet. At 4 years old, Ricky insisted that his parents put a diaper on him so that he could squat down behind the couch and relieve himself.

Ricky also experienced sensory disturbances. He could not tell the difference between stomach pains related to hunger and those associated with needing to pass stool. He was also very sensitive to any pressure around his wrists, waist, or legs and would only wear loose-fitting clothing and pants with elastic waistbands. I suspected his aversion to any tightness on his body was based on having the umbilical cord wrapped around him in the womb and being held down when initially circumcised and later when given enemas.

Ricky could not handle transitions well and demonstrated intense separation anxiety when his mother dropped him off at the daycare center on her way to work. He desperately clung to Pooh Bear and his "blankie" (blanket) that he had since birth. If he left home without them, he would have a meltdown, sobbing inconsolably until his mother or father retrieved them.

Ricky's infant traumas appeared to be the source of his subsequent ongoing symptoms. My working hypothesis was that Ricky's separation anxiety and ongoing digestive and sensory disturbances were related to his birth trauma and subsequent painful medical procedures. It was clear that Ricky's early traumas would need to be accessed and processed.

Accompanied by his parents, Ricky, a frail child, walked slowly into my office, clutching his Pooh Bear and dragging his worn and faded blanket. It was apparent that every day was a struggle for him and his parents as well, who had dark circles under their eyes and appeared exhausted. They had tried different diets, behavior therapy, and mineral oil treatment, but Ricky's severe bowel problems persisted. Therapy was their last hope, as the pediatric gastroenterologist was considering surgery.

I believe in the power of even young children to heal their inner wounds when provided a vehicle to do so. I mapped out a strategy by using his inseparable Pooh Bear as a projection of Ricky in play therapy. Pooh Bear had been with Ricky since birth, making him a perfect transitional representation of Ricky. My operating premise was that Ricky's early traumatic events had become segmented in a frozen infant state that carried the implicit traumatic memories, resulting in ongoing symptoms involving his genitalia and pelvic area.

I introduced myself to Ricky, explaining that I help children with bad things that happen to them when they are born, making them hurt and scared. I got out my toy medical kit and indicated that when Pooh Bear was born, he had a hard time because his body got hurt. He felt really scared. I explained that it was too much for Pooh Bear to handle and that there was a Little Pooh Bear inside of Pooh Bear that felt all of these hurts and scared feelings. I suggested that Ricky could be "Dr. Ricky" and help the Little Pooh Bear inside of Pooh Bear feel better and heal from all of the scary and bad feelings from which he got hurt at birth. Ricky enthusiastically agreed.

Dr. Ricky proceeded to open the medical kit and take Pooh Bear's temperature, listen to his heart, give him a shot, and put a bandage on his arm. I explained that it was important for Little Pooh Bear to know that he was safe now and is able to heal from the bad, scary, and painful feelings he felt when he was born. I indicated that Dr. Ricky could help Little Pooh Bear. I said, "Little Pooh Bear is safe now and all of his body parts are safe," as I listed his head, arms, wrist, legs, ankles, stomach, and private parts. I continued to repeat that all of his body parts were now healing with Dr. Ricky's care. I asked Dr. Ricky how old Little Pooh Bear was and he said, "Zero years old." Ricky seemed to unconsciously connect with his own birth trauma and this intervention seemed to resonate with him, as he administered to Little Pooh Bear.

I further explained that Little Pooh Bear needed lots of love and care, and now that he was healing from the bad, scary things that happened when he was born, he would be able to eat food and have it go down his stomach, and it would provide him with energy to play and have fun. What he does not need will go out of his body when he poops. I indicated that it was safe to feel his body when he has to poop and that Little Pooh Bear would not need to be afraid anymore, because he is safe now; he is healing from the scary, bad things that happened when he was born, and he is getting lots of love and care. I also indicated that it is through all of Dr. Ricky's and Pooh Bear's love that Little Pooh Bear can grow up to be Pooh Bear's age. I counted from 0 to 4 years old. During this intervention, I did not make any reference to Ricky himself.

That evening, Ricky told his mother that he had a Little Ricky inside of him and when he eats, Little Ricky tastes the food and chews it. Then, the food goes down into his stomach and comes out when he poops. Ricky had symbolically related the story to himself. He was able to self-reflect and to make the projective link between Little Pooh Bear and a younger part within himself. Ricky's mother was stunned, because she had been in the session and knew that I had never suggested that Ricky had a little Ricky inside of himself.

The intervention had a dramatic impact on Ricky's behavior. He began to have bowel movements every third day—which was remarkable given that he had only been having them once a week, at best, prior to the intervention with Pooh Bear. A week later, when Ricky returned with Pooh Bear, I asked how old Little Pooh Bear was and Ricky responded, "Three years old." Ricky also enthusiastically told me that he had a Little Ricky inside of him who was now 3 years old and explained the same process that was occurring within himself.

Despite his improvement, Ricky still wanted a diaper put on him before defecating. I suggested that we teach Little Pooh Bear how to use the toilet. Ricky picked a plastic lid that had a raised handle for the "toilet." Ricky took Pooh Bear's fat legs and worked very hard to stuff them under the narrow space between the lid and the handle so that Little Pooh Bear could sit on the "toilet." Ricky's mother whispered to me that she felt he was reenacting being held down for his circumcision and when he was given an adult enema.

Naming each of his body parts, I stressed that "all" of Little Pooh Bear was safe, and it was now safe for him to use the toilet. I suggested that Dr. Ricky could now teach Little Pooh how to use the toilet. After this intervention, Ricky no longer required a diaper to defecate and sat on the toilet when he needed to have a bowel movement. Shortly thereafter, it was time to integrate Little Pooh Bear, since Ricky indicated that he was now 4 years old—the current age of big Pooh Bear (and Ricky)—and Little Pooh Bear no longer felt afraid and hurt. I suggested to Ricky that since Little Pooh Bear felt so much better, he could join as one with Pooh Bear as I clasped my hands together. Ricky agreed. Ricky held Pooh Bear and I said, "Little Pooh Bear is joining with Pooh Bear as one big, wonderful Pooh Bear! All of Little Pooh Bear's feelings, thoughts and the way his body feels, are now one with Pooh Bear. Little Pooh Bear can feel his body, eat food, and go to the bathroom now without any problems. His body feels much better and is safe now. He is one with Pooh Bear." Ricky reported that Little Pooh Bear was now one with Pooh Bear and that his Little Ricky had become one with him also!

Remarkable changes occurred immediately. Ricky began having daily bowel movements. One day, he forgot his Pooh Bear and "blankie" when he went to his daycare center. Rather than having a total meltdown, Ricky did not even realize their absence until it was time to leave. He was fine without them—a major feat! He also separated easily from his parents, handled transitions well, and appeared relaxed and happy. Most of his food allergies cleared up, and he no longer had digestive problems.

I suggested that a child's self-defense class could help increase Ricky's sense of empowerment. Ricky and his parents agreed. Ricky later proudly showed me the different positions he had learned. Ricky became very confident and connected to his body. He no longer insisted on loose-fitting clothes and was able to wear jeans with a normal waistband and shirts that had cuffs. When Ricky entered kindergarten, he was outgoing and considered a leader among his classmates. He and his parents have periodically visited me to keep me informed of his progress. Ricky is currently in middle school and continues to do well.

The example just cited epitomizes how an infant can be severely impacted by birth and medical trauma (Chapter 1). Developing interventions that access an early implicit memory system for processing is critical to healing and integrating infant states.

Intensive Assessment and Integrative Treatment With Sarah (Atypical DID Adolescent)

I introduced 17-year-old Sarah (Waters, 2005) in Chapter 4 when describing how useful the Adolescent Multidimensional Inventory of Dissociation V.6.0 (A-MID) was in detecting her hidden 7-year-old self-state. Sarah's mother brought her daughter to me for treatment due to Sarah's total amnesia for her past and her inability to retain memory for her current life. She could not perform in school and had to resign from her job and peer activities. She also did not recognize her house, parents, or peers—including her current boyfriend and therapist of the past year! Sarah reported that each time she entered her therapist's office, she did not know whom "the lady" was. Sarah slightly recognized her older sister. Sarah's therapist, who was treating Sarah for anorexia, was against Sarah being seen by a specialist in dissociation, thinking that her condition could worsen. However, Sarah was already completely debilitated and her parents were committed to finding her help.

During the intensive 2-day evaluation, which her parents and sister attended, Sarah described the precipitating events prior to her amnesia.

Shortly after her inpatient release and after celebrating a school banquet with her family and sister, she began to faint repeatedly and was taken to the local hospital emergency department with complete amnesia. While in the emergency department, Sarah experienced severe pain in her ankle and could barely walk. Although numerous exams and X-rays found no organic cause, she limped for several weeks with pain.

During the first day of the evaluation, Sarah, who was bright, articulate, and highly motivated, denied all forms of trauma or abuse. When she was asked to check inside of her mind about what might account for her amnesia, she learned that she had not only a 7-year-old self-state but also a controlling and critical part of her. She was developmentally reaching a critical age in which individuation and separation are decisive developmental milestones to prepare for adulthood. However, as Sarah faced this developmental crisis, the emerging needs of the hidden Little Girl began to surface. The Little Girl wanted to play, relax, and have fun, which had become an anomaly in Sarah's life, due to the Critical Part, who persistently told her to do more and to do it perfectly—join every civic group available, get straight As, and so forth. In order to resolve this intense conflict, the Control Part was created to essentially take control of the situation and protect the Little Girl's wishes. The main mechanism that the Control Part used to accomplish this was taking away Sarah's memory. This allowed the Little Girl to emerge and fulfill her desires to play and have fun. The Little Girl also played a central role in Sarah's year-long battle with anorexia, because Sarah kept seeing herself as needing to be little, through the eyes of the hidden Little Girl. So she starved herself.

Through a dissociative treatment framework including a psychodynamic approach, extensive cognitive reprocessing, reframing, and cooperation occurred between Sarah and her self-states. A contract was established in which the Control Part agreed to give back Sarah's memory if Sarah agreed to relax more and have fun, which would meet the child-state's need. Sarah quickly accepted that growing up does not mean that one cannot have fun, and that retaining the child-like qualities of spontaneity and playfulness are crucial to a healthy adult lifestyle. The Critical Part agreed to be renamed Advisor and accepted that it is impossible to be perfect and to please everyone. Advisor was encouraged to relax and to help Sarah by being assertive and set realistic expectations and limits for herself.

The second morning of the evaluation, there was a marked improvement in Sarah's affect, memory, appearance, and overall outlook. Sarah remembered the entire first day of the evaluation, and her parents were delighted that Sarah had joked with them and spontaneously recalled information from the previous evening. The reason for Sarah's split was still unknown. She denied all forms of abuse, including witnessing domestic violence. However, because Sarah feared angering anyone and went to great lengths to please others in order to avoid conflict, even apologizing for things that were not her fault, I wondered whether there was some incident that was associated with anger.

I reframed the question about witnessing domestic violence, asking, "Was there any arguing between your parents or anyone else that ever scared or upset you?" Sarah immediately reported a continuous vivid memory of witnessing an altercation between her parents when she was 7 years old. Her parents had returned home from a party and were screaming at each other. Her father hit the wall with his fist and then left the house, leaving her mother crying. Since she was daddy's girl and not close to her mother, Sarah immediately experienced loss and abandonment, even though he returned the next day. Her parents never spoke of this incident, nor was Sarah able to receive comfort and reassurance to overcome her lingering fear of losing her father, who was a powerful figure in her life. Even though this was an isolated incident, it shattered her sense of security and contradicted her belief that she had a perfect family. This pivotal traumatic incident caused her to dissociate and fueled her need to be perfect in order to avoid reexperiencing loss and abandonment.

The mystery of Sarah's ankle pain also needed to be resolved. I queried her about any injuries she had when she was 7—the time of her splitting. She smiled, realizing the connection to an incident at 7 years old when she had fallen from a tree and was taken to the emergency department with a badly sprained ankle, causing her to limp for several weeks. When the child dissociative state emerged and once again was taken to the emergency department, it triggered her memory of her sprained ankle. I explained somatoform dissociation to Sarah (Nijenhuis, 1999), in which pain may occur with the reactivation of a traumatic memory.

Sarah resided 500 miles away from my office. Because of lack of resources in the area where she lived, and the considerable progress and willingness Sarah and her dissociative states displayed, I proposed integration. I explained what integration involved and provided the integration message to her and her self-states, saying that all of their qualities and skills would join together as one. They agreed. I initially did a fusion exercise with hypnotic suggestion to age progress the child state to Sarah's age. I then asked the three dissociative states to imagine forming a circle with Sarah. As I counted from 1 to 10, they came closer to Sarah and, at 10, they integrated.

During the evaluation, I met with the parents to explore their family history and at the conclusion of the second day, a family therapy meeting was held to explain the cause of Sarah's dissociation. Sarah explained to her family that her child state did not recognize her parents, because they had changed so much. She slightly recognized her older sister who looked more similar to how she looked 10 years ago. The child state also did not recognize the interior of their home, because it had been completely remodeled and redecorated.

In addition, everyone was able to openly express with much emotion their memory of the parents' altercation and Sarah's parents apologized to her. I encouraged Sarah and her mother to strengthen their attachment by spending more time together, and recommended that Sarah's mother seek therapy for her disrupted attachment with her own mother, who was hospitalized throughout Sarah's mother's childhood for mental illness.

I had made a recording for Sarah on visualizing a safe place so that she could listen to this when she returned home. She agreed to see another therapist who had some knowledge about dissociation. In a follow-up contact, Sarah was attending college. She had no further episodes of amnesia and was eating normally. Sarah was able to resolve her severe dissociation and eating disorder with intensive 2 days of evaluation and treatment. It should be noted that, although Sarah had severe dissociation, she did not have a severe trauma history. In addition, she was a highly motivated, intelligent teenager with a supportive family. All of these contributed to the success of her treatment in such a brief time span.

Let us examine how metaphors can be used for integration.

USE OF METAPHORS FOR INTEGRATION

The child's interests, activities, and culture can provide metaphors that help the child understand the importance of integration (see Chapter 7, where metaphors are discussed in the context of stabilization). These symbols can then remind children throughout their lives of oneness, strength, and recovery.

Celebration of the integration will reinforce the child's unity. Silberg (2013) suggests that parents and therapists write the child a congratulatory letter, celebrating the progress and changes that the child has achieved. The letter can be added to an integration ceremony that includes serving the child's favorite dessert. In fact, the child's favorite dessert can, in and of itself, provide a metaphor that helps the child achieve integration.

The Child's Favorite Dessert

Making the child's favorite dessert can be used as a metaphor for integration as well as reinforce equality and respect among self-states. I explain to the child that all of the ingredients that make up the dessert are important to making the dessert delicious; if even one ingredient is omitted, the dessert would not be as tasty. This metaphor provides a means to communicate to the child that all of the child's parts are equally important in making the child unique and special. If any part is omitted, this would impact the child's uniqueness and abilities. This metaphor also promotes blending of the dessert ingredients to symbolize blending of the selves into one— an integration exercise. When integration is achieved, then the child and parents can bake the child's favorite dessert and bring it to the therapy session to celebrate.

Miranda

Eight-year-old Miranda used the favorite dessert intervention to help achieve stabilization and integration (see Chapter 7, where this intervention is described). When Miranda discussed her favorite dessert—pumpkin pie—as a metaphor for her self-states' showing internal cooperation and appreciation, Miranda revealed that the pumpkin was actually one of her self-states, Miranda Sue, who contained unresolved feelings for her biological mother, who was named Sue. After recording a goodbye letter to her birth mother, Miranda Sue resolved this loss. She then was able to accept her adoptive mother and put extra pumpkin in the pie, to mean "extra love" that she could now give to her adoptive mother. She then was able to spontaneously integrate with Miranda.

Lisa

Lisa's adoptive mother, Sandra, altered the procedure when she and Lisa made Lisa's favorite dessert—butterscotch and chocolate cookies. Lisa, whose case was introduced in Chapter 4, was removed from her Asian biological mother at birth and placed in a foster home until she was adopted at 4 months of age. Lisa arrived in the United States with a painful swollen gum that the pediatric dentist ruled was from an unknown trauma. After extensive trauma processing (Chapter 10), Lisa was ready to integrate.

Sandra had several decorative mixing bowls and allowed Lisa to choose one to represent herself. Lisa picked a lovely blue-and-white bowl. Sandra then explained that all of the ingredients represent Lisa's good and bad feelings and experiences. She told Lisa to taste each ingredient and say whether or not she liked it. When Lisa did not like the vinegar, cinnamon, and baking soda, Sandra engaged Lisa in a discussion of what the bad taste reminded her of. Lisa recounted some of her traumas (e.g., when her foster mother cut her gum). Lisa associated the good tasting ingredients with positive feelings and experiences. For example, these reminded Lisa of times when her adoptive mom cuddled her and when her adoptive dad took her fishing. Then, Sandra had Lisa measure out all of the ingredients and put the ingredients (i.e., the good and bad experiences/feelings that had happened to Lisa) in the "beautiful Lisa bowl," making sure that Lisa understood that the ingredients related to all of the experiences and feelings that she and her parts held.

When the cookies were done, Sandra made a brilliant analogy and asked Lisa whether an ingredient that she did not like, for example, the cinnamon, ruined the cookies when it was added along with all of the other ingredients. Lisa replied, "No." Her mother then said, "Lisa, all those bad things that happened to you don't have to wreck you. You can still be beautiful! This bowl is the beautiful you and what did we put in the bowl? Good and bad things. Did the bad things make the cookies taste yucky?" Lisa again said, "No." Her mom said, "You can still be happy even if bad things happen to you. You can be one happy Lisa with all your parts!" Lisa beamed. She was finally able to release the deep shame she held about her early trauma. She was able to accept all parts of herself and integrated.

After Lisa integrated, she reminded me of a bright, shining star. Her eyes and smile shined. In the farewell session, Lisa enthusiastically told me about her first day in fourth grade when she was surrounded by lots of friends asking her questions about her summer vacation. She was so excited. This was remarkable, because Lisa had been unable to attend school full time and had no friends when I saw her initially. After 1½ years of intensive therapy, Lisa was able to self-regulate, handle transitions that would previously send her into a tailspin, show humor with family instead of defensiveness, and had a radiant smile.

The Child's Favorite Sport

I have used the child's favorite sport's team as an integration metaphor to promote internal awareness, partnership, and equality among the child's inner team. I explain that all team members have to watch, listen, and learn all of the maneuvers to perform well. I then note that a similar process is required between the child and his or her parts in order for the child to be successful and happy. The child can be encouraged to draw a picture of the child playing his or her favorite sport at the time of integration to symbolize the joining together of the parts as one. I explain that joining together will enhance the child's skills and performance in his or her favorite sport and other activities. I relay the integration message and suggest that all the parts' qualities, feelings, thoughts, sensations, and memories are joining together as one with the child.

During the stabilization phase, Miranda used a soccer game as a symbol to promote internal cooperation and teamwork among her self-states. This symbol was then used throughout her treatment and eventual integration. At age 8, she drew a final picture representing herself integrating as she played soccer. As I guided her, she looked at her picture as she imagined all of her parts joining with her as one (Figure 13.4).

Circle Visualization Technique

Sometimes, I will have children visualize in their mind all the parts joining hands in a circle, and then walking closer and closer to each other until the parts are joined within the child. I then repeat the integration message, emphasizing that they are combining their special qualities and strengths into one self. I tell them that I will count from 1 to 5, and at 5, they will integrate.

Figure 13.4 *Miranda's integration drawing of her and her self-state playing soccer together. (Used with permission.)*

Using Cultural Symbols for Integration

When working with children of diverse cultures, the inclusion of cultural symbols in integration ceremonies can be helpful. For example, when I worked with a Native American boy, I used the Native American circle-of-life symbol to represent his integration and suggested that his parts were encompassed in the circle of life, joining together as one. He focused on the center of a circle-of-life symbol that held the words "learning, self, beauty, harmony, and balance," as he brought all of his parts to the center to join with him. I elaborated on all of their special qualities comprising peace and unity.

Cathy: The Use of Multiple Integration Techniques

I describe Cathy's process in more depth to highlight the use of numerous integration techniques in children with multiple self-states. Cathy, whose case was first introduced in Chapter 4 and continued in Chapters 7, 8, and 10, had experienced sadistic abuse at the hands of her adopted father after being sent to live with him after her mother was seriously injured in an automobile accident. Cathy had developed numerous self-states as a result of her adoptive father's abuse (e.g., forced to take cold showers, made to sleep with wet clothes on, placed for hours in an unheated storage room, beatings, and screaming in her face). After Cathy's self-states (Inside Mom, The Friend [formerly The Dad], The Brother, Little Sister, and Crystal) processed their physical and emotional abuse by her adoptive father, they were ready to integrate.

I asked Cathy whether she would like to draw a picture that symbolized her integration. Instead, Cathy wanted to paint a picture of her self-states and herself joining together. She painted herself in the center of the picture surrounded by her self-states who were connected to each other with lines (Figure 13.5). Cathy represented her self-states with colored circles. Each of them has colored headbands, signifying their different emotions.

Cathy explained her painting, saying,

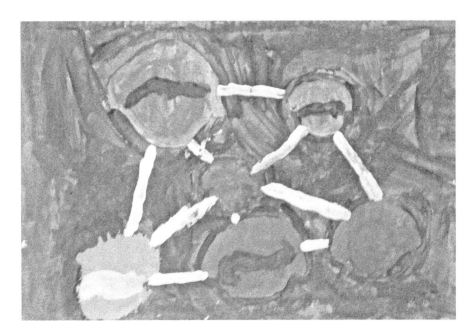

Figure 13.5 *Cathy's self-states connected to each other. (Used with permission.)*

This is me because I am in the center. All of these white lines mean that we are connected. I think the most important thing about the picture, if you notice, is that they are not just attached to me; they are attached to each other! That means that we have to work to fit the puzzle pieces together. The biggest thing about that is they have to get to know each other. They have to get along. If they get along, I'm going to get along with other people. When they are all together, I will be so much more and I will be getting along with other people.

I was struck by the fact that Cathy recognized the importance of her self-states connecting with each other as well as with her. She also understood that if they integrated within her, her relationships with others would improve. She was demonstrating important metacognitive skills.

Cathy identified the circles as Little Brother, Mom, Crystal, Little Sister, Little Brother, and The Friend. She then stated that Little Brother had integrated with her and she wanted to change the color of his headband to pink—the same color as her own headband. I asked her what the headbands signified.

Cathy: "These are their different emotions."
Therapist: "Are those the emotions you also experience when they experience them?"
Cathy: "Sort of. Not sure. [*She often experienced amnesia at those times.*] That might be part of my bipolar because they're feeling it." She pointed to her picture and continued, "So this one might be feeling an emotion, but this one might be feeling a different emotion, and they all might be feeling different emotions all at once. So I'm crying, laughing, mad."

I was amazed at Cathy's insight on how she was now able to "connect the dots" with her expression of emotions, being a direct result of her parts expressing various emotions. I responded by saying, "Before you came to see me, you were diagnosed with bipolar disorder. It really wasn't bipolar; it was dissociation. Because parts of you were feeling different things, people thought it was bipolar because they only saw the emotions and didn't understand where they came from. Is there anything else you want to say about the picture?"

Cathy: "Actually yes!" She again said how she and Little Brother should have the same colors, as they are now integrated.

Therapist: "What do we want to do with all of them?"

Cathy: "We want them to connect with me like little puzzle pieces."

Therapist: "So there will only be just you?"

Cathy: "Yes!"

Therapist: "Anything else you want to say about your picture?"

Cathy: "Only one more thing. Everybody should be connected as soon as possible because I think that would be really nice to be *just me!*"

Therapist: "Ask them if they are willing to work on that with you and me to be all connected with you?"

Cathy: "Yeah!"

Cathy's internal self-states were ready to integrate with her after the completion of significant trauma processing. Because I respected and appreciated Cathy's self-states and what they did to help her survive, Cathy had learned to appreciate them as well. Cathy and I gained their trust and when the time came to integrate, none of them resisted. This is what I mean when I say that integration begins when the dissociative child enters the therapeutic environment.

In the follow-up session, Cathy wanted to sculpt her head out of clay with braided hair to signify how they were joining with her together as one. She took the clay and meticulously made tiny braids of hair with different-colored clay to symbolize her parts. She even formed the nose with braided colors. While she worked on the sculpture, we continued to talk about how all of them were joining together more and more within her. Cathy related that all her self-states spontaneously integrated within her, except one— The Friend.

In the next session, we sat on the floor playing with a magnet set as Cathy posed the problem of how to integrate The Friend. She said she was not sure how to do this, because The Friend is male and she is female. This had not been a problem when she integrated with Little Brother. (I suspect this was because she and Little Brother were so close to each other and he was younger; so his maleness had never been an issue for her.) I began to talk with her about androgynous qualities—those that both males and females possess—and how she and The Friend might have some common qualities.

Cathy then came up with an integration game we could play. She suggested that we stand about 5 feet apart. I would represent The Friend, and she would be herself. We would each take turns, saying what we like to do, and if the other one liked to do the same thing, we each would take a step closer to the other. If the other did not like that activity, we would each take a step backward. When our bodies were right next to each other, then The Friend would integrate within her. I praised her for coming up with such a creative game, while I thought to myself how she must feel safe with me to engage in a game in which we would be in such close proximity with each other. We began the game, and each turn resulted in a step closer together. In about a minute, we were standing closely together. Cathy happily announced that The Friend had integrated.

Prior to seeing me, Cathy had been diagnosed with attention deficit hyperactivity disorder (ADHD) and bipolar disorder. She was prescribed medications for inattention, dysregulated mood, and also an antipsychotic because she reported hearing voices. Although she had disclosed signifi-cant trauma, dissociation was not considered when assessing the origin of her voices. While in treatment with me, her mother had taken her off of all medications because of her lack of improvement. When Cathy fully inte-grated, her transformation was dramatic. Every aspect of her life improved. She seemed brighter, and she was focused in school and at home. Her memory was excellent, and she began getting As in many of her classes. Her peer relationships also improved considerably, and she was no longer teased at school. She developed healthy, close friendships; slept well; and most importantly, started to enjoy life.

Let us look at some guidelines for assessing childhood dissociation.

GUIDELINES FOR ASSESSING CHILDHOOD INTEGRATION

When a child reports that the self-states are integrated, how can you be certain that integration has actually occurred? I have provided numer-ous examples of significant changes that integrated children have exhib-ited. The following are guidelines to assist the caregivers and therapists to assess for integration in children and adolescents with dissociation (adapted from Waters & Silberg, 1998a). These guidelines also describe improvement in domains of impairment noted in children with complex trauma (Cook et al., 2005).

1. Subjective Report of a Unified Self and Accompanying Sensory Changes

Self-report of unity by the child is one assessment criterion, particularly if the child is articulate and specific about the changes he or she has experienced, as covered in the other indicators given next. Also, children will often describe sensory changes when integrated. For example, they may describe that their hearing, sight, touch, taste, and smell are clearer and more distinct, very similar to what has been reported in the adult literature (e.g., Kluft, 1988). For example, after integration, Martha reported that colors were more distinct and her vision was clearer.

However, there are times that the child's report of unification is questioned when a caregiver or therapist witnesses a continuation of the child's dissociative behaviors or affect. In these cases, the child may report integration in order to avoid having to deal with traumatic material or take responsibility for his or her behavior. There may also be a self-state that is fearful of disclosing the trauma. In some instances, the child may also engage in playful tactics to please or fool the therapist to believe that integration has occurred. If the child's report of integration is questionable, it is advisable to sensitively address with the child what is underlying the child's report of unification, and develop a cooperative plan to motivate the child to continue with treatment.

2. Disappearance of Core Dissociative Signs

The child who has achieved integration no longer exhibits significant memory lapses. The child is no longer perplexed about current events that he or she participated in and has no difficulty recalling them. Although the child may not recall all of the past traumatic memories, the child is no longer plagued with memory problems that impair his or her functioning. Auditory and visual hallucinations have ceased. The child does not display any depersonalization or derealization; the child feels connected somatically and perceives the physical environment with clarity.

3. Lack of Fluctuating Behavior

The child demonstrates consistent likes and dislikes (e.g., food, dress, and activities). Preference in things such as clothing, food, activities, and music may change with the child's development, but the child's preferences no longer change suddenly, dramatically, erratically, or frequently.

4. Changes in Physical Characteristics

Significant physical changes may be noted in a child after integration, including changes in his or her voice, facial expressions, body posture, and gait. The child's face may appear more relaxed, and most notably, the eyes may appear brighter, softer, and more open. Circles under the eyes may not be as dark or may disappear. The complexion may have more color, and the forehead may appear smooth without lines between the brows. The body posture may be more erect, and the head may be held straighter. The child may have a spring in his or her step, and the child's voice may develop a more musical lilt. These changes in voice, facial appearance, and body movement are a consistent presentation, contrary to extreme variations noted prior to the integration. Many of these physiological changes were observable in the children whose cases were highlighted throughout this book.

5. Affect Regulation

The integrated child no longer exhibits a cycle of hyperarousal and hypoarousal (i.e., dissociation). Moods are more consistent and predictable. The child has an expanded capacity to handle difficult feelings and disappointments, and the child's moods are not as intense, erratic, or volatile. The child shows more resilience and can return to a playful state soon after experiencing conflict and difficult emotions. Parents notice a more cheerful disposition, and that the child smiles more readily. The child can demonstrate humor, a characteristic noted with Lisa.

6. Improved Cognitive Abilities

Because children no longer react to unresolved traumatic triggers, the higher parts of their brain—the thinking parts—are functioning better. As a result, children display improved cognitive functioning. They often demonstrate the following: the capacity to use metacognitive skills; clearer, more organized, and logical thought processes; an ability to better manage divergent thoughts and feelings; more consistency in learning and increased attention span in school; an improvement in completing homework; and improved school performance. For example, Fagan and McMahon (1984) reported a 14-point improvement in IQ in a child after integration.

7. Improved Attachment and Family Relationship

There is a more consistent attachment behavior exhibited by the child toward his or her parents. The child is able to give and receive affection. The child displays more trust with less frequent episodes of testing. The child may be more willing to participate in family activities and may be more willing and able to comply with parental requests (e.g., chores, homework).

8. Improved Peer Relationships

After integration, the child is better able to form meaningful peer relationships and maintain them over time. The child is also able to cooperate in group activities and is more capable of sharing with peers. The child may begin to receive invitations from school friends to attend activities and reciprocates. The child is better at negotiating activities with peers, rather than resorting to bullying or intimidation if the child does not get his or her way. Lisa, Rudy, and Cathy made significant changes in these areas. After integrating, their socialization skills and peer relationships improved greatly, resulting in invitations to indulge in activities with peers.

9. Behavioral Improvement in a Wide Variety of Settings

The child displays improved impulse control across a variety of settings along with an increased capacity to manage frustrations. The child is better able to handle transitions, as noted with Ricky and Lisa, often resulting in the parents feeling more comfortable with exposing the child to unfamiliar people and settings. In addition, the child may display more sensitivity to others and respect for other people's property.

10. Increased Self-Esteem, Interest in Hobbies, Special Projects, and Age-Appropriate Pursuits

The child expresses a more positive self-image. The child may show an increased interest in extracurricular activities offered through the school or in the community, and may begin to participate in them (e.g., sports, dancing, skating, swimming, or learning a musical instrument). The child expresses anticipation and enthusiasm about activities. When conflicts or obstacles occur, the child has a more optimistic approach to solving them. There is a significant shift from a sense of hopelessness and despair to a sense of hope for the future.

POSTINTEGRATION

It should be noted that integration does not mean that there will be no more struggles for the child. Because of the child's former reliance on dissociation, he or she will need to do some "catching up" in areas that the dissociation impaired, particularly with mastering earlier developmental skills and assimilating information that was not learned about managing daily life. For example, the child will need help with coping and problem-solving skills, along with managing interpersonal relationships and conflicts. The child may also experience an existential crisis about the meaning of life. He or she may continue to have lingering feelings of guilt about the abuse and philosophical questions of why God allowed the abuse to happen. Silberg (2013) suggests bringing in a religious figure that aligns with the youth's beliefs (such as a pastor or rabbi) to discuss the youth's questions and concerns.

Postintegration Relapse

It is not unusual for some fragmentation to occur after integration. There are a variety of reasons that this may happen. The following are some situations that can overwhelm children's new coping skills, causing them to revert to their dissociative defenses (adapted from Waters & Silberg, 1998a; reprinted with permission).

1. New Traumatic Memories Surface as a Result of the Triggering of a Previously Unknown Trauma

After integration, an event may trigger a memory of a trauma that the child had not previously remembered. These memories may elicit intense bodily sensations and feelings of pain and fear. Even when strategies have been discussed to deal with such occurrences, the feelings may be too overwhelming for the child to manage and a self-state that managed prior traumas may reappear. Once the child and the self-state are able to receive the necessary reassurance and support and are able to process the new memory, reintegration can occur rapidly. For example, after integration, a sexually abused 10-year-old girl was eating a piece of meat and choked. She had a flashback of oral penetration—a new memory. She was terrified. The self-state that experienced this trauma reappeared. After trauma processing, this self-state quickly reintegrated.

2. Emergence of a Hidden Self-State Previously Unknown to the Child That Was Not Ready to Reveal Itself at an Earlier Time

Sometimes, a new self-state will appear that was not a part of the trauma processing. For example, 4 months after 10-year-old Randy integrated, he was playing with neighborhood children and another boy teased him. Suddenly, an 18-year-old self-state emerged. This self-state had dealt with verbal abuse by his biological father. Randy ran inside the house, grabbed a kitchen knife, and chased the neighbor boy with the knife. Once Randy and his self-state were able to process their memories of emotional abuse, the previously unknown self-state readily integrated and Randy had no further dissociative relapses.

3. Incomplete Processing of a Traumatic Memory

Children may become restless with therapy or want to avoid painful memories. Although the therapist may use creative techniques to make the processing of the trauma engaging and less stressful, some states may not be ready to deal with their feelings. They may appear to be engaged in the therapeutic exercises, but may only be doing so to please the therapist, parents, or other self-states. Once it is apparent that integration of a self-state did not actually occur, the therapist must review with the self-state the short-term and long-term benefits of working through the materials and ask the other integrated parts to share how much better they have felt and the rewards they have received as a result of resolving the trauma. Brief therapy breaks and negotiations for desirable activities after processing painful material are techniques that may be helpful in such cases.

4. Revictimization

Therapists need to be aware of the child's family environment, assess the parents' ability to deal with stress, and use appropriate child management techniques. When there is an emergence of a new state or a former state, the therapist needs to ask the child whether he or she has been revictimized. A referral to Child Protective Services may be warranted, and interventions to stabilize the child and make the environment safe may be necessary before the dissociative coping can be resolved.

5. Major Environmental Stressors, Such as Divorce, Death of a Loved One, Change in Placement, or Court Appearances

These types of changes, particularly if they are sudden and the child does not have time to prepare for them, can cause the child to feel extremely vulnerable and overwhelmed. A self-state who dealt with similar past stressors may reappear. Once the child and self-state are helped to develop coping skills to manage anxiety and stress, and are able to grieve their losses, the state is likely to rejoin with the child.

6. Major Developmental Stressors, Especially During Adolescence

Adolescents usually experience varying degrees of anxiety, identity confusion, sexual fears, peer difficulties, and parental discord as they struggle with assuming more independence. Sexually abused dissociative children who have successfully achieved personality integration at an earlier age may need to reprocess the trauma during sexual maturation. If they continue to reside in a dysfunctional family, they are particularly vulnerable to dissociating again. One 13-year-old girl dissociated anew when she reached her teen years. She continued to reside in a dysfunctional family environment that was characterized by parental divorce and alcoholism and began to engage in promiscuous behavior, substance abuse, and truancy. With the pressures of adolescence and the instability of her home environment, she was unable to maintain her unified self.

In summary, when a previously integrated child relapses, the therapist should try to uncover the underlying reasons for the setback, move to create an environment of increased safety for the child, and help the child with any unresolved feelings and thoughts that led to the refragmentation.

CONCLUSION

Although working with dissociative youth is demanding, watching their fractured selves become integrated is the most gratifying work I have ever done. These children can now reclaim their childhood and go on to lead healthy productive lives. They are now free from the burden of their past. One teenager I worked with aptly described how she felt after integration in the following untitled poem (reprinted with permission from Waters & Silberg, 1998a):

> *I come to you now, and bring nothing in my hand.*
> *I bring myself to you wiped away from anger.*
> *I come to you today free from abuse and pain.*
> *I come to you now and give to you my love.*
> *I come to you this day showing how I changed.*
> *So, now that I am here empty handed,*
> *But with a fulfilled heart.*
> *Take me under your wings and wrap me in your innocence.*
> *I am now FREE.*

INTERNET RESOURCES AND ADDITIONAL READINGS

INTERNET RESOURCES ON TRAUMA AND DISSOCIATION

Child Trauma Academy: childtrauma.org
International Society for the Study of Trauma and Dissociation (ISSTD): www.isst-d .org
ISSTD's Child Adolescent Dissociative Treatment Guidelines: www.isst-d.org
ISSTD's FAQs for parents on child adolescent dissociation: www.isst-d.org/default .asp?contentID=100
ISSTD's FAQs for teachers on child adolescent dissociation: www.isst-d.org/ default.asp?contentID=101
International Society for Traumatic Stress Studies: www.istss.org
International Society on Violence, Abuse, and Trauma: ivatcenters.org
Leadership Council on Child Abuse and Interpersonal Violence: www.leadership council.org
National Child Traumatic Stress Network: www.nctsnet.org
Trauma Institute and Child Trauma Institute: www.childtrauma.com

INTERNET RESOURCES ON EMDR THERAPY

EMDR International Association: www.EMDRIA.org
Training information on EMDR: www.emdr.org

PARENTING RESOURCES

Parent Websites

www.ATTACH.org
www.kidsinthehouse.com

Books for Parents

Growing Up Again: Parenting Ourselves, Parenting Our Children (1998) by Jean Illsley Clarke and Connie Dawson

Children Are Wet Cement (2002) by Anne Ortlund

Between Parent and Child: The Bestselling Classic That Revolutionized Parent-Child Communication (2003) by Haim G. Ginott and Alice Ginott

Brain-Based Parenting: The Neuroscience of Caregiving for Healthy Attachment (2012) by Daniel A. Hughes and Jonathan Baylin

The Whole-Brain Child: 12 Revolutionary Strategies to Nurture Your Child's Developing Mind (2012) by Daniel Siegel and Tina Payne Bryson

Parenting from the Inside Out: How a Deeper Self-Understanding Can Help You Raise Children Who Thrive (10th anniversary edition, 2013) by Daniel Siegel and Mary Hartzell

No-Drama Discipline: The Whole-Brain Way to Calm the Chaos and Nurture Your Child's Developing Mind (2014) by Daniel Siegel and Tina Payne Bryson

CHILDREN'S BOOKS ON TRAUMA

Slaying the Dragon by Ricky Greenwald
www.slayingthedragon.com

A Fairy Tale by Ricky Greenwald
www.childtrauma.com/publications/books/fairy-tale

The Child Abuser's Secret Book of Tricks by Ricky Greenwald
www.childtrauma.com/publications/books/child-abuser

Tuxy the Mistreated Kitten: A Story about Physical and Verbal Abuse by Jamie Henle

Tuxy the Forgotten Kitten: A Story about Neglect by Jamie Henle

Telly the Turtle Learns to Come Out of Her Shell: A Story about Repairing Attachment Wounds by Jamie Henle

CHILDREN'S BOOKS ON DISSOCIATION

All the Colors of Me: My First Book About Dissociation (Gomez & Paulsen, in press)
Rob the Robin and the Bald Eagle by Madge Bray

CHILDREN'S EMDR BOOKS AND WORKBOOKS

My EMDR Workbook (n.d.) by Robbie Adler-Tapia and Maura Tapia
www.drrobbie.org

Dark Bad Day Go Away (2009) by Ana Gomez
www.anagomez.org/dark-bad-daygo-away-book-children-about-trauma-and-
emdr-therapy-second-edition

Buddy the EMDR Dog (2008) by Isabelle and Cécile Meignant
emdrresources.com/oscommerce/product_info.php?products_id=160

Butterfly Hug: An Explanation of EMDR for Children (2008) by Karin Gertner
emdrresources.com/oscommerce/product_info.php?products_id=166

Goodbye Yucky Thoughts and Feelings: An EMDR Workbook for Children (2004) by
Ann P. Waldon
emdrresources.com/oscommerce/product_info.php?products_id=146

Hello Strength and Bravery: A Resource Workbook for Children (2006) by Ann P. Waldon
emdrresources.com/oscommerce/product_info.php?cPath=21_87&products_
id=147

APPENDIX B

CHECKLISTS FOR CHILDREN

THE CHILD DISSOCIATIVE CHECKLIST
Discussion by Ann Aukamp, MSW, BCD[1]

The child dissociative checklist (CDC) is a tool that compiles observations by an adult observer regarding a child's behaviors on a 20-item list. Behaviors that occur in the present and for the past 12 months are included. As a research tool, the CDC can quantify dissociative behavior for dimensional approaches and can generate cutoff scores that categorize children into low and high dissociation groups. Research shows that healthy nonmaltreated normal children usually score low on the CDC, with younger children scoring slightly higher. As a group, maltreated children score higher than those with no trauma history; however, as a group they still score substantially lower than children diagnosed with a dissociative disorder. Generally, scores of 12 or more can be considered tentative indications of sustained pathological dissociation.

As with any screening tool, a trained clinician should assess the child in a face-to-face interview before a diagnosis is confirmed. As a clinical tool, the CDC has multiple uses. It can be a routine screening instrument used in a clinic setting as a standalone tool or in addition to other reporting tools for parents. In special circumstances, teachers or others who know the child reasonably well could be asked to complete the checklist. In these circumstances, allowances need to be made for the observer's familiarity with the child and also the observer's opportunity to observe the child at night. If the observer has no nighttime observation of the child, items 17 and 18 should be ignored (Putnam, 1997).

For finer screening, the CDC could also be administered sequentially in an interval-based series. Putnam notes that nondissociative children often increase their scores by a small amount (1–3 points) over the first few completions, because the questions draw attention to minor dissociative behaviors that had not previously been noticed.

Finally, the CDC can be used as a rough index of treatment progress. Although evidence for this use is limited, it seems that the CDC provides a reasonable indication of whether a child is improving over time or with treatment. Putnam reports consistent results on several children from the CDC and also clinical observations (Putnam, 1997).

Users of the CDC are cautioned that CDC scores reported in the literature for the various groups are means that reflect the "average" child in a given group. Individual children in any of the groups can, and often do, exhibit varying scores on the CDC. Thus, a high score does not prove a child has a dissociative disorder, nor does a low score rule it out. Also, since the CDC reports observers' ratings of a child, variations in the observers' interpretations of behavior as well as actual variations in child behavior may affect the variance. This is a potential complication in any observer-based assessment, but it may be especially important when observers are drawn from those whose perceptions may be clouded by their attachment to the child (Putnam, 1997).

NOTE

1. From the International Society for the Study of Trauma and Dissociation website (www.isst-d.org).

REFERENCE

Putnam, F. W. (1997). *Dissociation in children and adolescents: A developmental perspective.* New York, NY: Guilford Press.

Child Dissociative Checklist (CDC), Version 3

Frank W. Putnam, MD

Date: _____   Age: _____   Sex: M F   Identification: _____

Below is a list of behaviors that describe children. For each item that describes your child NOW or WITHIN THE PAST 12 MONTHS, please circle 2 if the item is VERY TRUE of your child. Circle 1 if the item is SOMEWHAT or SOMETIMES TRUE of your child. If the item is NOT TRUE of your child, circle 0.

0 1 2   1. Child does not remember or denies traumatic or painful experiences that are known to have occurred.

0 1 2   2. Child goes into a daze or trance like state at times or often appears "spaced-out." Teachers may report that he or she "daydreams" frequently in school.

0 1 2   3. Child shows rapid changes in personality. He or she may go from being shy to being outgoing, from feminine to masculine, and from timid to aggressive.

0 1 2   4. Child is unusually forgetful or confused about things that he or she should know, e.g. may forget the names of friends, teachers or other important people, loses possessions or gets easily lost.

0 1 2   5. Child has a very poor sense of time. He or she loses track of time, may think that it is morning when it is actually afternoon, gets confused about what day it is, or becomes confused about when something has happened.

0 1 2   6. Child shows marked day-to-day or even hour-to-hour variations in his or her skills, knowledge, food preferences, and athletic abilities, e.g. changes in handwriting, memory for previously learned information such as multiplication tables, spelling, use of tools or artistic ability.

0 1 2   7. Child shows rapid regressions in age-level behavior, e.g. a twelve-year-old starts to use baby talk, sucks thumb or draws like a four-year-old.

0 1 2   8. Child has a difficult time learning from experience, e.g. explanations, normal discipline or punishment do not change his or her behavior.

0 1 2   9. Child continues to lie or deny misbehavior even when the evidence is obvious.

0 1 2   10. Child refers to himself or herself in the third person (e.g. as she or her) when talking about self, or at times **insists** on being called by a different name. He or she may also claim that things that he or she did actually happened to another person.

0 1 2   11. Child has rapidly changing physical complaints such as headache or upset stomach. For example, he or she may complain of a headache one minute and seem to forget about it the next.

0 1 2   12. Child is unusually sexually precocious and may attempt age-inappropriate sexual behavior with other children or adults.

0 1 2   13. Child suffers from unexplained injuries or may even deliberately injure self at times.

0 1 2   14. Child reports hearing voices that talk to him or her. The voices may be friendly or angry and may come from "imaginary companions" or sound like the voices of parents, friends or teachers.

0 1 2   15. Child has a vivid imaginary companion or companions. Child may insist that the imaginary companion(s) is responsible for things that he or she has done.

0 1 2   16. Child has intense outbursts of anger, often without apparent cause, and may display unusual physical strength during these episodes.

0 1 2   17. Child sleepwalks frequently.

0 1 2   18. Child has unusual nighttime experiences, e.g. may report seeing "ghosts" or that things happen at night that he or she can't account for (e.g. broken toys, unexplained injuries).

0 1 2   19. Child frequently talks to himself or herself, may use a different voice or argue with self at times.

0 1 2   20. Child has two or more distinct and separate personalities that take control over the child's behavior.

THE ADOLESCENT DISSOCIATIVE EXPERIENCES SCALE
Discussion by Ann Aukamp, MSW, BCD

The Adolescent Dissociative Experiences Scale (A-DES) is a public domain, 30-item self-report instrument that is appropriate for those aged 10 to 21. It is a screening tool that fits an adolescent's phase-appropriate development. Modeled after the adult DES, the A-DES was developed by a group organized by Judith Armstrong, PhD, Frank Putnam, MD, and Eve Bernstein Carlson, PhD. Preliminary studies suggest that the A-DES is a reliable and valid measure of pathological dissociation in adolescents. Dissociative adolescents (diagnosed independently of the A-DES) scored significantly higher than other adolescent inpatients (Putnam, 1997). However, older adolescents with psychotic disorders scored almost as high as dissociative adolescents.

The A-DES is not a diagnostic tool. Its items survey dissociative amnesia, absorption and imaginative involvement (including confusion between reality and fantasy), depersonalization, derealization, passive influence/interference experiences, and identity alteration. The A-DES is scored by summing item scores and dividing by 30 (the number of the items). Overall scores can range from 0 to 10. Armstrong, Putnam, Carlson, Libero, and Smith (1997) gave both the A-DES and the DES to a sample of college subjects and found that their scores on each correlated well (Putnam, 1997). The A-DES score approximates the DES score divided by 10. Adolescents with DID typically score between 4 and 7.

As you consider using the A-DES, please consult the current literature and/or your more experienced colleagues to update yourself about any changes or evolving areas of knowledge. Although the A-DES might be used to screen for dissociative experience in large populations in a short period or as the basis for a differential diagnosis by a clinician learning about dissociation, its primary use is in the evaluation of dissociative symptoms for individual patients. Clinicians may learn nearly as much from exploring the reasons that patients choose to endorse certain items as they would from looking at test scores. Sidran Foundation offers the A-DES along with a short manual about it for a nominal fee. The Sidran Foundation can be reached at (410) 825-8888, via e-mail: sidran@access .digex.net, or on the Internet at www.sidran.org. You may also download the A-DES from this site.

REFERENCE

Putnam, F. W. (1997). *Dissociation in children and adolescents: A developmental perspective.* New York, NY: Guilford Press.

Adolescent Dissociative Experiences Scale-II (A-DES)

Judith Armstrong, PhD
Eve Bernstein Carlson, PhD
Frank Putnam, MD

DIRECTIONS

These questions ask about different kinds of experiences that happen to people. For each question, circle the number that indicates how much that experience happens to you. Circle a "0" if it never happens to you; circle a "10" if it is always happening to you. If it happens sometimes but not all of the time, circle a number between 1 and 9 that best describes how often it happens to you. When you answer, only say how much these things happen when you HAVE NOT had any alcohol or drugs.

EXAMPLE:

0   1   2   3   4   5   6   7   8   9   10
(never)   (always)

Date _____   Age _____   Sex: M F _____

1. I get so wrapped up in watching TV, reading, or playing a video game that I don't have any idea what's going on around me.

    0   1   2   3   4   5   6   7   8   9   10
    (never)   (always)

2. I get back tests or homework that I don't remember doing.

    0   1   2   3   4   5   6   7   8   9   10
    (never)   (always)

3. I have strong feelings that don't seem like they are mine.

   0   1   2   3   4   5   6   7   8   9   10
   (never)   (always)

4. I can do something really well one time and then I can't do it at all another time.

   0   1   2   3   4   5   6   7   8   9   10
   (never)   (always)

5. People tell me I do or say things that I don't remember doing or saying.

   0   1   2   3   4   5   6   7   8   9   10
   (never)   (always)

6. I feel like I am in a fog or spaced out and things around me seem unreal.

   0   1   2   3   4   5   6   7   8   9   10
   (never)   (always)

7. I get confused about whether I have done something or only thought about doing it.

   0   1   2   3   4   5   6   7   8   9   10
   (never)   (always)

8. I look at the clock and realize that time has gone by and I can't remember what has happened.

   0   1   2   3   4   5   6   7   8   9   10
   (never)   (always)

9. I hear voices in my head that are not mine.

   0   1   2   3   4   5   6   7   8   9   10
   (never)   (always)

10. When I am somewhere that I don't want to be, I can go away in my mind.

    0   1   2   3   4   5   6   7   8   9   10
    (never)   (always)

11. I am so good at lying and acting that I believe it myself.

    0   1   2   3   4   5   6   7   8   9   10
    (never)   (always)

12. I catch myself "waking up" in the middle of doing something.

    0   1   2   3   4   5   6   7   8   9   10
    (never)   (always)

13. I don't recognize myself in the mirror.

    0   1   2   3   4   5   6   7   8   9   10
    (never)   (always)

14. I find myself going somewhere or doing something and I don't know why.

    0   1   2   3   4   5   6   7   8   9   10
    (never)   (always)

15. I find myself someplace and I don't remember how I got there.

    0   1   2   3   4   5   6   7   8   9   10
    (never)   (always)

16. I have thoughts that don't really seem to belong to me.

    0   1   2   3   4   5   6   7   8   9   10
    (never)   (always)

17. I find that I can make physical pain go away.

    0   1   2   3   4   5   6   7   8   9   10
    (never)   (always)

18. I can't figure out if things really happened or if I only dreamed or thought about them.

    0   1   2   3   4   5   6   7   8   9   10
    (never)   (always)

19. I find myself doing something that I know is wrong, even when I really don't want to do it.

    0   1   2   3   4   5   6   7   8   9   10
    (never)   (always)

20. People tell me that I sometimes act so differently that I seem like a different person.

    0   1   2   3   4   5   6   7   8   9   10
    (never)   (always)

21. It feels like there are walls inside of my mind.

    0   1   2   3   4   5   6   7   8   9   10
    (never)   (always)

22. I find writings, drawings or letters that I must have done but I can't remember doing.

    0   1   2   3   4   5   6   7   8   9   10
    (never)   (always)

23. Something inside of me seems to make me do things that I don't want to do.

    0   1   2   3   4   5   6   7   8   9   10
    (never)   (always)

24. I find that I can't tell whether I am just remembering something or if it is actually happening to me.

    0   1   2   3   4   5   6   7   8   9   10
    (never)   (always)

25. I find myself standing outside of my body, watching myself as if I were another person.

    0   1   2   3   4   5   6   7   8   9   10
    (never)   (always)

26. My relationships with my family and friends change suddenly and I don't know why.

    0   1   2   3   4   5   6   7   8   9   10
    (never)   (always)

27. I feel like my past is a puzzle and some of the pieces are missing.

    0   1   2   3   4   5   6   7   8   9   10
    (never)   (always)

28. I get so wrapped up in my toys or stuffed animals that they seem alive.

    0   1   2   3   4   5   6   7   8   9   10
    (never)   (always)

29. I feel like there are different people inside of me.

    0   1   2   3   4   5   6   7   8   9   10
    (never)   (always)

30. My body feels as if it doesn't belong to me.

    0   1   2   3   4   5   6   7   8   9   10
    (never)   (always)

QUESTIONS TO ASK CHILDREN, PARENTS, AND THERAPISTS

QUESTIONS TO ASK PARENTS ABOUT DISSOCIATIVE SYMPTOMS

The following is a list of questions to ask parents that will assist in identifying dissociative symptoms in children. Depending on parental responses, some questions may not be necessary. This is a guide for the clinician to use with discretion. Many of these questions correlate with the International Society for the Study of Trauma and Dissociation's frequently asked questions (FAQs) for parents (www.isst-d.org). (Although these questions apply to both boys and girls, for simplicity, male gender is used.)

- Does your child have extreme switches in mood and behavior? If so, describe these times and what you notice about his behavior and affect. Does he seem different during these episodes, and if so, in what ways?
- Does your child deny his aggressive or disruptive behavior even when you have witnessed it? How does he respond to you at these times? Does he continue to deny his behavior even after he is disciplined? Does he deny other behaviors or situations that are not problematic (e.g., conversations or family/social/school activities)?
- Does your child have memory problems for events that he should recall, such as holidays and birthdays, past or present?
- Does your child adamantly deny that you told him to do his homework or chores when you were facing him, engaging with him in the conversation, and he wasn't occupied with any other activity, such as electronic games?
- Does your child look and behave differently at times that are not attributable to physical illness? Describe these times in detail.
- Does your child prefer a favorite food, activity, clothing, etc., but at other times hate it? Please explain in detail.

- Do you see your child staring, unresponsive, like he is in his own world (not including when playing video games or watching television)? How often and for how long? Afterward, can he explain where his mind was?
- Do you notice any changes in the child's eyes (e.g., blinking, fluttering, eye rolling) and/or notice changes in voice and/or mannerisms during these times? Please describe. Are there other changes associated with these mannerisms (e.g., memory, mood, or behavior disturbances)?
- Has your child ever told you that he hears voices or sees things or people that are not heard or seen by others? Please describe those times. Do you notice other changes during those times (e.g., memory, mood, or behavior disturbances)?
- Have you heard your child talk to himself? Does he sound like he is using a different voice during those times? Does he seem younger or older, or act very differently? Does he have memory problems during those times?
- Does (or did) your child have imaginary playmates? When were you aware of them? Describe what you have noticed. Does he have memory problems and/or act differently during this time?
- Does your child have somatic complaints that do not have a medical cause? (If so, ask for details and if other changes are noticed when he is having these problems.)

SUGGESTED QUESTIONS TO ASK CHILDREN SUSPECTED OF BEING DISSOCIATIVE

The following are questions to explore dissociative symptoms with children and adolescents. Depending on the age and developmental level of the child, modification or reframing of the questions may need to occur. It is also important to pace the questions according to the child's ability to manage them.

- Have you ever had imaginary friends? Did (or do) they seem real to you? If so, in what way?

- Do you find yourself zoning out and not aware of what is happening in the here and now? *If the answer is affirmative, follow up with these questions:*
  - How often does this happen? What was going on just prior to zoning out? What were you feeling or thinking just before you zoned out? How long do these periods last? What is the shortest and longest amount of time? Where do you go in your mind? (Child may not know.) Do other people notice this, like parents, teachers, and if so, what do they say to you? Do you have control over it or does it just happen?
- Do you sometimes not remember drawing, playing games, doing chores, homework, problem behaviors, or other activities that others indicate you did? *If the answer is affirmative, follow up with these questions:*
  - How often does this occur? What seems to be occurring when the memory problems happen (e.g., are you mad, under stress, having a conflict with someone)? During these episodes, do you hear any voices or see things that are not there later?
- Do you have a hard time remembering scary or bad things that happened to you? *If the answer is affirmative, ask the child to elaborate.* (Be aware that you may not want to pursue too many details about trauma, as the child may not be ready to disclose them or strong enough to handle the disclosure. You may witness some dissociative shifting that is diagnostic. Notice the child's reactions and follow sound therapeutic guidelines and principles.)
- Do you ever have a hard time recognizing or remembering your parents, siblings, friends, teachers, etc.? *If the answer is affirmative, follow up with these questions:*
  - When does this tend to occur (e.g., when you wake up in the morning, at bedtime, during times of stress)? Who do you have a hard time remembering or recognizing? Do you hear voices during these times? What are you feeling and thinking when this occurs? How often does this occur? Do you tell anyone about not remembering people?
- Do you have a hard time remembering something you did, like homework? Do you get homework back and not remember doing it? Please describe those times.

- Do you ever see things or people and later realize that what you saw wasn't there or you aren't sure if they were there? *If the answer is affirmative, follow up with these questions:*
  - Please describe what you saw. When do you see them? How often do you see them? What were you doing, feeling, or thinking at the time? When you saw (insert what was said), did you hear voices at the same time; if so, what did they say?
- Some kids who have been through similar situations have reported hearing voices either inside or outside of their minds. Have you had this happen to you? *If the answer is affirmative, follow up with these questions:*
  - Do the voices seem friendly, angry, sad, scared, etc.? What do they say? How often do you hear them? What is happening just before you hear them? What feelings do you have when you hear them? What thoughts do you have when you hear them? Do you talk to them?
- Do you ever see things, objects, or people and later realize that what you saw wasn't there or you weren't sure if they were there? *If the answer is affirmative, follow up with these questions:*
  - Please describe what you saw. When do you see them? How often do you see them? What were you doing, feeling, or thinking at the time? When you saw objects or people, did you hear voices at the time and if so, what were they saying?
- When you had (insert recent behavioral problem), what was going on inside of your mind? Ask the child if he would be willing to draw what he experienced in his mind at that time.

THERAPIST READINESS CHECKLIST FOR TRAUMA WORK WITH CHILDREN USING EYE MOVEMENT DESENSITIZATION AND REPROCESSING (EMDR)
Adapted from Paulsen (2009)

This is a guide for therapists to assess whether a child or an adolescent with dissociation or complex trauma is ready for trauma processing. This is a guideline to help alert clinicians to the areas of knowledge needed and skill level necessary to do trauma processing using EMDR with children. Treating dissociative children and adolescents with EMDR therapy

requires specialized training in trauma, dissociation, adaptive information processing (AIP) theory, and EMDR therapy for safe trauma processing. Specialized training and knowledge are important, because children
with dissociation can exhibit destructive or suicidal behavior. Employing
a phase treatment model, with emphasis on stabilization and a supportive environment prior to trauma work, can lead to successful trauma processing. Specific areas for therapists to consider their readiness, prior to
doing trauma processing, are given next. Chapters refer to the chapter in
this book where the topic is discussed.

- Knowledge about various forms of traumatic experiences, such as
  abuse, neglect, witnessing violence, medical interventions, etc., that
  can cause trauma and dissociation
- Knowledge of research on trauma, attachment impairment (Chapters
  1 and 6), and family violence, and how these influence the development of dissociative symptoms/disorders in children and adolescents
- Knowledge of basic child development (e.g., Erikson's psychosocial
  phases) and how trauma can disrupt development and lead to the
  formation of self-states (Chapter 1)
- Knowledge of family systems theory (e.g., Satir, 1983) and the family's
  influence on the child's dissociative defenses (Chapters 1 and 6)
- Knowledge about research on neurobiology of trauma and how
  trauma impairs memory and consciousness (Chapter 1)
- Knowledge of dissociative theories (e.g., discrete behavior states,
  affect avoidant theory, structural dissociation theory, and betrayal
  trauma) (Chapter 1)
- Knowledge of phase-oriented treatment for children and adolescents with dissociation (see www.isst-d.org; Waters, 2016 [this book])
- Knowledge of AIP theory (Shapiro, 2001) and EMDR therapeutic
  phases (Chapter 12)
- Recognize dissociative symptoms and disorders in children and adolescents (Chapters 2, 3, and 4)
- Knowledge of trauma and dissociative checklists for children (e.g.,
  child dissociative checklist [CDC], Adolescent Dissociative Experiences Scale [A-DES], Briere's Child Trauma Symptom Checklist)
  (Chapter 4)
- Knowledge of comorbidity and differential diagnoses of childhood
  dissociation (Chapter 3) and awareness that comorbid symptoms
  may be contained in different self-states

- Evaluate the child's environment at home, in school, and in the community for safety and support
- Follow guidelines for treatment of dissociative children (www.isst-d.org) and EMDR therapy (Chapter 12)
- Incorporate stabilizing techniques that include self-states when using EMDR therapy (Chapter 12)
- Incorporate supportive caregivers/parents/others in child's treatment (Waters, 1996)
- Incorporate child-friendly techniques (e.g., play, art, and sand tray therapies) throughout treatment
- Consult with schools and provision of techniques to help them manage the child/adolescent with dissociation
- Awareness that hidden self-states may be contributing to symptoms and explore them before proceeding with trauma processing
- Knowledge of techniques to titrate trauma processing (Kluft, 1988; Levine, 2010; Ogden, Mitton, & Pain, 2006) and adapt them for child-friendly use
- Incorporate relevant self-states in trauma processing, and make arrangements for other self-states to be in internal safe places or play a supportive role when using EMDR therapy
- Flexible approach during treatment to maintain stabilization (e.g., a new self-state emerges that needs to be attended to), particularly during trauma processing
- Be aware of any counter-transference and seek consultation if necessary

REFERENCES

Kluft, R. P. (1988). Playing for time: Temporizing techniques in the treatment of multiple personality disorder. *American Journal of Clinical Hypnosis, 32,* 90–98.

Levine, P. A. (2010). *In an unspoken voice: How the body releases trauma and restores goodness.* Berkeley, CA: North Atlantic Books.

Ogden, P., Minton, K., & Pain, C. (2006). *Trauma and the body: A sensorimotor approach to psychotherapy.* New York, NY: W. W. Norton.

Paulsen, S. (2009). *Looking through the eyes of trauma and dissociation: An illustrated guide for EMDR therapists and clients.* Charleston, SC: Booksurge.

Satir, V. (1983). *Conjoint family therapy.* Palo Alto, CA: Science and Behavior Books.

Shapiro, F. (2001). *Eye movement desensitization and reprocessing: Basic principles, protocols, and procedures* (2nd ed.). New York, NY: Guilford Press.

Waters, F. S. (2016). *Healing the fractured child: Diagnosis and treatment of youth with dissociation.* New York, NY: Springer Publishing Company.

Waters, F. S. (1996). Parents as partners in the treatment of dissociative children. In J. L. Silberg (Ed.), *The dissociative child: Diagnosis, treatment, and management.* Lutherville, MD: Sidran Press.

ASSESSMENT GUIDELINE FOR CHILDREN WITH COMPLEX TRAUMA AND DISSOCIATION: READINESS TO DO TRAUMA WORK USING EMDR
Adapted from Paulsen (2009)

This is a guide for therapists to assess whether a child or an adolescent with dissociation or complex trauma is ready for trauma processing using EMDR.

Client Readiness Checklist

- Is the child in a safe environment?
- Does the child have supportive caregivers to comfort the child?
- Do the child and the self-states have a positive relationship with you?
- Does the child's system understand EMDR and trauma work?
- Are destructive, self-harming symptoms attributed to self-states alleviated or decreased?
- Has the child learned safe place imagery, self-soothing, and containment exercises?
- Are destructive or self-harming self-states practicing safe discharge of negative affect?
- Is the child able to practice these exercises outside of therapy (i.e., home, school)?
- Has the child developed sensory awareness across self-states?
- Are self-states, especially perpetrating, disruptive, and younger self-states, oriented to present time, place, and person most of the time?
- Has the child developed ego strength to tolerate intense affect?
- Do older, stronger resource parts of the child's system agree to help with younger, frail child parts?

- Are angry/protective self-states on board with the plan to process trauma?
- Do you have consent from the child's self-system to process trauma?
- Do self-states understand that they are in the same body, in present time, and do they agree to work for healing and wholeness of the entire self?
- Is the child able and willing to use imagery to titrate affect (i.e., manage the feelings in small amounts)? (e.g., Small children can be shown how to indicate amounts by holding their hands apart and changing the span between them.)

APPENDIX D

Tools to Use

THE 4 L's

Motto: We do much better when we work together! (Figure D.1)

Look: Every part of me looks through our eyes on the outside so that we all know where we are and what is going on in the here and now.

Listen: Every part of me listens with our ears so that we can hear what is going on in the here and now.

Learn: Every part of me learns with our brain what the teachers tell us, and what our parents and others tell us so that we know how to do many things.

Love: Every part of me lets our hearts love all parts of ourselves and love the good people in our life. Be loving, kind, and respectful to all parts of us, the good people in our lives, and even those who are not nice to us.

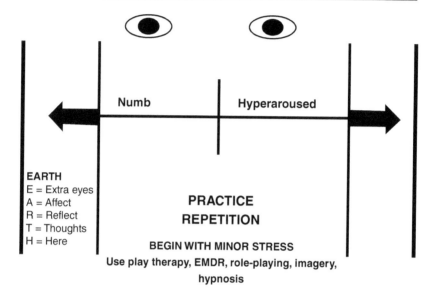

Figure D.1 *EARTH: Building self-reflection and expanding window of tolerance.*
© Waters, F. 2015.

REFERENCES

Achenbach, T. (1992). *Manual for the Child Behavior Checklist/2-3 and 1992 profile.* Burlington: University of Vermont Department of Psychiatry.

Adler-Tapia, R. L. (2009). *My EMDR workbook.* Retrieved from http://www.drrobbie.org/store.html

Adler-Tapia, R. L. (2012). *Child psychotherapy: Integrating developmental theory into clinical practice.* New York, NY: Springer Publishing Company.

Adler-Tapia, R. L., & Settle, C. S. (2008). *EMDR and the art of psychotherapy with children.* New York, NY: Springer Publishing Company.

Adler-Tapia, R. L., & Settle, C. S. (2009a). EMDR assessment and desensitization phases with children: Step-by-step directions. In M. Luber (Ed.), *Eye movement desensitization and reprocessing (EMDR) scripted protocols: Special populations* (pp. 67–96). New York, NY: Springer Publishing Company.

Adler-Tapia, R. L., & Settle, C. S. (2009b). Evidence of the efficacy of EMDR with children and adolescents in individual psychotherapy: A review of the research published in peer-reviewed journals. *Journal of EMDR Practice and Research, 3*(4), 232–247.

Ainsworth, M. D. S., Blehar, M. C., Waters, E., & Wall, S. (1978). *Patterns of attachment: A psychological study of the strange situation.* Hillsdale, NJ: Lawrence Erlbaum.

Alao, A. O., Tyrrell, C., Yolles, J. C., & Armenta, W. (2000). Dissociation and schizophrenia. *Journal of Trauma & Dissociation, 1*(1), 91–98. doi:10.1300/J229v01n01

Alexander, P. C. (2013). Relational trauma and disorganized attachment. In J. D. Ford & C. A. Courtois (Eds.), *Treating complex traumatic stress disorders in children and adolescents: Scientific foundations and therapeutic models* (pp. 39–61). New York, NY: Guilford Press.

Althoff, R. R., Ayer, L. A., Rettew, D. C., & Hudziak, J. J. (2010). Assessment of dysregulated children using the Child Behavior Checklist: A receiver operating characteristic curve analysis. *Psychological Assessment, 22*(3), 609–617. doi:10.1037/a0019699

American Academy of Child and Adolescent Psychiatry. (1997). Summary of the practice parameters for the assessment and treatment of children, adolescents and adults with ADHD. *Journal of the American Academy of Child & Adolescent Psychiatry, 36,* 1311–1317.

American Psychiatric Association. (2013). *Diagnostic and statistical manual of mental disorders* (5th ed.). Washington, DC: Author.

Anderson, R. (2014). Pharmaceutical industry gets high on fat profits. *BBC Business News.* Retrieved from www.bbc.com/news/business

Armstrong, J. G., Putnam, F. W., Carlson, E. B., Libero, D. Z., & Smith, S. R. (1997). Development and validation of a measure of adolescent dissociation: The Adolescent Dissociative Experiences Scale. *Journal of Nervous and Mental Disease, 185*(8), 491–497. Retrieved from http://www.ncbi.nlm.nih.gov/pubmed/9284862

Arseneault, L., Cannon, M., Fisher, H. L., Polanczyk, G., Moffi, T. E., & Caspi, A. (2011). Childhood trauma and children's emerging psychotic symptoms: A genetically sensitive longitudinal cohort study. *American Journal of Psychiatry, 168*, 65–72.

Baita, S. (2007, November). *What's inside my head? How to explore and explain trauma and dissociation to children.* Paper presented at the meeting of the International Society for the Study of Trauma and Dissociation, Philadelphia, PA.

Baita, S. (2011). Dalma (4 to 7 years old)—"I've got all my sisters with me." Treatment of dissociative identity disorder in a sexually abused young child. In S. Wieland (Ed.), *Dissociation in traumatized children and adolescents: Theory and clinical interventions* (pp. 41–88). New York, NY: Routledge.

Baker, D., Hunter, E., Lawrence, E., Medford, N., Patel, M., Sierra, M., . . . David, A. S. (2003). Depersonalisation disorder: Clinical features of 204 cases. *British Journal of Psychiatry, 182*, 428–433. doi:10.1192/bjp.02.399

Barach, P. M. (1991). Multiple personality disorder as an attachment disorder. *Dissociation, 4*(3), 117–123.

Barletto Becker, K., & McCloskey, L. A. (2002). Attention and conduct problems in children exposed to family violence. *American Journal of Orthopsychiatry, 72*(1), 83–91.

Belli, H., Ural, C., Vardar, M. K., Yesilyurt, S., & Oncu, F. (2012). Dissociative symptoms and dissociative disorder comorbidity in patients with obsessive-compulsive disorder. *Comprehensive Psychiatry, 53*(7), 975–980. doi:10.1016/j.comppsych.2012.02.004

Berthoud, H. R., & Neuhuber, W. L. (2000). Functional and chemical anatomy of the afferent vagal system. *Autonomic Neuroscience, 85*(1–3), 1–17.

Betensky, M. (1977). The phenomenological approach to art expression and art therapy. *Art Psychotherapy, 4*, 173–179.

Birmaher, B., Axelson, D., Goldstein, B., Strober, M., Gill, M. K., Hunt, J., . . . Keller, M. (2009). Four-year longitudinal course of children and adolescents with bipolar spectrum disorders: The course and outcome of bipolar youth (COB) study. *American Journal of Psychiatry, 166*(7), 795–804.

Birmaher, B., Axelson, D., Strober, M., Gill, M. K., Chiappetta, L., Ryan, N., . . . Hunt, J. (2006). Clinical course of children and adolescents with bipolar spectrum disorders. *Archives of General Psychiatry, 63*(2), 175–183. doi:10.1001/ archpsyc.63.2.175.Clinical

Birmes, P., Brunet, A., Carreras, D., Ducasse, J. L., Charlet, J. P., Lauque, D., . . . Schmitt, L. (2003). The predictive power of peritraumatic dissociation and acute stress symptoms for posttraumatic stress symptoms: A three-month prospective study. *American Journal of Psychiatry, 160,* 1337–1339.

Blader, J., & Carlson, G. (2006). Increased rates of bipolar disorder diagnoses amongst U.S. child, adolescent and adult inpatients, 1996–2004. *Biological Psychiatry, 62,* 107–114.

Blatner, A. (2000). *Foundations of psychodrama: History, theory, and practice* (4th ed.). New York, NY: Springer Publishing Company.

Blaustein, M. E., & Kinniburgh, K. M. (2010). *Treating traumatic stress in children and adolescents: How to foster resilience through attachment, self-regulation and competency.* New York, NY: Guilford Press.

Blizard, R. A. (2003). Disorganized attachment, development of dissociated self states, and a relational approach to treatment. *Journal of Trauma & Dissociation, 4*(3), 27–50. doi:10.1300/J229v04n03

Bowlby, J. (1953). *Child care and the growth of love.* Baltimore, MD: Pelican Books.

Bowlby, J. (1960). Grief and mourning in infancy and early childhood. *Psychoanalytic Study of the Child, 15,* 9–52.

Bowlby, J. (1961). The Adolf Meyer lecture: Childhood mourning and its implications for psychiatry. *American Journal of Psychiatry, 118,* 481–497.

Bowlby, J. (1973). *Attachment and loss, Vol. 2: Separation.* New York, NY: Basic Books.

Bowlby, J. (1980). *Attachment and loss, Vol. 3: Loss: Sadness and depression.* New York, NY: Basic Books.

Bowlby, J. (1982a). Attachment and loss: Retrospect and prospect. *American Journal of Orthopsychiatry, 52*(4), 664–678.

Bowlby, J. (1982b). *Attachment and loss, Vol. 1: Attachment* (2nd ed.). New York, NY: Basic Books.

Brand, B. L., Loewenstein, R. J., & Spiegel, D. (2014). Dispelling myths about dissociative identity disorder treatment: An empirically based approach. *Psychiatry, 77*(2), 169–189.

Bray, M., & Wheeler, J. (2015). *Rob the robin and the bald eagle.* Vincennes, IN: Artsake.

Bremner, J. D. (2002). Neuroimaging studies in post-traumatic stress disorder. *Current Psychiatry Reports, 4*(4), 254–263. Retrieved from http://www.ncbi.nlm .nih.gov/pubmed/12126593

Bremner, J. D. (2005). Effects of traumatic stress on brain structure and function: Relevance to early responses to trauma. *Journal of Trauma & Dissociation, 6*(2), 51–68. doi:10.1300/J229v06n02

Brenner, S. L., Southerland, D. G., Burns, B. J., Wagner, H. R., & Farmer, E. M. Z. (2014). Use of psychotropic medications among youth in treatment foster care. *Journal of Child & Family Studies, 23,* 666–674.

Bridge, J. A., Iyengar, S., Salary, C. B., Barbe, R. P., Birmaher, B., Pincus, H. A., . . . Brent, D. A. (2007). Clinical response and risk for reported suicidal ideation and suicide attempts in pediatric antidepressant treatment: A meta-analysis of randomized controlled trials. *JAMA, 297*, 1683–1696.

Briere, J. (1996). *Trauma Symptom Checklist for Children professional manual*. Odessa, FL: Psychological Assessment Resources.

Briere, J. (2005). *Trauma Symptom Checklist for Young Children*. Lutz, FL: Psychological Assessment Resources.

Briere, J., Johnson, K., Bissada, A., Damon, L., Crouch, J., Gil, E., . . . Ernst, V. (2001). The Trauma Symptom Checklist for Young Children (TSCYC): Reliability and association with abuse exposure in a multi-site study. *Child Abuse & Neglect, 25*, 1001–1114. Retrieved from http://www.ncbi.nlm.nih.gov/pubmed/11601594

Brisch, K. H. (1999). *Treating attachment disorders: From theory to therapy*. New York, NY: Guilford Press.

Briscoe-Smith, A. M., & Hinshaw, S. P. (2006). Linkages between child abuse and attention-deficit/hyperactivity disorder in girls: Behavioral and social correlates. *Child Abuse & Neglect, 30*(11), 1239–1255. Retrieved from http://www.pubmedcentral.nih.gov/articlerender.fcgi?artid=1934403&tool=pmcentrez&rendertype=abstract

Buckley, P. F. (1999). The role of typical and atypical antipsychotic medications in the management of agitation and aggression. *Journal of Clinical Psychiatry, 60*(Suppl. 10), 52–60.

Bukstein, O. G., & Horner, M. S. (2010). Management of the adolescent with substance use disorders and comorbid psychopathology. *Child & Adolescent Psychiatric Clinics of North America, 19*, 609–623.

Butcher, J. N., Williams, C. L., Graham, J. R., Archer, R. P., Tellegen, A., Ben-Porath, Y. S., & Kaemmer, B. (1992). *Minnesota Multiphasic Personality Inventory–Adolescent version (MMPI-A): Manual for administration, scoring and interpretation*. Minneapolis: University of Minnesota Press.

Carlson, V., Cicchetti, D., Barnett, D., & Braunwald, K. (1989). Disorganized/disoriented attachment relationships in maltreated infants. *Developmental Psychology, 25*, 525–531.

Caroff, S. N., Mann, S. C., & Campbell, E. C. (2000). Atypical antipsychotics and neuroleptic malignant syndrome. *Psychiatric Annals, 30*, 314–321.

Casile, A., Caggiano, V., & Ferrari, P. F. (2011). The mirror neuron system: A fresh view. *The Neuroscientist, 17*(5), 524–538. Retrieved from http://www.ncbi.nlm.nih.gov/pubmed/21467305

Castonguay, L. G., Boswell, J. E., Zack, S. E., Baker, S., Boutselis, M. A., Chiswick, N. R., . . . Holtforth, M. G. (2010). Helpful and hindering events in psychotherapy: A practice network study. *Psychotherapy: Theory, Research, Practice, and Training, 47*, 327–344.

Centers for Disease Control and Prevention. (2013). *National Health Interview Survey*. Atlanta, GA: Author. Retrieved from www.cdc.gov/nchs/nhis.htm

Chu, J. A. (1998). *Rebuilding shattered lives: The responsible treatment of complex post-traumatic and dissociative disorders*. New York, NY: Wiley.

Chu, J. A., & Dill, D. L. (1990). Dissociative symptoms in relation to childhood physical and sexual abuse. *American Journal of Psychiatry, 147*(7), 887–892. Retrieved from http://www.ncbi.nlm.nih.gov/pubmed/2104510

Chu, J. A., Frey, L. M., Ganzel, B. L., & Matthews, J. A. (1999). Memories of childhood abuse: Dissociation, amnesia, and corroboration. *American Journal of Psychiatry, 156*(5), 749–755.

Clark, M. S., Jansen, K. I., & Cloy, J. A. (2012). Treatment of childhood and adolescent depression. *American Family Physician, 86*(5), 442–448.

Cloitre, M., Stolbach, B. C., Herman, J. L., Pynoos, R., Wang, J., & Petkova, E. (2009). A developmental approach to complex PTSD: Childhood and adult cumulative trauma as predictors of symptom complexity. *Journal of Traumatic Stress, 22*(5), 399–408.

Coffey, S. F., Schumacher, J. A., Brimo, M. L., & Brady, K. (2005). Exposure therapy for substance abusers with PTSD: Translating research to practice. *Behavior Modification, 29*, 10–38.

Cohen, B. M., & Cox, C. T. (1989). Breaking the code: Identification of multiplicity through art production. *Dissociation, 2*, 132–137.

Connor, D. F., Fletcher, K. E., & Swanson, J. M. (1999). A meta-analysis of clonidine for symptoms of ADHD. *Journal of the American Academy of Child & Adolescent Psychiatry, 38*, 1551–1559.

Connor, D. F., Grasso, D. J., Slivinsky, M. D., Pearson, G. S., & Banga, A. (2013). An open-label study of guanfacine extended release for traumatic stress related symptoms in children and adolescents. *Journal of Child & Adolescent Psychopharmacology, 23*(4), 244–251.

Cook, A., Spinazzola, J., Ford, J., Lanktree, C., Blaustein, M., Cloitre, M., . . . van der Kolk, B. (2005). Complex trauma in children and adolescents. *Psychiatric Annals, 35*(5), 390–398.

Coons, P. M. (1996). Clinical phenomenology of 25 children and adolescents with dissociative disorders. *Child and Adolescent Psychiatric Clinics of North America, 5*(2), 361–373.

Cooper, W. O., Callahan, S. T., Shintani, A., Fuchs, D. C., Shelton, R. C., Dudley, J. A., . . . Ray, W. A. (2014). Antidepressants and suicide attempts in children. *Pediatrics, 133*(2), 204–210.

Cooper, W. O., Habel, L. A., Sox, C. M., Chan, K. A., Arbogast, P. G., Cheetham, T. C., . . . Ray, W. A. (2011). ADHD drugs and serious cardiovascular events in children and young adults. *New England Journal of Medicine, 365*, 1896–1904.

Cordón, I. M., Pipe, M. E., Sayfan, L., Melinder, A., & Goodman, G. S. (2004). Memory for traumatic experiences in early childhood. *Developmental Review, 24*(1), 101–132. doi:10.1016/j.dr.2003.09.003

Corell, C. U., Manu, P., Olshanskiy, V., Napolitano, B., Kane, J. M., & Malhotra, A. K. (2009). Cardiometabolic risk of second-generation antipsychotic medications during first-time use in children and adolescents. *JAMA, 302,* 1765–1773.

Costello, I., Long, P. F., Wong, I. K., Tuleu, C., & Yeung, V. (2007). *Pediatric drug handling.* New York, NY: Pharmaceutical Press.

Courtois, C. A. (2004). Complex trauma, complex reactions: Assessment and treatment. *Psychotherapy: Theory, Research, Practice, Training, 41,* 412–425.

Cox, C. T., & Cohen, B. M. (2005). The unique role of art making in the treatment of dissociative identity disorder. *Psychiatric Annals, 35*(8), 695–697.

Cromer, L. D., Stevens, C., & Deprince, A. P. (2006). The relationship between executive attention and dissociation in children. *Journal of Trauma & Dissociation, 7,* 135–153.

Crossley, M. L. (2000). *Introducing narrative psychology: Self, trauma and the construction of meaning.* Buckingham, UK: Open University Press.

Daitch, C. (2007). *Affect regulation toolbox: Practical and effective hypnotic interventions for the over-reactive client.* New York, NY: W. W. Norton.

Damásio, A. R. (1994). *Descartes' error: Emotion, reason and the human brain.* New York, NY: Picador.

D'Andrea, W., Ford, J., Stolbach, B., Spinazzola, J., & van der Kolk, B. A. (2012). Understanding interpersonal trauma in children: Why we need a developmentally appropriate trauma diagnosis. *American Journal of Orthopsychiatry, 82*(2), 187–200. doi:10.1111/j.1939-0025.2012.01154.x

Danylchuk, L. (2015). *Embodied healing: Using yoga to recover from extreme stress.* Kindle Publishing Package.

Davis, C. G., Nolen-Hoeksema, S., & Larson, J. (1998). Making sense of loss and benefiting from the experience: Two construals of meaning. *Journal of Personality and Social Psychology, 75,* 561–574.

DeBellis, M. D., Keshavan, M. S., Clark, D. B., Casey, B. J., Giedd, J. N., Boring, A. M., . . . Ryan, N. D. (1999). Developmental traumatology Part II: Brain development. *Biological Psychiatry, 5,* 1271–1284.

Deblinger, E., Mannarino, A. P., Cohen, J. A., Runyon, M. K., & Steer, R. A. (2011). Trauma-focused cognitive behavioral therapy for children: Impact of the trauma narrative and treatment length. *Depression and Anxiety, 28,* 67–75.

Dell, P., & O'Neil, J. (Eds.). (2009). *Dissociation and the dissociative disorders: DSM-V and beyond.* New York, NY: Routledge.

Dell, P. F. (2004). *Adolescent Multidimensional Inventory of Dissociation v. 6.0* [measurement instrument]. Retrieved from http://www.bainbridgepsychology.com/Adolescent_MID_reformatted.doc

Dell, P. F. (2006). A new model of dissociative identity disorder. *Psychiatric Clinics of North America, 29,* 1–26.

Demitrack, M., Putnam, F., Brewerton, T., Brandt, H., & Gold, P. (1990). Relation of clinical variables to dissociative phenomena in eating disorders. *American Journal of Psychiatry, 147,* 1184–1188.

Dieleman, G. C., Dierckx, B., & Hofstra, M. B. (2011). *Psychofarmaca in de KJP: formularium voor de kinder- en jeugdpsychiatrische praktijk* [Psychotropic drugs in the KJP: Formulary for the child and adolescent psychiatric practice]. Assen, The Netherlands: Van Gorcum.

Diseth, T. H. (2006). Dissociation following traumatic medical treatment procedures in childhood: A longitudinal follow-up. *Development and Psychopathology*, *18*(1), 233–251. Retrieved from http://www.ncbi.nlm.nih.gov/pubmed/16478561

Dodge, N. N., & Wilson, G. A. (2001). Melatonin for treatment of sleep disorders in children with developmental disabilities. *Journal of Child Neurology*, *16*, 581–584.

Egli-Bernd, H. (2011). EMDR in dissociative processes within the framework of personality disorders: The impact of cognitions in the EMDR process: The "Dialogue Protocol." *Journal of EMDR Practice and Research*, *5*(3), 131–139. doi:10.1891/1933–3196.5.3.131

Eich, J. E. (1980). The cue-dependent nature of state-dependent retrieval. *Memory & Cognition*, *8*, 157–173.

Elbrecht, C. (2012). *Trauma healing at the clay field: A sensorimotor art therapy approach.* Philadelphia, PA: Jessica Kingsley.

Endo, T., Sugiyama, T., & Someya, T. (2006). Attention-deficit/hyperactivity disorder and dissociative. *Psychiatry and Clinical Neurosciences*, *60*, 434–438.

Erikson, E. H. (1963). *Childhood and society* (2nd ed.). New York, NY: W. W. Norton.

Erikson, E. H. (1968). *Identity: Youth and crisis.* New York, NY: W. W. Norton.

Evers-Szostak, M., & Sanders, S. (1992). The Children's Perceptual Alteration Scale (CPAS): A measure of children's dissociation. *Dissociation*, *5*, 91–97.

Fagan, J., & McMahon, P. (1984). Incipient multiple personality in children. *Journal of Nervous and Mental Disease*, *172*, 2–36.

Farber, S. K. (2008). Dissociation, traumatic attachments, and self-harm: Eating disorders and self-mutilation. *Clinical Social Work Journal*, *36*(1), 63–72.

Farrington, A., Waller, G. D., Smerden, J. D., & Faupel, A. W. (2001). The Adolescent Dissociative Experiences Scale: Psychometric properties and difference in scores across age groups. *Journal of Nervous and Mental Disease*, *189*, 722–727.

Farrone, S. V., Biederman, J., Morley, C. P., & Spencer, T. J. (2008). Effect of stimulants on height and weight: A review of the literature. *Journal of the American Academy of Child & Adolescent Psychiatry*, *47*, 994–1009.

Fedorowicz, V. J., & Fombonne, E. (2005). Metabolic side effects of atypical antipsychotics in children: A literature review. *Psychopharmacology*, *19*, 533–550.

Ferenczi, S. (1949). Confusion of tongues between the adult and the child. *International Journal of Psychoanalysis*, *30*, 225–230. (Original work published 1933)

Findling, R. L., Robb, A., Nyilas, M., Forbes, R. A., Jin, N., Ivanova, S., . . . Carson, W. H. (2008). A multiple-center, randomized, double-blind, placebo-controlled study of oral aripiprazole for treatment of adolescents with schizophrenia. *American Journal of Psychiatry, 165*, 1432–1441.

Finkelhor, D., Ormrod, R. K., Turner, H. A., & Hamby, S. L. (2007). Measuring poly-victimization using the Juvenile Victimization Questionnaire. *Child Abuse & Neglect, 29*, 1291–1312.

Fleming, J. (2012). The effectiveness of eye movement desensitization and reprocessing in the treatment of traumatized children and youth. *Journal of EMDR Practice and Research, 6*(1), 16–26.

Foa, E. B., Zinbarg, R., & Olasov Rothbaum, B. (1992). Uncontrollability and unpredictability in posttraumatic stress disorder: An animal model. *Psychology Bulletin, 112*, 218–238.

Foote, B., & Park, J. (2008). Dissociative identity disorder and schizophrenia: Differential diagnosis and theoretical issues. *Current Psychiatry Reports, 10*, 217–221. Retrieved from http://www.ncbi.nlm.nih.gov/pubmed/Waters_99638_QA_14_409-412_AppA_11-24-15 18652789

Ford, J. D. (2009). Neurobiological and developmental research: Clinical implications. In C. A. Courtois & J. D. Ford (Eds.), *Treating complex traumatic stress disorders: An evidence-based guide* (pp. 31–58). New York, NY: Guilford Press.

Ford, J. D. (2011). Complicated forms of trauma-related reactions: Assessing child and adolescent complex traumatic stress reactions. *Journal of Child & Adolescent Trauma, 4*, 217–232.

Ford, J. D., & Connor, D. F. (2009). ADHD and posttraumatic stress disorder. *Current Attention Disorders Reports, 1*, 60–66. doi:10.1007/s12618-009-0009-0

Ford, J. D., Ellis, C. G., Davis, W. B., & Fleischer, A. (2007). Child maltreatment, other trauma among children with oppositional defiant and attention deficit hyperactivity disorders exposure, and posttraumatic symptomatology. *Child Maltreatment, 5*(3), 205–217.

Forgash, C. (2005, May). *Deepening EMDR treatment effects across the diagnostic spectrum: Integrating EMDR and ego state work.* Presented at the two-day workshop, New York. Retrieved from http://live.online.se/emdr2/bildarkiv/DEEPENINGEMDRtx.pdf

Forgash, C., & Copeley, M. (Eds.). (2008). *Healing the heart of trauma and dissociation with EMDR and ego state therapy.* New York, NY: Springer Publishing Company.

Forgash, C., & Knipe, J. (2008). Integrating EMDR and ego state treatment for clients with trauma disorders. In C. Forgash & M. Copeley (Eds.), *Healing the heart of trauma and dissociation with EMDR and ego state therapy* (pp. 1–59). New York, NY: Springer Publishing Company.

Fraiberg, S. (1982). Pathological defenses in infancy. *Psychoanalytic Quarterly, 51*(4), 612–635.

Franklin, M. (1992). Art therapy and self-esteem. *Art Therapy: Journal of the American Art Therapy Association, 9*, 78–84.

Freud, S. (2001). Some points for a comparative study of organic and hysterical paralyses. In J. Strachey & A. Strachey (Eds.), *Standard edition of the complete psychological works of Sigmund Freud, 1*. London, UK: Hogarth. (Original work published 1893)

Frewen, P. A., & Lanius, R. A. (2006). Neurobiology of dissociation: Unity and disunity in mind–body–brain. *Psychiatric Clinics of North America, 29*(1), 113–128. Retrieved from http://www.ncbi.nlm.nih.gov/pubmed/16530589

Freyd, J. (1996). *Betrayal trauma: The logic of forgetting childhood abuse*. Cambridge, MA: Harvard University Press.

Friedrich, W. N. (1997). *Child Sexual Behavior Inventory: Professional manual*. Odessa, FL: Psychological Assessment Resources.

Fromm, E. (1965). Hypnoanalysis: Theory and two case examples. *Psychotherapy: Theory, Research, and Practice, 2*, 127–133.

Frost, J., Silberg, J. L., & McIntee, J. (1996). *Imaginary friends in normal and traumatized children*. Paper presented at the 13th International Conference on Dissociative Disorders, San Francisco, CA.

Fuller-Tyszkiewicz, M., & Mussaph, A. J. (2008). The relationship between dissociation and binge eating. *Journal of Trauma & Dissociation, 9*(4), 445–462.

Gaensbauer, T. J. (1996). Developmental and therapeutic aspects of treating infants and toddlers who have witnessed violence. *Bulletin of Zero to Three/ National Center for Infants, Toddlers and Families, 16*, 15–20.

Gaensbauer, T. J. (2002). Representations of trauma in infancy: Clinical and theoretical implications for the understanding of early memory. *Infant Mental Health Journal, 23*(3), 259–277.

Gallese, V., Fadiga, L., Fogassi, L., & Rizzolatti, G. (1996). Action recognition in the premotor cortex. *Brain, 119*, 593–609.

Gallup, T. (2007). *Stone crazy: A crazy little series*. Mackinac Island, MI: Mackinac Island Press.

George, C., Kaplan, N., & Main, M. (1996). *Adult attachment interview protocol* (3rd ed.). Unpublished manuscript, University of California at Berkeley.

Gershuny, B. S., Baer, L., Jenike, M. A., Minichiello, W. E., & Wilhelm, S. (2002). Comorbid posttraumatic stress disorder: Impact on treatment outcome for obsessive-compulsive disorder. *American Journal of Psychiatry, 159*, 852–854.

Giaconia, R. M., Reinherz, H. Z., Hauf, A. C., Paradis, A. D., Wasserman, M. S., & Langhammer, D. M. (2000). Comorbidity of substance use and post-traumatic stress disorders in a community sample of adolescents. *American Journal of Orthopsychiatry, 70*, 253–262.

Giaconia, R. M., Reinherz, H. Z., Paradis, A. D., & Stashwick, C. K. (2003). Comorbidity of substance use disorders and posttraumatic stress disorder in adolescents. In P. Ouimette & P. J. Brown (Eds.), *Trauma and substance abuse: Causes, consequences, and treatment of comorbid disorders* (pp. 227–242). Washington, DC: American Psychological Association.

Gibbons, K. (2014). Houdini. *Multichannel News, 35*(32), 23.

Goldsmith, R. E., Cheit, R. E., & Wood, M. E. (2009). Evidence of dissociative amnesia in science and literature: Culture-bound approaches to trauma in Pope, Poliakoff, Parker, Boynes, and Hudson (2007). *Journal of Trauma & Dissociation, 10*(3), 237–260. Retrieved from http://www.ncbi.nlm.nih.gov/pubmed/19585333

Gomez, A., & Paulsen, S. (in press). *All the colors of me: My first book about dissociation.*

Gomez, A. M. (2007). *Dark, bad day . . . go away: A book for children about trauma and EMDR.* Phoenix, AZ: Author.

Gomez, A. M. (2013a). Advanced preparation strategies for dissociative children. In A. M. Gomez (Ed.), *EMDR therapy and adjunct approaches with children: Complex trauma, attachment, and dissociation* (pp. 151–178). New York, NY: Springer Publishing Company.

Gomez, A. M. (2013b). *EMDR therapy and adjunct approaches with children: Complex trauma, attachment, and dissociation.* New York, NY: Springer Publishing Company.

Graf, P., & Masson, E. J. (1993). *Implicit memory: New directions in cognition, development, and neuropsychology.* Hillsdale, NJ: Lawrence Erlbaum.

Grasso, D., Greene, C., & Ford, J. D. (2013). Cumulative trauma in childhood. In J. D. Ford & C. A. Courtois (Eds.), *Treating complex traumatic stress disorders in children and adolescents: An evidence-based guide* (pp. 79–99). New York, NY: Guilford Press.

Gray, G. C. (2013). The ethics of pharmaceutical research funding: A social organization approach. *Journal of Law, Medicine & Ethics, 41*(3), 629–634.

Greenwald, R. (1999). *Eye movement desensitization and reprocessing (EMDR) in child and adolescent psychotherapy.* New York, NY: Jason Aronson.

Griens, A. M., Jansen, J. M., Kroon, J. D., Lukaart, J. S., & Van der Vaart, R. J. (2014). *Data en feiten 2014* [Data and facts 2014]. The Hague, The Netherlands: The Dutch Foundation for Pharmaceutical Statistics (SFK). Retrieved from www.skf.nl

Grossman, G. A. (1997). Effects of childhood trauma and dissociation with substance abusing adolescents. *Dissertation Abstracts International: Section B: The Sciences and Engineering, 58*(3-B), 1531.

Hairmann, S. W., & March, J. S. (1996). SSRI-induced mania. *Journal of the American Academy of Child & Adolescent Psychiatry, 35*, 4–5.

HaLevi, E. (2008, February 7). Sderot teacher's song empowers children in face of rockets. *Arutz Sheva Israel National News.* Retrieved from http://www.israelnationalnews.com/News/News.aspx/125183#.U3uT6S9Q1YI

Hardy, L. T. (2007). Attachment theory and reactive attachment disorder: Theoretical perspectives and treatment implications. *Journal of Child & Adolescent Psychiatric Nursing, 20*(1), 27–39.

Harmon, R. J., & Riggs, P. D. (1996). Clonidine for PTSD in preschool children. *Journal of the American Academy of Child & Adolescent Psychiatry, 35*(9), 1247–1249.

Harris, J. (2005). The increased diagnosis of "juvenile bipolar disorder": What are we treating? *Psychiatric Services*, *56*(5), 529–531. doi:10.1176/appi.ps.56.5.529

Harrison, A. G., & Wilson, J. B. (2005). Inattention and dissociation: Overlapping constructs? *ADHD Report*, *13*(3), 9–12.

Heinicke, C. M. (1956). Some effects of separating two-year-old children from their parents: A comparative study. *Human Relations*, *9*, 105–176.

Heinicke, C. M., & Westheimer, I. (1965). *Brief separations*. New York, NY: International Universities Press.

Hesse, E., & Main, M. (2000). Disorganized infant, child, and adult attachment: Collapse in the behavioral and attentional strategies. *Journal of the American Psychoanalytic Association*, *48*, 1097–1127.

Hetrick, S. E., McKenzie, J. E., Cox, G. R., Simmons, M. B., & Merry, S. N. (2012). Newer generation antidepressants for depressive disorders in children and adolescents. *Cochrane Database of Systematic Reviews*, *14*, 11.

Hilt, R. J., Chaudhari, M., Bell, J. F., Wolf, C., Koprowicz, K., & King, B. H. (2014). Side effects from the use of one or more psychiatric medications in a population-based sample of children and adolescents. *Journal of Child & Adolescent Psychopharmacology*, *24*(2), 83–89.

Hinshaw-Fuselier, S., Boris, N. W., & Zeanah, C. H. (1999). Reactive attachment disorder in maltreated twins. *Infant Mental Health Journal*, *20*(1), 42–59.

Honig, A., Romime, M. A. J., Ensink, B. J., Escher, S. D. M. A. C., Pennnings, M. H. A., & deVries, M. W. (1998). Auditory hallucinations: A comparison between patients and nonpatients. *Journal of Nervous & Mental Disease*, *186*(10), 646–651.

Hornor, G. (2008). Reactive attachment disorder. *Journal of Pediatric Health Care*, *22*(4), 234–239. doi:10.1016/j.pedhc.2007.07.003

Hornstein, N. L., & Putnam, F. W. (1992). Clinical phenomenology of child and adolescent dissociative disorders. *Journal of the American Academy of Child & Adolescent Psychiatry*, *31*, 1077–1085.

Hov, I., Bjartnes, M., Slordal, L., & Spigset, O. (2012). Are drugs taken as prescribed? *Tidsskrift for den Norske Laegeforening*, *132*(4), 418–422.

Howell, E. F. (2011). *Understanding and treating dissociative identity disorder: A relational approach*. New York, NY: Routledge.

Huemer, J., Erhart, F., & Steiner, H. (2010). Posttraumatic stress disorder in children and adolescents: A review of psychopharmacological treatment. *Child Psychiatry & Human Development*, *41*, 624–640.

Hughes, D. A. (2009). *Attachment-focused parenting: Effective strategies to care for children*. New York, NY: W. W. Norton.

Hughes, D. A., & Bylin, J. (2012). *Brain-based parenting: The neuroscience of caregiving for healthy attachment*. New York, NY: W. W. Norton.

Hulette, A. C., Fisher, P. A., Kim, H. K., Ganger, W., & Landsverk, J. L. (2008). Dissociation in foster preschoolers: A replication and assessment study. *Journal of Trauma & Dissociation*, *9*(2), 173–190. doi:10.1080/15299730802045914

Hulette, A. C., Freyd, J. J., & Fisher, A. P. (2011). Dissociation in middle childhood among foster children with early maltreatment experiences. *Child Abuse & Neglect, 35*, 123–126.

Hyun, M., Friedman, S., & Dunner, D. (2000). Relationship of childhood physical and sexual abuse in adult bipolar disorder. *Bipolar Disorders, 2*, 131–135.

Iacoboni, M. (2009). Imitation, empathy, and mirror neurons. *Annual Review of Psychology, 60*, 653–670. doi:10.1146/annurev.psych.60.110707.163604

International Society for the Study of Trauma and Dissociation. (2011). Guidelines for treating dissociative identity disorder in adults, third revision. *Journal of Trauma & Dissociation, 12*, 115–187.

ISSD Task Force on Children and Adolescents. (2004). Guidelines for the evaluation and treatment of dissociative symptoms in children and adolescents. *Journal of Trauma & Dissociation, 5*(3), 119–150. Retrieved from http://www.isst-d.org/downloads/childguidelines-ISSTD-2003.pdf

Jackson, J. H. (1931/1932). *Selected writings of John Hughlings Jackson* (Vols. 1 and 2). London, UK: Milford.

Jain, R., Segal, S., Kollins, S. H., & Khayrallah, M. (2011). Clonidine extended-release tablets for pediatric patients with ADHD. *Journal of the American Academy of Child & Adolescent Psychiatry, 50*, 171–179.

Janet, P. (1907). *The major symptoms of hysteria*. London, UK: Macmillan.

Jarero, I., Artigas, L., Mauer, M., Alcala, N., & Lupez, T. (1999, November). *EMDR integrative group treatment protocol and the butterfly hug*. Paper presented at the annual meeting of the International Society for Traumatic Stress Studies, Miami, FL.

Johnson, K. A., Barry, E., Bellgrove, M. A., Cox, M., Kelly, S. P., Daibhis, A., . . . Gill, M. (2008). Dissociation in response to methylphenidate on response variability in a group of medication naive children with ADHD. *Neuropsychologia, 46*, 1532–1541.

Jovasevic, V., Corcoran, K. A., Leaderbrand, K., Yamawaki, N., Guedea, A. L., Chen, H. J., . . . Radulovic, J. (2015). GABAergic mechanisms regulated by miR-33 encode state-dependent fear. *Nature Neuroscience, 18*, 1265–1271. doi:10.1038/nn.4084

Kagan, R. (2004). *Rebuilding attachments with traumatized children: Healing from losses, violence, abuse, and neglect*. New York, NY: Haworth Press.

Kaplow, J. B., Hall, E., Karestan, C. K., Dodge, K. A., & Amaya-Jackson, L. (2008). Dissociation predicts later attention problems in sexually abused children. *Child Abuse & Neglect, 32*(2), 261–275.

Keck Seeley, S. M., Perosa, S. L., & Perosa, L. M. (2004). A validation study of the Adolescent Dissociative Experiences Scale. *Child Abuse & Neglect, 28*(7), 755–769. doi:10.1016/j.chiabu.2004.01.006

Kisiel, C., McClelland, G., & Torgersen, E. (2013). *Understanding the impact of dissociation in Illinois Child Welfare: Relationship to risk behaviors and trauma symptoms, and intensity of services*. Unpublished manuscript.

Kisiel, C., Stolbach, B., & Silberg, J. (2013). *Understanding and addressing dissociation within child serving systems: A missing link?* National Child Traumatic Stress Network All-Network Conference, Philadelphia, PA.

Kisiel, C. L., & Lyons, J. S. (2001). Dissociation as a mediator of psychopathology among sexually abused children and adolescents. *American Journal of Psychiatry, 158*(7), 1034–1039. Retrieved from http://www.ncbi.nlm.nih.gov/pubmed/11431224

Kluft, R. (1985). Childhood multiple personality disorder: Predictors, clinical findings, and treatment results. In R. Kluft (Ed.), *Childhood antecedents of multiple personality disorder* (pp. 167–196). Washington, DC: American Psychiatric Press.

Kluft, R. P. (1988). Playing for time: Temporizing techniques in the treatment of multiple personality disorder. *American Journal of Clinical Hypnosis, 32*, 90–98.

Kluft, R. P. (1990). The slow leak technique. In C. Hammond (Ed.), *Handbook of hypnotic suggestions and metaphors* (pp. 529–530). New York, NY: W. W. Norton.

Kluft, R. P. (1993). The initial stages of psychotherapy in the treatment of multiple personality disorder patients. *Dissociation, 6*(2/3), 145–161.

Kluft, R. P. (2013). *Shelter from the storm: Processing the traumatic memories of DID/DDNOS patients with the fractionated abreaction.* North Charleston, SC: CreateSpace Independent Publishing Platform.

Knipe, J. (2008). *The CIPOS method: Procedures to therapeutically reduce dissociative processes while preserving emotional safety.* Master class at the EMDR European Conference, London, UK.

Korn, D. L., & Leeds, A. M. (2002). Preliminary evidence of efficacy for EMDR resource development and installation in the stabilization phase of treatment of complex posttraumatic stress disorder. *Journal of Clinical Psychology, 58*(12), 1465–1487.

Laddis, A., & Dell, P. F. (2012). Dissociation and psychosis in dissociative identity disorder and schizophrenia. *Journal of Trauma & Dissociation, 13*(4), 397–413. doi:10.1080/15299732.2012.664967

Lanius, R. A., Williamson, P. C., Hopper, J., Densmore, M., Boksman, K., Gupta, M. A., . . . Menon, R. S. (2003). Recall of emotional states in posttraumatic stress disorder: An fMRI investigation. *Biological Psychiatry, 53*(3), 204–210. doi:10.1016/S0006-3223(02)01466-X

Lanius, U. F., & Paulsen, S. L. (2014). Toward an embodied self: EMDR and somatic interventions. In U. F. Lanius, S. L. Paulsen & F. M. Corrigan (Eds.), *Neurobiology and treatment of traumatic dissociation: Towards an embodied self* (pp. 447–469). New York, NY: Springer Publishing Company.

Lanius, U. F., Paulsen, S. L., & Corrigan, F. M. (Eds.). (2014). *Neurobiology and treatment of traumatic dissociation: Towards an embodied self.* New York, NY: Springer Publishing Company.

Larose, M. E. (1988). The use of art therapy with juvenile delinquents to enhance self-image. *Art Therapy: Journal of the American Art Therapy Association, 4*, 99–104.

Lederman, J., & Fink, C. (2003). *The ups and downs of raising a bipolar child: A survival guide for parents.* New York, NY: Fireside.

Leonard, H. L., March, J., Rickler, K., & Allen, A. J. (1997). Pharmacology of the selective serotonin reuptake inhibitors in children and adolescents. *Journal of the American Academy of Child & Adolescent Psychiatry, 36*, 725–736.

Levine, P. A. (2010). *In an unspoken voice: How the body releases trauma and restores goodness.* Berkeley, CA: North Atlantic Books.

Levine, P. A., & Frederick, A. (1997). *Waking the tiger: Healing trauma.* Berkeley, CA: North Atlantic Books.

Levine, P. A., & Kline, M. (2007). *Trauma through a child's eyes: Infancy through adolescence.* Berkeley, CA: North Atlantic Books.

Levy, B. F. (2007). The broad relationship between bipolar disorder and disorders of psychological trauma—time-limited to life-long need for mood stabilizers. *Journal of Psychological Trauma, 6*(2–3), 99–125. doi:10.1300/J513v06n02

Libby, A. M., & Riggs, P. D. (2008). Integrated substance use and mental health services for adolescents: Challenges and opportunities. In Y. Kaminer & O. G. Bukstein (Eds.), *Adolescent substance abuse psychiatric comorbidity and high-risk behaviors* (pp. 435–452). New York, NY: Taylor & Francis.

Lightstone, J. (2004). Dissociation and compulsive eating. *Trauma & Dissociation, 5*(4), 17–32.

Liotti, G. (1999). Disorganization of attachment as a model for understanding dissociative psychopathology. In J. Solomon & C. George (Eds.), *Attachment disorganization* (pp. 291–317). New York, NY: Guilford Press.

Liotti, G. (2004). Trauma, dissociation, and disorganized attachment: Three strands of a single braid. *Psychotherapy: Theory, Research, Practice, Training, 41*(4), 472–486. doi:10.1037/0033–3204.41.4.472

Liotti, G. (2006). A model of dissociation based on attachment theory and research. *Journal of Trauma & Dissociation, 7*(4), 55–73. doi:10.1300/J229v07n04

Liotti, G. (2009). Attachment and dissociation. In P. F. Dell & J. A. O'Neil (Eds.), *Dissociation and the dissociative disorders: DSM-V and beyond* (pp. 53–65). New York, NY: Routledge.

Lochner, L., Seedat, S., Hemmings, S. M. J., Kinnear, C. J., Corfield, V. A., Niehaus, D. J. H., . . . Stein, D. J. (2004). Dissociative experiences in obsessive-compulsive disorder and trichotillomania: Clinical and genetic findings. *Comprehensive Psychiatry, 45*(5), 384–391.

Loewenstein, R. J., Spiegel, D., & Hermann, R. (2014). Dissociative amnesia: Epidemiology, pathogenesis, clinical manifestations, course, and diagnosis. *UpToDate.* Retrieved from http://www.uptodate.com/contents/dissociative-amnesia-epidemiology-pathogenesis-clinical-manifestations-course-and-diagnosis

Lombardo, G. T. (2006). *Understanding the mind of your bipolar child: The complete guide to the development, treatment, and parenting of children with bipolar disorder.* New York, NY: St. Martin's Press.

Looff, D., Grimley, P., Kuller, F., Martin, A., & Shonfield, L. (1995). Carbamazepine for PTSD. *Journal of the American Academy of Child & Adolescent Psychiatry, 34*(6), 703–704.

Lopez, B. H. (2004). Mortise and tenon. In B. H. Lopez, *Resistance* (pp. 39–52). New York, NY: Knopf.

Lopez, B. H. (2010, Fall). A dark light in the west: Racism and reconciliation. *The Georgia Review*, pp. 365–386.

Lopez, B. H. (2013, January). Sliver of sky: Confronting the trauma of sexual abuse. *Harper's*, pp. 41–48.

Lovett, J. (1999). *Small wonders: Healing childhood trauma with EMDR*. New York, NY: The Free Press.

Lowenstein, R., & Brand, B. (2014, October). Treating complex trauma survivors. *Psychiatric Times*, p. 40.

Lyons-Ruth, K. (1996). Attachment relationships among children with aggressive behavior problems: The role of disorganized early attachment patterns. *Journal of Consulting and Clinical Psychology, 64*, 64–73.

Lyons-Ruth, K. (1999). The two-person unconscious: Intersubjective dialogue, enactive relational representation, and the emergence of new forms of relational organization. *Psychoanalytic Inquiry, 19*, 576–617.

Lyons-Ruth, K. (2003). Dissociation and the parent–infant dialogue: A longitudinal perspective from attachment research. *Journal of the American Psychoanalytic Association, 51*(3), 883–911.

Lyons-Ruth, K., Dutra, L., Schuder, M. R., & Bianchi, I. (2006). From infant attachment disorganization to adult dissociation: Relational adaptations or traumatic experiences? *Psychiatric Clinics of North America, 29*(1), 63–86, viii. Retrieved from http://www.pubmedcentral.nih.gov/articlerender.fcgi?artid=2625289&tool=pmcentrez&rendertype=abstract

Lyons-Ruth, K., & Spielman, E. (2004). Disorganized infant attachment strategies and helpless-fearful profiles of parenting: Integrating attachment research with clinical intervention. *Infant Mental Health Journal, 25*(4), 318–335.

Macfie, J., Cicchetti, D., & Toth, S. L. (2001). Dissociation in maltreated versus nonmaltreated preschool-aged children. *Child Abuse & Neglect, 25*, 1253–1267.

Main, M., & Hesse, E. (1990). Parents' unresolved traumatic experiences are related to infant disorganized attachment status: Is frightened and/or frightening parental behavior the linking mechanism? In M. T. Greenberg, D. Cicchetti, & E. M. Cummings (Eds.), *Attachment in the preschool years: Theory, research and intervention* (pp. 161–182). Chicago, IL: University of Chicago Press.

Main, M., & Solomon, J. (1986). Discovery of an insecure-disorganized/disoriented attachment pattern: Procedures, findings and implications for the classification of behavior. In T. B. Brazelton & M. Yogman (Eds.), *Affective development in infancy* (pp. 95–124). Norwood, NJ: Ablex.

Malinosky-Rummel, R. R., & Hoier, T. S. (1991). Validating measures of dissociation in sexually abused and nonabused children. *Behavioral Assessment*, *13*, 341–357.

Marcovitch, H. (2007). Misconduct by researchers and authors. *Gac Sanit*, *21*(6), 492–499.

Marks, R. P. (2011). Jason (7 years old)—Expressing past neglect and abuse: Two-week intensive therapy for an adopted child with dissociation. In S. Wieland (Ed.), *Dissociation in traumatized children and adolescents: Theory and clinical interventions* (pp. 97–140). New York, NY: Routledge.

McLeer, S. V., Deblinger, E., Henry, D., & Orvaschel, H. (1992). Sexually abused children at high risk for post-traumatic stress disorder. *Journal of the American Academy of Child & Adolescent Psychiatry*, *31*, 875–879.

McLewin, L., & Muller, R. (2006). Childhood trauma, imaginary companions, and the development of pathological dissociation. *Aggression and Violent Behavior*, *11*(5), 531–545. doi:10.1016/j.avb.2006.02.001

McNevin, S. H., & Rivera, M. (2001). Obsessive compulsive spectrum disorders in individuals with dissociative disorders. *Journal of Trauma & Dissociation*, *2*(4), 117–131.

McShane, J. M., & Zirkel, S. (2008). Dissociation in the binge–purge cycle of bulimia nervosa. *Journal of Trauma & Dissociation*, *9*(4), 463–479.

McVoy, M., & Findling, R. L. (2013). *Clinical manual of child and adolescent psychopharmacology* (2nd ed.). Washington, DC: American Psychiatric Publishing.

Merry, S. N., & Andrews, L. K. (1994). Psychiatric status of sexually abused children 12 months after disclosure of abuse. *Journal of the American Academy of Child & Adolescent Psychiatry*, *33*(7), 939–944.

Milot, T., Plamondon, A., Ethier, L. S., Lemelin, J. P., St. Laurent, D., & Rousseau, M. (2013). Validity of CBCL-derived PTSD and dissociation scales: Further evidence in a sample of neglected children and adolescents. *Child Maltreatment*, *18*(2), 122–128. doi:10.1177/1077559513490246

Moore, T. (2007, June). *The nature and role of relationships in early childhood intervention services*. Paper presented at the Second Conference of the International Society on Early Intervention, Zagreb, Croatia. Retrieved from http://www.rch.org.au/uploadedFiles/Main/Content/ccch/TM_ISEIConf07_Nature_role_rships.pdf

Moskowitz, A. (2011). Schizophrenia, trauma, dissociation, and scientific revolutions. *Journal of Trauma & Dissociation*, *12*, 347–357.

MTA Cooperative Group (Multimedia Treatment of Attention Deficit Hyperactive Disorder Study). (1999). A 14-month randomized clinical trial of treatment strategies for ADHD. *Archives of General Psychiatry*, *56*(12), 1073–1086.

Muller, R. T. (2010). *Trauma and the avoidant client: Attachment-based strategies for healing*. New York, NY: W. W. Norton.

Muris, P., Merckelbach, H., & Peeters, E. (2003). The links between the Adolescent Dissociative Experiences Scale (A-DES), fantasy proneness, and anxiety symptoms. *Journal of Nervous and Mental Disease*, *191*, 18–24.

Music, G. (2011). *Nurturing natures: Attachment and children's emotional, sociocultural and brain development.* New York, NY: Psychology Press.

National Institutes of Health. (2000). National Institutes of Health Consensus Development Conference statement: Diagnosis and treatment of ADHD. *Journal of the American Academy of Child & Adolescent Psychiatry, 39*, 182–193.

National Scientific Council on the Developing Child. (2014). *Excessive stress disrupts the architecture of the developing brain* (Working Paper No. 3). Retrieved from www.developingchild.harvard.edu

Nemzer, E. D. (1998). Psychopharmacologic interventions for children and adolescents with dissociative disorder. In J. L. Silberg (Ed.), *The dissociative child: Diagnosis, treatment, and management* (pp. 235–270). Lutherville, MD: Sidran Press.

Nijenhuis, E. R. S. (1999). *Somatoform dissociation: Phenomena, measurement, and theoretical issues.* Assen, The Netherlands: Van Gorcum.

Nijenhuis, E. R. S. (2004). *Somatoform dissociation: Phenomena, measurements, and theoretical issues* (2nd ed.). New York, NY: W. W. Norton.

Nijenhuis, E. R. S., & den Boer, J. A. (2009). Psychobiology of traumatization and trauma-related structural dissociation of the personality. In P. F. Dell & J. A. O'Neil (Eds.), *Dissociation and the dissociative disorders: DSM-V and beyond* (pp. 337–367). New York, NY: Routledge.

Nilsson, D., & Svedin, C. G. (2006). Dissociation among Swedish adolescents and the connection to trauma: An evaluation of the Swedish version of Adolescent Dissociative Experiences Scale. *Journal of Nervous and Mental Disease, 194*, 684–689.

O'Donnell, M. L., Creamer, M., & Pattison, P. (2004). Posttraumatic stress disorder and depression following trauma: Understanding comorbidity. *American Journal of Psychiatry, 161*, 1390–1396.

Oedegaard, K. J., Neckelmann, D., Benazzi, F., Syrstad, V. E. G., Akiskal, H. S., & Fasmer, O. B. (2008). Dissociative experiences differentiate bipolar-II from unipolar depressed patients: The mediating role of cyclothymia and the Type A behaviour speed and impatience subscale. *Journal of Affective Disorders, 108*(3), 207–216. doi:10.1016/j.jad.2007.10.018

Ogawa, J., Sroufe, A., Weinfield, N., Carlson, E., & Egeland, B. (1997). Development and the fragmented self: Longitudinal study of dissociative symptomatology in a nonclinical sample. *Development and Psychopathology, 9*, 855–879.

Ogden, P., & Fisher, J. (2015). *Sensorimotor psychotherapy: Interventions for trauma and attachment.* New York, NY: W. W. Norton.

Ogden, P., & Gomez, A. M. (2013). EMDR therapy and sensorimotor psychotherapy with children. In A. M. Gomez (Ed.), *EMDR therapy and adjunct approaches with children* (pp. 247–271). New York, NY: Springer Publishing Company.

Ogden, P. K., Minton, K., & Pain, C. (2006). *Trauma and the body: A sensorimortor approach to psychotherapy.* New York, NY: W. W. Norton.

Olfson, M. (2007). *Rates of bipolar diagnosis in youth rapidly climbing, treatment patterns similar to adults.* Retrieved from http://www.nih.gov/news/pr/sep/2007/nimh-03.htm

Omer, H., & Alon, N. (1994). The continuity principle: A unified approach to disaster and trauma. *American Journal of Community Psychology, 22,* 237–287.

O'Shea, K. (2009). The EMDR early trauma protocol. In R. Shapiro (Ed.), *EMDR solutions II: For depression, eating disorders, performance, and more* (pp. 313–334). New York, NY: W. W. Norton.

Pae, C. U., Lim, H. K., Peidl, K., Ajwani, N., Serretti, A., Patkar, A. A., & Lee, C. (2008). The atypical antipsychotics olanzapine and risperidone in the treatment of PTSD: A meta-analysis of randomized, double-blind, placebo-controlled clinical trials. *International Clinical Psychopharmacology, 23*(1), 1–8.

Palidofsky, M., & Stolbach, B. C. (2012). Dramatic healing: The evolution of the trauma-informed musical theatre program for incarcerated girls. *Journal of Child & Adolescent Trauma, 5,* 239–256.

Papolos, D., & Papolos, J. (2000). *The bipolar child: The definitive and reassuring guide to childhood's most misunderstood disorder.* New York, NY: Broadway Books.

Parens, E., & Johnston, J. (2008). Understanding the agreements and controversies surrounding childhood psychopharmacology. *Child and Adolescent Psychiatry & Mental Health, 2*(1), 5.

Parry, P. I., & Levin, E. C. (2011). Pediatric bipolar disorder in an era of "mindless psychiatry." *Journal of Trauma & Dissociation, 13,* 51–68. doi:10.1080/1529973 2.2011.597826

Paulsen, S. (2009). *Looking through the eyes of trauma and dissociation: An illustrated guide for EMDR therapists and clients.* Charleston, SC: Booksurge.

Pavuluri, M. N., Henry, D. B., Carbray, J. A., Sampson, G. A., Naylor, M. W., & Janicak, P. G. (2006). A one-year open-label trial of risperidone augmentation in lithium nonresponder youth with preschool-onset bipolar disorder. *Journal of Child and Adolescent Psychopharmacology, 16,* 336–350.

Perls, F., Hefferline, R., & Goodman, P. (1951). *Gestalt therapy: Excitement and growth in the human personality.* New York, NY: Delta Publishing.

Perry, B. (2003). Complex PTSD in children: Brain and behavior. In P. Stein & J. Kendall (Eds.), *Psychological trauma and the developing brain: Neurologically based interventions for troubled children* (pp. 97–132). New York, NY: Taylor & Francis.

Perry, B. D. (2001). The neurodevelopmental impact of violence in childhood. In D. Schetky & E. P. Benedek (Eds.), *Textbook of child and adolescent forensic psychiatry* (pp. 221–238). Washington, DC: American Psychiatric Press.

Perry, B. D. (2006). Applying principles of neurodevelopment to clinical work with maltreated and traumatized children. In N. B. Webb (Ed.), *Working with traumatized youth in child welfare* (pp. 27–52). New York, NY: Guilford Press.

Perry, B. D., Pollard, R., Blakely, T., Baker, W. L., & Vigilante, D. (1995). Childhood trauma, the neurobiology of adaptation and use-dependent development of the brain: How states become traits. *Infant Mental Health Journal, 16*(4), 271–291.

Peterson, G. (1990). Diagnosis of childhood multiple personality. *Dissociation, 3*, 3–9.

Pica, M., Beere, D., & Maurer, L. (1997). The overlap between dissociative and obsessive-compulsive disorders: A theoretical link. *Dissociation, 10*(1), 38–43.

Pittman, J. F., Keiley, M. K., Kerpelman, J. L., & Vaughn, B. E. (2011). Attachment, identity, and intimacy: Parallels between Bowlby's and Erikson's paradigms. *Journal of Family Theory & Review, 3*(1), 32–46. doi:10.1111/j.1756-2589 .2010.00079.x

Pobric, G., Mashal, N., Faust, M., & Lavidor, M. (2008). The role of the right cerebral hemisphere in processing novel metaphoric expressions: A transcranial magnetic stimulation study. *Journal of Cognitive Neuroscience, 20*, 170–181.

Pollak, S. D., Cicchetti, D., Klorman, R., & Brumaghim, J. T. (1997). Cognitive brain event-related potentials and emotion processing in maltreated children. *Child Development, 68*, 773–787.

Pollak, S. D., Klorman, R., Thatcher, J. E., & Cicchetti, D. (2001). P3b reflects maltreated children's reactions to facial displays of emotion. *Psychophysiology, 38*, 267–274.

Pollak, S. D., & Tolley-Schell, S. A. (2003). Selective attention to facial emotion in physically abused children. *Journal of Abnormal Psychology, 112*, 323–338.

Porges, S. (2011). *The polyvagal theory: Neurophysiological foundations of emotions, attachment, communication and self-regulation.* New York, NY: W. W. Norton.

Porges, S. (2014a, October 15). Beyond the brain: Using polyvagal theory to help patients "reset" the nervous system after trauma [Webinar with Stephen Porges and Ruth Buczynski]. In NICABM webinar series *Rethinking Trauma.*

Porges, S. (2014b, February 1). The polyvagal theory [Webinar with Stephen Porges and Maggie Phillips]. In webinar series *Innovations in Trauma Therapy Conference.*

Porter, D. M., & Bell, C. C. (1999). The use of clonidine in PTSD. *Journal of the National Medical Association, 91*(8), 475–477.

Potgieter-Marks, R. (2012). When the sleeping tiger roars: Perpetrator introjects in children. In R. Vogt (Ed.), *Perpetrator introjects: Psychotherapeutic diagnostics and treatment models* (pp. 87–110). Kröning, Germany: Asanger.

Potgieter-Marks, R. (2015). Jason (7 years old)—Expressing past neglect and abuse: Two-week intensive therapy for an adopted child with dissociation. In S. Wieland (Ed.), *Dissociation in traumatized children and adolescents: Theory and clinical interventions* (2nd ed., pp. 89–134). New York, NY: Routledge.

Preston, J. D., O'Neal, J. H., & Talaga, M. C. (2010). *Child and adolescent clinical psychopharmacology made simple* (2nd ed.). Oakland, CA: New Harbinger Publications.

Putnam, F. W. (1989). *Diagnosis and treatment of multiple personality disorder.* New York, NY: Guilford Press.

Putnam, F. W. (1997). *Dissociation in children and adolescents.* New York, NY: Guilford Press.

Putnam, F. W., Helmers, K., & Trickett, P. K. (1993). Development, reliability, and validity of a child dissociation scale. *Child Abuse & Neglect, 17*, 731–741.

Putnam, F. W., Hornstein, N. L., & Peterson, G. (1996). Clinical phenomenology of child and adolescent dissociative disorders: Gender and age effects. *Child & Adolescent Psychiatric Clinics of North America, 5,* 303–442.

Rauch, S. L., van der Kolk, B. A., Fisler, R. E., Alper, N. M., Orr, S. P., Savage, C. R., . . . Pitman, R. K. (1996). A symptom provocation study of posttraumatic stress disorder using positron emission tomography and script-driven imagery. *Archives of General Psychiatry, 53*(5), 380–387. doi:10.1001/archpsyc.1996.01830050014003

Raven, D. (2004). *Art expression: An alternative coping strategy for self-injury* (Unpublished master's thesis). Northern Michigan University, Marquette, MI.

Raven, D., LaDuke, M., & Waters, F. S. (2014). *Adolescents with dissociation in residential substance abuse treatment* (An unpublished study).

Read, J., van Os, J., Morrison, A. P., & Ross, C. A. (2005). Childhood trauma, psychosis and schizophrenia: A literature review with theoretical and clinical implications. *Acta Psychiatrica Scandinavica, 112,* 330–350.

Reinders, A. A. T. S., Nijenhuis, E. R. S., Paans, A. M. J., Korf, J., Willemsen, A. T. M., & den Boer, J. A. (2003). One brain, two selves. *Neuroimage, 20,* 2119–2125.

Reinders, A. A. T. S., Willemsen, A. T. M., Vos, H. P. J., den Boer, J. A., & Nijenhuis, E. R. S. (2012). Fact or factitious? A psychobiological study of authentic and simulated dissociative identity states. *PLoS One, 7*(6), e39279. doi:10.1371/journal.pone.0039279

Rizzolatti, G., Fadiga, L., Gallese, V., & Fogassi, L. (1996). Premotor cortex and the recognition of motor actions. *Cognitive Brain Research, 3,* 131–141.

Robb, A. S., Cueva, J. E., Sporn, J., Yang, R., & Vanderburg, D. G. (2010). Sertraline treatment of children and adolescents with PTSD: A double-blind, placebo-controlled trial. *Journal of Child and Adolescent Psychopharmacology, 20*(6), 463–471.

Robertson, J. (1952). *Film: A two-year old goes to the hospital.* New York, NY: New York University Film Library.

Robertson, J., & Bowlby, J. (1952). Responses of young children to separation from their mothers II: Observations of the sequences of response of children aged 18 to 24 months during the course of separation. *Courrier du Centre International de l'Enfance, 2,* 131–142.

Rodenburg, R., Benjamin, A., de Roos, C., Meijer, A. M., & Stams, G. J. (2009). Efficacy of EMDR in children: A meta-analysis. *Clinical Psychology Review, 29*(7), 599–606.

Ross, C. A., & Keyes, B. (2004). Dissociation and schizophrenia. *Journal of Trauma & Dissociation, 5*(3), 69–83.

Ross, C. A., & Keyes, B. (2008). Dissociation and schizophrenia. *Journal of Trauma & Dissociation, 5*(3), 69–83.

Ross, C. A., Miller, S. D., Reagor, P., Bjronson, L., Fraser, G., & Anderson, G. (1990). Schneiderian symptoms in multiple personality disorder and schizophrenia. *Comprehensive Psychiatry, 31,* 111–118.

Rynn, M. A., Siqueland, L., & Rickels, K. (2001). Placebo-controlled trial of sertraline in the treatment of children with generalized anxiety disorder. *American Journal of Psychiatry, 158*, 2008–2014.

Salinger, T. (2015, November 19). Indiana girl, 12, killed stepmother because creepy clown character 'Laughing Jack' told her to do it. *New York Daily News.* Retrieved from http://www.nydailynews.com/news/crime/indiana-girl-12-killed-stepmom-laughing-jack-article-1.2440821

Sanders, S. (1986). The Perceptual Alteration Scale: A scale measuring dissociation. *American Journal of Clinical Hypnosis, 29*(2), 95–102.

Sanders-Woudstra, J. A. R. (1978). The importance of psychodynamics in relation to psychopharmacology. *Advances in Biological Psychiatry, 2*, 61–69.

Sar, V., Akyüz, G., Oztürk, E., & Alioğlu, F. (2013). Dissociative depression among women in the community. *Journal of Trauma & Dissociation, 14*(4), 423–438. doi:10.1080/15299732.2012.753654

Sar, V., Onder, C., Killicaslan, A., Zoroglu, S. S., & Alyanak, B. (2014). Dissociative identity disorder among adolescents: Prevalence in a university psychiatric outpatient unit. *Journal of Trauma & Dissociation, 15*(4), 402–419.

Sar, V., & Oztürk, E. (2009). Psychotic presentations of dissociative identity disorder. In P. F. Dell & J. A. O'Neil (Eds.), *Dissociation and the dissociative disorders: DSM-V and beyond* (pp. 535–545). New York, NY: Routledge.

Sar, V., Oztürk, E., & Kundakci, T. (2002). Psychotherapy of an adolescent with dissociative identity disorder. *Journal of Trauma & Dissociation, 3*(2), 81–95.

Satir, V. (1965). The family as a treatment unit. *Confinia Psychiatrica, 8*, 37–42.

Satir, V. (1983). *Conjoint family therapy* (3rd ed.). Palo Alto, CA: Science and Behavior Books.

Satir, V. (n.d.). *Virginia Satir quotes.* Retrieved from http://www.brainyquote.com/quotes/quotes/v/virginiasa175186.html

Saunders, B. E. (2003). Understanding children exposed to violence: Toward an integration of overlapping fields. *Journal of Interpersonal Violence, 18*(4), 356–376. doi:10.1177/0886260502250840

Scaer, R. (2001). *The body bears the burden: Trauma, dissociation and disease.* New York, NY: Haworth Medical Press.

Schäfer, I., Harfst, T., Aderhold, V., Briken, P., Lehmann, M., Moritz, S., . . . Naber, D. (2006). Childhood trauma and dissociation in female patients with schizophrenia spectrum disorders: An exploratory study. *Journal of Nervous & Mental Disease, 194*(2), 135–138.

Schauer, M., & Elbert, T. (2010). Dissociation following traumatic stress. *Zeitschrift Für Psychologie/Journal of Psychology, 218*(2), 109–127. doi:10.1027/0044-3409/a000018

Scheck, M., Schaeffer, J. A., & Gillette, C. (1998). Brief psychological intervention with traumatized young women: The efficacy of eye movement desensitization and reprocessing. *Journal of Traumatic Stress, 11*, 25–44.

Schneeberger, A. R., Muenzenmaier, K., Castille, D., Battaglia, J., & Link, B. G. (2014). Use of psychotropic medication groups in people with severe mental illness and stressful childhood experiences. *Journal of Trauma & Dissociation, 15*(4), 494–511.

Schore, A. (2002). Advances in neuropsychoanalysis, attachment theory, and trauma research: Implications for self psychology. *Psychoanalytic Inquiry, 22*, 433–484.

Schore, A. N. (1994). *Affect regulation and the origin of the self: The neurobiology of emotional development*. Hillsdale, NJ: Lawrence Erlbaum.

Schore, A. N. (2000). Attachment and the regulation of the right brain. *Attachment & Human Development, 2*(1), 23–47. doi:10.1080/146167300361309

Schore, A. N. (2009). Attachment trauma and the developing right brain: Origins of pathological dissociation. In P. F. Dell & J. A. O'Neil (Eds.), *Dissociation and the dissociative disorders: DSM-V and beyond* (pp. 107–141). New York, NY: Routledge.

ScienceDaily. (2015, August 17). How traumatic memories hide in the brain, and how to retrieve them. Retrieved from http://www.sciencedaily.com/releases/2015/08/150817132325.htm

Scutti, S. (2015, August 17). Memories of child abuse, other traumas hide in the brain; changing patient state of mind may help retrieve them. *Medical Daily.* Retrieved from http://www.medicaldaily.com/memories-child-abuse-other-traumas-hide-brain-changing-patient-state-mind-may-help-348164

Semerari, A., Carcione, A., Dimaggio, G., Nicolò, G., & Procacci, M. (2007). Understanding minds: Different functions and different disorders? The contribution of psychotherapy research. *Psychotherapy Research, 17*(1), 106–119. doi:10.1080/10503300500536953

Shackman, J. E., Shackman, A. J., & Pollak, S. D. (2007). Physical abuse amplifies attention to threat and increases anxiety in children. *Emotion, 7*, 838–852.

Shapiro, F. (1995). *Eye movement desensitization and reprocessing: Basic principles, protocols, and procedures*. New York, NY: Guilford Press.

Shapiro, F. (2001). *Eye movement desensitization and reprocessing: Basic principles, protocols, and procedures* (2nd ed.). New York, NY: Guilford Press.

Shi, L. (2014). Treatment of reactive attachment disorder in young children: Importance of understanding emotional dynamics. *American Journal of Family Therapy, 42*(1), 1–13. doi:10.1080/01926187.2013.763513

Shin, J.-U., Jeong, S. H., & Chung, U.-S. (2009). The Korean version of the Adolescent Dissociative Experience Scale: Psychometric properties and the connection to trauma among Korean adolescents. *Psychiatry Investigation, 6*(3), 163–172.

Shin, L. M., McNally, R. J., Kosslyn, S. M., Thompson, W. L., Rauch, S. L., Alpert, N. M., . . . Pitman, R. K. (1999). Regional cerebral blood flow during script-driven imagery in childhood sexual abuse-related PTSD: A PET investigation. *American Journal of Psychiatry, 156*(4), 575–584.

Shirar, L. (1996). *Dissociative children: Bridging the inner and outer worlds*. New York, NY: W. W. Norton.

Siegel, D. (1999). *The developing mind: Toward a neurobiology of interpersonal experience*. New York, NY: Guilford Press.

Siegel, D., & Payne Bryson, T. (2012). *The whole-brain child: 12 revolutionary strategies to nurture your child's developing mind*. New York, NY: Random House.

Siegel, D., & Payne Bryson, T. (2014). *No-drama discipline: The whole-brain way to calm the chaos and nurture your child's developing mind*. New York, NY: Random House.

Siegel, D. J. (2010). *The mindful therapist: A clinician's guide to mindsight and neural integration*. New York, NY: W. W. Norton.

Silberg, J. (Ed.). (1996). *The dissociative child: Diagnosis, treatment, and management*. Lutherville, MD: Sidran Press.

Silberg, J. (Ed.). (1998). *The dissociative child: Diagnosis, treatment, and management* (2nd ed.). Lutherville, MD: Sidran Press.

Silberg, J. (2013). *The child survivor: Healing developmental trauma and dissociation*. New York, NY: Routledge.

Silva, R. R., Munoz, D. M., Alpert, M., Perlmutter, I. R., & Diaz, J. (1999). Neuroleptic malignant syndrome in children and adolescents. *Journal of the American Academy of Child & Adolescent Psychiatry, 38*, 187–194.

Sim, L., Friedrich, W. N., Davies, W. H., Trentham, B., Lengua, L., & Pithers, W. (2005). The Child Behavior Checklist as an indicator of posttraumatic stress disorder and dissociation in normative, psychiatric, and sexually abused children. *Journal of Trauma Stress, 18*, 697–705.

Simeon, D., Guralnik, O., Schmeidler, J., Sirof, B., & Knutelska, M. (2001). The role of childhood interpersonal trauma in depersonalization disorder. *American Journal of Psychiatry, 158*, 1027–1033.

Simeon, D., Smith, R. J., Knutelska, M., & Smith, L. M. (2008). Somatoform dissociation in depersonalization disorder. *Journal of Trauma & Dissociation, 9*(3), 335–348. doi:10.1080/15299730802139170

Sinason, V. (Ed.). (2002). *Attachment, trauma and multiplicity: Working with dissociative identity disorder*. New York, NY: Routledge.

Smits, M. G., Van Stel, H. F., Van der Heijden, K. B., Meijer, A. M., Coenen, A. M., & Kerkhof, G. A. (2003). Melatonin improves health status and sleep in children with idiopathic chronic sleep-onset insomnia: A randomized placebo-controlled trial. *Journal of the American Academy of Child & Adolescent Psychiatry, 42*, 1286–1293.

Sobol, B., & Schneider, K. (1998). Art as an adjunctive therapy in the treatment of children who dissociate. In J. L. Silberg (Ed.), *The dissociative child: Diagnosis, treatment, and management* (2nd ed., pp. 219–230). Lutherville, MD: Sidran Press.

Solomon, J., & George, C. (1999). *Attachment disorganization*. New York, NY: Guilford Press.

Solomon, R. M., & Shapiro, F. (2008). EMDR and the Adaptive Information Processing Model: Potential mechanisms of change. *Journal of EMDR Practice and Research, 2*(4), 315–325. doi:10.1891/1933–3196.2.4.315

Souza, T., & Spates, C. R. (2008). Treatment of PTSD and substance abuse comorbidity. *Behavior Analyst Today, 9*, 11–26.

Spence, W., Mulholland, C., Lynch, G., McHugh, S., Dempster, M., & Shannon, C. (2011). Rates of childhood trauma in a sample of patients with schizophrenia as compared with a sample of patients with non-psychotic psychiatric diagnoses. *Journal of Trauma & Dissociation, 7*(3), 7–22. doi:10.1300/J229v07n03

Spitz, R. A. (1952). *Psychogenetic disease in infancy (an attempt at their classification).* Retrieved from https://www.youtube.com/watch?v=VMWb8rfU-rg

Stamatakos, M., & Campo, J. V. (2010a). Posttraumatic stress disorder in children and adolescents: A review of psychopharmacological treatment. *Child Psychiatry & Human Development, 41*, 624–640.

Stamatakos, M., & Campo, J. V. (2010b). Psychopharmacologic treatment of traumatized youth. *Current Opinion in Pediatrics, 22*, 599–604.

Steele, K., Dorahy, M. J., van der hart, O., & Nijenhuis, E. R. S. (2009). Dissociation versus alterations in consciousness: Related but different concepts. In P. Dell & J. O'Neil (Eds.), *Dissociation and the dissociative disorders: DSM-V and beyond* (pp. 155–169). New York, NY: Routledge.

Steele, W., & Raider, M. (2001). *Structured sensory interventions for children, adolescents and parents (SITCAP™).* New York, NY: Edwin Mellen Press.

Steinberg, A. M. (1994). *Structured Clinical Interview for DSM-IV Dissociative Disorders (SCID-D).* Washington, DC: American Psychiatric Press.

Steinberg, A. M., & Brymer, M. J. (2008). The UCLA PTSD Reaction Index. In G. Reyes, J. Elhai, & J. Ford (Eds.), *Encyclopedia of psychological trauma* (pp. 673–674). Hoboken, NJ: Wiley.

Steinberg, A. M., Brymer, M. J., Kim, S., Briggs, E. C., Ippen, C. G., Ostrowski, S. A., . . . Pynoos, R. S. (2013). Psychometric properties of the UCLA PTSD Reaction Index: Part I. *Journal of Traumatic Stress, 26*, 1–9. doi: 10.1002/jts.21780

Steptoe, A. S. (2000). Control and stress. In G. Fink (Ed.), *Encyclopedia of stress* (Vol. I, pp. 526–532). San Diego, CA: Academic Press.

Stern, D. N., Sander, L., Nahum, J., Harrison, A., Lyons-Ruth, K., Morgan, A., . . . Tronick, E. Z. (1990). Non-interpretative mechanisms in psychoanalytic therapy: The "something more" than interpretation. *International Journal of Psychoanalysis, 79*, 903–922.

Stevens, J. E. (2013). Nearly 35 million U.S. children have experienced one or more types of childhood trauma. *ACES Too High News.* Retrieved from http://acestoohigh.com/2013/05/13/nearly-35-million-u-s-children-have-experienced-one-or-more-types-of-childhood-trauma

Steward, G. (1999). *Interview with Stan Freberg.* Retrieved from http://www.crazycollege.org/fweb.htm

Stien, P., & Kendall, J. (2004). *Psychological trauma and the developing brain: Neurologically based interventions for troubled children.* Binghamton, NY: Haworth.

Stinehart, M. A., Scott, D. A., & Barfield, H. G. (2012). Reactive attachment disorder in adopted and foster care children: Implications for mental health professionals. *Family Journal*, *20*(4), 355–360. doi:10.1177/1066480 712451229

Stolbach, B. C. (1997). The Children's Dissociative Experiences Scale and Post-traumatic Symptom Inventory: Rationale, development, and validation of a self-report measure. *Dissertation Abstracts International*, *58*(3), 1548B.

Stolbach, B. C. (2005). Psychotherapy of a dissociative 8-year-old boy burned at age 3. *Psychiatric Annals*, *35*(8), 685–694.

Stosny, S. (1995). *Treating attachment abuse: A compassionate approach*. New York, NY: Springer Publishing Company.

Strawn, J. R., Keeshin, B. R., DelBello, M. P., Geracioto, T. D., Jr., & Putnam, F. W. (2010). Psychopharmacologic treatment of posttraumatic stress disorder in children and adolescents: A review. *Journal of Clinical Psychiatry*, *71*, 932–941.

Struik, A. (2014). *Treating chronically traumatized children: Don't let sleeping dogs lie!* New York, NY: Routledge.

Taylor, M., Carlson, S. M., Maring, B. L., Gerow, L., & Charley, C. (2004). The characteristics and correlates of high fantasy in school-aged children: Imaginary companions, impersonation and social understanding. *Developmental Psychology*, *40*, 1173–1187.

Teicher, M. H., Samson, J. A., Polcari, A., & McGreenery, C. E. (2006). Sticks, stones, and hurtful words: Relative effects of various forms of childhood maltreatment. *American Journal of Psychiatry*, *163*(6), 993–1000. Retrieved from http://www.ncbi.nlm.nih.gov/pubmed/16741199

Terr, L. (1990). *Too scared to cry*. New York, NY: Basic Books.

Thomaes, K., Dorrepaal, E., Draijer, N., Jansma, E. P., Veltman, D. J., & Van Balkom, A. J. (2014). Can pharmacological and psychological treatment change brain structure and function in PTSD? A systematic review. *Journal of Psychiatric Research*, *50*, 1–15.

Tippett, K. (Producer). (2013). *Bessel van der Kolk on restoring the body: Yoga, EMDR, and treating trauma* [On Being]. Podcast retrieved from http://www.onbeing .org/program/restoring-the-body-Bessel-van-der-kolk-on-yoga-emdr-and-treating-trauma/5801

Tolmunen, T., Maaranen, P., Hintikka, J., Kylmä, J., Rissanen, M., Honkalampi, K., & Laukkanen, E. (2007). Dissociation in a general population of Finnish adolescents. *Journal of Nervous and Mental Disease*, *195*, 614–617.

Turner, H. A., Finkelhor, D., & Ormrod, R. (2010). Poly-victimization in a national sample of children and youth. *American Journal of Preventive Medicine*, *38*, 323–330.

Tuval-Mashiach, R., Freedman, S., Baragai, N., Boker, R., Hadar, H., & Shalev, A. Y. (2004). Coping with trauma: Narrative and cognitive perspectives. *Psychiatry*, *67*, 280–293.

Twardosz, S., & Lutzker, R. J. (2010). Child maltreatment and the developing brain: A review of neuroscience perspectives. *Aggression and Violent Behavior*, *15*, 59–68.

Twombly, J. H. (2012). Overt and covert perpetrator ego states in dissociative disordered patients. In R. Vogt (Ed.), *Perpetrator introjects: Psychotherapeutic diagnostics and treatment model* (pp. 133–147). Kröning, Germany: Asanger.

van der Hart, O., & Dorahy, M. J. (2009). Dissociation: The history of a construct. In P. F. Dell & J. A. O'Neil (Eds.), *Dissociation and the dissociative disorders: DSM-V and beyond* (pp. 3–26). New York, NY: Routledge.

van der Hart, O., Nijenhuis, E., & Steele, K. (2006). *The haunted self: Structural dissociation and the treatment of chronic traumatization*. New York, NY: W. W. Norton.

van der Hart, O., van Ochten, J. M., van Son, M. J. M., Steele, K., & Lensvelt-Mulders, G. (2008). Relations among peritraumatic dissociation and posttraumatic stress: A critical review. *Journal of Trauma & Dissociation*, *9*(4), 481–505. doi:10.1080/15299730802223362

van der Heijden, K. B., Smits, M. G., Van Someren, E. J., Ridderinkhof, K. R., & Gunning, W. B. (2007). Effects of melatonin on sleep, behavior and cognition in ADHD and chronic sleep onset insomnia. *Journal of the American Academy of Child & Adolescent Psychiatry*, *46*, 233–241.

van der Kolk, B. (2005). Developmental trauma disorder: Toward a rational diagnosis for children with complex trauma histories. *Psychiatric Annals*, *35*(5), 401–408.

van der Kolk, B. (2014). *The body keeps the score: Brain, mind, and body in the healing of trauma*. New York, NY: Viking.

van der Kolk, B. A. (1996). The complexity of adaptation to trauma: Self-regulation, stimulus discrimination, and characterological development. In B. A. van der Kolk, L. Weisaeth, & A. C. McFarlane (Eds.), *Traumatic stress: The effects of overwhelming experience on mind, body, and society* (pp. 182–234). New York, NY: Guilford Press.

van der Kolk, B. A., Greenberg, M. S., Orr, S. P., & Pitman, R. K. (1989). Endogenous opioids, stress induced analgesia, and posttraumatic stress disorder. *Psychopharmacology Bulletin*, *25*, 417–421.

van der Kolk, B. A., van der Hart, O., & Marmar, C. R. (1996). Dissociation and information processing in posttramatic stress disorder. In B. A. van der Kolk, A. C. MacFarlane, & L. Weisaeth (Eds.), *Traumatic stress: The effects of overwhelming experience of mind, body, and society* (pp. 46–74). New York, NY: Guilford Press.

Varese, F., Barkus, E., & Bentall, R. P. (2012). Dissociation mediates the relationship between childhood trauma and hallucination-proneness. *Psychological Medicine*, *42*(5), 1025–1036.

Vásquez, D. A., de Arellano, M. A., Reid-Quiñones, K., Bridges, A. J., Rheingold, A. A., Stocker, R. P. J., & Danielson, C. K. (2012). Peritraumatic dissociation and peritraumatic emotional predictors of PTSD in Latino youth: Results from the Hispanic family study. *Journal of Trauma & Dissociation, 13*(5), 509–525. doi:10.1080/15299732.2012.678471

Vermetten, E., Schmahl, C., Lindner, S., Loewenstein, R. J., & Bremner, J. D. (2006). Hippocampal and amygdalar volumes in dissociative identity disorder. *American Journal of Psychiatry, 163*(4), 630–636.

Vogel, M., Spitzer, C., Kuwert, P., Möller, B., Freyberger, H. J., & Grabe, H. J. (2009). Association of childhood neglect with adult dissociation in schizophrenic inpatients. *Psychopathology, 42*, 124–130. doi:10.1159/000204763

Vogt, R. (Ed.). (2012). *Perpetrator introjects: Psychotherapeutic diagnostics and treatment models*. Kröning, Germany: Asanger.

Wang, D., Li, Z., Li, L., & Hao, W. (2014). Real-world, open-label study to evaluate the effectiveness of mirtazapine on sleep quality in outpatients with major depressive disorder. *Asia-Pacific Psychiatry, 6*(2), 152–160.

Warner, E., Cook, A., Westcott, A., & Koomar, J. (2011). *SMART: Sensory motor arousal regulation treatment*. Brookline, MA: Trauma Center.

Waters, F. S. (1991, May). *Assessing and treating children with dissociation*. Workshop presented at the Eastern Regional Conference on Multiple Personality and Dissociative Disorders, Alexandria, VA.

Waters, F. S. (1993, June). *Dissociation in childhood and adolescents*. Workshop presented at the Fifth Anniversary Eastern Regional Conference on Abuse and Multiple Personality, Alexandria, VA.

Waters, F. S. (1996, November). *Quadri-theoretical model for the treatment of children with dissociation*. Paper presented at the meeting of the International Society for the Study of Trauma and Dissociation, San Francisco, CA.

Waters, F. S. (1998a). Parents as partners in the treatment of dissociative children. In J. L. Silberg (Ed.), *The dissociative child: Diagnosis, treatment, and management* (pp. 273–295). Lutherville, MD: Sidran Press.

Waters, F. S. (1998b). Therapeutic phases in the treatment of dissociative children. In J. L. Silberg (Ed.), *The dissociative child: Diagnosis, treatment, and management* (pp. 135–165). Lutherville, MD: Sidran Press.

Waters, F. S. (1999). *Children with dissociative disorders and OCD following traumatic experiences*. (Unpublished study)

Waters, F. S. (2000). Obsessive compulsive behaviors in dissociative children. *ISSD News, 18,* 3, 5.

Waters, F. S. (2005). Atypical DID adolescent case. *ISSD News, 23*(3), 1–2, 4–5.

Waters, F. S. (2013). Assessing and diagnosing dissociation in children: Beginning the recovery. In A. Gomez (Ed.), *EMDR therapy and adjunct approaches with children: Complex trauma, attachment, and dissociation* (pp. 129–149). New York, NY: Springer Publishing Company.

Waters, F. S. (2015). Ryan (8 to 10 years old)—Connecting with the body: Treatment of somatoform dissociation (encopresis and multiple physical complaints) in a young boy. In S. Wieland (Ed.), *Dissociation in traumatized children and adolescents: Theory and clinical interventions* (2nd ed., pp. 135–190). New York, NY: Routledge.

Waters, F. S., & Adler-Tapia, R. L. (2009, November). *EMDR for children with trauma and dissociation: Case conceptualization from stabilization to integration.* Workshop presented at the 26th Annual Conference of the International Society for the Study of Trauma and Dissociation, Washington, DC.

Waters, F. S., Laddis, A., Soderstrom, B., & Yehuda, N. (2007). *Differential diagnostic issues in dissociative and bipolar disorders in children and adults.* In F. S. Waters (Chair), Symposium conducted at the meeting of the 24th International Society for the Study of Trauma and Dissociation, Philadelphia, PA.

Waters, F. S., & Silberg, J. L. (1997). Therapeutic phases in the treatment of dissociative children. In J. L. Silberg (Ed.), *The dissociative child: Diagnosis, treatment, and management* (2nd ed., pp. 135–165). Lutherville, MD: Sidran Press.

Waters, F. S., & Silberg, J. L. (1998a). Promoting integration in dissociative children. In J. L. Silberg (Ed.), *The dissociative child: Diagnosis, treatment, and management* (2nd ed., pp. 167–190). Lutherville, MD. Sidran Press.

Waters, F. S., & Silberg, J. L. (1998b). Therapeutic phases in the treatment of dissociative children. In J. L. Silberg (Ed.), *The dissociative child: Diagnosis, treatment, and management* (pp. 135–165). Lutherville, MD: Sidran Press.

Waters, F. S., & Stien, P. (2000, November). *Etiology and treatment of OCD symptoms in dissociative children.* ISSTD's 17th International Fall Conference, San Antonio, TX.

Waters, F. S., Yehuda, N., & Potgieter-Marks, R. (2011). *But they are too young to be traumatized.* Workshop presented at the 28th International Conference on the Study of Trauma and Dissociation, Montreal, Canada.

Watkins, H. (1993). Ego-state therapy: An overview. *American Journal of Clinical Hypnosis, 35,* 232–240.

Watkins, J. G. (1988). The management of malevolent ego states in multiple personality disorder. *Dissociation, 1*(1), 67–72.

Watkins, J. G., & Watkins, H. H. (1988). The management of malevolent ego states in multiple personality disorder. *Dissociation, 1*(1), 67–72.

Watkins, J. G., & Watkins, H. H. (1997). *Ego-states: Theory and therapy.* New York, NY: W. W. Norton.

Watson, D., Wu, K. D., & Cutshall, C. J. (2004). Symptom subtypes of obsessive-compulsive disorder and their relation to dissociation. *Journal of Anxiety Disorder, 18*(4), 435–458.

White, M. K. (2007). *Maps of narrative practice.* New York, NY: W. W. Norton.

White, M. K., & Epston, D. (1990). *Narrative means to therapeutic ends.* New York, NY: W. W. Norton.

Wieland, S. (2008, April). *What to do if the mother of a dissociative child has disorganized attachment.* Workshop conducted at the 1st Conference of European Society for Trauma and Dissociation, Amsterdam, The Netherlands.

Wieland, S. (Ed.). (2011). *Dissociation in traumatized children and adolescents: Theory and clinical interventions*. New York, NY: Routledge.

Wieland, S. (2015a). Joey (11 to 12 years old)—Moving out of dissociative protection: Treatment of a boy with dissociative disorder not elsewhere classified following early family trauma. In S. Wieland (Ed.), *Dissociation in traumatized children and adolescents: Theory and clinical interventions* (2nd ed., pp. 191–260). New York, NY: Routledge.

Wieland, S. (Ed.). (2015b). *Dissociation in traumatized children and adolescents: Theory and clinical interventions* (2nd ed.). New York, NY: Routledge.

Wigren, J. (1994). Narrative completion in the treatment of trauma. *Psychotherapy: Theory, Research, Practice, Training, 31*, 415–423.

Wolff, P. H. (1987). *The development of behavioral states and the expression of emotions in early infancy*. Chicago, IL: University of Chicago Press.

Wozniak, J., Crawford, M. H., Biederman, J., Faraone, S. V., Spencer, T. J., Taylor, A., & Blier, H. K. (1999). Antecedents and complications of trauma in boys with ADHD: Findings from a longitudinal study. *Journal of the American Academy of Child & Adolescent Psychiatry, 38*, 48–55.

Yehuda, N. (2005). The language of dissociation. *Journal of Trauma & Dissociation, 6*(1), 9–29. doi:10.1300/J229v06n01

Yehuda, N. (2015). *Communicating trauma: Clinical presentations and interventions with traumatized children*. New York, NY: Routledge.

Yehuda, N., Stolbach, B., & Waters, F. S. (2008, November). *When caring hurts: Medical trauma and dissociation in children*. Panel discussion conducted at the 25th Anniversary ISSTD Annual Conference, Chicago, IL.

Yoshizumi, T., Hamada, S., Kaida, A., Gotow, K., & Murase, S. (2010). Psychometric properties of the Adolescent Dissociative Experiences Scale (A-DES) in Japanese adolescents from a community sample. *Journal of Trauma & Dissociation, 11*(3), 322–336. Retrieved from http://www.ncbi.nlm.nih.gov/pubmed/20603766

Zeanah, C. H., Scheeringa, M., Boris, N. W., Heller, S. S., Smyke, A. T., & Trapani, J. (2004). Reactive attachment disorder in maltreated toddlers. *Child Abuse & Neglect, 28*, 877–888. doi:10.1016/j.chiabu.2004.01.010

Zoroglu, S., Sar, V., Tuzun, U., Tutkun, H., & Savas, H. A. (2002). Reliability and validity of the Turkish version of the Adolescent Dissociative Experiences Scale. *Psychiatry and Clinical Neurosciences, 56*, 551–556.

INDEX

AA. *See* Alcoholics Anonymous

abstract painting, 324–328

Achenbach, T., 74, 115

adaptive information processing (AIP), 353–355, 359, 437
  vs. dissociative theories, 355

A-DES. *See* Adolescent Dissociative Experiences Scale

ADHD. *See* attention deficit hyperactivity disorder

Adler-Tapia, R. L., xix, 102, 293, 354, 355, 357, 359, 364, 366–368, 370, 372–374, 377, 381

Adolescent Dissociative Experiences Scale (A-DES), 111–113, 173, 322, 425
  correlates to MMPI-A, 112–113

Adolescent Dissociative Experiences Scale-II (A-DES), 427–431

Adolescent Multidimensional Inventory of Dissociation V.6.0 (A-MID), 113, 322

adolescents
  art therapy interventions for, 321–352
  assessment of, 101
  differential diagnoses, 69, 79, 88–93
  dissociation, warning signs of, 47–48
  dissociative symptoms, 109–112
  Fine Line Between Life and Death intervention, 330–332
  intensive assessment and integrative treatment in, 397–400
  medication for, 253–259
  psychopharmacological interventions, 250–253
  sexualized self-state of, 53–54
  time of identity vs. role confusion, 158–160

adoption ceremonies, 169–170

adrenergic agonists, 277–279
  clonidine, 278–279

affect avoidance theory, 11–12

adaptive information processing (AIP), xxviii

Ainsworth, M. D. S., 21

AIP theory. *See* adaptive information processing (AIP)

Alcoholics Anonymous (AA), 245, 308, 350

All the Colors of Me: My First Book About Dissociation (Gomez & Paulsen), 139

A-MID. *See* Adolescent Multidimensional Inventory of Dissociation V.6.0

anatomical changes in dissociative patients, 256

Angry Part vs. Intuitive Part, 247

angry self-states, 168, 171, 183

ANP. *See* apparently normal personality

CPSIA information can be obtained
at www.ICGtesting.com
Printed in the USA
BVHW041756061020
590426BV00012B/108